WARDROBE
STRATEGIES
FOR
WOMEN

WARDROBE STRATEGIES FOR WOMEN

Judith Rasband
Conselle Institute of Image Management
Provo, Utah

This book was previously published by Delmar Publishers,
a division of International Thomson Publishing Inc.

Fairchild Publications, Inc.
New York

Dedication

Dedicated to my parents,
Maxine and Lisle Packard, remembered for their
unfailing support and encouragement.
They taught me the value of an education.

Second Printing, 2002 by Fairchild Publications, Inc.

Copyright © 1996
Delmar Publishers, a division of International Thomson Publishing Inc.

Library of Congress Catalog Card Number: 2001093659

ISBN: 1-56367-259-6

GST R 133004424

Printed in the United States of America

Contents

Preface

The end purpose of all fashion classes is, logically, the creation of materials, designs, and clothing able to meet the wardrobe needs of the people—materials, designs, and clothing that can be sold to the buying public.

Wardrobe Strategies for Women was written to set forth realistic ways women might approach clothing selection, coordination, evaluation, and planning to efficiently and effectively meet wardrobe needs. It was written to provide solid information essential to that process and to the development of wardrobe management skills for life.

Virtually every woman will find a wealth of valuable information, theoretical and practical, that can be used in daily life. Those working in, or intending to work in, fashion-related fields will find information they can apply to themselves and to others in a professional setting.

Organization and Content

Wardrobe Strategies for Women contains twelve chapters that correspond to one of twelve wardrobe strategies. Because we learn by repetition, each chapter begins with a list of **Objectives** and a preview of **Main Points** that alerts the reader to what she can expect to learn from the chapter. Supporting information follows, with actual material for the reader to learn from. The **Review** reminds the reader of what she has studied. As long as both **Main Points** and the **Review** are deliberately short, this type of repetition can benefit the reader. It serves to guide the reader, and if the reader retains nothing more, it is likely she will remember these repeated points.

Within each chapter, the wardrobe strategy is presented first in terms of "**Rely on . . .**" It is often followed by a related counter strategy or possibly a companion strategy.

Chapters 1 and 2 set the stage for the topics that follow and establish the importance and usefulness of the information presented in the text. It provides the rationale for spending time and effort in learning about clothing and

wardrobing as a lifetime skill. It is expected that topics introduced in these chapters may be developed in coursework to follow.

Chapters 3 through 7 set forth fashion design traits consumers can rely on. They present basic theory helpful in gaining an understanding of the elements and principles of design as the reader will deal with them in wardrobe selection, coordination, and evaluation. **Chapter 8** treats all the elements of design in terms of personal style identification, development, and refinement.

Chapter 9 outlines cluster wardrobe planning and building. This may be considered the core chapter, with companion videotaped programs serving as needed illustrations throughout the course of study.

All chapters to this point have prepared the reader with information necessary to evaluate her own wardrobe successfully, as detailed and discussed in **Chapter 10**. This chapter talks the reader through the most complex and crucial task in wardrobing—the task of evaluating an actual wardrobe. Experience shows that embarking on a wardrobe evaluation without essential information leads to confusion, frustration, and lack of follow-through or follow-up. Positioned at this non-traditional point in the text, the reader is better prepared and more easily recognizes the ramifications of what she is dealing with in each piece of clothing encountered.

Chapters 11 and 12 present practical information needed to get a good return from the clothing investment in terms of care and cost. Shopping strategies seem a natural conclusion to the text as one exits from the course and into the real world, eager to apply what has been learned throughout the text.

Note: If the reader in a particular curriculum has already completed a course giving equal attention to all the elements of design, portions of these chapters may serve as reference and review only. Many readers, however, have not previously experienced direct application of theory to the actual wardrobing process. Chapters 3 through 8 are intended to prepare the reader for an advanced class on the elements and principles of visual design, so needed by the serious student in fashion design and fashion merchandising but missing from many curriculums.

Wardrobe Strategies for Women concludes with a **Parting Note** intended to encourage and instill confidence in the reader. In the face of a multitude of fashion choices and endless decisions the reader will encounter, inevitable mistakes can occur as she learns through repeated practice. These closing remarks give readers permission to make a mistake, survive, and still progress in their learning.

Special Features

The presentation of material is designed to be "user friendly," encouraging self-help and self-study attitudes on the part of the reader.

Charts and illustrations, original to *Wardrobe Strategies for Women,* appear as Figures and Tables. They serve to summarize vast amounts of detailed information and help the reader to visualize cause-and-effect relationships.

Photographs are extensive and provide examples essential to the text and contribute to the visual appeal of the book.

Tips From the Pros and **Query Boxes** are interspersed throughout the chapters. They establish a rapport with the reader, dispense special points of information, or engage the reader in making a thoughtful choice.

Newspaper articles ending each chapter are intended to casually acquaint the reader with the author as they interject related information in a lighter journalistic format and present author participation within the larger fashion field. These articles also serve as subtle evidence of fashion journalism as a career option.

Review Quizzes, Discussion Questions, and innovative end-of-chapter **Exercises** are included at the end of each chapter, positioned to reinforce and apply learning. Exercises are very practical in nature. Readers are immediately encouraged and instructed in ways to apply their reading in a realistic manner—to act on what they've read and learned about.

A series of six **Video Programs** accompany the text. These thirty-minute tapes in twelve parts visually restate the wardrobe strategies and illustrate the cluster concept in action, according to the different needs and goals of many different women. The content of these programs earned four-star ratings from the Video Rating Guide for Libraries. They are highly recommended in the *American Library Journal* reviews and in *Booklist.*

Instructor's Guide

An *Instructor's Guide* is available to complement the text and video programs. It serves to clarify the author's intent and logic regarding the text. It contains presentation and demonstration outlines, Review Quiz keys, and a test bank of questions for each chapter.

Acknowledgments

Sincere thanks go to Lorraine Conger for her very creative illustrations accompanying the text; to Linda Davis for computer-rendered tables and selected figures; to Peter Hansen for highly skilled video direction and editing; and to my associates Heidi Nelsen, Angela Lutzow, Kathy Adams, and Helen Vanderbeek for special assignment assistance and continued support.

Photographic contributions graciously supplied by Madeleine Direct, Eddie Bauer, All Week Long by Eddie Bauer, Clifford & Willis, and J. Crew, among others, are sincerely appreciated.

I am grateful for the time spent by reviewers and thank them for helpful suggestions. These experienced professionals include: Lori Battistone, ICM School of Business, Pittsburgh, Pennsylvania; Nancy Bredemeyer, Indian River Community College, Fort Pierce, Florida; Leslie Burns, Oregon State University, Corvallis, Oregon; E. Marie Cory, University of Arizona, Tucson, Arizona; Holga Garza, Skyline Career Development Center, Dallas, Texas; Patsy Hallman, Stephen Austin University, Nadogdoches, Texas; and Teresa Robinson, Middle Tennessee State University, Murfreesboro, Tennessee.

These acknowledgments would be incomplete if I did not recognize the family love, encouragement, and continued support I received throughout the duration of this project. My family is my greatest joy.

Judith Rasband

WARDROBE STRATEGIES FOR WOMEN

Chapter 1
Clothing: A Powerful Resource

Learning Objectives

Your goal in completing this chapter is to be able to:

- Accept your clothing as a personal resource.
- Recognize basic clothing needs and cite examples.
- Identify the elements of personal appearance (image).
- Improve your awareness and perception of clothing cues.
- Become more objective in your interpretation of clothing cues.
- Increase your ability to project your clothing message.
- Recognize the ways clothing influences you and your life.
- Anticipate situations in which your clothing is particularly important.
- Define the difference between a cluster, a wardrobe, and add-on pieces.
- Resolve to create a wardrobe that meets your needs and goals.

Preview Main Points

1. Rely on clothing as a resource, a tool you can control and use to help you achieve your goals.

2. Clothing is a basic human need — physically, psychologically, socially, and aesthetically.

3. Clothing is a universal element in nonverbal communication.

4. Clothing directly affects the way you think, the way you feel, the way you act, and the way others react to you.

5. Clothing, or wardrobe, management is the process of evaluating and controlling the use and effect of your clothing on you and others.

6. Ideally, the end purpose of all clothing design, manufacturing, selection, or sales effort is the creation of a wardrobe that meets the needs of the individual wearer.

1.

Rely on clothing as a resource, a tool you can control and use to help you achieve your goals.

A **resource** is anything available to use to your advantage, as an aid to meet a need or achieve a goal. Time, money, property, energy, food, and clothing qualify as resources. This book focuses on clothing as a resource. It may seem like common sense that people use their clothing as a resource. Common sense, however, is not always practiced when it comes to clothes. Few people are aware of the many ways clothing can be used to their advantage. This book provides a base of essential information to build on.

To begin, we are born without any preconceived ideas about ourselves. As we grow older, we gain experience with ourselves, with our surroundings, and with others. We perceive our bodies and begin to develop ideas about ourselves that impact our lives.

Body image is your perception of your physical self — the mental image and ideas you have about your body. It begins to develop early in life and evolves over time.

Body image can be positive or negative, accurate or inaccurate, particularly as we form this image in comparison with others and in relation to cultural fashion ideals. An accurate, objective body image is necessary and plays a significant part in clothing selection and appearance. Clothing becomes part of your body image, acting much like a "second skin" in establishing new physical boundaries for yourself.

Self-image is how you perceive the combination of all of your characteristics — your physical self including body image, your psychological self, social self, and so forth. It is how you see and judge yourself as a whole. Again, self-image can be positive or negative, accurate or inaccurate, particularly as we rely on feedback from others in forming our self-image. Your self-image helps determine what type of clothing is consistent with your self-image and flattering to your body image, depending on the various roles, activities, and occasions in your life. (See Figure 1–1.)

Self-esteem is how you feel about yourself — your general feelings of self-worth based on self-image and the amount of esteem others have for you. Social approval and acceptance play a significant part in the development of self-esteem. A negative body image or self-image, combined with negative response from others, can lower self-esteem. A person with low self-esteem can learn to use clothing to enhance appearance and thus raise self-esteem. In fact, anyone can use clothing to enhance appearance and boost self-esteem.

Self-confidence refers to your belief, trust, and reliance on yourself — your appearance, skills, and abilities you can count on to meet your needs. Appearance is

Figure 1–1. This young woman is comfortable and confident about herself. *(Courtesy J. Crew; photographer Franz Walderdorff)*

just one factor in the development of self-confidence. Self-confidence increases when you know how to use your clothing to help develop, maintain, and modify your appearance according to your needs.

Self-competence refers to specific abilities you possess and skills you have mastered. Like body image and self-image, self-image and self-esteem, self-confidence and self-competency can be seen as cyclical, because one influences the other. When confident in yourself, you are better able to develop talents, skills, and abilities that, in turn, instill more self-confidence. Competencies move you toward self-actualization and the accomplishment of your goals. (See Figure 1–2.)

For example, *when confident in your ability to learn, you can move ahead in learning wardrobe evaluation, planning, and shopping skills. Capable and competent in the selection and use of your clothing, you may feel more confident in tackling a particular project or in meeting and working with others. Dress may be comfortably and appropriately casual, businesslike, or dressy depending on the project, occasion, or setting.*

Figure 1–2. Competency in the closet often reflects competency in the workplace. *(Courtesy Madeleine Direct)*

Figure 1–3. Congratulations! Graduation Day. *(Courtesy Bud Neslen)*

Self-actualization is based on the root word *actual* and refers to the process of making something actual or real — the process of bringing something into reality. It refers to the use of your resources and abilities in ways that maximize your potential to achieve your goals. Preoccupation with clothing or anxiety over appearance interferes with your potential. The person who uses clothing as a resource to present herself in ways that meet her needs is less likely to dwell on clothing or to receive negative responses to her appearance. She is more likely to realize her potential as she strives to reach her goals. (See Figure 1–3.)

Goals are those things you want or hope to obtain or achieve. Your ability to reach your goals is influenced in varying degrees by body image, self-image, self-esteem, self-confidence, self-competence, and self-actualization. Clothing can influence each of these, independently or in turn. (See Figure 1–4.)

2.

Clothing is a basic human need — physically, psychologically, socially, and aesthetically.

Food, clothing, and shelter are ranked among basic human needs, in terms of survival. This book concentrates on clothing needs and ways, or strategies, to meet those needs.

Basic Clothing Needs

Clothing needs can be **physical**, in terms of physical survival, safety, health, and comfort. Clothing functions as a second skin or covering to protect your body from the environment — from injury due to the cold, sun, fire, wind, water, and plants, or attack by humans, animals, insects, or germs.

For example, at six feet tall Liz has great difficulty meeting her need for clothing that fits her figure. Clothing that is too short is physically uncomfortable for her, even to the point of chafing or cutting into her skin.

Clothing needs can be **psychological**, in terms of mental health and psychological comfort. Clothing functions as a second skin or an extension of yourself — your body and your psyche — to establish and maintain or protect your body image, self-image or self-concept, self-confidence, and self-esteem or self-respect.

For example, chemotherapy patients often experience hair loss. With a bald head, most women feel particularly exposed and vulnerable. An attractive scarf, head wrap, turban, or wig meets the need for psychological comfort as it serves to maintain self-image and self-confidence.

Developmental Levels Leading to the Achievement of Goals

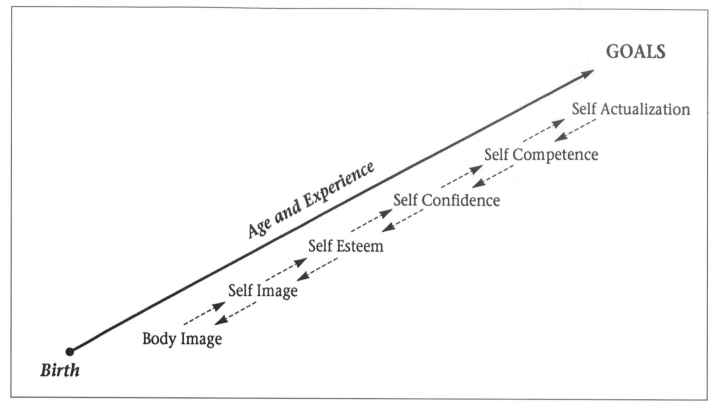

Figure 1–4.

Clothing needs can be **social**, in terms of acceptance, assignment, belonging, and modesty. Clothing functions to establish, identify, and maintain social roles, and to aid group interaction within the family, the community, and the workplace.

For example, a Girl Scout generally feels more like she belongs to the group when she's wearing the Girl Scout uniform. She is also recognized by others as a member of that group.

Clothing needs can be **aesthetic**, in terms of the art elements and principles of design. Clothing functions as a second skin to enhance appearance, as a medium for aesthetic creative self-expression, and adornment or decoration, and as a source of beauty.

For example, Elaine likes to wear a lovely hand-painted scarf of her own creation tied over her left shoulder. Elaine's figure is asymmetrical, with her left shoulder being lower than her right. The decorative scarf visually lifts her left shoulder, improving the apparent balance of her figure.

A piece of clothing can meet a single need or be designed and selected to meet many needs at once.

For example, compare the strictly physical needs met by a beekeeper's suit, with the largely aesthetic needs met or fulfilled by a hand-beaded dress. On the other hand, consider a favorite and well-worn blazer jacket, designed to be warm and to fit comfortably. Psychologically, it provides a protective layer between the wearer and others while it empowers the wearer with self-confidence, credibility, and authority in both leadership and professional situations. Aesthetically, when made up in a beautiful fabric and color, it enhances the appearance of the wearer.

Meeting Clothing Needs

Basic clothing needs must be met at all stages in life or the effort to fill the need can get in the way or interfere with developmental tasks, activities, and goals. (See Figure 1–5.)

When clothing needs are met, your mind is free from concern about your clothing and appearance. You are able to concentrate on other important endeavors. Other people are better able to see you as you want to be seen, and to concentrate on you and the activity or purpose at hand.

When clothing needs are not met, your mind is occupied with concern about yourself or others in terms of clothing and appearance. You are conscious of self, or self-conscious. Your mind is not able to concentrate or focus on other important matters. Your goals are realized less quickly or less often.

For example, without a jacket or coat on a cold day, wearing clothing two sizes too small, or sweats to a wedding, your thoughts are distracted or preoccupied by the shivers, by clothes cutting into your body, or by thoughts of what you wish you'd worn. You are not able to concentrate on matters of the moment.

Figure 1–5. Meeting family clothing needs contributes to successful family interaction. *(Courtesy All Week Long by Eddie Bauer; photographer Howard Frye)*

Needs versus Wants

The words "I need" are often used when what you really mean is "I want." Parents are quick to point out, "You may want it, but you don't need it" or "You don't really need a new pair of pants. You already have three pairs." Once needs are met, people begin to notice or focus on wants — the desire for something that will give you more confidence, satisfaction, pleasure, or happiness than you think you now have.

Actual clothing needs are few, primarily for survival, and are influenced by our environment and life-style. Clothing wants, however, are endless and are influenced by values, attitudes, friends, and peers. Display and media advertising expose us to endless goods and services that make us dissatisfied with what we have. It is essential to reconsider actual needs versus wants if you hope to resist the temptation to acquire and overextend your resources. (See Table 1–1.)

3.

Clothing is a universal element in nonverbal communication.

Verbal communication depends on words and sound. Nonverbal communication occurs through sight and touch. Call it what you like; your visual image, personal appearance, or self-presentation communicates to one and all within view.

Elements of Visual Image

Four elements combine to create personal appearance or visual image:

- Clothing, including accessories.
- Grooming, including body hygiene, hair care, skin care, nail care, makeup for women, and so forth.
- Body language, including figure or body type, personal coloring, posture, gestures, eye contact, facial expressions, and so forth.
- Manners, including polite behavior toward others and general etiquette.

Together, these elements create a unique and memorable image of you, either as a first impression or as an image that comes immediately to the minds of those who know you.

By its very presence, the visibility of clothing is accessible to others. This allows clothing to make statements, to project or reflect messages about the wearer and the situation, occasion, or activity. (See Figure 1–6, page 8.)

Query Box

What can you do to reverse the growing trend for carrying to an extreme the desire for physically comfortable and socially casual clothes?

Occasionally, comfortable and casual clothes are exactly right. Imagine wearing, however, only T-shirts and jeans all of the time — at any age. You immediately limit the range of feelings that a variety of clothes can stimulate, reflect, or project. Putting forth no thought or effort in dress, you gradually lose the ability to coordinate or create attractive and versatile outfits. Looking and feeling only comfortable and very casual, you gradually become psychologically uncomfortable with people in situations where dressier clothes are the tradition. Feeling uncomfortable, you gradually limit your association with those people. Wearing extremely casual clothing every day, you never look special. You never feel special. All occasions are the same. You are always the same. Facets of your personality and potential are not discovered and not developed. Experience supports the finding that when people stop dressing for different occasions they stop doing and going.

Consider, that when you give some thought and effort to dressing in a variety of ways for a variety of moods and occasions, you become more creative, individual, confident, and competent. You become more involved with more people, in more places and in more pursuits. Productivity increases. You are more likely to become self-actualized and to accomplish your goals.

Table 1–1 Life-Cycle Clothing Needs

	Physical	Psychological	Social	Aesthetic

Infant	*Physical needs are of prime importance. Diapers and sleepwear are worn most often.*
	
	Warm/cool enough
	Soft and flexible
	Lightweight
	Absorbent
	Germ-free
	Nonallergenic
	Easy care
	  Washable
	  Quick dry
	  No-iron
	Safety features
	  No pins, ribbons, or
	    drawstrings
	  Flame retardant
	Easy on/off
	  Larger openings
	  Elastic
	  Snaps
		When physical needs are met, psychological development proceeds unhindered.	*Social reactions occur from birth.*
			
			  Clean
			  Attractive to others
				An infant is not yet aware of beauty in clothing.

Toddler and Preschool	*Physical needs continue to be most important—influenced by rapid growth and active play.*
	
	Protective
	Safety features
	  Bright, visible colors
	  Knee padding
	  No pins, cuffs, drawstrings
	  Rubber-soled shoes,
	  Sleep feet
	  Flame retardant
	Comfortable
	Nonrestricting
	Durable, tightly woven
	Reinforced
	Easy on/off
	Easy care
	Growth features
	  Separates
	  Stretch fabrics
	  Adjustable buttons & straps
	  Ease pleats/tucks
	  Wide seam allowances
	    & hems
	Flexible soled shoes
		Psychological development begins to be influenced more specifically by clothing that fosters a sense of independence.
		
		  Self-help features
		    Front openings
		    Larger openings
		    Large, easy fasteners
		    Large armholes
		    Elasticized waistbands
		    Shoelaces with tips
		    Clothes marked F and B
		    Shoes marked L and R
		  Value formation
		  Personality formation
			Social interaction accelerates. Social development is influenced more specifically by clothing that contributes to acceptance and security.
			
			  Attention-getting
			  Attractive to others
			  Affordable
			    (within social environment)
				Aesthetic preferences form and influence selection. Preferences are more freely expressed.
				
				  Colorful
				  Decorative

Table 1–1 Life-Cycle Clothing Needs *(continued)*

	Physical	Psychological	Social	Aesthetic
Elementary School	*Physical needs are not as important, but must still be considered.* Protective incl. safety features Growth features Durable	*Psychological needs assume greater importance, influenced by the need for self-respect and worthiness.* Suited to age Value formation Personality reflecting Self-esteem building	*Social needs assume greater importance. Social development is influenced more specifically by clothing that fosters a sense of belonging and security.* Reasonably similar to friends Attention-getting Attractive Affordable	*Aesthetic preferences vary from personal to peer group.* Colorful Decorative
Teen Age	*Physical growth can be rapid, then stops.* Growth features incl. Separates Loose fit Raglan sleeve Ease pleats or tucks Elastic waistline	*Emphasis is now on psychological needs as clothing influences maturation.* Value reinforcing Personality reflecting Confidence building Self-esteem building	*Emphasis is now on social needs. Active sports, dating, and possible employment influence needs.* Reasonably fashionable Reasonably similar to friends Versatile Attractive Affordable	*Personal aesthetic preferences may give in to peer pressure. This is a good time for developing personal style.* Flattering Outlet for creativity and personal expression
Adult	*The body has stopped growing, reducing the need for new clothes.* Classic styling Suited to climate Maternity clothing for women	*With maturity comes the need for personal independence and individuality.* Suited to personality Suited to values Confidence building	*Emphasis is on the personal suitability of clothing for life-style, social roles, and goals — college, military service, employment, marriage, childbearing, sports, and social occasions.* Separates Suited to roles Versatile Attractive Affordable	*Personal aesthetic preferences are more stable and freely expressed.* Enhancing Flattering fit Well made Well coordinated Creative outlet contributes to personal fulfillment

Middle–Age and Elderly	*Physical needs again become very important. With advancing age the body begins to soften and sag while joints stiffen.*
	
	Comfortable
	Warm or cool enough
	Nonirritating to sensitive skin
	Easy care
		Psychologically, clothing can help maintain self-image and self-esteem.
		
		Attractive
		Self-help features
		  Medium-to-large easy fasteners
		  Velcro closures
		  Larger neck and armholes
		  Slip-on shoes
			Socially, clothing can help maintain an active life-style.
			
			Attractive
			Interesting
			Motivating
			Affordable
				Aesthetic needs counter the effect of physical changes occurring with increasing age and help maintain an attractive appearance.
				
				Enhancing
				Styled or altered to fit and flatter
				  Collar
				  Loose fit
				  Elastic waistlines

Figure 1–6. A sarong skirt, reflecting cultural influence, is paired with a professional-looking linen jacket. It makes an interesting combination for warm weather casual business dress. *(Courtesy All Week Long by Eddie Bauer; photographer David Martinez)*

Figure 1–7. Traditional German-Austrian influence is reflected in modern-day fashion. *(Courtesy Madeleine Direct)*

For example, in her book, The Language of Clothes, *Alison Lurie (1981) explains: "Long before I am near enough to talk to you on the street, in a meeting, or at a party, you announce your sex, age, and class to me through what you are wearing — and very possibly give me important information (or misinformation) as to your occupation, origin, personality, opinions, tastes, sexual desires, and current mood. I may not be able to put what I observe into words, but I register the information unconsciously; and you simultaneously do the same for me. By the time we meet and converse we have already spoken to each other in an older and more universal tongue." (p. 3).*

Clothing Cues

Specific characteristics, traits, or design details in clothing function as symbols or cues to communicate a message. There is no such thing as neutral clothing. Any and every detail speaks out, although the meaning of the clothing may be unclear and the interpretation may be inaccurate. (See Table 1–2.)

For example, some individuals may wear a Christian or Greek cross to symbolize religious belief and/or cultural association. Others, however, may wear a necklace with these symbols out of pure aesthetic interest. Top-stitching on a garment collar or lapel may signal appropriateness for a sportive, more casual occasion, while lapels buttoned back reflect traditional Tyrolian influence.

The specific message depends on: the characteristic cue or combination of cues; the people involved; the social context — the place, situation, occasion, or activity; and the period in time.

Different cues are noticed by different people, depending on their own background or frame of reference. (See Figure 1–7.) Even the same cue may carry or project different meanings to different people, depending on their background and historic position in time.

Table 1–2 Clothing Cues

	Message	Some Clothing Characteristic or Cues
Occasion	• Casual, informal, sporty/sportive	• Crew or V-necklines, convertible collars, shoulder and skirt yokes, jumper, T-shirt, shorts, jeans, sweaters, blazer, parka, canvas shoes, sandals, sweats, caps
	• Dress business-like, leadership	• 2–3 piece matched suit, firm to crisp fabric, straight and A-line skirts, shirtwaist dress, coatdress, overcoat, pumps
	• Dressy, formal, sophisticated, glamour	• Wider scoop or lower neckline, strapless, long fitted sleeves, Juliet sleeve, trumpet sleeve, draped bodices and skirts, long skirt, palazzo pants, satin or beaded dress, tuxedo, long skirt, cummerbund, sparkling jewelry, patent leather shoes
	• Lounging, sleeping	• P.J.'s, nightgown, negligée, caftan, night shirt, flannel, satin or chiffon, lace, slippers, robe
Personality	• Energetic, fun, friendly, approachable, outgoing	• Full-curved lines, bright colors, gathers, pleats, knits, plaids, prints, polka dots, soft fabrics, bold contrast, scoop neckline, open collar, short or puffed sleeves, colorful trims, casual larger jewelry
	• Serious, stern, aloof, authoritative	• Straight lines, restrained curves, dark or dull colors, black, gray, firm or stiff fabric, small patterns, pinstripes, high or buttoned collar, long sleeves, straight and A-line skirts, matched suit, coatdress, minimal trim, small to medium conservative jewelry
	• Calm, quiet, gentle, ladylike, supportive	• Solid colors, subtle color contrasts, small and floral prints, fitted styles, princess seamlines, soft, thin, delicate sheer fabrics, soft gathers and flair, bows, small or delicate jewelry
Values	• Wants to save valuable time	• Easy-care fabric of manmade fibers or blended fibers; shops the catalogs, organized wardrobe
	• Wants the best dollar value, the most for the money	• Basic classic styles, durable fabrics, sales important, clothes in excellent condition
	• Values creativity as important	• Unusual clothing combinations, adds personal touch, self-made
	• Appreciates beautiful things	• Well-designed, high-quality clothing, harmonious color schemes, artistic mix of textures
	• Wants to be part of the group and put others at ease	• Clothing like friends, follows the leader's dress or what's in fashion, clothing appropriate for the occasion
	• Wants to influence others opinion and actions	• Tailored looks
	• Likes to impress others, to be the best dressed	• Expensive, designer, or name-brand clothes, one-of-a-kind
	• Believes in practicality and modesty, with attention away from the body	• Nonskimpy, loose-fitting styles, opaque fabrics
	• Wants to be comfortable	• Soft fabrics in simple, loose-fitting styles, nonirritating styles and fabrics
	• Prefers the natural, "real" thing	• Real leather and suede, 100% wool or silk, real gemstones

For example, a diamond ring worn on the third finger of the right hand may not even be noticed by a young teen, but could be noticed immediately by a young adult; it could be perceived as a wedding band by someone in Europe, but assumed by an observer in America to communicate a change of hand due to divorce.

Change the cue (alter, remove, cover, uncover), the combination of cues, or the situation, and you change the message. Each piece of clothing, including accessories, serves as a cue.

For example, it is common for women or men in business suits to remove their jackets or loosen their ties after work to communicate a less formal situation. This action may even occur within a business situation to project a more relaxed attitude and more informal interaction between the business associates. Closely related, a cotton knit T-shirt generally projects a comfortable, relaxed mood and is considered appropriate for strictly casual occasions. During the mid 1980s, however, T-shirts began to be worn in combination with contemporary business suits and jackets. The combination of traditional cues worn in a nontraditional way served to soften the look of a business suit and communicate a more comfortable, relaxed attitude about business in general. The look tends to be most acceptable in creative or casual business settings.

Theatrical costume designers rely on clothing cues to set the stage for a character and stimulate audience response. (See Figure 1–8.) They are responsible, in part, for the believability of the character and the reactions of the audience. Results are recognized to be so powerful that awards are given annually in the form of a Tony, an Oscar, or an Emmy.

In everyday life as well, it is essential that you become aware of your own clothing cues, the messages you are sending, and their potential for response. These cues set the parameters of expectation and behavior. When those parameters or limits are incorrect, communication breaks down. Sending a clothing message that is inconsistent, incongruent, or incompatible with your values, your personality, your role, or the occasion serves only to distract and confuse the viewer.

For example, a professional woman dressed in ruffles and frills or a tight-fitting skirt is less likely to be perceived as being serious about her work. This, in turn, influences office relationships.

Clothing Expectations and Stereotypes

We have expectations of people's clothing and appearance for specific occasions based on what is socially and culturally acceptable for the time and place — or upon experience alone.

For example, you would interpret a man dressed in a tuxedo seen on the occasion of a wedding differently than if you saw the man wearing a tuxedo on the occasion of an informal backyard barbecue, and still differently if you

Figure 1–8. Everyone, especially the kids, recognize and trust Snow White.

saw him in a tuxedo and mask on the occasion of a Halloween party.

In addition, value conflicts between people, such as parent and child or employer and employee, can occur because the individuals disagree on their expectations of appropriate dress. The workplace is known for attention to professional appearance. Not all people want to comply, and yet by dressing to meet the expectations of those you work for and with, you can create a more positive impression about yourself and your abilities. You can establish or maintain your credibility and exert a more significant influence.

In general, there are four types of business or work environments, each with typical expectations about appearance. (See Table 1–3.)

In order to make the world a simpler place, we often stereotype people by our preconceived ideas of what specific clothing pieces or combinations mean. We thereafter presume similarly dressed people possess common personality or behavioral characteristics as well.

For example, the "Patty Perfect" stereotype comes complete with prim-and-proper posture, a never-ending smile,

Table 1–3 Professional Image Types

Image Type	Typical Fields	Expected Traits	Recommended Dress
Executive and Administrative	Banking and finance Law Military Management Personnel	Authoritative Knowledgeable Organized Efficient Trustworthy Formal manner	Conservative cut Traditionally classic Tailored styles, including matched suits, coat-dress Predictable use of line, color, and texture
Sales and Service	Education Real estate Insurance Travel Counseling Health care Hospitality	Authoritative Knowledgeable Efficient Trustworthy Friendly Approachable Helpful	Softly tailored, more casual tailored looks Less predictable Unmatched suits, sport coats, sweaters, slacks, skirts, dresses Possible uniform dress
Creative and Communications	Fashion Art, music Theater, TV Architecture Interior design Computer Research	Creative Artistic Sensitive Individual Up-to-date Knowledgeable Efficient	Trend-setting styles are acceptable or required Tailored to casual tailored Unpredictable, unique use of line, color, and texture
Physical Labor	Construction Transportation Industrial Factory Maintenance	Hard working Dependable Strong Informal Efficient	Durable work clothes Classic tailored styles and colors; durable fabrics Possible uniform dress

clothes perfectly put together, flawless makeup, and the latest hairstyle. The nineties BMOC (big-man-on-campus) wears the J. Crew look and walks with a confident swagger, while the traditional Ivy Leaguer is described wearing a V-neck sweater, button-down Oxford cloth shirt, twill pants or shorts, and loafers. The typical cheerleader sports long "swishy" hair or a ponytail and a short pleated skirt. "Suits" is the name applied to corporate businessmen, reflecting a fixed mental image of severely tailored business suits. Skimpy, extremely tight-fitting clothes and excess makeup on women bring to mind negative stereotypes.

In making extended assumptions, we often use ourselves as a frame of reference for comparison.

For example, a teenager may perceive someone in her thirties as old, and an older person may perceive the same person as young. Or a person may remind us of a friend, relative, or TV star, and we automatically transfer the friend's or relative's or TV star's characteristics to that person. The perceptions are true only in comparison to ourselves.

In general, if you want to be associated with a stereotypical trait or set of traits recognized by others, it is to your advantage to adopt them in your appearance. (See Figure 1–9.) Conversely, if you don't want to be seen in a predictably stereotypical manner, it is to your advantage to avoid those traits in your appearance.

Figure 1–9. In professional dress, dark-light contrast is often used to draw attention to the face. *(Courtesy Madeleine Direct)*

Figure 1–10. Dark glasses and rolled bandana typify the serious exercise biker. *(Courtesy Heidi Neslen)*

4.

Clothing directly affects the way you think, the way you feel, the way you act, and the way others react to you.

You must be aware of the effects of your clothing in your life — in your home, school, community, workplace, and so forth. Your clothing is continually at work; you can't hide it. It can work for you or against you. It can help you reach your goals, or be a tremendous liability that holds you back without your ever knowing why. (See Figure 1–10.)

For example, Liz, a young college student, needs afford-able, durable, easy-care, comfortable, and casual clothing to meet her daily needs. She wants to feel, behave, and be seen as a competent, responsible student and a friendly, fun-to-be-with, feminine young woman. She chooses clothing pieces in blue chambray, blue denim, and red cotton broadcloth, in a mix of solid colors and floral prints, in shirts, pants, and skirts, in softly tailored and feminine styles to allow her a wide range of looks for her many moods and occasions.

Universal Effects of Clothing

You can't afford to think negative thoughts about your-self and others — or to harbor a negative self-image. Clothing can help you create a positive appearance, maintain positive thoughts, and a positive self-image.

You can't afford to feel self-conscious, uncomfortable, unproductive, inferior, or full of self-doubt. Clothing can be a fast, effective tool to increase self-acceptance, self-confidence, and overcome feelings of anxiety or inability.

You can't afford to act awkward, insecure, or out-of-place. Nor can you afford to act in a defensive, defiant,

Table 1–4

All-Occasion Image Makers	All-Occasion Image Breakers

• Appropriate
    for the occasion
    for the person
	• Inappropriate
	    for the occasion
	    for the person

• Reasonably fashionable	• Out of date
• Harmony between style lines and shapes, fabrics, colors, and patterns	• Clashing style lines and shapes, fabrics, colors, and patterns
• Tasteful use of accessories	• Too many accessories
• One focal point	• Too many focal points
• Neat, orderly	• Visible labels, hanger loops, cleaner's tags
• Good quality	• Poor quality
• Well fitted	• Poor fit
• Well cared for clean and in good repair	• Poor care, dirty, wrinkled, or ripped

arrogant, affected, superior, or conceited manner. Clothing is one of the most effective tools you can use to improve behavior and increase performance, allowing you to act more at ease, secure, and competent, and to perform or produce well.

You can't afford to be seen as pretentious, irresponsible, ineffective, or unproductive. These perceptions lead to negative reactions and responses from others.

Clothing is an available and effective tool to help you create a positive impression, and to project your personality traits, values, attitudes, interests, and abilities. It also allows others to more easily perceive these traits and to recognize your credibility and abilities. It invites them to become acquainted with the unique individual inside your well-managed visual image, to regard you favorably and with continued interest. (See Table 1–4.)

T I P

FROM THE PROS

You have to work harder to overcome a bad impression, as people tend to skew all information that follows to fit the previous impression. **A good impression is like an investment** you can always draw on. A bad impression is a continual drain on your resources.

5.

Clothing, or wardrobe, management is the process of evaluating and controlling the use and effect of your clothing on you and others.

The effect of your clothing and appearance is something you can analyze or evaluate and generally control or manage, in much the same way you manage your other resources — time, money, meals, and so forth. (See Figure 1–11.)

The clothing management process involves continual evaluation, planning, selection, coordination, purchase, and care. The entire process is a necessary life skill. Strategies, guidelines, suggestions, direction, and advice you can adapt and apply to your own wardrobe follow throughout the remainder of this book.

For example, (1) evaluating the fit of your clothing can reveal fitting problems that attract attention to your body. Once aware of the fitting problems, you can take steps to select clothing that fits well, flatters your figure, and directs attention where you want it. (2) Planning for a first job interview, you are smart to dress in more professional, tailored-looking clothes. (3) If you want to get the most for

Figure 1–11. An effective wardrobe includes casual as well as business and dressy clothing. Each can energize you for the specific occasion. *(Courtesy of Esprit)*

your clothing dollar, plan your purchases, select more durable fabrics, and care for them properly.

Key Words in Clothing Management

While there is no one-and-only right way to look, "attractive" and "appropriate" are words to keep in mind when selecting your clothes. Rather than dressing by habit, impulse, imitation, pressure, or trial and error, dress as a result of thoughtful decisions and choices. Think in terms of dressing appropriately for:

- The occasion, situation, or activity, and in relation to purpose and goals.
- The person, the people, or the group you will be, or wish to be, involved with — their mood, values, attitudes, and interests.
- You as an individual — for your physical body, your personality, mood, values, attitudes, and interests.

T I P
☞
FROM THE PROS

If you are unsure about what to wear on a certain occasion, ask a friend who has been to a similar event; call the host or person in charge of the event, talk to a parent, teacher, or local newspaper fashion editor. Adapt advice to your needs, preferences, and ability to provide.

Key Situations

Time and attention to the message you create with your clothing and appearance are important in three general situations:

- Whenever the other person does not know you.
- Whenever the other person's opinion or reaction to you is important to the achievement of your goals — any time you want or need to influence the opinion or action of another person.
- When your mood or confidence level needs a lift.

A few such occasions include the first day of class, a blind date, a job interview, an appearance in court, or the day you have to present a report, make a sale, or participate on a committee.

T I P
☞
FROM THE PROS

In all cases, learn to manage your clothing as a resource, a tool to help you think, feel, and act your personal and professional best; to create a positive first and lasting impression about yourself. With thought and practice, you can create an attractive appearance — authentic, appropriate, and acceptable — that allows you to forget yourself.

While there is no great mystery surrounding clothing and image management, some people seem to have more natural talent or ability. They always seem to look attractive, appropriate and absolutely terrific. Others have to work at it a bit. The good news is that clothing management skills can be learned, then practiced to become almost automatic. Resolve now to take charge and make your clothes work for you on all occasions.

Fashion Therapy

Fashion therapy is a facet of image management, with more attention directed to the effects of clothing on the wearer, rather than on the response of others. People often get caught up in fashion for the sake of fashion and they forget about function. In fashion therapy, clothing is used as a resource that literally empowers you with a better ability to think, feel, and do the things you want to. Looking better always helps to solve problems related in some way to personal appearance. (See Figure 1–12.)

For example, Loya is a graduate student who lives with rheumatoid arthritis, a progressively disabling disease. Due to limited arm movement, she requires easy on-and-off clothing with front openings. Pullover sweaters, wrap-around blouses, and tie belts are among her favorite clothes. She is conscious of the weight of her clothing, as heavy clothes make her shoulders ache. Because her elbows will no longer straighten, she prefers to wear long-sleeved blouses and dresses, which make the problem unnoticeable to others. If she wants to wear short sleeves in warm summer weather, she seeks out blouses with

Figure 1–12. While pregnancy is a time of continual adjustment, clothing helps to maintain a positive body image, and competency in the workplace.

Figure 1–13. Cluster dressing for the "me" of the moment.
(Courtesy Clifford & Wills; photographer Val Ostrowsky)

neckline emphasis to draw attention away from her arms. She wears little jewelry, particularly rings, because they draw attention to her hands. She looks for shoes with lower heels to aid her balance, and to provide proper support and comfort. She says that one of the most important things she's learned when not feeling well, is to keep herself looking well. When attractive and well-fitted clothing is worn, personal appearance is enhanced and self-confidence can be increased.

6.

Ideally, the end purpose of all clothing design, manufacturing, selection, or sales effort, is the creation of a wardrobe that meets the needs of the individual wearer.

A **wardrobe** is a large group of clothes and accessories, generally brought together over an extended period of time, and serving all the needs of the owner.

A **cluster** is a smaller group of about five to twelve coordinated clothing pieces and accessories in a wardrobe, brought together over a shorter period of time, and serving limited situational needs, or expanded over a longer period of time to meet most of the needs of the owner. Ideally, a complete wardrobe is made up of one or more clusters. (See Figure 1–13.)

Looking Good Isn't Necessarily Vanity

Say the word *fashion* to any woman between the ages of ten and eighty, and you are likely to get one of two very opposite reactions. They either love it or they hate it. As a result, they pay too much or too little attention to it.

In one extreme, the individual slavishly follows every fashion trend and fad to the point of becoming a fashion victim. Clothing is acquired and retired with little regard for function or finance.

In the other extreme, the woman puts little to no thought or attention and effort into building a workable wardrobe. For some women, just thinking about their wardrobes brings on an anxiety attack. Given the complexity of women's fashion and the overwhelming variety to choose from, these women harbor a literal fear of fashion.

While some women admit to a fear of fashion, others, and men in particular, cultivate an attitude of indifference, allowing themselves to ignore it, make jokes about it, or put it down. Individuals in this latter group aren't aware or won't admit the ways in which their clothes influence their lives. They prefer to see it merely as superficial gloss.

Your image — the way you care for and carry yourself, the clothes you wear, your personal style, your poise and presence — is part of who you are, reflecting the way you think, feel, act, and live. Personal appearance creates a memorable image, reflecting your personality, values, attitudes, interests, roles, and often your goals.

The thought, time, energy, and money it takes to manage your clothes and put together an appearance you feel good about is not a matter of vanity or frivolity. It's a matter of good sense, self-worth, and provident living. A positive personal appearance is an open invitation to others to become acquainted with the person behind the well-presented image.

It would be foolish to assume that the woman who wears a suit, a pretty blouse, a great pair of jeans or applies lipstick and blusher relies solely on looks for self-esteem, self-confidence or self-expression. A positive personal appearance is not an end in itself. Yet it is still an important attribute, one ranking right up there with intelligence, knowledge, effort, and ability.

My approach to wardrobing isn't so much about fashion as it is about function. It isn't so much about style as it is about life-style and personal style. It's not about ego. It's about self-concept and self-esteem and self-confidence. It's not just about money. It's about management — the management of your resources; your money, your time, your energy, and your clothing. It's about using your clothing as a resource, a tool to help you meet your needs and accomplish your goals. With today's personal and professional demands, your wardrobe has to work as hard as you do.

Add-ons are those clothing pieces added on to the original cluster to expand the cluster.

The advantage of a coordinated cluster is the versatility and flexibility it affords. Change the pieces and you change your appearance according to the mood and occasion. Both a cluster and a complete wardrobe evolve or change over time, reflecting changes in the wearer's needs, based on changes in the body, personality, moods, values, attitudes, roles, goals, and so forth. The evolution of a cluster or a wardrobe reflects the evolution of the person as she or he matures over time.

The goal of this book is to provide you with accurate information for your task of selecting clothing and assembling a cluster or clusters of clothes — a workable wardrobe that meets your needs. Wardrobe skills are skills for a lifetime.

TIP
❧
FROM THE PROS
Today's women and men have more roles to fill than at any previous time in history. Each role is associated with a different look appropriate for the role — a look that communicates values, attitudes, moods, intentions, goals, and actions of the person in the role. Different personality traits come out in different roles to different degrees. "There are a lot of me's inside." This sentence expresses the complexity of today's woman and the multiple me's that her wardrobe must reflect. Dressing to accommodate and reflect each "me" is an effective way to nurture each part of that woman and assist in the development of the person striving for self-actualization or fulfillment.

Review Main Points

Your clothing is a personal resource that meets basic needs — physical, psychological, social, and aesthetic. When clothing needs are met, you are better able to forget about your clothes and appearance and concentrate on more important matters. Visible to you and others, clothing communicates a great deal about people and about social situations. Change the clothing cues and you change the message. Whether or not we purposely use clothing to project a specific message or image, we perceive appearance and form impressions based upon a person's clothing and the situation. The accuracy of these impressions will depend upon the clothing cues themselves and the awareness and abilities of the wearer and the viewer. The message we convey through our clothes may be interpreted differently in different situations and by different people. The way we look affects the way we think, feel, act, and the way others react to us. With these points in mind, it is wise to evaluate and manage our clothes in ways to help us achieve our goals — in the home, school, community, and workplace. A wardrobe with clusters of clothes that meet your needs can help you achieve your goals, both personal and professional.

Review Questions

1. Clothing needs can be classified as being _____, _____, _____, or _____.

2. Clothing appropriate for the occasion meets a _____ need.

3. Three elements that combine to create a unique and memorable image of you include your _____, your _____, and your _____.

4. Clothing has the ability to project and reflect messages about people simply because it is _____.

5. Different clothing _____ may be noticed by different _____, due to different backgrounds, frames of reference, or points of view.

6. Sneakers tend to project a _____ mood, occasion, or activity, while patent leather shoes communicate a _____ occasion.

7. Easy-care, durable fabrics tend to reflect the value or _____ of saving _____ and money.

8. _____ on clothing tend to reflect the wearer's need to impress others.

9. The way you look influences the way you _____, the way you _____, and the way you _____.

10. You can't afford to let your clothing make you feel _____ or act _____.

11. Clothing management is the process of evaluating and _____ the effect of your clothing on you and on others.

12. A small group of coordinated clothes is called a _____.

Discussion Questions

#1 What are some of your own clothing needs — or, what do you need your clothing to do for you — physically, psychologically, socially, and aesthetically?

Notes: _____

_____

_____

#2 What stereotypes are you aware of — in your school, town, region, or country — or, in your age group, your parents' age group, your grandparents' age group? What clothing cues describe these stereotypes?

Notes: _____

_____

_____

_____

_____

#3 If you were being interviewed for an award, a scholarship, or a job, what personal characteristics would you want your appearance to say? What details of dress might serve as cues to communicate those characteristics?

Notes: _____

_____

_____

_____

_____

#4 What situations can you remember when what you were wearing influenced yourself and others noticeably? What did you think? How did you feel? How did you act? How did others react or respond to you?

Notes: _____

_____

_____

_____

_____

#5 In the future, how might you manage your clothing selection to put you more at ease, to lift your spirits, to feel more attractive, to feel more self-confident, to act more friendly, or be seen as more friendly, to act or appear more knowledgeable and in charge?

Notes: _____

_____

_____

_____

_____

(Courtesy Madeleine Direct)

• What is your first impression about the person in the photograph?

_____

_____

_____

_____

_____

_____

• What were the cues, the details of dress or image, that stimulated your impression?

_____

_____

_____

_____

_____

_____

Exercise 1–2   First Impressions

(Courtesy Madeleine Direct)

What are your impressions or assumptions about the person in the photograph? What were the cues, the details of dress or image, that stimulated your responses?

Gender Projected:	Cues:
Age Projected:	Cues:
Activity Projected:	Cues:
Personality Traits Projected:	Cues:
Values Projected:	Cues:

Exercise 1–3   Clothing Needs and Wants   Name _____

Interview someone you know about her clothing needs.

• Make up your own list of five questions to ask.
• Allow ten to fifteen minutes for the interview.
• Take detailed notes or tape record your interview.
• Analyze the responses of the person you interviewed, identifying her specific clothing needs and wants, her apparent personality traits, and clothing values that seem to be reflected in the responses.
• Record your impressions and assumptions and turn in with your notes or tape.

Interviewed: Family Member _____   Female _____

Friend _____ , ___   Male _____

Other _____   Age Approx. _____

Item/Statement	Personality Trait Reflected	Values Reflected

Clothing Needs

Item/Statement	Personality Trait Reflected	Values Reflected

Clothing Wants

Exercise 1–4   Inappropriate Dress: Not "The Real Me"

Name _____

Experience the effect of clothing on you and others. Dress inappropriately for some activity or occasion — in some way inappropriate for your age, your personality, your values, your figure, or your perception of the occasion itself. A subtle approach often gets the best results. The options are endless, but don't go so far as to dress in a way that will create serious problems for you. Consider wearing:

- Clothing with a noticeable food spot on the front.
- A shirt with a rip in the underarm seam.
- Clothing overly dressy or overly casual for the occasion.
- Mismatched clothes, shoes, or earrings.
- More jewelry than is usual for you.
- A clothing style associated with a celebrity but not suited to you.
- Clothing associated with someone older or younger than you are.
- Clothes that do not fit, borrowed from a neighbor if necessary.
- An outfit more or less creative than is usual for you.

As with any experiment, there are a few rules.

1. Don't tell anyone what you are doing. Even one person knowing that this is an assignment will spoil the results of the experience.
2. Keep accurate mental or written notes throughout the experience — notes about what you're thinking, what and how you are feeling, how you are acting, and how others are reacting or responding to you.
3. Record your experience on the exercise form provided.
4. Ponder the results of your experience and draw some conclusions about the influence of your clothes.
5. Be prepared to discuss your experience in class.

Describe the situation:
Describe your clothing:
What thoughts went through your mind?
How did you feel?
How did you act? What did you do?
How did other people react or respond to you? Who were the people?
Conclusions and special comments:

Exercise 1–5 Appropriate Dress: "The Real Me" Name_____

Repeat Exercise 1–4, this time wearing clothing totally appropriate for you and the occasion — looking the way you'd like to be seen and remembered by someone significant in your life. Compare experiences from Exercises 1–4 and 1–5, then draw some conclusions.

Describe the situation:
Describe your clothing:
What thoughts went through your mind?
How did you feel?
How did you act? What did you do?
How did other people react or respond to you? Who were the people?
Conclusions and special comments:

Chapter
2
Clothing as Wearable Art

Learning Objectives

Your goal in completing this chapter is to be able to:

- Recognize your clothing as pieces of wearable art.
- List the elements and principles of design.
- Identify the dominant line, shape, color, texture, and/or pattern in any garment or outfit.
- Explain the difference between dominant and subordinate points of interest.
- Recognize your artistic input as you select and coordinate your clothes.
- Describe ways you become part of the composition with your clothes.
- Discuss repetition/reinforcing and contrast/countering as ways of controlling attention and the resulting visual effects in your clothes.
- List factors contributing to life-style and personal style.
- Recognize the influence of life-style and personal style on clothing needs.
- Identify factors contributing to your life-style and personal style.

Preview Main Points

1. Rely on your clothing as an art form — personal pieces of wearable art.

2. Think of yourself as an artist as you select and coordinate your clothes and build your wardrobe.

3. Think of yourself as part of the artistic composition with your clothes.

4. As with any art form, select your clothing to be in harmony with your life-style and your personal style, together they determine your needs.

5. Identify the specific factors that contribute to your life-style and personal style.

1.

Rely on your clothing as an art form — personal pieces of wearable art.

Clothing is an art form you can see, touch, and at times even hear as it stimulates your senses every bit as much as a painting, a piece of sculpture, or a song. Because you can wear this art form, clothing can be seen as wearable art. In this broad sense, all clothing qualifies as wearable art, not just pieces of hand-rendered art that can be displayed on the human body. (See Figure 2–1.)

Elements of Design

All clothing is a combination or composition of lines, shapes, color, texture, and pattern — commonly called the artistic **elements of design**, the basic components, or the media of clothing design. Each element of design has its own exciting set of characteristics that no other element provides or can imitate. (See Table 2–1.)

Figure 2–1a, b, c, d. Examples of wearable art. Some are simple while others are more complex. *(a & b: Courtesy Putman Photography; c & d: Courtesy Roberta Glidden)*

Table 2–1 Elements and Principles of Design

Design Elements	Design Principles
Media Components to Manipulate: • Line • Shape • Color • Texture • Pattern	Guidelines and Goals: • Balance • Proportion • Scale • Rhythm • Emphasis • Harmony • Unity

Line refers to a narrow, elongated mark that connects two or more points. Line encloses and divides space, creating shapes. Seamlines divide and enclose space on a garment.

Shape or form refers to the area or space enclosed by a line, creating the outer edge or outline of an object. The outer edge or silhouette of a garment is a shape. Shapes within a garment might include sleeves, cuffs, pockets, shirt yokes and plackets, skirt gores, and so forth.

Color is a sensation experienced when colored light waves stimulate the eye. Light waves may emanate from a light source or be reflected from the pigmented surface of an object, such as clothing. Colors in the visible hue spectrum include red, orange, yellow, green, blue, and violet.

Texture refers to the surface quality of something, such as fabric — the way it looks, feels, and possibly sounds if rubbed.

Pattern is an arrangement of lines, shapes, and color printed onto or woven into a fabric.

Principles of Design

The generally accepted goals for any art form, including clothing, include balance, proportion and scale, rhythm, emphasis, and harmony. They are commonly called the **principles of design**. The principles of design also serve as guidelines for selecting and using the elements of design and for critically evaluating the success of a clothing composition. (See Table 2–1.)

Balance refers to how lines, shapes, colors, textures, and patterns are used to break up an area or space and how they are distributed or grouped within a garment or an outfit. When balance is achieved, it appears that weight (visual and actual) is evenly distributed — from side to side and top to bottom. A feeling of stability, rest, and equilibrium results. Symmetry is a factor in balance.

Symmetrical balance results when both sides of a garment are the same. The design space is broken into equal parts. Design details divide the garment equally, side to side. Balance is achieved because the design details are distributed equally on both sides. The finished effect is more formal, serious, and stable. The body is basically symmetrical. Most clothing designed is symmetrical.

Asymmetrical balance results when the sides of a garment are different. The design space is broken into unequal parts. Design details divide the garment unequally, side to side. Balance is achieved when more design details are added to the smaller side, balancing the undetailed or empty larger side. (See Figure 2–2.) The finished effect is generally less formal and more interesting, even exciting. A garment can be asymmetrical in design, or be made to appear asymmetrical with the use of accessories on one side.

Proportion refers to how lines and shapes divide the garment or outfit into parts. It involves the relationship of one part or space compared to another part or space, compared to the whole garment, and to the body — in terms of areas, amounts, parts, ratios, distance, and degrees. (See Figure 2–3.) A garment is generally more interesting and pleasing if divided into unequal parts, and if the parts are in scale with the body. Color, texture, and pattern also influence the appearance of proportional areas. When achieved, garment proportions flatter the body proportions. When parts do not relate well to one another, they appear out of proportion.

Scale refers to the size relationship of one shape compared to another. Relative differences in scale are generally described in terms of small, medium, and large. (See Figure 2–4.) When achieved, there is one consistent size or a gradual transition from one size to another — between garment shapes, and between the garment and the body. When one shape overpowers another, they are said to be out of scale.

Figure 2–2. Asymmetrical balance is seen in the design of the sweater and bracelets. One-to-one proportions work due to the width of the upper body compared to the lower body. *(Courtesy Madeleine Direct)*

Figure 2–4. The white collar is relatively large-scale. *(Courtesy Madeleine Direct)*

Proportional Areas or Ratios

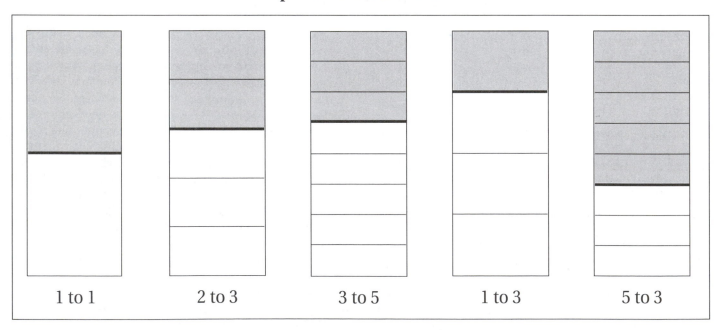

1 to 1   2 to 3   3 to 5   1 to 3   5 to 3

Figure 2–3.

Rhythm refers to how attention is led around the garment or the outfit. It is used to provide a transition between areas of the garment. It unifies the entire design. Rhythm is achieved when the lines, shapes, colors, textures, or patterns are arranged in such a way as to lead the eye around the garment to a point of emphasis. When achieved, there is a sense of smooth, orderly, organized movement.

For example, plaids that don't match at the seams interrupt the smooth flow of lines. Plaids that match are rhythmically more pleasing.

Rhythmic movement can be created by several means.

- Repetition of design elements or details repeated within the design.
- Progression or gradation in the size of lines and/or shapes, color values and/or intensities, or textures.
- Alternation of two or more lines, shapes, colors, textures, or patterns.
- Continuous line movement created by a line, a line of shapes, colors, or textural trims.
- Radiation of lines, shapes, colors, or textural folds inward or outward from a central point.

Emphasis refers to the use of line, shape, color, texture, or pattern to create a dominant focal point or center of interest in a garment or an outfit — a point for the eye to rest on. Conflicting parts, areas, or points of emphasis are distracting and confusing. When good emphasis is achieved, there is only one dominant point or most important point of emphasis in the garment or the outfit. If there are subordinate points of emphasis or interest, they are smaller or less obvious in their claim for attention. Emphasis is usually employed to draw attention to a pleasing area on the body or near the face. Emphasis occurs at the point of greatest visual interest or contrast. Emphasis can be created by the following means.

- Contrast in line direction, shape, color, texture, or decorative detail.
- Repetition or concentration of lines, shapes, colors, eye-catching texture, or pattern in one area.
- Reinforcement of a design detail by trim in that same area.

Harmony refers to the use of lines, shapes, colors, textures, and patterns in repetitious or similar ways, appropriate for the wearer, the purpose, idea, concept, or theme — with just enough variety to avoid boredom but not so much variety as to create conflict. Harmony is achieved when all design details relate consistently to one another, to the occasion, and to the wearer. If a garment is not well balanced, is out of proportion, has several spotty points of emphasis, or does not fit, the garment will not appear harmonious.

Unity refers to a sense of completeness. Nothing is left out or undone. When achieved, the garment or outfit appears as a finished, totally integrated, unified composition.

For example, quoting Marion L. Davis, from her textbook Visual Design In Dress *(p. 24), "One might compare clothing design to preparing a dish [of food]. The ingredients of eggs, sugar, and flour would compare with the elements such as line and shape as visual ingredients or media to be manipulated. Principles would compare to the recipe telling what to do with the ingredients and how to do it."* A completely harmonious and unified appearance is your ultimate goal.

All clothing is designed, defined, and discussed in terms of the elements and principles of design. Each element and principle of design is individual and can be studied separately, yet when combined into an art form such as clothing, each is interrelated and interdependent to the other.

For example, lines form the shape of a garment. The shape determines where light will fall on the garment, and the fabric's texture influences the color of light reflected to the eyes. Lines lead attention rhythmically around the garment, possibly to a point of emphasis. Lines within the garment determine proportions, and lines, shapes, colors, textures, and patterns influence apparent balance.

TIP
&
FROM THE PROS

Analyze and evaluate often the way in which each element is used and each principle is achieved in dress, whether in window and floor displays, magazines, or on an individual. You will learn as you look. This exercise is essential for students in any fashion-related field.

Harmony in Dress

Nature has a habit of combining the elements in such a way that is never rigidly absolute, is seldom regular, and yet is always logical. In the search for beauty, interest, and harmony, we strive to combine similarity with variety — repetition with contrast.

In all art forms, including dress, the main parts of the composition must be similar. Without similarity among the parts, our senses would become confused, and we would be uncomfortable. People tend to feel secure with similarity. Similarity is desirable, but we don't want everything so much the same that the composition becomes boring, predictable, or obvious.

It is important, therefore, to introduce some variety, some contrast or difference in the parts. Without variety our senses cannot be fully stimulated. People are excited by the unexpected. They enjoy a new or surprise element. Variety is desirable, but you don't want so much variety that the different elements begin to conflict. Too much variety results in conflict, confusion, and mixed messages.

If you always wear clothes with similar lines and shapes, similar colors, and similar fabric, people become so accustomed to seeing you look the same that soon they hardly notice you. Some variety or contrast — a new style, color, or fabric — is good to relieve the monotony, to create renewed interest and to attract some attention to your uniqueness.

On the other hand, if everything you wear is totally different from the day before, or every element within the outfit is unrelated to the others, the effect becomes confusing. The clothes clash. You loose your identity altogether as all attention is attracted to the clothes. Some similarity or repetition is necessary to provide a stable base or framework.

In an attempt to avoid both boredom and confusion, you should compromise between similarity and variety, achieving needed balance between repetition and contrast. The problem is how to get the various parts of an outfit to cooperate in creating a single theme, mood, or message.

The compromise and balance you seek is achieved when you learn to control the *amounts* of similarity and variety — repetition and contrast — included in any one garment or outfit. It is most easily achieved when you understand and apply the concept of dominance and subordinance. (See Figure 2–5.) Therein lies the logic that can guide you in combining or coordinating your clothes for a beautifully harmonious effect that allows you to express your individuality.

Dominant and Subordinate Elements

The principles of design demand that within the use of each element one line, one shape, one color, one texture, and one pattern is always (1) dominant over all other use of the same element; (2) all other uses are subordinate by degree; and (3) that within the garment design or outfit as a whole, one point or area is dominant over all else. Lack of attention to the complete concept leads to many of the common mistakes in dress.

The **dominant** line, shape, color, texture, pattern, and point of emphasis in a design attracts the eye first and holds attention for longer periods of time.

Attention may go to **subordinate** lines, shapes, colors, textures, patterns, or points if present in the design. However, because subordinate points are smaller or less obvious, attention is always drawn back to the dominant, and finally to the overall dominant point of emphasis in the entire garment or outfit.

For example, *visualize an elegant outfit composed of charcoal gray wool flannel slacks and jacket with red satin ¾-inch binding around the collar, paired with an ivory chiffon blouse, and gold jewelry. Lines are straight, and are therefore the dominant line type. Shapes are relatively angular. Colors include gray as the dominant color used in the largest amount. Ivory is subordinate. Red, we might say, is sub-subordinate and gold is used least.*

Textures include a chiffon fabric as dominant, it being

Figure 2–5. Within these cluster pieces, there is an interesting variety of light and dark color, solid color, and stripe fabric. Color contrast in the stripes on the collar create a dominant point of emphasis. Stripes on the sleeve cuff are subordinate points. Jewelry contributes to emphasis around the face and works well together because the necklace is relatively medium in scale while the earrings are relatively large in scale. *(Courtesy Clifford & Wills; photographer Val Ostrowski)*

somewhat grainy. Flannel is subordinate to the chiffon, being quite smooth with a softly napped surface. Since it is very smooth, satin has a still lesser degree of surface texture, and gold has the least amount of textural interest, since it is not only smooth but used least. None of the colors and textures conflict with the other or fight for attention.

The dominant point of emphasis in the whole outfit is at the collar, where attention is always drawn to the red/gray color contrast and the soft luster or shine from the red satin. Attention goes briefly to the shiny gold jewelry in terms of size — larger gold earrings, medium-sized bracelet, and relatively smaller belt buckle — but always comes back to rest around the totally dominant collar with its red satin binding.

Advancing and Receding Elements

Elements of design used in ways that appear to move toward or jump out at you are said to **advance** — or to be **advancing**. They are generally dominant and noticed first. (See Figure 2–6.) Elements used in ways that appear to blend in or back away from you are said to **recede** — or to be **receding**. They tend to be subordinate, attracting less attention. (See Table 2–2.)

Yang and Yin

The ancient Chinese concept of opposing characteristics or traits in nature is described with the terms yang and yin. (See Figure 2–7.) The concept relates directly to dominance and subordinance, advancing and receding. **Yang** represents dominant, advancing, assertive traits. **Yin** represents subordinate, receding, receptive traits. More specifically, to the Chinese, yin means gentleness and softness — the grace of the willow tree, and the delicacy of the moon. Yang means strength and vigor — the sturdiness of the pine tree, and the force of the sun.

Bell Northrup, formerly of the Teachers College at Columbia University, adapted the yang-yin concept in a published paper entitled "An Approach to the Problem of Costume and Personality." Within Northrup's paper, the terms *yin* and *yang* are used to classify, describe, and compare a person's physical and psychological or personality traits, as well as design elements or clothing traits. The work has been widely accepted and applied. (See Table 2–3, page 33.)

Figure 2–6. Pearlized buttons reflect the light and appear to advance from the soft, light-absorbing washed silk and melton wool fabrics. *(Courtesy Madeleine Direct)*

Chinese Symbol for Yin and Yang

Figure 2–7.

Table 2–2 Elements of Design

	Receding Elements	Advancing Elements
Line	• Curved • Broken • Thin • Horizontal	• Straight • Solid • Thick • Vertical
Shape	• Curved • Broken spaces	• Straight, angled • Open spaces
Color	• Cool • Dark • Dull, muted • Weak contrasts	• Warm • Light • Bright • Strong contrasts
Texture	• Soft • Pliable • Lightweight • Thin • Dull, absorb light • Smooth • Coarse • Sheer	• Crisp • Firm • Heavyweight • Thick • Shiny, reflect light • Rough • Fine • Opaque
Pattern	• Natural • Stylized • Smaller scale • All-over	• Geometric • Abstract • Larger scale • Spaced or spotty

Table 2–3 Traits That Reflect Opposites

Yin	Yang
Physical Traits	
Receding	*Advancing*
• Short	• Tall
• Small boned	• Large boned
• Delicate, rounded features	• Large, angular features
• Delicate, lighter coloring	• Strong, darker coloring
• Fine-textured skin	• Slightly coarse skin
• Softly curled or tossled hair	• Sleek, tailored, controlled hair
• Light movement	• Vigorous movement
• Graceful walk	• Purposeful walk
• Youthful	• Mature
Personality Traits	
Receptive	*Assertive*
• Gentle	• Forceful
• Dependent	• Independent
• Impulsive	• Deliberate
• Idealistic	• Realistic
• Pliant	• Firm
• Yielding	• Decisive
• Subtle	• Direct
• Demure	• Daring
• Friendly	• Reserved
• Ladylike	• Businesslike
• Informal	• Formal
• Warm	• Cool
• Naïve	• Sophisticated
• Open	• Closed
• Fragile	• Stable
Clothing Traits	
Receding/Receptive	*Advancing/Assertive*
• Curved lines	• Straight lines
• Broken lines	• Solid, unbroken lines
• Curved shapes and silhouette	• Angular shapes and silhouette
• Small-scale shapes and patterns	• Large-scale shapes and patterns
• Soft, light colors	• Bold, dark colors
• Pliable fabric	• Firm fabric
• Lightweight	• Heavyweight
• Fine, smooth textures	• Coarse, rough textures
• Few or weak, subtle contrasts	• More or strong, bold contrasts
• Untailored	• Tailored

It should be noted:

- Within Western society, the yin-yang concept has no relevance to good and evil or to sexuality and virility. The terms can be objectively applied to describe physical and psychological characteristics in both women and men, as well as clothing characteristics. You can observe yang women and yin men, or yin traits that surface in men on occasion, and dominant yang traits that surface in women, also dependent on the occasion or situation.

- Seldom is a person yin or yang exclusively; instead, and like the symbol, a person is a combination of both, with one type dominant and the other type subordinate. Both are equally important and interdependent. (See Figure 2–8.)

- Often, a person has physical traits in conflict with psychological or personality traits, or with personality traits needed in a particular role.

- A person's clothing preferences may clash with the physical body or dominant personality traits.

- Sometimes, a needed or desirable physical effect creates an undesirable psychological effect and vice versa.

For example, Liz has dominant yang physical and psychological traits combined with some yin traits. She is six feet tall and large boned, yet blonde with softly curled hair and light, graceful movements. Liz is independent, deliberate, direct, and forceful, yet idealistic, friendly, and warm. Heather's petite figure and delicate, cute features conflict with her firm, formal, direct, and businesslike personality traits so essential in her professional role. Della's preference for feminine yin clothing traits can clash with her strong, direct, formal, and sophisticated personality. Pastels flatter Gina's personal coloring, but they do not reflect her outgoing, vivacious personality. Carefully selected clothing will be useful to blend and balance these contradictory traits.

- You also differ in yang and yin traits that emerge according to your role or mood of the moment — feeling, acting, and appearing more yin on one occasion and more yang on another.

For example, you might feel, act, and appear more yang, closed or cool in a professional setting with business associates, and more yin, open or warm in the home with family members. You might feel and act more yang engaged in active sports, but more yin when out on a date. A dominant yang woman might feel more feminine and be willing to appear more yin during pregnancy and when with her children, while a dominant yin woman assumes more yang personality and clothing traits when filling a leadership role.

Degrees of Difference

In considering clothing needs and preferences in relation to physical and psychological traits, there are no

Figure 2–8. Linen/rayon separates combine for a dominantly yang appearance. A leather belt and tortoise-shell buttons reinforce the image. A lacy scoop-neck tank top and soft knit sweater introduce degrees of yin femininity to the outfit. *(Courtesy Clifford & Wills; photographer Val Ostrowski)*

absolutes, no right or wrong responses. Instead, there are degrees of difference in clothing needs and preference from one person to another, from one place to another, from one occasion to another, and from one day to another. Individual differences become more apparent when opposite traits are observed and considered side by side. Therefore, within this book, you will work often with opposing yang and yin traits, and with a continuum between extreme opposites.

Curved lines	Straight lines
Small scale	Large scale
Weak contrasts	Strong contrasts
Pliable	Firm
Casual	Formal

It is somewhere in between those opposites, on a huge middle ground, that you will find what works best for you. It will be up to you to decide which traits more nearly reflect your general needs and preferences, or where they appear to be on that continuum between opposing traits.

You will learn to borrow and blend selected traits from one side or the other, depending on your purpose. This is a matter of delicate balance and therein lies the art of successful dressing.

You can better use the elements and principles of design to create the type of appearance you need or want when you have a basic knowledge and understanding of them. While this book is not intended to present the elements and principles of design in all their intricate detail, chapters three through six include essential information helpful in applying a specific wardrobe strategy.

2.

Think of yourself as an artist as you select and coordinate your clothes and build your wardrobe.

You may not be a professional fashion designer, creating original pieces of clothing, but you are very much involved in the process of design as you select and coordinate lines, shapes, colors, textures, and patterns; as you put together each outfit you wear; and as you add new pieces of clothing to your wardrobe.

Again, some people may seem to have more natural talent and ability — but like any task, *you can learn the skills* necessary to manipulate the elements of design in ways attractive and appropriate to meet your needs. Once learned and practiced, you will feel more confident about what you choose to wear, which frees you to have fun with fashion.

In addition, you can enjoy the results of your artistic effort all day long, as you take your "design" with you wherever you go. That can be fun as well as functional.

Query Box

You can add your own creative touch to your clothes if you choose.

Which fashion art appeals to you?

Yarn Crafts	Stitching Crafts	Dyeing/Printing
Weaving	Sewing	Tie Dying
Knitting	Embroidery	Batik Printing
Crocheting	Appliqué	Block Printing
Tatting	Patchwork	Silk Screen Printing
Lacemaking	Quilting	Photo Printing
Macramé	Beadwork	Painting
Braiding	Quillwork	

3.

Think of yourself as part of the artistic composition with your clothes.

Clothing offers a practicality no other art form offers. You can wear it on your body — at which point *you become part of the artistic composition.* This is a concept that is often overlooked.

Your own body lines and shapes, coloring, texture, and subtle patterns are seen in combination with your clothing lines and shapes, colors, textures, and patterns. One influences the appearance of the other.

Just as the addition of a new piece of furniture contributes to the interior design of a room, the addition of a new piece of clothing or an accessory contributes to the total design of your wardrobe — and to the exterior design of yourself.

Creativity and Individuality

Like all art, clothing is a medium for self-expression, creativity, and individuality. Clothing is so continually present, so easily observable, and so highly personal that it becomes a ready means to create a picture or reflection of your inner self.

The artistic approach to clothing selection and coordination encourages **creativity**. You can manipulate the artistic media, those elements of design — line, shape, color, texture, and pattern. You can create any desired effect, in any specific outfit, in ways that will enhance your own attractiveness. Once thought and effort have been put into the artistic composition of an outfit, you can reassemble and enjoy the same outfit time and time again. That is particularly effective on those occasions when time is short, and you can't give much thought or attention to your clothes.

The artistic approach to clothing selection and coordination encourages **individuality**. Dressing is truly an art when it relates to or expresses the individual person within. When the details of dress are appropriate for your physical, psychological, social, and aesthetic needs, the picture you present will more likely be an accurate image of you. Each outfit you create becomes an accurate statement about the artist — and that's you!

Reinforcing and Countering

You can manipulate the elements of design to further control attention and create virtually any cue or visual effect you want or need for an attractive and appropriate appearance. Two effective ways of controlling attention and resulting visual effect are repetition or reinforcing, and contrast or countering.

Reinforcing or **repetition** occurs when an element of design repeats and therefore strengthens or emphasizes

Most people want to be attractive, but all too often they assume an attractive appearance just "happens." Some view it as a matter of luck, or an inherent trait. Others continually wish, watch, and wait for some sort of "magic" that will make them instantly attractive. However, it just doesn't work that way. It takes knowledge, thought, and effort. For those who really want to create an attractive appearance, the artistic approach holds the most hope and help.

the effect of an existing characteristic. (Think "same or similar.") In dress, this technique must be evaluated in terms of the effect you want to create. Generally, it is used to emphasize a body characteristic you see as pleasing, but it is also used to strengthen a particular personality trait.

For example, narrow vertical lines and spaces in the clothing design will repeat and reinforce or emphasize a tall, thin person's height and lack of weight or bony angularity. Round shapes repeat and therefore emphasize a rounded, more weighty body shape. Cinnamon rust in clothing repeats and therefore emphasizes auburn hair coloring. Angular clothing and accessory lines will reinforce and play up an angular jaw as well as an exacting personal temperament.

Countering or **contrast** occurs when an element of design contrasts and therefore weakens, minimizes, or camouflages the effect of an existing characteristic. (Think "opposing.") Again, this technique must be evaluated in terms of the effect you want to create. Generally, however, it is used to minimize or camouflage a body characteristic you consider less pleasing, but may also be used to play down a particular personality trait.

For example, if you don't want to call attention to a red, ruddy complexion, don't choose to wear a kelly green shirt. Green, the complementary color to red, can be expected to contrast too greatly, therefore emphasizing the red. For a pleasing visual effect on the figure, curved lines and shapes in clothing will contrast, counter, fill out, and camouflage a thin, angular figure. Straighter lines and slightly angled shapes will effectively counter the curves of a rounded figure. Curved lines may also be used to help soften a generally assertive personality.

Both repetition and contrast may be used in a single garment or outfit to draw attention away from a body area where it is not wanted, and to focus attention on another area where it is considered more pleasing or purposeful.

For example, Randy was assigned to give a classroom report. He chose to layer two shirts, the top-layer shirt having a row of buttons to lead attention up and away from the lower torso, where a color contrasting collar served to hold attention near the face — exactly where he wanted it.

While there are no rigid rules, there is a point beyond which the overuse of repetition or contrast becomes obviously and clumsily apparent.

For example, very thin legs will be emphasized by a very wide, bouffant skirt. The differences are too great. When contrast or countering is carried to an extreme, the effectiveness of the technique is lost.

Know that you can wear virtually any line, color, texture, or pattern you need or want to wear. Avoid a set of rigid rules. When it comes to clothing design and coordination, there is an infinite variety of combinations, with exceptions to nearly every rule. Each new outfit presents a new set of circumstances. With you as the artist, keep in mind that it's not only what you wear, it's how you wear it.

Keep in mind that throughout this book, advice and guidelines are approached in terms of what you *can* do, as opposed to what you *should* do. It's up to you to decide what you *will* do, based on your individual needs and purposes, in harmony with the principles of design.

4.

As with any art form, select your clothing to be in harmony with your life–style and your personal style; together they determine your needs.

&

We have more clothing options today than ever before. The time is right to choose what works for you — for the way you live and the way you need or want to look and be seen. You can be as practical as you need to be, yet creative, individual, and attractive at the same time. To guide you in your choices, examine your life-style and your personal style.

Life–style and Personal Style

Life-style refers to the way you live: where you live, the geographical environment, including natural resources; the general climate and weather; how you live, including your finances, the pace and places of your life, and your social roles and goals. (See Figure 2–9.) Life-style determines many of your clothing needs and what you choose to wear at any given time. Life-style can change gradually as you age and mature, or abruptly as you move to another role or another place. This, in turn, can lead to changing clothing needs.

Personal style puts the focus on the person, describes who you are, and develops in response to your life-style; your personality traits and moods; your values, attitudes, and interests; your body build and personal coloring.

Figure 2–9. Housing is a factor that influences life-style. *(Courtesy a–d: Heidi Neslen; e: photograph by Arien Whidden)*

Personal style in dress evolves over time, changing according to what you need, what you love and feel comfortable about wearing. Personal style is evident in the usual clothes you choose to wear and the way you usually choose to wear them — how you consistently put the clothes together to meet your needs, in ways unique to you.

For example, consider a young woman in transition from student to assistant editor at a performing arts magazine. Recognizing the need to feel and appear more secure, responsible, and authoritative in her professional role, yet aware of her lifelong need for creative self-expression in her dress, she gradually put together a wardrobe of traditionally styled suits, blouses, and jacket-dresses in surprise colors and textures, paired with eye-catching antique jewelry. Years later, arthritis took its toll on her hands, making it impossible to fasten tiny clasps. She adapted or gave away short necklaces. She gave away bracelets and rings that drew attention to her hands. She concentrated on her collection of longer necklaces that slipped easily over her head, and on clip earrings, both of which held attention near her face. Pins that could be adapted became pendants on long chains.

Life-style and personal style are each individual and can be discussed separately, yet each is interrelated and interdependent. (See Table 2–4.) Life-style influences the limits of your personal style and personal style influences your decisions regarding life-style. Personal style reflects life-style to a large degree. Both evolve over time.

For example, Lisa had an interest in horses, ranching, and western clothing. Living and working in a northeastern city limited her association with any of these interests. Her wardrobe reflected a more formal, refined way of life. To pursue her interests, she chose to vacation in the American Southwest at a working ranch. This practice turned into a lifelong summer tradition that included a casual cluster of Western clothes.

1.

2.

3.

4.

5.

6.

7.

8.

9.

10.

Figure 2–10. Many looks for many moods and occasions.
(Courtesy Louise Young)

Table 2–4

Life-style Factors	Personal Style Factors
• Geographic location • Climate/weather • Pace of life • Finances • Situation/occasion • Roles	• Life-style • Personality • Values • Body build • Coloring

Wardrobing should provide for the physical, psychological, social, and aesthetic needs specific to your stage in life, in harmony with your life-style and personal style. Pay attention to the future and the potential changes in your life.

For example, at age twenty-four, Chelsey was expecting her first child. Her wardrobe consisted of separates. To accommodate her expanding figure, she acquired a few loose-fitting first-layer maternity pieces and was surprised to discover how much more comfortable she felt with the added ease. Knowing pregnancy would not last long, and not wishing to invest a lot of money on maternity clothes, she tapped into her husband's wardrobe, adopting a sweater and vest to layer over her own casual clothes, and a terry-cloth robe to wear as a swimsuit cover-up. Liking vested looks long after the nine months were past, she incorporated them into her personal style of dress.

Remember to think of your wardrobe as an investment not only in the tangible garments you buy, but also in the intangible effects they leave on you — affecting the way you think, feel, act, and the way others react or respond to you. Your clothing is a valuable resource that helps you maintain a positive self-concept, improve self-presentation, and project a positive message to others. This, in turn, leads to success in all areas of your life.

5.

Identify the specific factors that contribute to your life-style and personal style.

Long before you begin planning a wardrobe, go shopping, or evaluate your wardrobe, you need to identify the factors contributing to your life-style and your personal style. Life-style is easier to evaluate than personal style,

and physical traits are easier to determine and describe than personality traits and values. Nevertheless, the better you recognize and understand your life and yourself, the better you will be able to develop personal style and provide for all your clothing needs. (See Figure 2–11.)

Figure 2–11. Exercise clothes reflect an important part of a woman's life. *(Courtesy Clifford & Wills; photographer Val Ostrowski)*

In Art, All Things Are Possible

Returning home from traveling in the United States, Canada and Europe, I am always asked, "What did you see?" "What did you do?" "What are they wearing?" A few even ask, "What did you learn?"

Aside from learning to negotiate the maze of narrow one-way streets and adjusting to living out of a suitcase, I've visited great buildings, the wonderful museums, and fashion houses from New York to Chicago and Los Angeles, from Toronto to Montreal and Vancouver, from Amsterdam to Vienna and Budapest, from Hamburg to Milan, Florence, and Rome, from Paris to Munich and Moscow.

I came away with a sure knowledge, a confirmation of what I know to be true — that in art, you can harmoniously combine virtually any line, shape, color, texture, or pattern with any other line, shape, color, texture, or pattern.

All too often, in considering the use of a line, color, or fabric, we accept the idea that "it can't be done." When it comes to clothing, someone often says, "You can't wear that line, that color, that fabric. It won't work," or "It's not your type."

Respond to this advice by saying to yourself, "It can be done. You just don't know how to do it." If it's something you'd really like to try, simply add, "I'll just have to learn how to do it — how to make it work for me."

It's not only artists and practitioners of today who place limits on artistic combinations. Each of the great masters of yesterday — some well known and some lesser known — had his own ideas, theories, and methods. Each was searching for truth in his use of line, shape, color, texture, and pattern. Each found a portion of that truth — some more than others.

As you study their ideas and look at their works, contradictions are evident even among the masters in painting. Michaelangelo and Leonardo da Vinci were often at odds. Perhaps this competitive spirit contributed to their individual greatness.

Ingres disagreed with Delacroix, arguing that line was more important than color. Rembrandt, Picasso, and Itten had opposing views on how to use color. Exactly how to use a line was as different for Ingres, Botticelli, and Credi, as was the use of texture for Chanel and St. Laurent.

Each artist had ideas and methods that rang true for what they were doing at the time. But given a different set of circumstances, a different goal, a different time, what didn't work for one, worked for another. What one didn't know how to do, another learned, and progress was made.

Who, thirty years ago, would have thought denim and lace would work together in the same outfit? Fashion experts said it wouldn't work. Along came Ralph Lauren and today we see lace trim and accessories paired with denim clothes of all sorts.

And so, with centuries of learning and examples to guide us, and having seen that virtually all things are possible, what a shame in this modern day to believe there is some limited way to use or combine a line, a shape, a color, a texture, or pattern — be it in a painting, a room, or in fashion.

I love the idea that you can wear virtually any line, shape, color, texture, or pattern that you want to wear. Keep in mind that it's not only what you wear, but how you wear it. Lines, shapes, colors, textures, and patterns *in combination* make the difference!

Think current and long term. What are your goals for the next one to three or five years? Visualize the following:

- Where you want to be.
- Whom you want to be with.
- What you want to be doing.
- What you want to be wearing.

This information will later allow you to plan for and purchase clothing that will make up a truly workable wardrobe, allowing you to appear as you want to be seen, and able to give you years of valuable service.

Looking Ahead

The wardrobe that works for one woman will be quite different from what works for another — as varied as the women themselves. When you analyze what makes the wardrobes work, however, you'll discover the women rely on several of the same strategies. They plan for and shop for the following:

- Basic style lines and shapes
- Classic style lines and shapes
- Separates
- Wardrobe neutral, muted colors
- All-season fabrics
- Classic patterns
- Clusters of clothes that work together

In the following chapters you will learn more about these strategies, and about the elements of clothing and design. This information will allow you to relate them more closely to your evolving personal style, life-style, and goals.

Review Main Points

Because all clothing is composed of lines, shapes, color, texture, and pattern, it qualifies as an art form and as wearable art simply because you wear it. The elements of artistic design include line, shape, color, texture, and pattern. A successful clothing design combines these elements according to the principles of design — with good balance, proportion, scale, rhythm, emphasis, harmony, and unity.

Attention may be drawn briefly to less obvious or subordinate lines, shapes, colors, textures, patterns, or points of emphasis. However, attention is always drawn emphatically back to the dominant line, shape, color, texture, or pattern and finally to the overall dominant point of interest in the entire garment or outfit. As with any artistic effort, you can increase your skill in selecting and coordinating your clothes, becoming part of the artistic composition with clothes that relate to you as an individual. Through reinforcing (repetition) and countering (contrast), you can select advancing or receding, yang or yin lines, shapes, colors, textures, and patterns, and use them in ways to control attention and create virtually any effect you need or want. In putting together a workable wardrobe, you should select clothes in harmony with your life-style and your personal style — in harmony with the location, situations, and occasions in your life, your body build, coloring, personality traits, and values.

Review Questions

1. Clothing is an art form, composed of the elements of design including
   _____, _____, color, _____, and pattern.

2. An area or space enclosed by a line is defined as a _____.

3. The surface look and feel of a fabric is called its _____.

4. A _____ results from the arrangement of lines, shapes, and color printed onto or woven into a fabric.

5. The principles of design or goals for any art form include balance,
   _____, scale, _____, _____, harmony, and unity.

6. When it appears that weight is evenly distributed from side to side and top to bottom, we say that _____ in the design has been achieved.

7. _____ refers to how and where attention is led in a garment or an outfit.

8. _____ is achieved in an outfit when all design details relate consistently to one another, to the occasion, and to the wearer.

9. To avoid distracting or confusing elements in a garment, there should be only _____ dominant focal point or center of interest in an entire garment or outfit.

10. Subordinate points of interest in an outfit call _____ attention to themselves.

11. Clothing is a ready medium for self-_____ and creativity.

12. To emphasize a body characteristic or personality trait you see as pleasing, repeat or _____ it with some detail of design.

13. Contrast or _____ with some detail of design can minimize or camouflage a body characteristic or personality trait you don't want to be noticed.

14. List four factors that determine life-style.

    _____   _____

    _____   _____

15. Personal style evolves in response to your _____,
_____, _____, and _____.

16. The _____ gives a garment its shape.

17. Shapes within a garment include _____ _____
_____ and _____.

18. A dress with a pocket on one side and off-center closure illustrates
_____ balance.

Discussion Questions

#1 As the artist in putting together an outfit you choose to wear, what are some
of the lines, shapes, colors, textures, and patterns you usually select and
ways you arrange, coordinate, or prefer to wear them? What might others
notice and remember about you as part of this artistic composition?

Notes: _____

_____

_____

_____

_____

#2 As you select the lines, shapes, colors, textures, and patterns in your clothes,
where do you prefer to direct attention? What kinds of effects do you want
to create with your clothes? What personality traits do you want to reinforce
or counter? What values do you want to reflect?

Notes: _____

_____

_____

_____

_____

#3 What are the occasions in your life, as compared to your parents, brothers,
sisters, friends, and neighbors? How do these differences influence differences in clothing needs and preferences? What occasions do you want to
add to your life-style in your future?

Notes: _____

_____

_____

_____

_____

Exercise 2–1 Week–at–a–Glance Activity Evaluation

Name_____

- Decide on a symbol and color for each of the major activities or roles in your daily life.
- Select colored pencils or crayons to fill in the following activity grid.
- Fill in each block of time with the appropriate symbol and color.
- Blocks of color represent the amount of time you spend in each activity or role. You can instantly see the comparative

portion of time spent in each activity or role. Relate this information to the kinds and amounts of clothing you need, and the portions of your clothing budget they'll each require.

- On the back of this page list and describe the type of clothing you will need for each activity or role.
- Compare your activity grid with other students' grids and note the differences.

	Monday	Tuesday	Wednesday	Thursday	Friday	Saturday	Sunday
6 AM							
7 AM							
8 AM							
9 AM							
10 AM							
11 AM							
12 PM							
1 PM							
2 PM							
3 PM							
4 PM							
5 PM							
6 PM							
7 PM							
8 PM							
9 PM							
10 PM							
11 PM							

☐ School ☐ Casual at-home ☐ Dressy day ☐ Exercise/sports

☐ Work/employment ☐ Casual away ☐ Dressy evening ☐ Sleep

❑ **School**

_____

_____

_____

❑ **Work/employment**

_____

_____

_____

❑ **Casual at-home**

_____

_____

_____

❑ **Casual away**

_____

_____

_____

❑ **Dressy day**

_____

_____

_____

❑ **Dressy evening**

_____

_____

_____

❑ **Exercise/sports**

_____

_____

_____

❑ **Sleep**

_____

_____

_____

Exercise 2–2   Life-style Evaluation

Name_____

Objectively identify factors that influence your life-style.

- Identify where you live.
- Identify what the climate is like.
- Identify the mood or atmosphere in your home, and in your workplace.
- Identify the pace of life in your home, and in your workplace.

- Identify the personal, professional, and social roles, activities, and occasions in your life.
- List four goals to be achieved within the next one to three years.
- Identify your approximate clothing budget or allowance.
- Identify the amount of time you have to shop for clothing.

Where do you live?

☐ Large city   ☐ Mid-size town   ☐ Small town   ☐ Rural

☐ Urban home   ☐ Urban apartment   ☐ Suburban home   ☐ Condominium

☐ Farm   ☐ Mobile home   ☐ Other _____

What is the climate like?

☐ Hot   ☐ Warm   ☐ Cool   ☐ Cold

☐ Humid/damp   ☐ Rainy   ☐ Snow   ☐ Windy

What is the mood or atmosphere and pace of life in your home?

☐ Relaxed   ☐ Hectic   ☐ Formal   ☐ Casual   ☐ Varied

What is the mood or atmosphere and pace of life in your workplace?

☐ Relaxed   ☐ Hectic   ☐ Formal   ☐ Casual   ☐ Varied

☐ Conservative   ☐ Creative   ☐ Sophisticated

What are the specific roles, activities, and occasions in your life?

FAMILY

☐ Single   ☐ Married   ☐ Divorced   ☐ Widowed

☐ Only child   ☐ Young children home   ☐ Teens at home   ☐ Grown children

HOMEMAKING TASKS

☐ Cleaning   ☐ Shopping   ☐ Cooking   ☐ Child care

☐ Full responsibility   ☐ Shared/assigned responsibilities   ☐ Housekeeper

EDUCATION

☐ Full-time   ☐ Part-time   ☐ Community/cont. ed.   ☐ Other _____

COMMUNITY CLUBS

☐ Member   ☐ Leadership   ☐ Volunteer service

☐ Daily   ☐ Weekly   ☐ Monthly   ☐ Annually

RELIGIOUS SERVICE

☐ Member   ☐ Leadership   ☐ Volunteer service

☐ Daily   ☐ Weekly   ☐ Monthly   ☐ Annually

PROFESSION/EMPLOYMENT

☐ Full-time   ☐ Part-time   ☐ Home-based   ☐ Outside home

☐ Executive/admin. ☐ Sales/service/education   ☐ Creative/communication

☐ Physical labor   ☐ Uniform   Title _____

ENTERTAINMENT/LEISURE TIME

Leisure time at home (reading, television, writing, sewing, painting, etc.)

☐ Daily   ☐ Weekly   ☐ Monthly

Activities _____

Casual dining out/party

☐ Weekly   ☐ Monthly   ☐ 1–4 times a year   ☐ Never

Dressy dining/party

☐ Weekly   ☐ Monthly   ☐ 1–4 times a year   ☐ Never

Formal dining/party

☐ Weekly   ☐ Monthly   ☐ 1–4 times a year   ☐ Never

Theater/symphony/ballet/opera

☐ Weekly   ☐ Monthly   ☐ 1–4 times a year   ☐ Never

Spectator sports (basketball, football, tennis, wrestling, etc.)

☐ Weekly   ☐ Monthly   ☐ 1–4 times a year   ☐ Never

Active sports/exercise

☐ Daily   ☐ 1–4 times weekly ☐ Other _____

Activity _____

Camping/fishing

☐ Often   ☐ Seldom   ☐ Never

Travel

☐ Weekly   ☐ Monthly   ☐ 1–4 times a year   ☐ Never

Destination(s) _____

Exercise 2–2 Life–style Evaluation (continued)

Name _____

List four goals you want to achieve within the next one to three years.

_____

_____

_____

_____

What is your approximate clothing budget or allowance?

Monthly _____

Seasonally _____

Annually _____

Approximately, how much time do you have to shop for clothing?

Monthly _____

Seasonally _____

Annually _____

Where do you usually shop?

☐ Department store _____

☐ Chain store _____

☐ Specialty store/boutique _____

☐ Discount store/outlet _____

☐ Catalog _____

☐ Television _____

☐ Other _____

Are you able and willing to make some of your own clothes?

☐ Yes   ☐ No

Are you able and willing to alter your own clothes as needed?

☐ Yes   ☐ No

Exercise 2–3 Writing to Learn About Yourself

Name _____

- Imagine the need to introduce yourself by letter to one of the following people:
  - Potential roommate
  - Personal shopper
  - Blind date
  - Family counselor
  - Foreign exchange family
  - Employment agency
- In each case, imagine that the person(s) you are paired with and the success of your association depends on the detailed description of factors contributing to your life-style and personal style.
- Write a three-to-four-page description of yourself in terms of these factors.
- Include any reasons that further explain your descriptions. For example, why you live where you do; why your pace of life is the way it is; why you think you possess certain values, personality traits, physical traits, spending habits, and so forth.
- Include short anecdotal examples if you like.

Exercise 2–4   Personal Style Evaluation, Part 1

Name_____

Objectively identify factors that influence your personal style.

- Identify your age group.
- Identify how you want to feel and appear in your home, in professional situations, and in social situations.
- Identify the personality traits that you think best describe you.
- Identify the values that determine your decision to buy an article of clothing.
- Identify how you want your clothing to fit.

What is your age group?

- ☐ Pre-teen
- ☐ 13–17
- ☐ 18–24
- ☐ 25–34
- ☐ 35–44
- ☐ 45–54
- ☐ 55–64
- ☐ 65+

How do you want to feel and appear in your home?

☐ Sporty	☐ Friendly	☐ Pretty	☐ Beautiful
☐ Fragile	☐ Romantic	☐ Practical	☐ Fashionable
☐ Older	☐ Younger	☐ Comfortable	☐ Creative
☐ Casual	☐ Feminine	☐ Sophisticated	☐ Knowledgeable
☐ Sexy	☐ Dramatic	☐ Dressy	☐ Capable
☐ Authoritative	☐ Approachable	☐ Wholesome	☐ Chic
☐ Sweet	☐ Cute	☐ Calm	☐ Appropriate
☐ Other _____			

How do you want to feel and appear in professional situations?

☐ Older	☐ Friendly	☐ Refined	☐ Beautiful
☐ Feminine	☐ Romantic	☐ Practical	☐ Fashionable
☐ Authoritative	☐ Younger	☐ Appropriate	☐ Creative
☐ Distinctive	☐ Efficient	☐ Sophisticated	☐ Knowledgeable
☐ Likeable	☐ Sexy	☐ Exotic	☐ Impressive
☐ Dramatic	☐ Elegant	☐ Pretty	☐ Glamorous
☐ Dependable	☐ Unobtrusive	☐ Fragile	☐ Approachable
☐ Conservative	☐ Gracious	☐ Organized	☐ Chic
☐ Successful	☐ Provocative	☐ Sweet	☐ Trustworthy
☐ Other _____			

How do you want to feel and appear in social situations?

☐ Calm	☐ Cute	☐ Modest	☐ Chic
☐ Authoritative	☐ Assertive	☐ Friendly	☐ Approachable
☐ Pretty	☐ Beautiful	☐ Sexy	☐ Romantic
☐ Practical	☐ Fashionable	☐ Older	☐ Younger
☐ Conservative	☐ Creative	☐ Likeable	☐ Feminine
☐ Sophisticated	☐ Knowledgeable	☐ Distinctive	☐ Elegant
☐ Confident	☐ Impressive	☐ Organized	☐ Ethnic
☐ Trustworthy	☐ Efficient	☐ Dependable	☐ Admired
☐ Appropriate	☐ Credible	☐ Glamorous	☐ Hard-working
☐ Provocative	☐ Rugged	☐ Dignified	☐ Compatible
☐ Understated	☐ Western	☐ Glitzy	☐ Dramatic
☐ Other_____			

What personality traits do you think best describe you?

☐ Relaxed, easy going   ☐ Warm, supportive   ☐ Cheerful, optimistic

☐ Cool, reserved, remote   ☐ Organized, efficient   ☐ Reliable, dependable, loyal

☐ Innocent, naïve   ☐ Mysterious, unpredictable ☐ Self-centered

☐ Pliant, easily influenced ☐ Sophisticated, chic   ☐ Depressed, blue

☐ Creative, original   ☐ Shy, quiet   ☐ Daring, adventurous

☐ Assertive, competitive   ☐ Impulsive, spontaneous   ☐ Sensitive

☐ Gentle, ladylike, subtle   ☐ Trustworthy   ☐ Considerate

☐ Analytical, methodical   ☐ Poised, calm, collected   ☐ Outgoing, friendly

☐ Strong willed, independent ☐ Flirtatious   ☐ Sweet

☐ Unpretentious   ☐ Tense, high strung   ☐ Forceful, direct, businesslike

☐ Energetic, active   ☐ Whimsical   ☐ Enthusiastic

☐ Dignified, regal, stately ☐ Receptive, cooperative   ☐ Demanding

☐ Provocative   ☐ Intimidating   ☐ Other _____

What values determine your decision to buy an article of clothing?

☐ Comfortable   ☐ Unique   ☐ Easy care   ☐ Color

☐ Beautiful   ☐ Lower price   ☐ Practicality   ☐ Like my friends

☐ Durable   ☐ Trendy   ☐ Expensive   ☐ Modest

☐ Brand/designer ☐ Plain   ☐ Versatile   ☐ Warm/cool enough

☐ Good fit   ☐ Impressive   ☐ Well made   ☐ Flatters figure

☐ Fast to put on ☐ Good fabric   ☐ Appropriate   ☐ Feel of the fabric

☐ Like famous person ☐ One-of-a-kind ☐ Timelessness ☐ Other _____

What type of clothing do you feel most comfortable wearing?

☐ Tailored   ☐ Feminine   ☐ Sportive   ☐ Elegant

☐ Artistic   ☐ Perky   ☐ Sexy   ☐ Exotic

☐ Romantic   ☐ Conservative   ☐ Dramatic   ☐ Offbeat

☐ Outdoorsy   ☐ Dressy   ☐ Casual   ☐ Softly tailored

☐ Formal   ☐ Classic   ☐ Trendy   ☐ Alluring

☐ Modest   ☐ Sophisticated ☐ Sporty   ☐ Simple

☐ Decorative   ☐ Gamin   ☐ Glamorous   ☐ Other _____

How do you like your clothing to hang and fit?

☐ Tight   ☐ Loose   ☐ Semi-fitted   ☐ Form-fitting

☐ Combination   ☐ Controlled   ☐ Unstructured   ☐ Comfortable

☐ Free-flowing   ☐ Other _____

Chapter
3

Basic Styles and Line Selection and Coordination

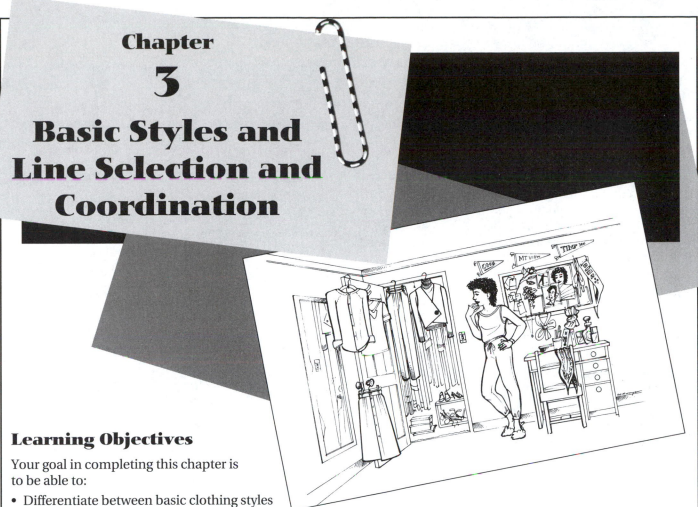

Learning Objectives

Your goal in completing this chapter is to be able to:

- Differentiate between basic clothing styles and costume styles.
- Recognize both basic and costume styles of clothing.
- Appreciate the value of basic clothing styles in a wardrobe.
- Recognize the value of separates and one-piece styles in a wardrobe.
- Understand and explain the functions of line.
- Describe how structural and decorative lines are formed in clothing.
- Identify the types of lines in clothing design.
- Recognize and locate line directions on a garment.
- Be aware of additional characteristics of line affecting clothing designs.
- Predict the effect of line on garment performance, mood, and message.
- Select clothing lines to meet your needs.
- Coordinate and combine two or more line types or directions harmoniously.
- Coordinate and combine basic and costume styles harmoniously.

Preview Main Points

1. Rely on basic styles, clothes that are simple in style lines and shape, that you can dress up and down or mix and match for a variety of good looks for many moods and occasions.

2. Acquire an occasional nonbasic, decorated, or "costume" piece of clothing for added interest.

3. Rely on separates, individual pieces in an outfit that can be mixed and matched with one another for variety and versatility.

4. Acquire an occasional one-piece garment, for interest as needed.

5. Knowing about line, as an element of design, will help you make wise consumer decisions about clothing selection and coordination.

6. Select clothing styles with lines that meet your individual needs or purposes — appropriate for your lifestyle, personal style, and for the fabric.

7. Coordinate or combine lines, as well as basic and costume styles, to achieve greater variety, interest, and individuality.

1.

Rely on basic styles, clothes that are simple in line and shape, that you can dress up and down or mix and match in a variety of good looks for many moods and occasions.

The more complicated our lives become, the more variety we need in our clothes and the more important basics become. Simple, plain styles with clean lines are the key to creating a variety of versatile outfits and good looks with your clothes.

The Beauty of Basics

- Basics do not attract a lot of attention to themselves.
- Basics have few design details and no decorations that would limit possible clothing combinations.
- Basics make good background pieces, easy to combine with other pieces of clothing and accessories, including those with many details or decorations.
- Basics take you anywhere — from day into evening with understated elegance.
- People don't quickly tire of basic styles.
- Basics are money savers, since they're easier to dress up or down.
- Virtually everyone can afford to buy basics; style is not a matter of money.

TIP

FROM THE PROS

Basics don't need to be boring. They're interchangeable and actually allow you more freedom to be creative as you make interesting and exciting changes in the looks of your clothes. All basics qualify as "look changers." As you experiment with basic styles, you give them life in the way you combine them — with color, texture, and pattern. You make them uniquely yours. You develop and refine your own personal style.

How to Recognize Basic Styles

To recognize basic styles, all you really have to do is look at the garment. The less detail, the more basic it becomes. If it's fairly plain, it's probably basic. If it's highly detailed or decorated, it's not. (See Figure 3–1.)

Basics are needed most by people who need to get as many looks from as few pieces of clothing as possible and by those employed in formal, conservative, or public and service-oriented businesses, such as banking and law, education and insurance — also by people in leadership positions.

Query Box

Which of these basic clothing styles have you tried? Which might you like to try?

T-shirts	straight-leg slacks
man-style sport shirts	palazzo pants
camp shirts	bell-bottom pants
crew-neck sweaters	harem pants
cardigan sweaters	blazer jackets
shirtwaist dresses	box jackets
sheath dresses	ponchos
cowl-neck sweater dress	capes
straight skirts	A-line skirts
duster coats	flared skirts
tuxedo coats	pleated skirts
pumps	bermuda shorts
clutch bag	stirrup pants
gold chain necklace	

(A complete list of basics would be very long. You have these and many other options.)

2.

Acquire an occasional nonbasic, decorated, or "costume" piece of clothing for added interest.

A costume piece of clothing is complete in itself, with details and decorative lines or shapes — or possibly accessorized — in ways that prevent its look from being changed easily. People not satisfied with their wardrobes often have a closet chock full of costume clothes. Clothing qualifies as costume if it:

- Is so unique, so flamboyant, fussy, or highly decorated you can't possibly change the way the clothes look or work together.

Query Box

Which of these costume clothing styles have you tried? Which might you like to try?

cowboy shirts	chesterfield jackets
prairie blouses	button-front skirts
sailor shirts	multi-tiered skirts
safari shirts	fringed-hem skirts
fringed vests	thigh-high slit skirts
pinafore	quilted parkas
safari jackets	reefer coats

Basic Styles

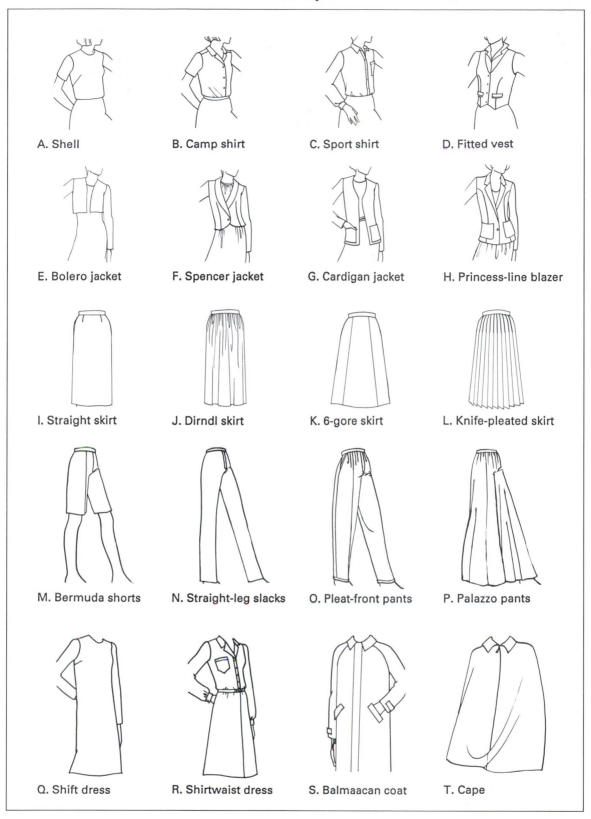

A. Shell

B. Camp shirt

C. Sport shirt

D. Fitted vest

E. Bolero jacket

F. Spencer jacket

G. Cardigan jacket

H. Princess-line blazer

I. Straight skirt

J. Dirndl skirt

K. 6-gore skirt

L. Knife-pleated skirt

M. Bermuda shorts

N. Straight-leg slacks

O. Pleat-front pants

P. Palazzo pants

Q. Shift dress

R. Shirtwaist dress

S. Balmaacan coat

T. Cape

Figure 3–1.

• Demands special costume accessories to complete the look — accessories that go with virtually nothing else.

• Is associated with a festive or literally "costume" occasion, such as a rodeo or a luau, Halloween or Mardi Gras.

How to Recognize Costume Styles

Each costume garment features distinctive lines or shapes — the yoke on a cowboy shirt, the ruffles on a prairie blouse, the collar on a sailor shirt, and so forth. (See Figure 3–2.) A complete list of costume styles would be shorter than a list of basics.

Some clothing styles are borderline, such as a sarong skirt, closely associated with a tropical holiday and lending itself harmoniously to fewer shirts and jacket styles than, say, a basic straight skirt which goes with virtually any top. Any garment that has decoration added, such as colored piping, stones or sequins, fancy buttons and pockets or epaulets qualifies as a costume piece of clothing.

Costume Styles

A. Peasant blouse B. Sailor shirt C. Safari shirt D. Western shirt

E. Oriental vest F. Embroidered sweater G. Hacking jacket H. Quilted parka

I. Side-button skirt J. Sarong K. Fanny wrap skirt L. Tiered skirt

M. Knickers N. Jeans O. Harem pants P. Overalls

Q. Costume dress R. Prairie dress S. Duffel coat

Figure 3–2.

More costume pieces can be included in wardrobes of people who don't have to worry about cost or closet space, and by those who work in creative businesses, such as art, music, theater, interior design, and fashion.

3.

Rely on separates, individual pieces of an outfit that can be mixed and matched with one another for variety and versatility.

❧

Clothing styles can be described in terms of separates, suits, and one-piece garments. Separates are clothes designed with lines that cover only part of the body — top or bottom. They include: blouses, shirts, sweaters, vests, tunics, and jackets on top, and skirts, slacks or pants, and shorts on the bottom.

Separates never have to be worn as part of a specific or matched suit, but are intended to be combined with other separates to complete an outfit. One advantage of separates is that they combine to project any mood, occasion, or personality trait you choose. So how do you feel today? With separates you can appear demure one day and dramatic the next, businesslike in the morning and sociable that evening, all depending on your mood and schedule.

Super Separates

Wardrobes composed predominantly of separates are highly recommended, because separates:

- Provide flexibility and versatility in a wardrobe.
- Can be purchased, replaced, or updated one at a time with less strain on a budget.
- Do wonders to camouflage a figure variation or create an attractive illusion about the figure.
- Allow you to split or mix sizes in tops and bottoms for a better fit.

Basic, classic separates are needed to build a wardrobe that works for the way you live.

Power Suits

Strictly speaking, a suit is two or more matched pieces of clothing intended to be worn together, never separated, and intended to pack authority. Quite the opposite of separates, matched suit pieces seldom lend themselves to mixing with other pieces, putting them into the costume category. (See Figure 3–3.) That doesn't mean you can't if the mix works, and providing that you wear both top and bottom pieces equally often. If you don't, one piece wears out before the other.

Many women can't even consider buying a matched suit with both pieces one size. Many figures demand different sizes in top and bottom. With a fabulous fit, however, a stunning suit can present a powerful image for those women in authoritative professional or leadership roles, and for those who lead a more formal life-style. One or two are probably enough in most wardrobes.

Figure 3–3. This power suit features peaked lapels. *(Courtesy Madeleine Direct)*

4.

Acquire an occasional one–piece garment, for interest as needed.

🖋

One-piece garments are full-length and complete on their own — although one-piece garments in simple, basic styles can be layered with separate tops. One-piece garments include dresses, jumpers (skirt-styling), jump-suits, rompers, and catsuits (pant-styling), robes, coats, and capes. (See Figure 3–4.)

Dress Options

Most women want some dresses in their wardrobe; some women prefer dresses altogether. Dresses can be uncomplicated, comfortable, and lovely to own. (See Figure 3–5.) A dress is ideal for those times when you just want to slip into something quickly and can't be bothered deciding what to mix or match with what. However, a wardrobe composed mainly of dresses can be limiting.

Dresses with eye-catching design details or decoration move into the costume category and do not combine well with layered tops. Close-fitting dresses can be difficult to fit. They don't flatter many figures. Even well-fitted basic dresses present problems because the plain and simple styling can be revealing and allow too much attention on the body silhouette. At that point even dresses need to be layered to camouflage various areas of the body.

Women not happy with their wardrobe, who feel bored with limited looks, often have too many dresses in their closet. One or two dresses or a jumper and one jumpsuit in a small cluster of clothes are generally enough. Carefully chosen, you can find wonderful basic dresses simple enough to layer with a shirt or blouse underneath, and a vest, sweater, or jacket over. Two-piece dresses are actually a separate skirt and top that work together to look like a one-piece dress. They fill a double bill, working as separates as well. A good two-piece dress is a terrific buy.

5.

Knowing about line, as an element of design, will help you make wise consumer decisions about clothing selection and coordination.

🖋

All design begins with a continuous mark, called a line. For the sake of understanding, be reminded that when a

One-Piece Clothing

A. Coat dress

B. Jumper

C. Caftan

D. Asymmetrical drape dress

E. Jumpsuit

F. Overalls

Figure 3–4.

continuous line encloses space, it creates a shape. Line and shape are the foundations of all clothing design. Line and shape are interrelated from the beginning of any clothing design. As a continuous line encloses and divides the area inside a garment, more shapes result. You can't deal with one without the other. Together, they create the endless variety of clothing styles. This section concentrates on line. A discussion of shape follows in Chapter 4.

Importance and Functions of Line

- Lines define the shape of the body and clothing.
- Lines divide spaces, creating proportional areas.
- Lines indicate direction.
- Lines lead attention throughout the garment, to a point of emphasis.
- Lines create powerful illusions about the size and shape of the body.
- Lines communicate visual meaning, messages, or moods.

Figure 3–5. Feminine elegance in a softly draped dress. (*Courtesy Madeleine Direct*)

How Lines Are Formed

Outlines are outside lines, created by the body's or the garment's outer edges. The outline is also known as the silhouette. Ideally, the clothing outline enhances the body outline.

Lines can be formed inside the garment outline. They include structural lines and decorative lines. (See Figure 3–6.)

Structural lines are woven or knitted into the fabric during manufacture and created during construction of the garment as a result of:

seamlines	tucks
dartlines	pleats
folds	gathers
edges	

Decorative lines are printed onto the fabric during manufacture, and formed when buttons, pocket flaps, trim, or special stitching is applied to the surface of the garment to change or enhance appearance. (See Figure 3–7.) Trims include:

ric-rac	braid
lace	ribbon
piping	ribbing
bands	panels
welt seams	lapped seams
top stitching	surface ruffles

Types of Lines

There are two general types of lines: straight and curved. (See Figure 3–7.)

Straight lines are crisp, flat, and rigid. They oppose the curved lines of the body to varying degrees.

Curved lines have some degree of roundness, from slight waves to circular. Slightly curved lines are often called restrained curves, while more circular lines are referred to as full-rounded curves. Curved lines conform more closely to the curves of the body.

Design Lines

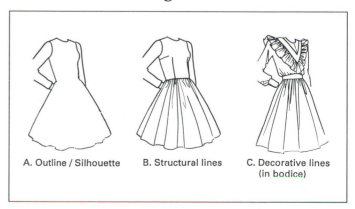

A. Outline / Silhouette   B. Structural lines   C. Decorative lines (in bodice)

Figure 3–6.

Line Types and Directions

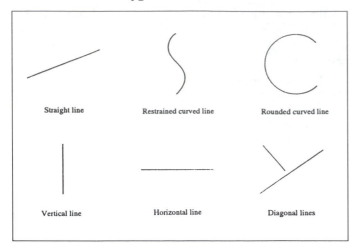

Figure 3–7.

Line Directions

The eye is first drawn to the line, then in the direction of the line until it meets another line and begins moving in that direction. Used in combination, attention will follow and come to rest on the dominant line. The length and strength of a line determines the amount of time the eye rests on it.

For example, the strength or effect of a line is directly related to the amount of time focused on a line. A line that extends from neck to hemline will appear longer and stronger, adding more height to a figure, than will a line that extends from neck to waistline.

There are three general line directions: vertical, horizontal, and diagonal.

Vertical lines go up and down. (See Figure 3–8.)

- One vertical line draws attention to itself, then up and down, creating the illusion of increased height and thinness.
- Several narrow vertical lines placed close together generally create the same illusion. Line width is key to the effect.
- Several medium to wide vertical lines, or vertical lines spaced widely apart, lead the eye across the body, visually measuring the space between the stripes. This creates the effect of increased width and decreased height.

Horizontal lines go across. (See Figure 3–9.)

- One horizontal line draws attention to itself, then from side to side, creating the illusion of width and decreased height.
- Several wide horizontal lines or horizontal lines widely spaced, create the same effect.

Figure 3–8. Structural vertical lines are created in the knitting process. *(Courtesy Madeleine Direct)*

- Several short, thin horizontal lines placed close together lead the eye up and down, creating the effect of slimness and increased height.

Diagonal lines slant at an angle.

- A diagonal line draws attention to itself, then up and down or side to side, depending on the angle or slant of the line.
- A long, thin, slightly diagonal line may appear to increase height.
- If the angle is more horizontal, the diagonal line appears to increase width.
- Several diagonal lines that form a chevron focus attention on the face or figure, depending on the direction in which the chevron points.
- A single chevron, such as a V-neck, focuses attention on the area where it is placed.

Figure 3–9. Horizontal stripes in graduated widths lead attention upward to emphasize the shoulder. *(Courtesy Madeleine Direct)*

Figure 3–10. Lines in opposition are evident in this sportive plaid shirt. *(Courtesy Eddie Bauer; photographer G. Remington)*

Arrangement of Lines

Lines in opposition are created when lines intersect, forming angles between opposing vertical, horizontal, and diagonal lines. Oppositional lines appear more severe, sharp, and precise. (See Figure 3–10.)

Lines in transition are created when one line changes direction smoothly into another direction, without sharp angles, leading the eye along the line. Transitional lines appear more soft and subtle.

Lines in radiation are created when lines spread or radiate from a central point or area, much like the rays of a sunburst, or spokes of a wheel. Lines that radiate cause the eye to move in several directions at once. The effect is one of activity. (See Figure 3–11, page 61.)

Additional characteristics of line affect the psychological mood and message of any given line, and the physical illusions the line creates. Some of those additional characteristics include:

- Long as compared to short.
- Thick as compared to thin.
- Even as compared to uneven.
- Sharp as compared to fuzzy.
- Solid as compared to porous.
- Unbroken as compared to broken.
- Dotted as compared to zig-zag, looped, and scalloped.

For example, long, unbroken lines communicate stability and continuity with a certain gracefulness, while short, broken lines communicate a staccato, disconnected feel-

Table 3–1 Line Type and Line Direction

	Message (Psychological Effect)	Illusion (Physical Effect)	Line Placements	
Straight	Forceful Rigid Strong Hard Formal Masculine Crisp	Increases, emphasizes, reinforces body lines and angles Counters curved lines	Closures Bateau necklines Notched collars Lapels Seamlines Slit necklines Dartlines Tucks	Pleats Folds Panels and insets Stripes Geometric shapes Tubular silhouettes A-line silhouettes
Curved	Gentle Romantic Fragile Soft Casual Feminine Graceful	Holds attention longer Increases, emphasizes, reinforces rounded soft-body curves Counters straight lines	Jewel necklines Scoop necklines U-shaped necklines Curved yokelines Princess seamlines Soft bows Ruffles Tiers Bouffant skirt	Full gathers Draped bodice Scalloped edges Ric-rac trim Buttons Full-rounded silhouette
Vertical	Formal Strong Dignity Stiff Businesslike Stately	Increases, emphasizes, reinforces length, height, narrowness, thinness Counters horizontal lines	Boat necklines Collars Yokelines Narrow lapels Narrow panels or gores Fabric insets Lengthwise grainline Lengthwise stripes Tucks Pleats	Folds Zippers CF, CB, side placket Row of buttons Slash pockets Ties Long sleeves High heels Tubular silhouettes
Horizontal	Restful Stable Calm Relaxed Casual Quiet Serene	Increases, emphasizes, reinforces width, bulk, shortness Counters vertical lines Placed high—appears taller Placed low—appears shorter	Bateau necklines Scoop necklines Square necklines Jewel necklines Bow ties Yoke lines Tucks Pleats Bands Horizontal stripes	Cuffs Waistline Belts Crosswise grainline Patch or flap pockets Slot pockets Wide-set double-breasted closure Bouffant skirt Platform shoes
Diagonal	Active Movement Unstable Excitement Interesting Dramatic Restless	Increases, emphasizes, reinforces the direction of the dominant angle Counters vertical and horizontal lines	V-shaped neckline Open collar Lapels Raglan sleeve seamlines French darts Closures Surplice closure Row of buttons Fabric inset	Gores Herringbone Zig-zag Ric-rac A-line skirt Flared skirt Shoe laces

Figure 3–11. Decorative diagonal lines radiate from center front outward, to emphasize the upper torso. *(Courtesy Madeleine Direct)*

ing. Zig-zag lines appear stiff, abrupt, and jerky, while scalloped lines impart the feeling of being busy, springy, and swirly.

You can combine various types and characteristics of line for endless effects. (See Table 3–2.)

Line Illusions

An illusion is a false perception or interpretation of something we see — something that deceives our eye when we look at it. An illusion makes something look quite different than it really is. Regardless of the facts, and according to our mind's eye, we tend to believe the illusion. Lines can be created, arranged, and controlled to create illusions. (See Figures 3–12 and 3–13, pages 64 and 65.)

A general goal in using clothing as a resource is to select and arrange design lines in ways that enhance the body — in ways that make the face and figure appear more nearly ideal. Clothing lines can be used in ways that emphasize the most attractive lines of the body and camouflage or counter those body lines we consider less attractive, in effect minimizing or eliminating them. Illusions are easier to control if you know some of the illusions that relate directly to clothing. When you know what illusion you want to create, you'll know how to do it.

Line and the Principles of Design

To appear harmonious, the size of clothing and accessory lines needs to be in proportion and scale for the

body. We compare the size of clothing lines to the size of the body. Small or narrow to medium lines appear harmonious on a smaller body. Medium-sized lines work well on a medium-sized body. Medium to large or wide lines appear in scale with a comparatively large body.

Dominant or decorative lines draw attention to themselves and therefore emphasize the area where they are placed. Use them only in places where you want to draw attention and emphasis.

For example, *adding braid around the collar and lapels of a jacket will draw attention to the chest and bust area, emphasizing a rounded chest or larger bust. The braid might be better applied to the collar only, or possibly on the collar and long sleeve hem, drawing attention to the face and hands instead.*

TIP

FROM THE PROS

Keep in mind, that because all elements of design are interrelated, **the ultimate effect of any line is influenced by the other elements** of design — the shapes, colors, textures, and patterns in the clothes. This influence is what makes so many "fashion rules" unreliable or invalid. The rule appears to work in one outfit, but not in another because the color, the fabric, the pattern, or the combination of clothes caused the effect to be different than expected. This influence is what gets so many people confused. As you study through Chapters 3–7, learning what the predictable effects of each element are, you will be better equipped to evaluate the total effect of any given garment or outfit.

6.

Select clothing styles with lines that meet your individual needs or purposes — appropriate for your life-style, personal style, and for the fabric.

🐚

- Choose style lines with characteristics appropriate for the mood, occasion, or activity. (See Table 3–2.)

- Choose style lines with characteristics that reflect the values of the wearer — what she or he believes to be valuable or important.

- Choose style lines with characteristics that are compatible with, or that reflect the wearer's personality.

- Choose style lines with characteristics that flatter the face and figure.

Table 3–2 General Perception of Line

	Message/Function	Characteristic Lines
Weather	To feel and appear warmer	Straight Vertical
	To feel and appear cooler	Restrained curves Full-rounded curves Horizontal
Occasion/Activity	To feel and appear casual/informal (casual business)	Restrained curves Vertical Horizontal
	To feel and appear dress-businesslike (formal business)	Straight Vertical
	To feel and appear dressy/formal	Restrained curves Full-rounded curves Horizontal and diagonal
Values	To save time	Few Simple
	To influence others	Straight
	To be comfortable	Restrained curves
	To save money	Few Simple
Personality	To feel and appear ingenue/romantic	Curved Broken
	To feel and appear happy, youthful, gamine, sportive	Straight
	To feel and appear dramatic/exotic	Straight Vertical and diagonal Solid
	To feel and appear mature, serious, somber, classic	Straight Few Solid

Table 3–2 General Perception of Line *(continued)*

	Message/Function	Characteristic Lines
Figure/Body Build	To maintain or decrease attention and apparent size—to appear taller, longer, narrower, thinner	Straight Vertical Narrow Solid Smooth
	To increase attention and apparent size—to appear shorter, wider, thicker	Curved Horizontal Wider Broken Fuzzy
Fabric	Lines demand thin, pliable drapey fabrics	Straight Restrained curves Full-rounded curves Vertical Gathers, folds, pleats Many
	Lines require crisp, stiff fabrics	Straight Full-rounded curves
	Lines can permit use of thick, bulky fabrics	Straight Restrained curves Horizontal Few

---

TIP

❧

FROM THE PROS

To determine the effect of a line on your figure, try the "blink test." Stand about five to eight feet in front of a full length mirror. Shut your eyes, relax, and clear your mind. When you open your eyes, be aware of where your attention is attracted and how the lines lead your attention throughout the garment or outfit. Generally, your attention will be drawn to the dominant point in the entire outfit. Ask yourself if the dominant area of attention, interest, or emphasis is where you want viewers to focus. If not, look for another style, one with lines leading to an area where you prefer viewers to focus attention. Try the "blink test" again.

Choose style lines with characteristics that look, feel, and hang appropriately for the fabric of the garment. Choose style lines that will coordinate with the existing wardrobe.

7.

Coordinate or combine lines, as well as basic and costume styles, to achieve greater variety, interest, and individuality.

In addition to style lines, the following discussion may acknowledge shape, color, fabric, and pattern in the clothes, as these elements of design are interrelated and influence your choice of clothes to be combined in any one outfit.

Harmony among Style Lines

To combine two or more pieces of clothing with different style lines, here is the general guideline. Select and com-

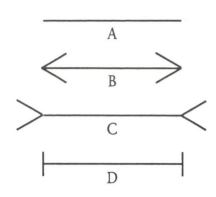
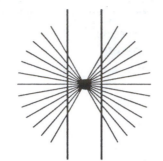
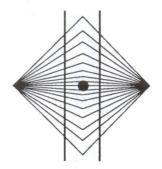

Center horizontal lines A-D are the same length. Each line appears a different length due to the illusory effects of the vertical lines and diagonal end lines.

Parallel lines appear to bow outward.

Parallel lines appear to bow inward.

Note: Clothing style lines appear to create illusions about the body size and shape. Learn to use them to your advantage.

Figure 3–12.

bine clothing **in terms of the activity, occasion, mood, values, and personality traits they communicate**, project, or reflect. The characteristics of line need to be somewhat similar for the clothes to appear like they belong together.

Combining basics with basics, or basics with a costume piece, is relatively easy. Being simple in design, there are few lines in the basic pieces to conflict with one another or a costume piece. Nonetheless, the lines in each piece can be any combination or arrangement of straight, curved, vertical, horizontal, diagonal, structural, or decorative lines. The lines in the basic pieces to be combined in one outfit must be considered in terms of what each communicates.

As you've learned, straight lines appear more assertive, controlled, cold, formal, and severe. Curved lines appear more approachable, relaxed, soft, warm, friendly, and feminine. Straight lines work well with other straight lines, and curved lines work harmoniously with other curved lines.

For example, *a straight skirt combines nicely with a blazer jacket, traditionally designed with straight lines. (The tubular shapes of the straight skirt, blazer sleeves, and blazer body also reinforce one another.)*

Women not satisfied with their wardrobes often combine clothes with lines that clash, conflict, or communicate contradictory traits — among themselves or with the wearer.

For example, *the look of a tailored blazer jacket does not combine well with the look of a ruffled skirt. The several straight lines of the jacket conflict with the many curved lines of the skirt. The personality or mood of the jacket is serious, the skirt is frivolous. Each piece communicates a different occasion — business and party.*

A Style of Your Own

Depending on the person wearing them, the lines that conflict may appear too severe and stern; too fussy and frilly; or too bold and brassy. The person may feel psychologically uncomfortable in the clothing, and observers may notice this.

For example, *a gentle, fun-loving, young woman may feel overwhelmed by the serious nature of a blazer jacket. She might look terrific in the jacket as far as others are concerned, but she may feel restricted. She might prefer a loose-fitting bomber jacket, swing coat, or a vest instead of a jacket. She has many other options.*

Experiment a little and discover which styles are most in harmony with you, the places you go, and what you do there. As you experiment, you may discover something you like to wear so well that it becomes your trademark — something so memorable, something so unique that it triggers an image of you in the minds of the people who know you. (See Figure 3–14, page 66.)

Line Illusions on the Figure

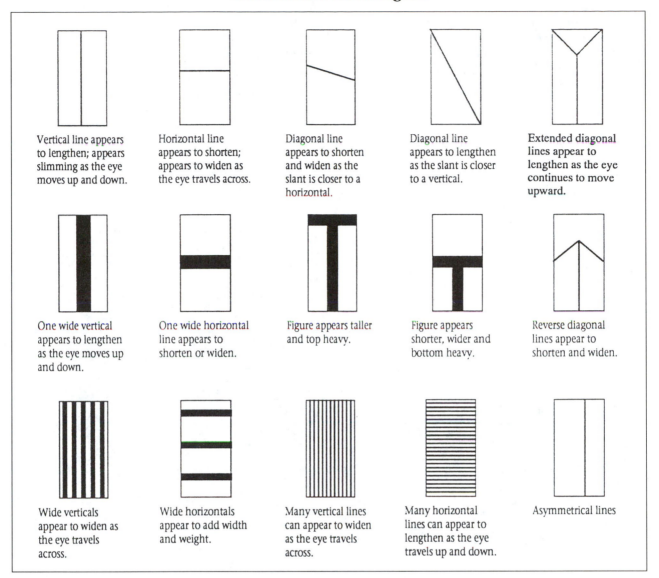

Figure 3–13.

Dominant/Subordinate Style Lines

In all cases, one line or group of similar, related lines must be dominant in the garment. Using all straight or all curved lines in a design, however, can become too repetitious, to the point of appearing monotonous or uninteresting. Some contrast in line can be more interesting, effective, and appealing, communicating subtle differences of mood, occasion, and personality. You can break the general guideline and combine basics or costume pieces with seemingly opposing lines communicating entirely different moods, but it takes extra thought and practice to make the outfit work. This is the guideline: **One line type and direction** (occasion, mood, or personality) **among the separates must be dominant and all others subordinate by descending degrees.** Stated another way, the mood, theme, or personality communicated by one line type, direction, and arrangement must be most obvious and most important —

dominant. Different lines can be introduced into the design, but they must be done so to a lesser degree — they must attract less attention. This requires a delicate balance.

In combining lines, your goal is to maintain the basic theme or mood, while achieving a more interesting balance between straight and curved lines, vertical, horizontal, and diagonal lines, lines in opposition, transition or radiation, and structural versus decorative lines.

For example, the lines of the blazer jacket and straight skirt communicate a similarly tailored and businesslike theme. Introducing a few curved lines into the outfit can soften or counter the total look, just a little, without conflicting with the business theme. Curved lines might be used to round the lapel points or shape the neckline on a blouse worn with the jacket. A flared skirt (triangular shape) could replace the straight skirt. In either case, the straight lines (and shapes) and tubular shapes remain dominant.

As another example, a peasant blouse and tiered, ruffled skirt are costume pieces designed with curved and full-rounded lines, many in the horizontal direction, and with gathers radiating from the scoop neckline, puffed sleeve line, waistline, and tiered seamlines. The dominant mood or personality of these pieces is happy, casual, care-free, free spirited, even frivolous.

You can counter the dominantly frivolous mood of these clothes simply by introducing some straighter lines. Add, for example, a basic vest designed with straight, vertical side-lines and a vertical center-front opening. Then add boots, the dominant outline on the sides of the boots being straight and vertical. (The frivolous feeling is further countered by using a firm, stiffer material for both vest and boots.)

The total look of the outfit is still dominantly carefree, casual, and fun. The more serious look of the vest is subordinate to the blouse and skirt; and the strong, stable, well-grounded look of the boots is subordinate to the vest, blouse, and skirt — sub-subordinate, we could say, within the total outfit.

To test the harmony of the combination, think in terms of amounts. There are more curved lines in the blouse and skirt, as compared to fewer straight lines in the vest and boots — in the total outfit. (In terms of fabric or texture, there is a greater amount of lightweight, pliable blouse and skirt fabric, as compared to lesser amounts of firm material in vest and boots. Color and pattern can further influence the final effect of an outfit like this.)

This flexible and creative way of combining lines opens up endless possibilities for greater individuality and subtle communication. Lines can be combined to reflect a woman as dramatic, demure, or a blend in between; as sportive, romantic, or a complementary combination of both; as a traditionally classic conservative, a trend-setting free spirit, or a mix in between. (See Figure 3–15.)

Figure 3–14. Dominant diagonal lines, forming a chevron, are created in this artistic quilted vest. *(Courtesy Roberta Glidden)*

Figure 3–15. Soft fullness in the skirt counters the tailored look of the jacket and vest. *(Courtesy Madeleine Direct)*

Beat the Heat in Style—with Loose Easy Lines

Loose, easy style lines are one of the keys to keeping cool in summer. The tips that follow are sure to help you keep your cool in comfort.

Select simple, loose-fitting, easy-to-move-in styles that cover your body without clinging or binding. Anything that's snug or tight against your body, including a belt, will make you feel warmer. Larger, loose necklines, wristlines, waistlines, and ankles offer a kind of built-in air conditioning, allowing air to circulate and cool you.

Avoid close-fitting necklines and collars. That high-button Victorian blouse may look charming in a climate-controlled dressing room but will only make you feel hot and claustrophobic outdoors. Open-collar shirts, V-necklines, scoop, boat, and sweetheart necklines are more comfortable choices.

Armholes should be cut wide and full. Look for styles with extended shoulder lines and deep-set or drop-shoulder sleeves. Cap, short, butterfly, or bell-style sleeves are smart choices. If sleeveless or capped only, check your mirror for straps and bra bands that might show.

Skirts should stand away from the body slightly, preferably in fabrics that don't require a slip to prevent seeing through or sticking to your skin. Rely on straight-hanging dirndl skirts, A-line skirts with an inverted center-front pleat, flared skirts, and free-flowing split-skirts. Skirt and pant waistbands will feel better in the heat if not too wide or snugly fitted. For a terrific evening look, try wearing palazzo pants or billowy harem pants.

A few dresses are good choices, ready for the hottest days of summer. They can look complete and polished worn alone. Drawstring waistlines are cooler than fitted or elasticized waistlines because they can be loosened as the temperature rises. Better yet, the coolest dress is one with lines that fall from the shoulders—without a waist at all. Shift and chemise style dresses do nicely in summer.

For business women, an open-collar shirtwaist dress or a lightweight coatdress can have the clout of a suit. A well-designed short-sleeve dress with a notched collar can look professional, yet feel several degrees cooler. Carry a jacket or keep one at the office for important meetings or business lunches. Choose a loose-fitting, unconstructed, unlined jacket—possibly with drop-shouldered, dolman- or kimono-styled sleeves. A cotton-knit cardigan knit sweater can be an alternate choice.

Sleeveless, cap, or short-sleeved tops, vests, and dresses will be coolest worn under your jacket. You could also choose a halter top if it's not too bare-cut from the shoulder. Wear your jacket at the office, removing it for a special evening occasion after work. If necessary, carry your jacket while commuting and put it on at the office. Fold it inside out to prevent soiling and reduce wrinkling.

Beware of overexposure at the office. It can strain the seams of good taste and cause an image problem. Camisole tops are seldom appropriate during business hours. Top a halter, V-back, or backless dress with a crisp looking jacket. And it's not lower necklines that are risky; it's visible cleavage. The higher the cleavage, the higher the neckline needs to be.

Wear lightweight jewelry with simple lines—possibly in mesh, frosted glass, silver, pale woods, and ivory. They tend to look and feel cooler than heavy, fussy jewelry. If you need a belt, think about a fabric, cord, or narrow leather belt. A wide plastic belt, pulled tight at the waist, only increases perspiration. A leather belt might absorb and give off moisture a little better, but heat and body moisture can cause the leather's dye to crack or bleed onto the garment. Try a longer, narrow belt wrapped loosely at the hip or buckled slightly loose at the waist.

Bare feet and legs in sandals are coolest, but are appropriate only for casual occasions or the most casual of business offices. Hosiery is essential for a dressy or professional look, and heat is seldom an excuse because most public and office buildings are air-conditioned. On those occasions when you feel the need for stockings, longer-length skirts and pants allow you to switch from pantyhose to knee-high stockings—they can make all the difference.

If necessary, commute bare-legged and put on stockings as soon as you arrive at your destination. Take them off again before you head home. Seek out summerweight or mesh sandal-foot hosiery and wear them with open-toe pumps or sling-back shoes that allow the air to circulate.

Review Main Points

The element, line, is used to design both basic and costume clothing styles. Basic styles are simple in design, while costume styles are more detailed or decorated, and are often associated with a particular person, place, or occasion. Basics feature only structural lines, allowing them to combine easily with many other clothing pieces. Costume pieces may feature several structural lines *and* decorative lines, making it more difficult to combine them with other clothing pieces. Build the bulk of your wardrobe around basic clothing styles. Gradually acquire needed or wanted costume styles. Rely on separates, acquiring a few one-piece garments. Each characteristic of line contributes to the total effect of the clothing. Lines can be manipulated to communicate messages, feelings, and moods, and to create a variety of illusions about the body. Because clothing styles interact with one another and with the wearer, their lines need to be compatible with one another and with the wearer, the time and place, and the fabric they are made of. In combining different line types and directions, one must be dominant, and all others subordinate, by degrees. Combining lines or basic and costume styles, in interesting and harmonious ways, is one of the keys to putting together an interesting, versatile, and fashionable wardrobe.

Review Questions

1. How can you recognize a basic style garment? _____
   _____.

2. What makes a garment a costume piece? _____
   _____.

3. Build the bulk of your wardrobe around _____ styles.

4. What is the disadvantage of a wardrobe composed of mostly one-piece garments?
   _____.

5. _____ and _____ are the foundations of all
   clothing design.

6. List two functions of the design element, line.
   _____   _____

7. Describe what is meant by structural lines as compared to decorative lines.
   _____
   _____

8. What makes rigid fashion "rules" so unreliable or invalid?
   _____

9. Horizontal lines appear to increase or emphasize _____.

10. What is an illusion? _____
    _____.

11. List four characteristics of a line that can affect the appearance of a garment
    and the illusions it may create.
    _____   _____

    _____   _____

12. Which of the following words does not belong in the group? Circle the word.
    diagonal   decorative   vertical   horizontal

13. Match the following characteristics of line to the appropriate mood or message it communicates.

    _____ curved   a. active, exciting, unstable

    _____ broken   b. gentle, feminine, happy

    _____ diagonal   c. strong, decisive, formal

    _____ straight   d. abrupt, sporty, casual

14. To keep your cool in hot and humid weather, select clothing with style lines
    that are
    _____ and _____.

15. What is the difference between dominant and subordinate points of
    interest?
    _____

Discussion Questions

#1 Discuss the illusory effects of the lines in clothes students are wearing. What occasions, moods, or themes are represented in the classroom? What feelings or personality traits are communicated by the various lines?

Notes: _____

_____

_____

_____

_____

_____

#2 If you were going to a job interview, where should the lines in your clothes lead? Where should the dominant focal point of emphasis be located? Why?

Notes: _____

_____

_____

_____

_____

_____

#3 What are some common fashion "rules" regarding line that don't always work, often prove untrue, and are unreliable or invalid?

Notes: _____

_____

_____

_____

_____

_____

#4 The same concepts and strategies that apply to women's clothing also apply to men's clothing. What are some examples of basic styles and costume styles in menswear?

Notes: _____

_____

_____

_____

_____

_____

Exercise 3–1   Line Recognition

Name _____

Look at what you are wearing.

- Identify, list, and checkmark which clothing pieces are basic in design; identify and checkmark costume pieces.
- Identify and list the structural and/or decorative lines formed in each item of clothing.
- Identify and list the type of lines—straight, restrained, or full-rounded curves—in each item.
- Identify and list the line directions—vertical, horizontal, or diagonal—in each clothing item.
- Work with a classmate and identify as above.

You–Clothing Item	Basic	Costume	Lines Formed (Structural/Decorative)	Line Type (Straight/Restrained/Curved)	Line Direction (Vertical/Horizontal/Diagonal)

Classmate–Clothing Item	Basic	Costume	Lines Formed (Structural/Decorative)	Line Type (Straight/Restrained/Curved)	Line Direction (Vertical/Horizontal/Diagonal)

Exercise 3–2   Line Preference

Name _____

Look in your closet, selecting five to ten favorite pieces of clothing and five to ten less favorite pieces of clothing.

- In the appropriate section—favorite/less favorite—place a checkmark in the column to identify the dominant kind of line formed—structural or decorative—and describe any special characteristics about these lines.
- Identify the dominant type of line—straight, restrained curve, or full-rounded curve.
- Identify the dominant line direction—vertical, horizontal, or diagonal.
- Check the appropriate column to identify the style as basic or costume.
- Identify the style as separate or one-piece.
- Total the number of lines identified in each column.
- Analyze how these line characteristics have influenced your preferences.

	Clothing Item	Lines Formed		Line Type		Line Direction			Basic	Costume	Separate	One-Piece
		Structural	Decorative	Straight	Curved	Vertical	Horizontal	Diagonal				
Favorite Clothes												
	TOTALS											
Less Favorite Clothes												
	TOTALS											

Conclusions:

Exercise 3–3   Local Store Experience

Look in a local clothing or fabric store for lines and styles you have never worn before. In front of a full-length mirror, experience the look and the feel of these fabrics and/or clothes.

Fabric Store Experience:

- To see how the fabric might look on you, drape it on your body to simulate a piece of clothing.
- Notice and record how the lines make you look and what they appear to communicate.

Clothing Store Experience:

- If possible, to see how the clothing will look on you, try it on.
- Notice and record how the garment looks and fits on your body.
- Notice and record what the lines appear to communicate.

Exercise 3-4   Basic/Costume Style Recognition

Name _____

• Collect five pictures of basic clothing pieces and accessories.
• Mount.
• Label.

• Collect five pictures of costume clothing pieces and accessories.
• Mount.
• Label.

Exercise 3–5   Line Coordination

Name_____

Find pictures of clothing pieces in lines you would like to combine into an outfit for yourself. Don't worry about color or textures now. Look for lines that can be expected to flatter your figure. Look for lines you can combine harmoniously. Mount and identify accordingly. Write a paragraph stating reasons for your choices.

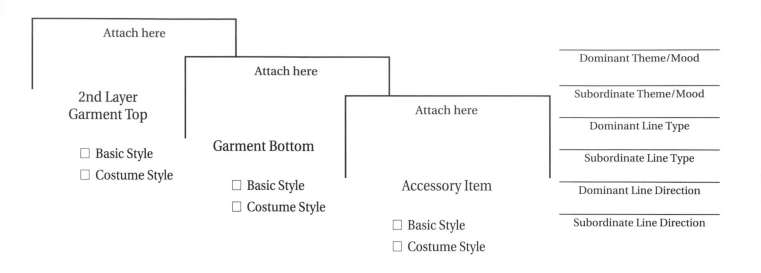

Attach here

2nd Layer
Garment Top

☐ Basic Style
☐ Costume Style

Attach here

Garment Bottom

☐ Basic Style
☐ Costume Style

Attach here

Accessory Item

☐ Basic Style
☐ Costume Style

_____
Dominant Theme/Mood
_____
Subordinate Theme/Mood
_____
Dominant Line Type
_____
Subordinate Line Type
_____
Dominant Line Direction
_____
Subordinate Line Direction

Attach here

2nd Layer Garment Top

☐ Basic Style
☐ Costume Style

Attach here

Garment Bottom

☐ Basic Style
☐ Costume Style

Attach here

3rd Layer
Garment Top

☐ Basic Style
☐ Costume Style

Attach here

Accessory Item

☐ Basic Style
☐ Costume Style

Attach here

Accessory Item

☐ Basic Style
☐ Costume Style

_____
Dominant Theme/Mood
_____
Subordinate Theme/Mood
_____
Dominant Line Type
_____
Subordinate Line Type
_____
Sub-subordinate Line Type
_____
Dominant Line Direction
_____
Subordinate Line Direction
_____
Sub-subordinate Line Direction

Exercise 3–6 Preferred Line Characteristics

Name _____

Plot your preferred line characteristics or traits on a continuum between opposites.

Receding—Yin   **Advancing—Yang**

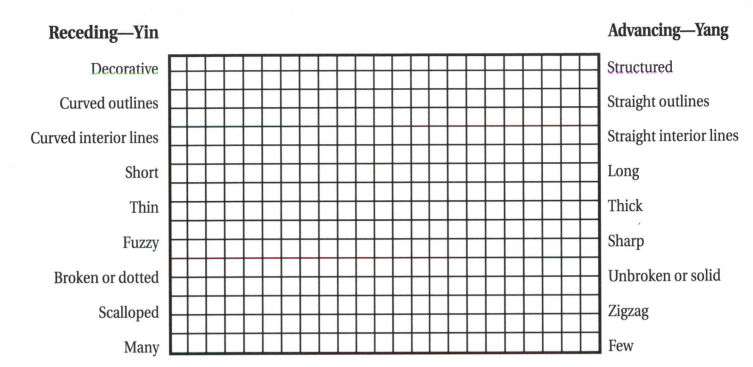

Receding—Yin	Advancing—Yang
Decorative	Structured
Curved outlines	Straight outlines
Curved interior lines	Straight interior lines
Short	Long
Thin	Thick
Fuzzy	Sharp
Broken or dotted	Unbroken or solid
Scalloped	Zigzag
Many	Few

Exercise 3–7   Personal Style File

Name_____

In newspapers, magazines, and catalogs, find pictures of clothes and accessories in styles you think you would like to own.

Put these pictures in a folder, file, or box for future reference. Group similar types of garments together—blouses and shirts together, jackets together, skirts together, dresses together, shoes together, jewelry together, and so forth.

Periodically, sort through your style file and discard pictures of those styles that no longer appeal to you.

There are sure to be some that you'll look at later and wonder, "Why did I ever like that?"

Add to your style file throughout your study in this book. Gradually, you'll accumulate a collection of pictured styles that represent your preferences and needs.

Later, as you plan a cluster of clothes, or consider additions to your wardrobe, your collection will serve as a guide, a reminder of the details of your personal style.

Update your style file, adding new pictures whenever you find styles you like.

Chapter

4

Classic Styles and Shape Selection and Coordination

Learning Objectives

Your goal in completing this chapter is to be able to:

- Differentiate between classic clothing styles and trendy or fad styles.

- Appreciate the value of classic clothing in a wardrobe.

- Understand and explain the functions of shape.

- Describe how background and foreground shapes are formed in clothing.

- Identify the types of shapes in clothing design.

- Be aware of additional characteristics of shape that affect a clothing design.

- Predict the effect of shape on garment performance, mood, and message.

- Recognize different types of body shapes, often called figure types.

- Select clothing style lines and shapes to meet your needs.

- Coordinate and combine two or more shapes harmoniously.

- Coordinate and combine classic and trend or fad styles harmoniously.

Preview Main Points

1. Rely on classic styles, clothes with design lines and shapes that fit and flatter most figures and are appropriate for many occasions.

2. Acquire an occasional fashion trend or fad item to update your classic wardrobe.

3. Knowing about shape, as an element of design, will help you make wise consumer decisions about clothing selection and coordination.

4. Become more aware of figure variations and body shapes, and how body shapes can relate to garment shapes.

5. Select clothing styles in shapes that meet your individual needs or purposes — appropriate for your lifestyle, personal style, and for the fabric.

6. Coordinate or combine shapes as well as separates in two or more styles to achieve greater variety, interest, and individuality.

1.

Rely on classic styles, clothes with design lines and shapes that fit and flatter most figures and are appropriate for many occasions.

The more complicated and costly our lives become, the more wear we need from our clothes and the more important classic clothing styles become. At some time, most clothing styles pass through a **fashion cycle**, wave, or curve. You can observe the predictable stages a clothing style goes through during its time as a **fashion trend**. These stages illustrate the relative position of classics and fads, from start to finish. (See Figure 4–1.) The average length of a fashion cycle is getting shorter, lasting only three to seven years.

Classy Classics

Once a new clothing style is introduced, it becomes a classic if it meets the following criteria:

- Classic styles satisfy many clothing needs for many people.
- Classic styles easily fit and flatter most figures.
- Most people have places to wear classic styles.
- Most people can afford to buy classic styles.

Clothes with classic styling are worn and seen often, causing them to become accepted in good taste by virtually everyone. At that point the style becomes a classic, core piece, retaining its appeal and ability to be worn for seven to ten years or more, without looking dated.

How to Recognize Classic Styles

To determine if a style is classic, look at the garment and ask yourself if the styling is extreme in any way — very wide or very big, very fitted or very tight, and so forth.

Query Box

Which of these classic clothing styles have you tried? Which might you like to try?

polo shirts	dirndl skirts
turtleneck shirts	knife-pleated skirts
cowboy shirts	straight-leg pants
single-breasted blazer	trouser-pleat pants
safari jackets	duffel coats
Chanel suits	trench coats
shirtwaist dresses	loop earrings
shetland sweaters	one-inch leather belts
cardigan sweater sets	penny loafers

(A complete list of classics would be very long. There are many options.)

The Fashion Curve

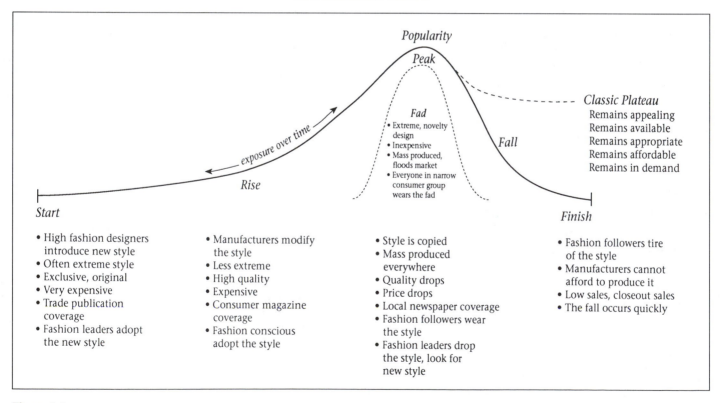

Figure 4–1.

The more moderate the design, the more classic it becomes. (See Figure 4–2.) Classics are never on the cutting edge of fashion, never extreme, never glitzy, tight, or revealing. Their styling changes very slowly and only slightly. Classics may be updated slightly in terms of current trends — say, toward slightly wider or narrower lapels or pant legs. Updated classics can become more fashionable at one time or another.

For example, *blazer jackets made fashion news in the late 1970s to early 1980s. They were appreciated, accepted, and appropriate in the 1990s, but were replaced as fashion*

Classic Clothing Styles

A. Camp shirt
B. Bowed blouse
C. Overblouse
D. Cap-sleeve jacket

E. Blouson jacket
F. Spencer jacket
G. Safari jacket
H. Pea coat

I. Inverted-pleat skirt
J. 4-gore flare skirt
K. Stitched-down pleated skirt
L. Shirtwaist dress

M. Walking short
N. Jeans
O. Gaucho pants
P. Surplice dress

Q. Smock dress
R. Wrap coat
S. Straight coat
T. Trench coat

Figure 4–2.

items with longer, fitted jackets with peaked lapels. Well designed, detailed, durable, easy to wear, and comfortable, the safari jacket is a fashion classic that makes fashion headlines from time to time.

Classics, then, are needed most by people who want their clothes to last as long as possible, and by people in leadership positions or politics. In these latter situations, classic clothes allow the wearer to relate more readily with a larger segment of an audience or voting population — people relate quickly and have more confidence in the long-term ability of the wearer. Present in any wardrobe as stable, core pieces, classics provide long-term, lasting value. Classic colors, fabrics, and patterns will be discussed.

2.

Acquire an occasional fashion trend or fad item to update your classic wardrobe.

Fads are short-lived, impractical, novelty, or high-fashion items, outdated within a few months because of more extreme lines and shapes.

How to Recognize Fads

Fads feature design lines and shapes that are relatively extreme in some direction or size — very wide or very narrow, very long or very short, very fitted or very tight, and so forth, including extreme colors, textures, and patterns. The more extreme the design, the more quickly it will come and go in terms of acceptability, popularity, or fashionability. (See Figure 4–3.)

Updating your classics with a periodic fad or high fashion piece allows you to have a bit of fun with your wardrobe. Carefully chosen, it makes you appear more in touch with today — open to new attitudes and ideas, modern methods and techniques. Even then, you are wise to avoid the more outrageous extremes, generally poorly designed and in poor taste. There are too many terrific clothes to choose from to risk money and reputation on something that doesn't present you well.

Individuals not satisfied with their wardrobes often have a closet full of fads and once trendy, but now outdated clothes. A wardrobe composed entirely of fashion trends or fads that go nowhere very appropriately, or go out of style all at once, leave you with nothing you want to wear or feel comfortable in even if *you do* want to wear them.

Avoid the Trend Trap

Leafing through spring and fall fashion magazines or catalogs, or strolling through the stores can keep you aware of new styles, fashion trends, and upcoming or current fads. Consider it research, prior to purchase. Cut or tear pictures from your magazines and catalogs. To become more familiar with them, tape them to your mirror or your closet door. Put them in your style file of looks to review and remind you of what you like.

Based on your own needs, decide what to adopt, adapt, or avoid before being pressured by your family, friends, or media advertisements. You are smart to:

- Avoid the most extreme styles.
- Buy into any new style on its upward rise, rather than at its peak or on its way out — with the exception of styles that become classic. Those you should continue to buy.

Trend and Fad Styles

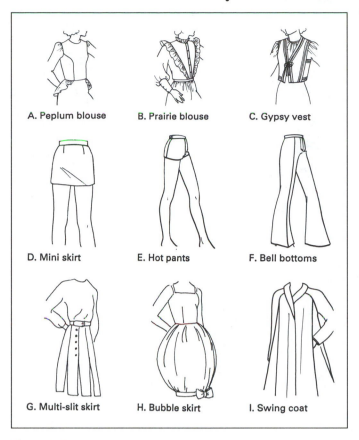

A. Peplum blouse B. Prairie blouse C. Gypsy vest

D. Mini skirt E. Hot pants F. Bell bottoms

G. Multi-slit skirt H. Bubble skirt I. Swing coat

Figure 4–3.

- Select only those new styles that provide new solutions to your clothing needs or problems.
- Select new styles that allow you a new degree of creativity and variety, while reflecting your own individuality and personal style.
- Buy fewer fad or trend items and then *only* after you have basic and classic clothes to work with.
- Pay low to moderate prices for fad items. Styles destined to become classics you can wait for until end-of-season sales.
- Wear a fad item often, so you can afford to toss it when it begins to look out of date. (See Figure 4–4.)

Wisely chosen, a fad item can provide a psychological boost, a touch of whimsy, or the surprise element that lets you have fun with fashion and show another side of yourself for a time. It's the kind of clothing you don't take too seriously. As with costume clothes, it's fine to have a few fad items, but not a whole closetful. Classics are what build more workable wardrobes.

More trend or fad items can be included in the wardrobes of people who don't have to worry about clothing cost or public response. For people who work in the more creative professions — such as art, music, theater, and interior design — there is even some general expectation that they will reflect more fashion-forward trends in their dress. Even they, however, must use wise judgment in what they buy or they risk looking like fashion victims,

getting negative responses from others, and losing their hard-earned dollars on clothes with short wear-lives.

Recognizing Basic Classics

Most basic styles are also classic, but not all classics are basic. Think about this for a moment. If the classic style is busy, with several lines and shapes, details or decoration, it isn't basic. (See Figure 4–5.) It's a classic costume piece.

For example, a safari style jacket is classic but not basic. Not simple or plain in design lines and shapes, a safari jacket is styled with shoulder epaulets or sleeve tabs, cuffed and/or roll-up sleeves, breast and/or hip pockets, and a fitted waistband or self-belt. Some may even feature a shoulder and/or hip yoke. These many design details are decoration enough, limiting your use of accessories to change the look or mood of the jacket. They cause the jacket to look sportive all the time. There is an indisputable costume look to the jacket, associated with an African bush hunt or safari holiday. A safari jacket has become a timeless travel piece, a classic, but it isn't a basic.

A safari jacket, however, is generally loose and fits easily over many figures. The design details are dominant, taking attention away from the body — the body becomes subordinate. That makes for an attractive appearance on virtually every body — women and men. Given today's more casual life-style, at work and at home, most people have plenty of places to wear a safari jacket. It's a true classic.

Figure 4–4. You'll have to wear this suit often to get your money's worth before the zipper look goes out of fashion. *(Courtesy Madeleine Direct)*

Figure 4–5. A Chanel suit is classic but not basic. Color contrasting binding or braid used on the jacket makes it difficult to combine with other clothing pieces. The costume jacket demands a matching, basic skirt. *(Courtesy Madeleine Direct)*

Some clothing styles are borderline.

For example, *jeans are classic garments that are not exactly basic. Traditionally designed with five pockets, metal rivets, and top stitching, you can change the way they look only so much. They always have a dominantly casual, sporty, or rugged look about them, associated with Western cowboy costumes, and appropriate for more casual occasions, including casual business.*

For example, *a classic peasant blouse (see Figure 3–2a, page 54), because of its lowered, gathered neckline and short, puffed sleeves, appears open and invites fun and friendly social interaction. It is not basic enough to lend itself to most business occasions, even under a blazer. Generally recognized as part of a traditional Austrian, German, or Gypsy costume, a peasant blouse is best worn on casual and social or party occasions.*

It is the *basic* classics that are needed most by people employed in more formal, conservative, or public and service-oriented business and professional roles, such as banking, law, education, insurance, and management.

The basics and the classics meet more needs for more people in more walks of life. They eliminate fashion confusion and frustration. Both basics and classics are fur-ther described in terms of colors, fabrics, and patterns, such as a bright yellow rain slicker, tweed blazer, plaid flannel shirt, and red-stripe tie. Basic, classic colors, fabrics, and patterns are discussed in the following chapters.

3.

Knowing about shape, as an element of design, will help you make wise consumer decisions about clothing selection and coordination.

The following section of this chapter concentrates on shape. For the sake of understanding, remember that a shape is created when a continuous line encloses space. Line and shape are the foundations of all clothing design. Line and shape are interrelated from the beginning of any clothing design. As a continuous line encloses and divides the area within a garment, more shapes result. You can't deal with one without the other. Together, they create the endless variety of clothing styles.

Figure 4–6. The full-rounded collar fills out the upper body, while the decorative beading frames the face beautifully and softly. *(Courtesy Madeleine Direct)*

Figure 4–7. The shape of this soft, sweater-knit coat is tubular. Pockets are angular. Sized appropriately, it flows easily over the figure. Clothing silhouette is dominant and the body is subordinate. *(Courtesy Madeleine Direct)*

Importance and Functions of Shape

- Shapes define the outer edge, outline, or silhouette of the body and clothing.
- Shapes define areas within a garment, including sleeves, cuffs, pockets, shirt yokes and plackets, and skirt gores. They can reinforce or counter the silhouette.
- Shapes add interest to a plain garment design.
- Shapes can create a point or area of emphasis.
- Shapes create powerful illusions about the size and shape of the body.
- Shapes communicate visual meaning, messages, or moods.

How Shapes Are Formed

In clothing, two kinds of shapes are formed: background shapes and foreground shapes.

Background shapes are those formed by the outline of the garment. They can appear as empty space, or as filled spaces if divided. A garment is designed in one or a combination of several shapes.

Foreground shapes are those formed by design details on the surface of the garment. They include collars, cuffs, pockets, bands, and trims. (See Figure 4–5). Foreground shapes tend to add some visual weight in the area where they are placed.

Types of Shapes

There are two types of shapes: angular and curved or rounded shapes.

Angular shapes are made with straight lines. Common angular shapes include the square, rectangle, triangle, diamond, pentagon, hexagon, and octagon. They appear crisp, flat, and rigid. They oppose the curved lines of the body to varying degrees.

Curved shapes have some degree of roundness, from wavy free forms to circles. Slightly curved shapes conform more closely to the curves of the body. (See Figure 4–6.)

Types of Garment Shapes

Tubular garment shapes and **rectangular garment shapes** are just that, rectangular with straight lines and tubes around the body. Taller than they are wide, the dominant lines are vertical. In clothing, they are in opposition to the body and the waistline is not always defined. (See Figure 4–7.)

Triangular garment shapes and spaces are composed of predominantly straight lines. They are narrower in the shoulders and wider at the hem. The waist may or may not be defined. Diagonal lines are dominant in the lower area of the garment. They repeat and emphasize straight edges and the angularity of the body shape, while they counter roundness. (See Figure 4–8.)

Inverted triangular shapes (wedge shapes) feature predominantly straight lines. They are wider in the shoulders and narrower at the hem. The waist may or may not

Common Types of Garment Shapes

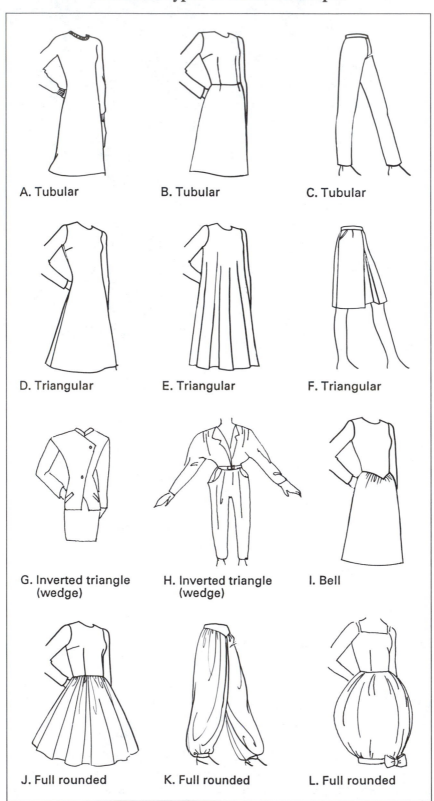

A. Tubular   B. Tubular   C. Tubular

D. Triangular   E. Triangular   F. Triangular

G. Inverted triangle (wedge)   H. Inverted triangle (wedge)   I. Bell

J. Full rounded   K. Full rounded   L. Full rounded

Figure 4–8.

be defined. Diagonal lines are dominant in the upper area. They tend to repeat and emphasize straight edges and the angularity of the body shape, while they counter roundness. (See Figure 4–8.)

Diamond garment shapes feature softly curved lines or fullness around the middle. They are narrower in the shoulder and at the hem, as compared to the waist. The waist is not generally defined. Softly curved diagonal lines are dominant. (See Figure 4–8.)

Hourglass garment shapes are designed with a mix of straight and softly curved lines. The garment is relatively fitted at the waist, emphasizing the waist area as compared to bust above and hips below. (See Figure 4–8.)

Bell garment shapes are similar to the triangular garment shapes, but combine straight lines with softly curved to full-rounded lines in the bottom half of the garment. They feature a mix of vertical and horizontal line directions, conforming more easily to the body. (See Figure 4–8.)

Rounded or curved garment shapes have more curved lines than other shapes. The shape changes depending on how full or rounded the curves are. They repeat and emphasize roundness and counter angularity in the figure. (See Figure 4–8.)

Additional geometric and free-form shapes may be introduced in dress design, creating endless psychological moods or messages and physical illusions. (See Table 4–1.)

Arrangement of Shapes on the Garment

Few shapes or no divided areas within a garment tend to increase apparent height and decrease width. No shapes within the garment can appear as empty background space and can put too much attention on the body beneath. A few well-chosen and well-placed shapes can camouflage and draw attention away from the body.

Many shapes or divided areas within a garment tend to decrease height and increase width. Too many shapes in a small space appear crowded and confusing.

Closely spaced shapes can visually narrow the area. Even a double-breasted jacket can flatter a larger figure if it fits well and the buttons are closely spaced.

Widely spaced shapes can visually widen or enlarge the area. Even widely spaced flowers, such as the shapes in a medium-scale floral print, can visually enlarge the figure it covers.

Illusions in Line and Shape

A visual or optical illusion is a false perception or misinterpretation of the visual cues — something that deceives your eye when you look at it. Illusions do not occur in isolation. They occur as the lines, shapes, colors, fabrics, and patterns interact with one another. Regardless of the facts, and according to your mind's eye, you tend to believe the illusion. Shapes, in addition to lines, can be manipulated and arranged to create illusions.

A general goal in using clothing as a resource is to select and arrange design shapes in ways that enhance the body — in ways that make the face and figure appear

Figure 4–9. Midriff, waist, and a high hip curve are effectively camouflaged in this comfortable sleeveless jacket. (*Courtesy Madeleine Direct*)

more nearly ideal. Clothing lines and shapes can be used in ways that emphasize the most attractive lines and shapes of the body and camouflage or counter those body lines and shapes considered less attractive, in effect minimizing or eliminating them. (See Figure 4–9.)

Shape and the Principles of Design

An asymmetrical figure can appear more nearly symmetrical and well-balanced when wearing clothing with asymmetrical lines or shapes, or by wearing the clothing in an asymmetrical way. The asymmetry of the body becomes less noticeable, as more attention goes to the clothing — clothing dominant, body subordinate.

For example, a shirt can be designed with an inset panel on one side only, or with a patch pocket on one side only. A dress or jacket can be styled with an off-center or side-front opening. Tie a neckline bow off-center, or place a pin on one side, each for an asymmetrical effect. A scarf or shawl can be draped over a low shoulder, to lift and balance the look of the body. Asymmetrical effects tend to appear more active and dramatic, drawing more attention to themselves and away from the body.

Table 4–1 General Perception of Shape

	Message/Function	Characteristic Shapes
Weather	To feel and appear warmer	Tubular Softly rounded
	To feel and appear cooler	Softly rounded Circular
Occasion/Activity	To feel and appear casual/informal (casual business)	Tubular Softly rounded
	To feel and appear dress-businesslike (formal business)	Angular Tubular Rectangular Triangular Inverted triangular
	To feel and appear dressy/formal	Softly rounded Bell Circular
Values	To save time, easy care	Softly rounded Rectangular Few shapes
	To impress or influence others	Tubular Form fitting Slim, sexy
	To be comfortable	Loose-fitting shapes
	To save money	Simple Few
Personality	To feel and appear ingenue/romantic	Rounded Many shapes Smaller
	To feel and appear happy, youthful, gamine, sportive	Angular Tubular
	To feel and appear dramatic/exotic	Angular Inverted Triangular triangular Hourglass Few Bell Larger Circular
	To feel and appear mature, serious, somber, classic	Tubular Rectangular

Table 4–1 General Perception of Shape (*continued*)

	Message/Function	Characteristic Shapes
Figure/Body Build	To maintain or decrease attention and apparent size — to appear taller, longer, narrower, thinner	Tubular Rectangular Triangular Narrower Few Empty
	To increase attention and apparent size — to appear shorter, wider, thicker	Square Circular Inverted triangle Hourglass Diamond Many Filled
Fabric	Shape demands thin, pliable drapey fabrics	Several to many seams or shapes Empty to filled space
	Shape requires crisp, stiff fabrics	Tubular Triangular Bell Circular Fewer seams or shapes Empty or filled space
	Shape can permit use of thick, bulky fabrics	Fewer seams or shapes Empty space

To appear balanced, the size of clothing and accessory shapes needs to be in proportion and scale with the body shape or form, including the bone structure. Compare the size of the body to the size of clothing and accessories — their overall size and the size of each detail. (See Table 4–2.)

For example, the smaller the body and bones, the smaller and fewer the design details must be. If proportionally too large, they appear to overwhelm a smaller figure. Conversely, the larger the body, the larger and more design details the figure can carry, without appearing overwhelmed.

Size, however, is relative. What appears large on a small-scale body may appear small on a large-scale body.

For example, jewelry may appear proportionally larger on a small-scale body but proportionally smaller on a large-scale body. A person may appear proportionally shorter standing next to a taller person, but proportionally taller when standing next to an even shorter person.

For this reason, you may not appear in harmony wearing the same jewelry as another woman.

When you look in the mirror, if attention is drawn to a proportionally long neck or square shoulders, to prominent breasts or large arms, to a prominent abdomen or wide hips, long arms or large ankles, you must then compare that part to the adjoining body part, to other parts, and to your whole body.

The size of clothing and accessory shapes can be used to create an attractive bridge or transition between body parts that are out of proportion, or out of balance, with one another. Call it image management or fashion therapy, it works!

For example, if a person's head and features are small but the body is relatively large, or vice versa, details in the hairstyle and neckline area need to be medium scale to visually fill out the head and bridge or minimize the difference in sizes.

Table 4-2 Scale (Size) Relationships

Body Build	Scale of Clothing Design Details and Accsessories
• Small bone structure • Short and narrow	Small to medium scale
• Medium bone structure • Short and wide • Moderate length and width • Tall and narrow	Medium scale
• Large bone structure • Tall and wide	Large to medium scale

As another example, if the bone structure of a person's head and features is small and the bone structure of the shoulders is medium, clothing details in the neckline and accessories placed in that area need to be medium, or small to medium — no larger or they will emphasize the difference in size. Several small details or accessories can also be arranged in a moderately sized grouping. If the bone structure or weight carried on the hips makes them even larger, clothing details and accessories positioned in that area need to be large to medium, no smaller or the contrast will be too great. Several small- to medium-scale details can also be arranged in a larger group and appear harmonious.

Decorative lines and foreground shapes call attention to themselves and therefore emphasize the area where they are placed. Use them only in places where you want to draw attention and therefore emphasize.

For example, a row of buttons or pocket flaps can lead attention around or up and down a garment. If placed on the bust, stomach, or buttocks, they draw attention to that spot. If the bust, stomach, or buttocks are larger than you want noticed, you won't want to place buttons or flap pockets there. If the bust is proportionally small or average and the stomach protrudes, breast pockets with a button and/or flap can draw attention away from the protruding stomach and fill out the bust.

TIP

FROM THE PROS

Because all the elements of design are interrelated, **the ultimate effect of any shape is influenced by the other elements** of design — the lines, colors, textures, and patterns in the clothes. This influence is what makes so many "fashion rules" unreliable or invalid. The rule appears to work in one outfit, but not in another because the color, the fabric, the pattern, or the combination of clothes causes the effect to be different than expected. This influence is what gets so many people confused. As you study Chapters 3 through 7, learning what the predictable effects of each element are, you will be better equipped to evaluate the total effect of any given garment or outfit.

4.

Become more aware of figure variations and body shapes, and how body shapes can relate to garment shapes.

Everybody is unique (see Figure 4–10), with few ideal figures existing. Virtually every figure has some **figure variations** — variations from that so-called ideal figure used as a standard for comparison and for clothing manufacture.

Figure 4–10. Figures can be very different from one another. Pregnancy introduces yet another dimension to those differences.

Fitting and Pattern Alteration: A Multi-Method Approach by Liechty, Pottberg, and Rasband, deals with eighty-five figure variations. A few of those variations include:

Long neck	Short neck
Square shoulders	Round shoulders
Forward arm joints	Inward rotation of the elbow
Large bust	Small bust
High waist	Low waist
Long lower torso	Short lower torso
Sway back	Sway front

It does not matter how many people have a particular figure variation. If it is you, your child, parent, sibling, student, customer, or client, you need to know how to recognize the variation and how to dress to camouflage or minimize it.

Body Shapes or Figure Types

A few specific figure variations occur in typical combinations — those having to do with horizontal width or the size of shoulders, bust, waist, hips, and thighs — combinations so typical that we tend to recognize the stereotypical shapes and give them names. Typical body shapes are often called **figure types**. They define how body parts relate proportionally to one another and to the total figure. (See Table 4–3.)

Ideal figure types, rare though they may be, are average in weight, appear similar in width in the shoulders and hips, with medium bust size and a small waist. They have a slightly curved abdomen, moderately curved buttocks, and slim thighs.

Tubular figure types are slim to thin and below the average weight range for their height, with generally straight body lines and bony angles. They have few to no obvious curves, with line movement in the vertical direction.

Rectangular figure types are average to above average weight range for their height. They are similar in width in the shoulders, waist, and hips/thighs. There is no defined waist curve or indentation. Body lines appear generally straight, with vertical line movement.

Triangular figure types are narrower in the shoulders and wider in the hips/thighs, with a low hip curve. They are often smaller in the bust and waist, narrower in the back, and rounder in the buttocks — generally straight lines above the waist and curved lines below. Emphasis is on the lower torso.

Inverted triangular figure types are wider in the shoulders and narrower in the hips/thighs, with a high hip curve. They are generally larger in the bust, wider in the back, and flatter in the buttocks — generally curved lines above the waist and straight lines below. Emphasis is on the upper torso.

Diamond figure types are wider in the midriff and waist area, narrower in the shoulders and hips/thighs, with a high hip curve and slim legs. The bust is often smaller and the buttocks flatter. Emphasis is on the waist area.

Hourglass figure types have full-rounded body lines, with proportionally larger shoulders, bust, hips, and buttocks and a proportionally small waist. Emphasis is on the bust and hips/buttocks, but may shift quickly to the contrast in size at the waist.

Rounded figure types are generally above the average weight range for their height. Being larger throughout the figure, body lines are full-rounded curves, with line movement in horizontal direction and emphasis on width.

Body shapes also vary vertically, from top to bottom. The figure may have a proportionally shorter torso (high waist) and longer legs, or longer torso (low waist) and proportionally shorter legs. (See Table 4–4, page 91.)

T I P

🌿

F R O M   T H E   P R O S

To determine your general figure type, try the time-tested "blink test." Dress in form-fitting clothing, in possibly a T-shirt and tights, tights and leotard, swimsuit, or underwear and follow the procedure described in Chapter 3. In this attire, your attention will generally be drawn to the largest area of your body shape. Then compare that area to other areas of your body and to the figure type descriptions above.

Note: Not every body conforms to one of these stereotypical figure types. If yours doesn't, simply become very aware of where your figure is proportionally narrower as compared to proportionally wider. If there is an area you determine to be too narrow or too wide, then select clothing styles to counter and create the illusion of a more nearly ideal figure. (Study typical countering techniques in Table 4–3, then adapt to your own figure.)

Figure Type	Characteristic Figure Variations	To Cover, Camouflage, Counter, and Create the Illusion of the Ideal Figure	
Tubular*	Slim to thin, below average weight range Straight body lines, angular, bony, no to few obvious curves Similar width in shoulders, waist, and hips Body appears balanced		Minimize thinness, bony angularity Emphasize anywhere Lead attention wherever you like Fill out above and below waist Loose fit above and below waist
Rectangular	Similar width in shoulders, waist, hips, and thighs Average to above ideal weight ranges Softly straight body lines No defined waist Often with high hip curve Body appears balanced		Minimize waist Emphasize center-front above the waist Lead attention inward at waist and up toward face Fill out slightly at shoulders Smooth, loose fit over entire figure
Triangular	Narrower shoulders, wider hips, and/or thighs Average to smaller bust, narrow back, smaller waist Low hip curve, rounded buttocks Possibly low waist, longer legs Straight upper body lines, curved lower body lines; appears bottom heavy		Minimize lower torso Emphasize upper torso Lead attention upward Fill out shoulders and upper torso with soft fullness and design details Smooth, loose fit below the waist
Inverted	Wider shoulders, narrower hips and thighs Average to larger bust, wider back, larger waist High hip curve, flatter buttocks, slim legs Possibly high waist, shorter legs Rounded upper body lines, straight lower body lines; appears top heavy		Minimize upper torso Emphasize center-front at neckline or anywhere below waist Lead attention inward at shoulders toward neck Fill out area below waist with soft fullness or design detail Smooth loose fit above the waist
Diamond	Wider midriff and waist Narrower shoulders, hips, and thighs Average to smaller bust High hip curve Flatter buttocks Mid-body heavy		Minimize midriff, waist, and high hip area Emphasize shoulder area Lead attention inward at waist and up to face Fill out shoulders and leg area Smooth, loose fit over mid-body area
Hourglass	Larger bust and possibly shoulders Wider back, small waist Larger hips and buttocks Rounded body lines Body appears balanced, but emphasizes full-rounded bust, hips, and buttocks		Minimize bust and hip fullness Emphasize shoulder and neckline area Lead attention upward toward face Fill out waist slightly Smooth, loose fit over entire figure
Rounded*	Larger to obese; above average weight range Larger figure with rounded body lines		Minimize body width and weight Emphasize shoulder and neckline area Lead attention inward at waist area and up to face Visually lengthen entire figure Smooth, loose fit over entire figure

* Weight loss or weight gain may cause the tubular and rounded figure types to appear more like another type.

Table 4-4   Recommended Style Lines and Shapes for Vertical Figure Type

Figure Type	Characteristic Figure Variations	To Cover, Camouflage, Counter, and Create the Illusion of the Ideal Figure	
High Waist	Shorter upper torso Longer lower torso or longer legs		Vertical design lines on tops Waistless dresses and coats Belt matches top Dropped waistline and hip yokes Horizontal design line on skirts and pants Design details at hem and below waist
Low Waist	Longer upper torso Shorter lower torso or shorter legs		Design details at neckline and above waist Horizontal design lines on tops Raised waistlines and midriff yokes Belt matches skirt or pants Waistless dresses and coats Vertical design lines on skirts and pants

From This Day Forward

Stop referring to your body as having figure problems, faults, flaws, defects, liabilities, and abnormalities. These words are self-defeating from the start. Be kind to yourself and more correctly call them *figure variations.* Ignore those social and cultural influences that cause you to feel dissatisfied with your body. Vow to be more objective as you evaluate your figure. Take joy in those areas where you are average/ideal, or nearly so. Recognize figure variations as something to work with. Remember, you don't have figure problems. You have fitting problems. And fitting problems can be solved — with the art of dress, and illusions in line, shape, color, fabric, and pattern.

TIP

&

FROM THE PROS

Accept those features about your face and figure you cannot change — your hereditary bone structure and pattern of weight distribution. Make them part of your individual beauty. Then work to change what you can and will — your posture and weight. Learn to cover, camouflage, or counter what you can to enhance your figure and create the illusion of your ideal face and figure. This is a wonderful growing experience that leads to self-acceptance, self-appreciation, self-confidence, and self-actualization.

TIP

&

FROM THE PROS

Sales associates working in fashion retailing need to recognize general body type the moment a potential customer enters the department or store. With an up-to-the-minute knowledge of the inventory, she can pull clothing styles, or direct the customer to clothing styles, that will most likely accommodate and flatter the customer's figure. Ability to explain the concept usually boosts credibility with the customer. Personal shoppers and image consultants benefit by this ability as well.

5.

Select clothing styles in shapes that meet your individual needs or purposes – appropriate for your life–style, personal style, and for the fabric.

- Choose style shapes with characteristics appropriate for the environment and the weather or season of the year.
- Choose style shapes with characteristics appropriate for the mood, occasion, or activity.
- Choose style shapes with characteristics that reflect the values of the wearer.
- Choose style shapes with characteristics that are compatible with, or that reflect, the wearer's personality. (See Table 4–1, page 86.)
- Choose style shapes, or silhouettes, with characteristics that flatter your face and figure. (See Tables 4–1, page 86; 4–2, page 88; and 4–5.)

Table 4–5 Recommended Style Lines and Shapes for the Face

Approximate	Hat and Hairstyle (To cover or counter)		Neckline and Collar Characteristics (To counter and create illusion of oval–shaped face)	
Oval/Ideal		Any style		Any style
Square		Add height Cover temples Diagonal bangs		Lead attention down Vertical V-shaped U-shaped Open collars Narrow lapels
Rectangle		Cover forehead Fill out at sides		Lead attention outward Horizontal Wide Scoop
Triangle		Fill out at temples Fill in at jaw		Lead attention down Vertical V-shaped U-shaped Narrow lapels Open collars
Inverted Triangle		Add height Cover temples Fill out at jaw		Lead attention outward Horizontal Wide Scoop Square
Diamond		Fill out at temples Fill out at jaw Cover ears		Lead attention outward Horizontal Wide Square Scoop
Circle/Round		Diagonal bangs Cover cheeks		Lead attention down Vertical V-shaped Open collars a little
Oblong		Cover partial forehead Fill out at cheeks		Lead attention outward Horizontal Wide Square Open collars wide

Common sense tells you to **avoid clothing styles that expose or emphasize** and, therefore, reinforce a figure variation that you don't want noticed.

For example, *strapless or sleeveless outfits expose the body to view and generally emphasize whatever is seen. Short sleeves expose the arm, shorts and short skirts expose the leg, and so forth. If that's not what you want, you'll need to cover up.*

Narrow shapes and tight-fitting or clingy fabric expose whatever body part is underneath, generally emphasizing it. If that's not what you want, you'll want slightly wider shapes and a looser fit. (Non-cling fabrics always look more attractive.) One of the kindest things you can do for your figure is to wear your clothing slightly loose rather than form fitting.

A helpful general guideline is to **look for clothing styles that will naturally accommodate your figure type** and any other figure variations. In other words, the garment shape makes visual sense, as it essentially repeats your body shape. Clothing styles in this shape are made for you. Selected in the right size, these styles *flow easily* over your entire figure, even areas where you may be larger. The clothing silhouette is dominant and your body is subordinate.

For example, *an A-line skirt or shirtwaist dress with a flared skirt easily accommodates the proportionally larger hip and thigh area of a triangular figure. A wedge-style chemise dress easily accommodates the proportionally larger shoulders of an inverted triangular figure, flowing easily over bust, midriff, and waist below. (Sizing may require minor adjustment or alteration for a fabulous fit. See* Fitting and Pattern Alteration *by Liechty, Pottberg, and Rasband, or* Fabulous Fit *by Rasband.)*

Another general guideline worth knowing is to **look for clothing styles that naturally cover, camouflage, counter, and minimize to create attractive illusions** about body areas that you may consider less attractive and reinforce or emphasize the most attractive characteristics about your figure. If better balance is needed, you're looking for clothing styles that will *fill out* smaller or narrower areas of your figure to counterbalance larger areas. In most cases, you want to lead attention in the opposite direction from the body. (See Table 4–3, page 90.)

For example, *that same shirtwaist dress, with moderate shoulder pads, slight gathering below the shoulder yoke, and blousing at the waist, works beautifully to fill out the upper body area, for better balance with the lower torso area of a triangular figure. Palazzo pants work to fill out the leg area of an inverted triangular or diamond-shaped figure for better balance with the top of the figure. At the same time, width at the hem of the pants will emphasize slim ankles. (Sizing may require some adjustment or alteration for a good fit.)*

- Choose style shapes with characteristics that look, feel, and hang appropriately for the fabric of the garment.
- Choose style shapes that will fit in well and coordinate with the existing wardrobe.

6.

Coordinate or combine shapes as well as separates in two or more styles, to achieve greater variety, interest, and individuality.

☙

In addition to style lines and shapes, the following discussion considers the color, fabric, and pattern of separates as they are interrelated and influence your choice of separates to be combined in any one outfit.

Harmony among Shapes and Styles

To combine two or more pieces of clothing with different shapes or styles, here is the general guideline. Select and combine the pieces **in terms of the activity, occasion, mood, values, and personality traits they communicate**, project, or reflect. The characteristic traits of both classics and trend pieces need to be somewhat similar for the clothes to appear like they belong together.

For example, *a casual/sporty cowboy shirt or a prairie blouse combines easily with equally casual/sporty jeans.*

Values and personality traits contributing to personal style are a little harder. It's a matter of deciding what design details are most important to you; it's a matter of likes and dislikes; a matter of deciding how severely or softly styled you want or need your clothes to be; a matter of yin and yang.

For example, *it's a matter of pairing a (satin) cowboy shirt with a (satin or velvet) tiered full skirt, as compared to pairing a (satin) cowboy shirt with a (gabardine) flared skirt.*

Women not satisfied with their wardrobe often combine clothes that clash, conflict, or communicate contradictory traits — among themselves or with the wearer. The combination or mix of design characteristics is very extreme — too extreme to appear harmonious. Remember, you want some but not too much difference for interest.

For example, *the very casual look of a cowboy or Western shirt conflicts with the obviously dressier look of traditional business suits and most evening clothes. The elements of design conflict — the style lines and shapes (as well as the colors, fabric, and/or patterns) communicate two very different occasions. The pieces need to be similar.*

A Style of Your Own

Depending on the person wearing them, the shapes that conflict may appear too severe, strict, and stern or too fussy, frilly, and frivolous in comparison to the person. The person may feel psychologically uncomfortable in the clothing and observers may also notice the conflict.

For example, *frilly, full-rounded shapes and ruffles on a dress may conflict with the personality of a generally calm, quiet, and reserved woman, causing her to feel and appear uncomfortably overdone, frivolous, and silly.*

So experiment a little and discover which styles are most in harmony with you, the places you go, and what you do there. As you experiment, you may discover something you like to wear so much that it becomes your trademark — something so unique to you that it triggers an image of you in the minds of the people who know you. It might be the particular shape in a piece of clothing or an accessory that marks your personal style.

Dominant/Subordinate Styles

In all cases, one shape or a group of similar, related shapes must be dominant in the garment. Using all the same shapes, or pairing all classic shapes can, in some instances, become too repetitious or monotonous. Introducing some contrast in shape and/or trendy styling can be interesting and effective, communicating subtle differences in mood, occasion, and personality. (See Figure 4–11.)

You can, therefore, break the general rule and combine different shapes and styles with seemingly opposing traits or entirely different moods, but it takes extra thought and practice to make the outfit work. This is the guideline: **One type of shape** (occasion, mood, or personality among the shapes) **must be dominant and all others subordinate by descending degrees**. Stated another way, the mood or personality conveyed by one garment must be dominant. Different shapes and different styles can be introduced into the design, but they must be done so to a lesser degree — they must attract less attention. This requires a delicate balance but can be done.

Figure 4–11. Traditional Spanish influence is evident in this creative combination of classic clothes. Body silhouette is subordinate. *(Courtesy Madeleine Direct)*

Table 4-6 Image Makers and Breakers in Line and Shape

Image Makers In Style Line and Shape	Image Breakers In Style Line and Shape
• Simple, basic style lines and shapes	• Cluttered style lines and/or shapes
• One dominant point of emphasis	• Several points of conflicting emphasis
• Updated classic styles	• Obviously out-of-date styles
• Pockets, buttons in scale with garment	• Oversize pockets, buttons on garment
• Smooth silhouette	• Visible bra or panty lines, visible body lines
• Smooth seamlines	• Sloppy, puckered, or ripped seamlines
• Smooth, easy fit	• Stress lines from tight fit
• Covers, camouflages, or counters figure variations	• Exposes or emphasizes figure variations
• Monogram or crest	• Suggestive slogan or picture on T-shirt

Thoughts and Feelings About Yourself

"But I can't wear those styles," a young woman wailed to her friends. They were all involved in an assignment to pick out clothing styles flattering to their figures to be presented in class the next day. "I look awful in that! I'm just too big! I hate this body! I won't do this!" and she slumped down in her chair, quitting before she began.

That's where I came in, catching sight of a girl quite average in height and weight; wondering where she got the idea that she was so big; and with questions that didn't end until we got to the bottom of her misconceptions about herself.

It didn't stop there. I placed a long distance call to her parents. Gradually, with time and fashion therapy at its most basic, we got the answers we needed — answers that allowed her to look at her body objectively for the first time in her life.

I learned that this girl was one of five girls in her family. She agreed that her parents were small in stature — what we'd call petite. Her mother was all of five feet tall, and her father, at five feet ten inches, was small boned with somewhat delicate features.

Of the five girls, my student was the tallest at five feet, six inches — and the biggest. Adding to that, she told me how her mother had, many times, introduced her to relatives and friends saying, "And now meet my big girl."

It was an innocent introduction on the part of the mother. She had no idea that her little girl was growing up thinking she was so big, complete with broad shoulders, big hips, big bottom, and big thighs by the time she was in high school.

But she wasn't that big. Her thighs were wider than her hips, but so what? Half the women in the world have wide thighs. And so, we began the process of figure evaluation to rebuild this girl's body image and self-concept, initially for the purpose of allowing her a full range of fashion options to choose from.

As a result of evaluating her figure and altering her attitude, she was able to dress in a way she wants to be seen. She was able to forget about herself and get on with the goals in her life.

What's important to note is that this experience is not an isolated incident. Whether due to the influence of parents, siblings, friends, teachers, television personalities, magazines, or movie stars, millions of people have negative body images, leading to poor self-concept and low self-esteem.

Our concept of self is learned through interaction with the ideas and reactions of others. As a small child, we see our body and begin to form opinions about it — it is strong, it is fast, it is beautiful, and so forth.

By the time we are old enough to be aware of the opinions of others, we also become aware of how those others view us. We listen to what they say about our bodies. In time, we notice how our bodies compare with the bodies of other children. We soon become concerned with how we look to others — if they like us, if they think we're beautiful. Their opinions are reinforced by mass media.

From the time we're old enough to watch TV, go to a movie, read a book or a magazine, and shop the malls, we're confronted with a cultural ideal of beauty. We're pressured to believe there is only one "right" way to look and that beauty comes in a perfect body.

Logically, we know this isn't true. But logic doesn't seem to serve us well when it comes to our appearance. Annie Raiphe put it well when she wrote, "Advertising doesn't create the inadequacy, it merely gives us the hammers with which to hit ourselves over the head!"

For some of us, the problem of self-criticism and self-hatred is lessened once we better understand how our body image and self-concept may have developed. Nonetheless, the greatest hurdle is to overcome our self-defeating negative attitude about our own body.

Necessary in this effort is personal commitment to self-acceptance and self-encouragement. It is essential that we take charge of our feelings of self-worth, that we take joy in our creation, that we take responsibility for an objective body image, along with responsibility for our appearance.

Once in control of our thoughts and feelings, as well as our appearance, attitudes and appearances can be changed. Once we begin to celebrate the way we are created, we can choose to dress in harmony with our own singular beauty. Growing further, we can communicate in a language of acceptance and encouragement that will carry over to our own families.

For example, the dominant mood or personality of a cowboy shirt and denim jeans is very casual and rather rugged. It packs some authority due to the shirt's collar with its angular points. You can counter the dominantly casual mood simply by changing to a (denim) skirt, for a slightly dressier, more feminine appearance. The total look is still dominantly casual and sporty, making the dressier, more feminine look of the skirt subordinate. Going further, you can romanticize the total look by adding a softly styled (lace) jabot at the neck or pairing the pieces with a wide-brimmed picture hat. Either of these accessory items is sub-subordinate to the skirt and to the total outfit. The jabot or hat add just a touch of femininity to the total look. To test the harmony of the combination, think in terms of size — the larger area of the total outfit, compared to the medium-size area for the skirt and the small-size area for the jabot or hat.

This flexible and creative way of dressing opens up the possibilities for greater individuality. If unsure, think in terms of having all pieces in the outfit the same or similar. Counter their mood or feeling with something small.

For example, a dominantly classic pant suit might benefit by adding a touch of the trendy — a small piece of popular jewelry, a trendy pocket square, the latest heel shape on the shoes, or a relatively small blouse in the latest style — as long as the mood and occasion agree. A small amount of trendy goes a long way and will balance a large amount of classic.

As with lines, shapes can be combined to reflect a woman as dramatic, demure, or a blend in between; as sportive, romantic, or a complementary combination of both; as a traditionally classic conservative, a trend-setting free spirit, or a mix in between.

Whatever the case, the style lines and shapes, the fabrics, colors, patterns, and quality of the clothes must combine harmoniously. (See Table 4–6.)

Review Main Points

The element, shape, is used to design basic and classic, costume and trendy clothing styles. Classic styles have a long and fashionable wearlife because they are designed to flatter many figures and are well accepted in many situations. Trendy styles are short lived, being more extreme in design, suitable for fewer people and fewer occasions. They move in and out of fashion quickly. Build the bulk of your wardrobe around classic clothing styles for long-term reliability and investment value. Gradually and cautiously, acquire trend or fad items. Each characteristic of shape contributes to the total effect of the clothing. Shapes can be manipulated to communicate messages, feelings, and moods, and to create a variety of illusions about the body. Because clothing styles interact with one another and with the wearer, clothing shapes, as well as classic and trendy styles, need to be compatible with one another and with the wearer, the time, and the place. In combining different types of shapes, one must be dominant, and all others subordinate, by degrees. Combining shapes or classic and trendy styles in interesting and harmonious ways is one of the keys to putting together an interesting, versatile, and fashionable wardrobe.

Review Questions

1. How can you recognize a classic style garment? _____
   _____
   _____.

2. What makes a style a fad? _____
   _____
   _____.

3. Build the bulk of your wardrobe around basic, _____ styles.

4. What is the positive side of buying an occasional fad item?
   _____.

5. List two examples each of classic and trendy fad clothing.

Classics	Trendy/Fads
_____	_____
_____	_____

6. List two functions of the design element, shape.

_____	_____

7. Match the following shapes to the words that describe them.

   _____ rectangular shape   a. wider waist

   _____ foreground shape   b. pocket, collar, button

   _____ inverted triangle   c. formed by the garment outline

   _____ background shape   d. wedge, wider on top

8. Name four of the eight typical body shapes or figure types.

_____	_____
_____	_____

9. A general goal in using clothing as a resource is that it should _____
_____.

10. Using the "blink test," how do you determine the effect of line and shape on
your body? _____
_____.

11. Asymmetrical clothing lines and shapes tend to make body asymmetry and
figure variations _____ noticeable.

12. Scale refers to the relative _____ of something.

13. To appear balanced, clothing and accessories need to be in scale with the
_____.

14. Which of the following words does not belong in the group? Circle the word.
balance   proportion   shape   scale

15. To appear harmonious, select and combine clothing styles in terms of the
_____, mood, and personality traits the clothes appear to
project or communicate.

Discussion Questions

#1 Discuss the illusory effects of the shapes in clothes students are wearing.
What occasions, moods, or themes are represented in the classroom? What
feelings or personality traits are communicated by the various shapes?

Notes: _____
_____
_____
_____

#2 What shapes in clothes are the majority of students wearing to class? Why
do you think these shapes are most popular? What effect do these shapes
have on appearance? What is the effect of these shapes on behavior?

Notes: _____
_____
_____
_____

#3 Identify the real worth of a person. Discuss the need and ways to overcome
a negative body image, and learn to accept the body you are born with.

Notes: _____
_____
_____
_____

Exercise 4–1   Shape Recognition

Name _____

Look at what you are wearing.

- Identify, list, and checkmark which clothing pieces are classic in design; list and checkmark trendy or fad items.
- Identify and list the background and/or foreground shapes formed in each item of clothing.
- Identify and list the type of shapes — angular and rounded shapes — in each item.
- Identify and list the specific types of garment shapes — tubular, triangular, inverted triangular, diamond, hourglass, bell, and rounded — in each clothing item.
- Work with a neighboring classmate and identify as above.

You – Clothing Item	Classic	Trendy/Fad	Shapes Formed (Background/Foreground)	Type of Shape (Angular/Rounded)	Garment Shape Type (Tubular/Triangular/Diamond, etc.)
Classmate – Clothing Item	Classic	Trendy/Fad	Shapes Formed	Type of Shape	Garment Shape Type

Exercise 4–2   Shape Preference

Name _____

Look in your closet, selecting five to ten favorite pieces of clothing and five to ten less favorite pieces of clothing.
- Identify the style as classic or trendy.
- In the appropriate section — favorite/less favorite — identify the kind of shape formed — background alone or with foreground shapes.
- Identify the type of foreground shapes — angular, rounded.
- Identify with a checkmark the garment shape type — tubular,

triangular, inverted triangular, diamond, hourglass, bell, or rounded.
- Describe any special characteristics about these shapes.
- Total the number of shapes identified in each column.
- Analyze how these shape characteristics have influenced your preferences.

Clothing Item	Classic	Trendy/Fad	Shapes Formed		Shape Type		Garment Shape Type						
			Background	Foreground	Angular	Rounded	Tubular	Triangle	Inverted Triangle	Diamond	Hour-glass	Bell	Rounded
Favorite Clothes													
TOTALS													
Clothing Item	Classic	Trendy/Fad	Background	Foreground	Angular	Rounded	Tubular	Triangle	Inverted Triangle	Diamond	Hour-glass	Bell	Rounded
Less Favorite Clothes													
TOTALS													

Conclusions:

Exercise 4–3   Local Store Experience

Name_____

Look in a local clothing store for shapes and styles you have never worn before. In front of a full-length mirror, experience the look and fit and feel of these shapes and styles.

Clothing Store Experience:

• Hold the garment up to you.
• Notice and record how the shapes make you look and what they appear to communicate.
• If possible, try it on to see how the clothing will look on you.
• Notice and record how the garment shape looks and fits on your body.
• Notice and record what the shapes appear to communicate.

Exercise 4–4   Classic/Trendy Style Recognition

• Collect five pictures of classic clothing pieces and accessories.
• Mount.
• Label.

• Collect five pictures of trendy clothing pieces and accessories.
• Mount.
• Label.

Exercise 4–5   Shape Coordination

Find pictures of clothing pieces in shapes you would like to combine into an outfit for yourself. Don't worry about color or textures now. Look for shapes that will accommodate and flatter your figure. Look for shapes you can combine harmoniously. Mount and identify accordingly. Write a paragraph stating the reasons for your choices.

A

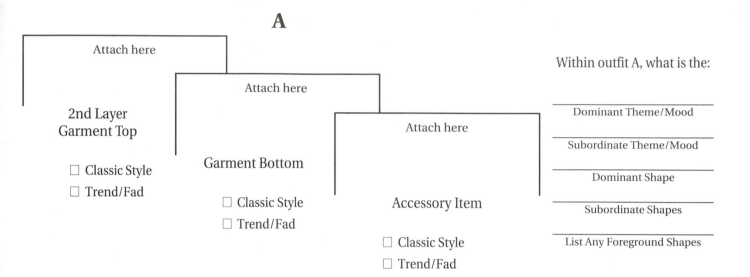

Attach here

2nd Layer Garment Top

☐ Classic Style
☐ Trend/Fad

Attach here

Garment Bottom

☐ Classic Style
☐ Trend/Fad

Attach here

Accessory Item

☐ Classic Style
☐ Trend/Fad

Within outfit A, what is the:

_____
Dominant Theme/Mood

_____
Subordinate Theme/Mood

_____
Dominant Shape

_____
Subordinate Shapes

_____
List Any Foreground Shapes

B

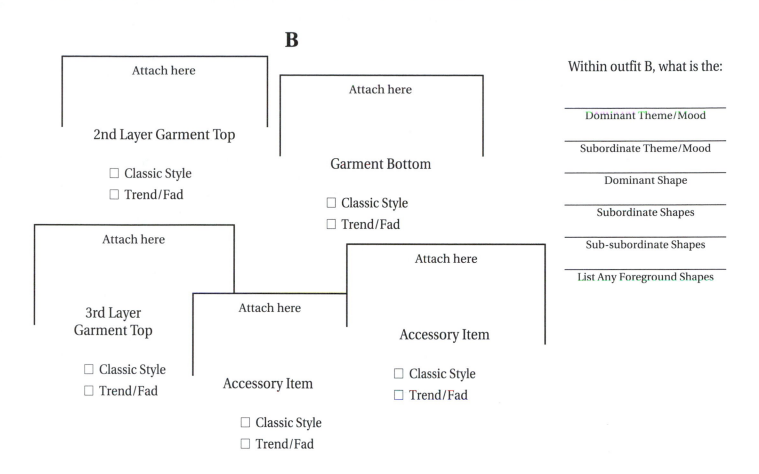

Attach here

2nd Layer Garment Top

☐ Classic Style
☐ Trend/Fad

Attach here

Garment Bottom

☐ Classic Style
☐ Trend/Fad

Attach here

3rd Layer
Garment Top

☐ Classic Style
☐ Trend/Fad

Attach here

Attach here

Accessory Item

☐ Classic Style
☐ Trend/Fad

Accessory Item

☐ Classic Style
☐ Trend/Fad

Within outfit B, what is the:

_____
Dominant Theme/Mood

_____
Subordinate Theme/Mood

_____
Dominant Shape

_____
Subordinate Shapes

_____
Sub-subordinate Shapes

_____
List Any Foreground Shapes

Exercise 4–6 Preferred Shape Characteristics

Name _____

Plot your preferred shape characteristics or traits on a continuum between opposites.

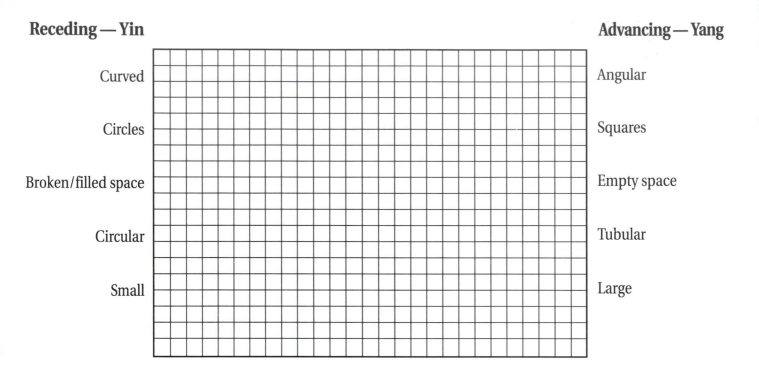

Receding — Yin

Curved

Circles

Broken/filled space

Circular

Small

Advancing — Yang

Angular

Squares

Empty space

Tubular

Large

Exercise 4–7   Personal Style Evaluation, Part 2

Name _____

Objectively identify factors that influence your personal style.

What is your approximate height?

☐ Shorter/petite   ☐ Average   ☐ Taller   ☐ Very tall

What is your appropximate weight?

☐ Under ideal range   ☐ Ideal range   ☐ Over ideal range

What is your approximate face shape?

☐ Oval   ☐ Oblong   ☐ Rectangle   ☐ Square

☐ Round   ☐ Triangular   ☐ Inverted triangle   ☐ "Heart"

☐ Diamond   ☐ "Pear"   ☐ Other _____

What are your facial characteristics?

☐ High forehead   ☐ Low forehead   ☐ Broad forehead   ☐ Narrow forehead

☐ Receding forehead ☐ Widow's peak

☐ Wide across cheeks ☐ Narrow across cheeks

☐ Wide, square jaw   ☐ Full, rounded jaw   ☐ Narrow jaw   ☐ Flat chin

☐ Rounded chin   ☐ Pointed chin   ☐ Double chin   ☐ Receding chin

☐ Prominent nose   ☐ Prominent lips   ☐ Other _____

What is your approximate posture type?

☐ Slumped, rounded back   ☐ Overly erect back

☐ Hips swayed back   ☐ Hips swayed front   ☐ Forward head

What is your approximate body/figure type?

☐ Triangular   ☐ Inverted triangle   ☐ Hourglass   ☐ Diamond

☐ Rectangular   ☐ Rounded   ☐ Tubular/thin   ☐ Ideal

☐ Short torso, long legs   ☐ Long torso, short legs

What are your figure variations?

☐ Neck short	☐ Neck long	☐ Neck wide	☐ Neck thin	☐ Neck average
☐ Shoulders narrow	☐ Shoulders broad	☐ Shoulders square	☐ Shoulders sloped	☐ Shoulders avg.
☐ Shoulders rounded	☐ Rt. shoulder high	☐ Left shoulder high		
☐ Collar bones prom.	☐ Chest shallow	☐ Chest barrel	☐ Sternum prominent	☐ Chest average
☐ Bust size A	☐ Bust size B	☐ Bust size C	☐ Bust size D	
☐ Rib cage short	☐ Rib cage long	☐ Midriff bulge	☐ Midriff flared	☐ Midriff average
☐ Waist small	☐ Waist large			☐ Waist average
☐ Hips narrow	☐ Hips wide	☐ Hip curve high	☐ Hip curve low	☐ Hips average
☐ Rt. hip high	☐ Left hip high	☐ Hip bones prominent		
☐ Thighs heavy outside		☐ Thighs heavy inside		☐ Thighs average
☐ Legs thin	☐ Legs heavy	☐ Legs short	☐ Legs long	☐ Legs average
☐ Knees thin	☐ Rt. knee high	☐ Left knee high		
☐ Calves flat	☐ Calves wide	☐ Calves bowed	☐ Ankles wide	
☐ Arms thin	☐ Arms heavy	☐ Upper arm heavy	☐ Elbow pronated	☐ Arms average
☐ Arms short	☐ Arms long	☐ Rt. arm high	☐ Left arm high	
☐ Hands small	☐ Hands large	☐ Fingers short	☐ Fingers long/slim	☐ Hands average
☐ Back narrow	☐ Back wide	☐ Shoulder blades prominent		☐ Back average
☐ Tummy flat	☐ Pop-tummy	☐ Tummy prominent	☐ Tummy low drop	☐ Tummy average
☐ Derriere flat	☐ Derriere large	☐ Derriere high	☐ Derriere low	☐ Derriere average

☐ Other _____

What sizes do you now wear?

	Ready-to-wear:	Pattern:
Blouse/shirt		
Straight skirt		
A-line, flared, or gathered skirt		
Pant		
Sweater		
Jacket		
Dress		
Coat		
Hosiery		
Shoes		
Belt		
Gloves		
Hat		
Ring		
Slip		
SPECIAL CONSIDERATIONS		

Chapter
5
Color Selection and Coordination

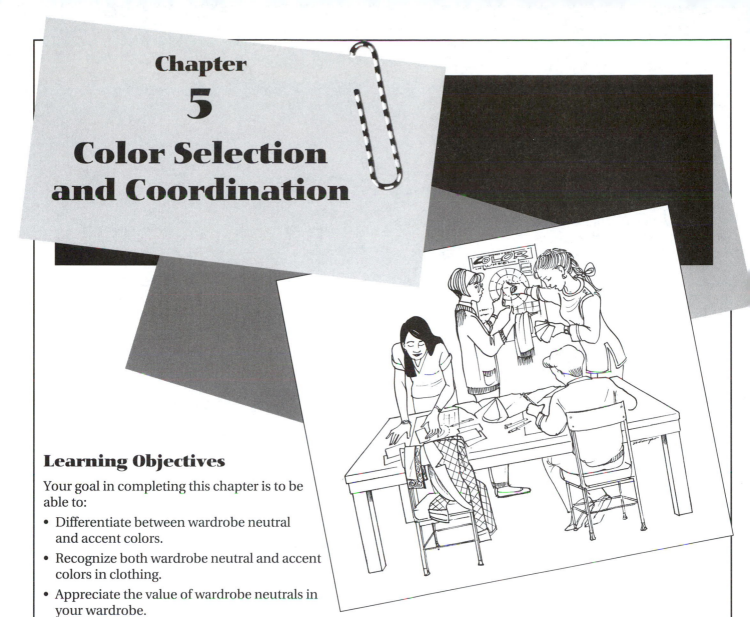

Learning Objectives

Your goal in completing this chapter is to be able to:

- Differentiate between wardrobe neutral and accent colors.
- Recognize both wardrobe neutral and accent colors in clothing.
- Appreciate the value of wardrobe neutrals in your wardrobe.
- Understand and explain the functions of color.
- Describe how wardrobe neutrals are formed.
- Identify the dimensions of color.
- Understand the process of simultaneous contrast in color.
- Be aware of additional characteristics of color that affect a clothing design.
- Predict the effect of color on garment performance, mood, and message.
- Recognize personal coloring.
- Become part of the color scheme with your clothes.
- Select clothing colors to meet your needs.
- Coordinate and combine two or more colors harmoniously.

Preview Main Points

1. Rely on wardrobe neutral colors, dulled or muted tones of every hue, as well as black, white, and gray.

2. Acquire contrasting accent colors in your wardrobe for added interest, variety, and personal style.

3. Become part of the color scheme with your clothes.

4. Knowing about color as an element of design will help you make wise consumer decisions about clothing selection and coordination.

5. Become more aware of personal coloring and how it can relate to clothing selection and coordination.

6. Select clothing in colors that meet your individual needs or purposes — appropriate for your life-style, personal style, and fabric.

7. Coordinate or combine colors, as well as basic and costume styles, to achieve greater variety, interest, and individuality.

1.

Rely on wardrobe neutral colors, dulled or muted tones of every hue, as well as black, white, and gray.

Considering the pace of life and cost of clothes, you need all the versatility in a wardrobe you can get. Wardrobe neutrals work to meet that need.

Black, white, and gray in their true form are neutrals without any hue or color and are called achromatic. As wardrobe neutrals, they may contain a slight amount of warm or cool hue — such as the warmer umber black or cooler blue-black.

Dulled, muted tones — such as the very traditional navy blue, burgundy, brown, tan, ivory, taupe, olive, forest green, teal, and plum — are wardrobe neutrals that coordinate easily to create a variety of versatile outfits and tasteful good looks with your clothes. Dulled, muted tones result from a mix of complementary warm and cool hues — colors that lie across from one another on the color wheel.

Wardrobe Neutrals Work Best

- Dulled tones are less intense and are able to coordinate well with a large variety of other colors, including personal coloring.
- Wardrobe neutrals do not attract a lot of attention to themselves.
- Wardrobe neutrals take you anywhere with understated elegance. While some may be more fashionable at one time or another, they are always well received.
- Wardrobe neutrals are subtle communicators, allowing the widest range of moods, occasions, and personality traits.
- People don't tire of wardrobe neutrals quickly.
- Wardrobe neutrals are money savers, since they combine easily with other colors.
- Everyone can afford to buy wardrobe neutrals; good taste is not a matter of money.

How to Recognize Wardrobe Neutrals

To recognize wardrobe neutrals, you have to look at the

Query Box

Which of these wardrobe neutrals have you tried? Which might you like to try?

black onyx	dusty rose
umber black	mauve
smoky gray	burgundy/wine
snow white	terra cotta/brick red
olive/khaki green	ivory/cream
sage gray-green	beige
forest/hunter green	khaki tan/sand
antique turquoise	camel
teal blue-green	shrimp/apricot
dusk blue-gray	cinnamon rust
navy blue	brown
plum/aubergine	taupe gray-brown

---

color. Your first impression of the color is usually right. The less bright the color, the more neutral it becomes. If it's fairly muted, it will probably work as a wardrobe neutral. (See Color Figure 1.) If it's bright, it won't.

Looking closer, if the warm color has a bit of cool blue, green, purple, or gray in it, or the cool color has a hint of warm orange, yellow, or gray in it, the color qualifies as dulled or muted — it's a wardrobe neutral. You will likely have to train your eye to detect the complementary color.

Because wardrobe neutrals contain both a warm and cool hue, they are attractive to most people. As you will learn, you can control the degree of dullness, lightness, and darkness with colors in combination to create the most attractive effect.

A few colors that qualify as wardrobe neutrals are not very complimentary to the skin, nor well accepted socially and aesthetically. Mustard yellow is just such a color. While slightly darker and duller, mustard is a color that often repeats and reinforces yellow skin coloration or clashes with skin and hair color altogether.

Wardrobe neutrals are needed most by people who want to get as many combinations from as few pieces of clothing as possible, and by those employed in formal, conservative, or public and service-oriented businesses — also by people in leadership positions. They're accepted by virtually everyone. Generally, you can rely on more of the lighter wardrobe neutrals in warm weather and darker wardrobe neutrals in cool weather.

2.

Acquire contrasting accent colors in your wardrobe for added interest, variety, and personal style.

Traditionally, an accent color is bright, strong, or intense. People not satisfied with their wardrobes often have a closet full of clothes in accent colors. On the other hand, the closet may contain only dull colors in need of something brighter to bring them to life.

A color qualifies as an accent color if it:

- is brighter than wardrobe neutral colors combined with it.
- is so bright, strong, or intense, so flamboyant you can't miss it — it may even overpower all other colors around it.
- demands special clothes and accessories in a narrow range of colors to complete the outfit — the clothes and accessories go with very few other clothes in the closet.

How to Recognize Accent Colors

Typically, accent colors are bright and bold. "Bright" says it all, but looking closely, you'll see that the colors appear pure, without any gray or complementary color mixed into them. (See Color Figure 25.)

Nontraditional wardrobe neutrals — such as shrimp, dusty rose, and seafoam green — often substitute for accent colors, simply because they are brighter than the other, more traditional, wardrobe neutrals they are combined with.

Within a cluster of clothes, accent colors are used in smaller amounts or in fewer clothing pieces. Traditionally bright accent colors can be included more easily in the wardrobes of people who don't have to worry about cost or critics, and by those who work in creative businesses, such as fashion, art, music, theater, and interior design.

Query Box

Which of these traditional accent colors have you tried? Which might you like to try?

shocking pink	lime green
fuchsia	kelly green
geranium red	bright turquoise
tangerine	ice blue
canary yellow	royal blue
chartreuse	orchid

TIP
FROM THE PROS

Red and royal blue are accent colors with wide social acceptance, often used for core pieces in a sportive or dramatic-looking cluster and combined with other equally strong accent colors. It takes more skill to build a workable cluster with these colors, a cluster that can't be missed. Red and royal blue are worn easily all year.

3.

Become part of the color scheme with your clothes.

It's time for a new attitude about color — a relaxed attitude that allows more flexibility and creativity than many people allow themselves. Too many people limit the colors they wear based on systems of personal color analysis and typing that divide them into categories and prescribe a particular group of colors they should wear for life.

In considering what colors you choose to wear, you need to recognize the physical, psychological, and cultural differences in color perceptions and interpretation. You need to be aware of the ways in which colors affect one another and cause them to appear to change. You need to know that personal coloring changes during your life due to age, diet, exposure to the environment, and health. Your color preferences also change as you mature, as you acquire new experiences and make changes in your goals and your life-style.

You can expect to look terrific wearing colors that repeat your hair, eyes, and cheek coloration, and in some variety of tints and shades. You can also expect that colors you've had positive experiences with in your life will be some of your favorite colors. They may or may not be one and the same colors.

This leads to a color concept you can use to expand the range of colors you can wear attractively and creatively. It's a simple strategy that reminds you to become part of the color scheme with your clothes.

Visualize, for a moment, a photograph or a painting hung on a wall in a room. In most cases, that picture is matted and framed to harmonize with the decor of the entire room. The composition is seen as part of the interior decoration. You and your clothing are not much different when you think about them being part of a single artistic composition — rather like your exterior decoration. In this sense, your clothing frames your figure and your face.

To appear harmonious and most attractive, both you and your clothes should look like they belong together. Ideally, your head and clothed body should appear balanced, with colors coming together in complete harmony. With this in mind, it helps to think of your head and face as being part of a pleasing color scheme with your clothes. There are two ways you can do this.

- **Repeat your most attractive personal coloring** — your hair color, your eye color, your skin, and warm cheek color — **in your clothing.** In other words, **take your personal coloring down into your clothing.** You can expect these colors to flatter you. (See Color Figure 40.)

For example, someone with blue or green eyes might choose as a wardrobe neutral color, smoky blue or olive green respectively, and thereby repeat a personal body color in a cluster of clothes. A blonde might easily choose to repeat hair color with clothing colors of camel, tan, ash, ivory, etc., depending on which hues most nearly match or blend harmoniously with hair color. Repeat both hair and eye color if you like.

- **Repeat your clothing color on or near your face** — with makeup, earrings, hair ornaments, headband, scarf, or hat. In other words, **take your clothing color up onto or near your face**. (See Color Figures 42–44.)

For example, coral , pink, red, or terra cotta clothing color is easy to bring up as lip color and/or blush color. Brown, blue, plum, teal, or olive clothing color can easily come up as shades in eye shadow, liner, or mascara. Black in clothing can be repeated with black earrings, hair ribbon, or hat — possibly in a two-color combination that includes black and the eye color or another clothing color. The options are many.

This simple strategy guarantees you of becoming an attractive part of the color scheme with your clothes. Additional options, such as analogous and complementary clothing contrast to personal coloring, are discussed later in this chapter. As you look through magazines and see pictures of clothing in colors you'd like to try, pull the pictures out and add them to your style file — in a file labeled color.

4.

Knowing about color, as an element of design, will help you make wise consumer decisions about clothing selection and coordination.

Color is the most obvious, powerful, stimulating, and demanding element of design. Color tends to be noticed first and remembered longest. Color is the most complex, creative, and confusing of the elements. Color is at once inviting and individual. It can also distract and disturb. Color evokes highly physical and emotional responses, which may be conscious or unconscious. Our reactions to color are immediate, inescapable, and long-lasting. While we may forget the texture and design details, we are more likely to remember the color and our reaction to it.

Importance and Functions of Color

- Color helps distinguish and identify objects and areas.
- Color draws attention, often to a point of emphasis.
- Color affects the body and the psyche.
- Color helps coordinate objects, such as clothing and accessories.
- Color creates powerful illusions about other colors, body size and shape, temperature, and distance.
- Color communicates visual meaning, messages, or moods.

How Color Is Formed

Light is an essential ingredient in the formation of color. Light is composed of electromagnetic waves of different lengths. Light waves may emanate from a light source or be reflected from the pigmented surface of an object, such as clothing. When light waves stimulate the retina of your eye and are interpreted by your brain, you experience the sensation of color. Colors in the visible spectrum include red, orange, yellow, green, blue, and violet. Eliminate light and there is no color.

Color and texture are interrelated. Objects or textural surfaces contain no color within themselves. When light strikes an object, certain rays are absorbed by the surface and others are reflected. (See Figure 5–1.) When all light is reflected, we see white. When all light is absorbed, we see black. For an object, including fabric, to appear a particular color, that color must be present in the light source.

For example, a certain fabric may absorb almost all color rays except red, which, when reflected to your eyes will create the sensation of red. A button that reflects primarily green light rays will appear green. If a leather shoe contains pigment that reflects a predominance of blue light rays, we say the shoe is blue. If mascara contains pigments capable of absorbing all light, we see it as black. Those mascaras that absorb lesser amounts of light may be seen as brown, gray, or navy blue, and so forth.

Together, color and texture create an endless variety of colors — literally thousands. This chapter concentrates on color. A discussion of texture and fabric follows in Chapter 6.

Color Illusions

An illusion makes something look quite different than it really is. Color is very good at creating illusions. Regardless of the facts, and according to our mind's eye, we tend to believe the illusion that color creates. By recognizing the illusions that color creates, you can select and arrange to create the illusions you want — they can be used to reinforce attractive personal coloring, or counter less attractive personal coloring or undesirable effects of color. In the following discussions, notice the illusions that color creates. (See color insert.)

The Color Wheel

Become familiar with the color wheel. (See Figure 5–2 and Color Figure 3.) While there are many different color wheels you can work with, the Prang or Brewster color wheel used in most schools and in this book, is the simplest and most familiar. It will meet your needs with reasonable accuracy and will help you visualize and compare color relationships in pigment. As you study the color wheel, notice that it is composed of twelve hues in an orderly arrangement.

Three Dimensions of Color

Rather than talk about types of color, we traditionally speak

1
THE STRATEGY

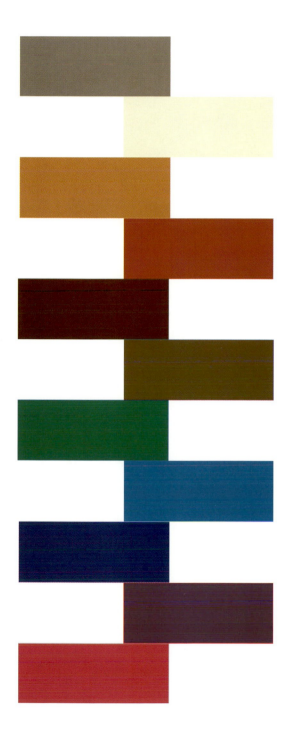

Color Figure 2 Achromatic Neutrals
Achromatic neutrals include black, white, and gray. They, too, function as wardrobe neutrals.

Color Figure 1 Wardrobe Neutrals
Wardrobe neutrals are muted chromatic hues that include taupe, ivory, tan, rust, brown, olive, forest, teal, navy, plum, and burgundy.

COLOR THEORY

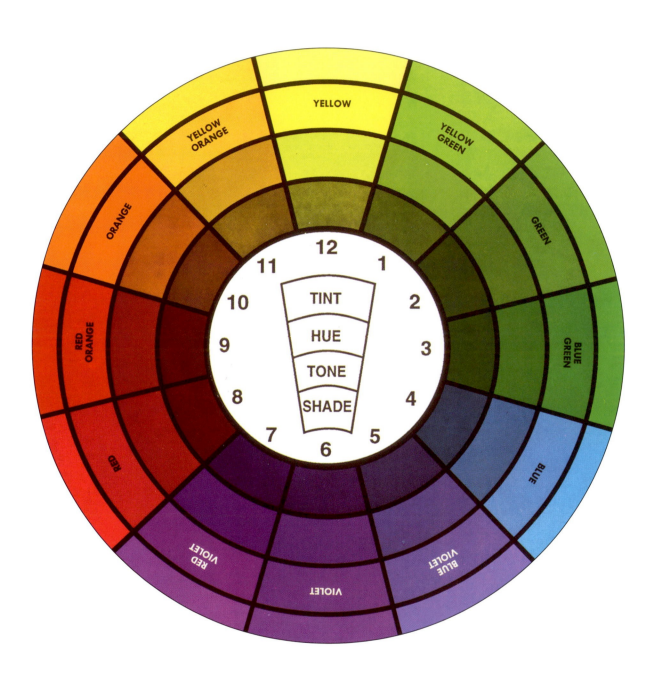

Color Figure 3 Color Wheel
This twelve-hue color wheel shows the relationships between colors. (Adapted from the Color Compass, ©1972, M. Grumbacher, Inc. All rights reserved. Used with permission.)

3

H U E : A Dimension of Color

Warm Hues
advance, enlarge, excite, and emphasize.

Cool Hues
recede, reduce, calm, and minimize.

Color Figure 4 Warm and Cool Hues

Hue

Hue appears more blue next to green.

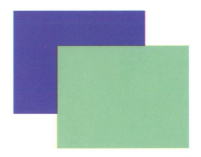

Hue appears more green next to blue.

Color Figure 5 Simultaneous Contrast

Warm Hues

Cool Hues

Analogous hues emphasize basic differences between one another. Colors predictably push apart in opposite directions on the color wheel. You see the basic hue plus the neighbor beyond.

Color Figure 6 Simultaneous Contrast

4

H U E : A Dimension of Color

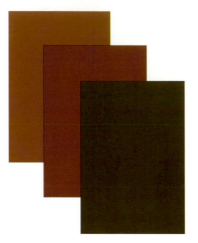

Color Figure 7 Simultaneous Contrast

Warm and cool versions of the same hue emphasize basic differences between one another or clash. Colors predictably push apart in opposite directions on the color wheel, with some browns appearing more orange, and others more blue.

Color Figure 8 Simultaneous Contrast

Warm and cool variations of achromatic neutrals

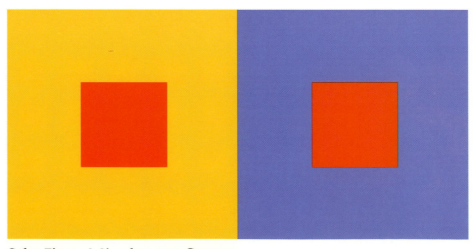

Color Figure 9 Simultaneous Contrast

The same hue can appear different on different backgrounds.

5

H U E : A Dimension of Color

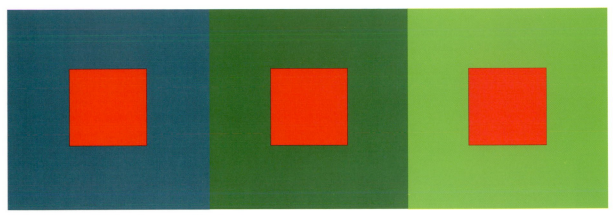

Color Figure 10 Simultaneous Contrast
Different hues can appear the same, or nearly the same, with slightly different backgrounds.

Color Figure 11 Simultaneous Contrast
Different surface hues can cause identical backgrounds to appear different.

Color Figure 12 Optical Mixing and Simultaneous Contrast
Viewed from some distance away, the mix of yellow and navy blue dots appears yellow green, particularly when seen next to green. The mix of more navy blue combined with yellow on green appears blue-green.

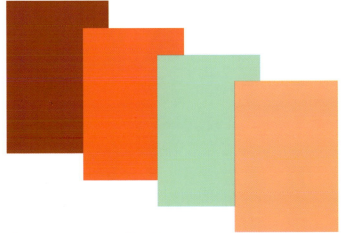

Color Figure 13 Colors in Combination
Apparently warm base hue and cool base hue combine harmoniously.

Color Figure 14 Colors in Combination and the Law of Areas
A small amount of cool hue balances and adds interest to a large area of warm hue and to a monochromatic color scheme of all warm hues, and vice versa.

6
VALUE: A Dimension of Color

Shade ◄——————— Darker   Lighter ——————► Tint

Color Figure 15 Value Scale in Gray

Light Values
advance, enlarge, excite, and emphasize.

Dark Values
recede, reduce, calm, and minimize.

Color Figure 16 Light and Dark Values

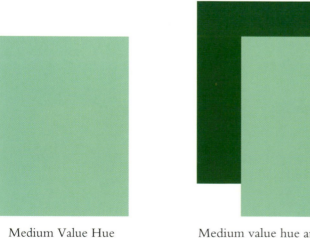

Medium Value Hue

Medium value hue appears lighter
next to low value hue.

Medium value hue appears darker
next to high value hue.

Color Figure 17 Simultaneous Contrast

VALUE: A Dimension of Color

Color Figure 18 Simultaneous Contrast
The same value can appear different on different backgrounds.

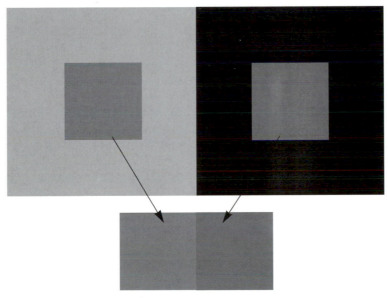

Color Figure 19 Simultaneous Contrast
Different values can appear the same, or nearly the same, with slightly different backgrounds.

Close Value Contrast

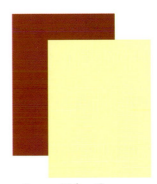

Strong Value Contrast

Color Figure 20 Colors in Combination

8
VALUE: A Dimension of Color

Color Figure 21 Opposite Value Afterimage

Stare at the yellow square for about one minute. Then look quickly at the colorless square in the middle and continue to stare at it. What color appears there? The opposite value is induced on the colorless surface as it stimulates the eyes. Repeat the experience looking at the black triangle.

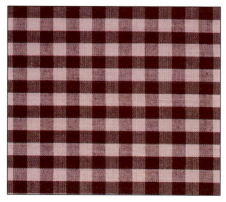

Color Figure 22 Irradiation or Spreading Effect

Reflected light rays radiate or spread over onto one another, causing black and white squares to appear to vibrate.

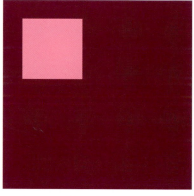

Color Figure 23 Colors in Combination and Law of Areas

A small area of light value balances and adds interest to a large area of dark and to a color scheme of all dark colors, and vice versa.

Natural value order

Reversal of natural value order – value discord or dissonance.

Color Figure 24 Colors in Combination

9

INTENSITY: A Dimension of Color

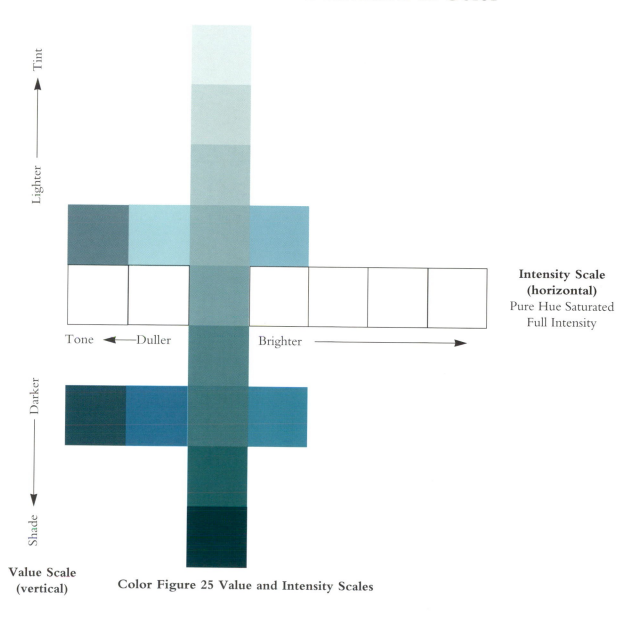

Tint

Lighter

Intensity Scale (horizontal)
Pure Hue Saturated
Full Intensity

Tone ← Duller   Brighter →

Darker

Shade

Value Scale (vertical)

Color Figure 25 Value and Intensity Scales

Bright Intensities
advance, enlarge, excite, and emphasize.

Dull Intensities
recede, reduce, calm, and minimize.

Color Figure 26 Bright and Dull Intensities

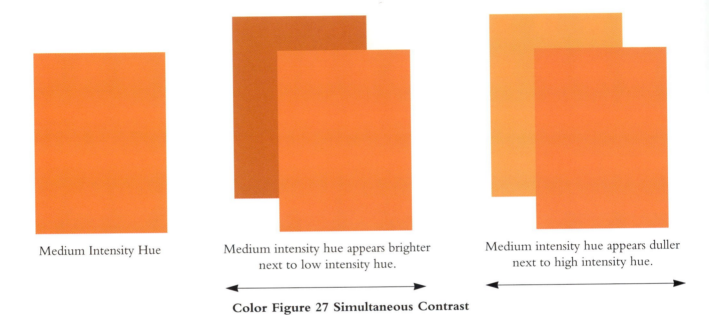

10
INTENSITY: A Dimension of Color

Medium Intensity Hue

Medium intensity hue appears brighter
next to low intensity hue.

Medium intensity hue appears duller
next to high intensity hue.

Color Figure 27 Simultaneous Contrast

Color Figure 28 Simultaneous Contrast
Different intensities can appear the same, or nearly the same, with slightly different backgrounds.

INTENSITY: A Dimension of Color

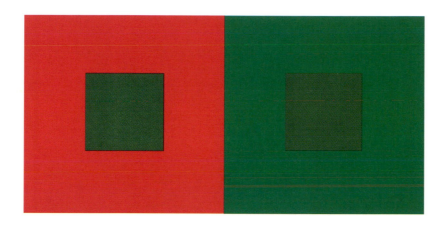

Color Figure 29 Simultaneous Contrast
The same intensity can appear different on different backgrounds.

Color Figure 30 Simultaneous Contrast
Complementary hue contrasts intensify the differences in one another.

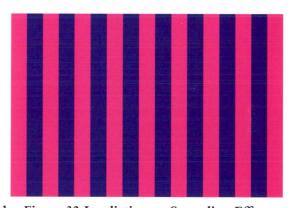

Color Figure 32 Irradiation or Spreading Effect
Reflected light rays (long and short wave lengths) radiate or spread over onto one another, causing intensely colored stripes to appear to vibrate.

Color Figure 31 Complementary Afterimage
Stare at the red square for about one minute. Then look quickly at the colorless square on the right and continue to stare at it. What color appears there? A complementary afterimage is induced on the colorless surface due to the intensity of the hue as it stimulates the eyes.

Color Figure 33 Adaptation of the Eye
Close one eye and stare at the vibrant red square about one minute. Then alternate eyes, closing one and opening the other to see the difference in hue that the unadapted eye sees, as compared to the adapted eye originally exposed to the intense hue.

12

INTENSITY: A Dimension of Color

Color Figure 34 Colors in Combination
Equal amounts of intense color fight for attention.

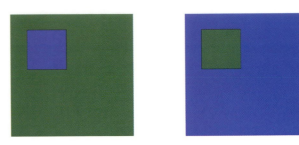

Color Figure 35 Colors in Combination and Law of Areas
A small amount of bright color balances and adds interest to a large area of dull and to a color scheme of all dull colors, while large areas of brightness overpower small dull areas.

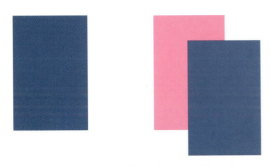

Color Figure 36 Colors in Combination
Dull, cool, hue appears brighter in combination with a warm hue.

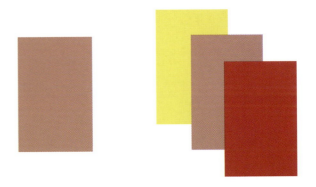

Color Figure 37 Colors in Combination
A dull hue becomes more attractive when used in combination with other hues of greater intensity and varying values.

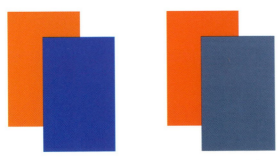

Color Figure 38 Colors in Combination
Full intensity complementary hues may overpower many people. Dulling the intensities makes the complementary hues more flattering on more people.

Color Figure 39 Colors in Combination
Virtually no one can wear black attractively in a combination like this. The pattern is too bold, with intense colors in equal amounts competing for attention with one another and with the wearer.

13
C O L O R   S C H E M E S

Color Figure 40 Colors in Combination
Add personal colors in combination with black to soften the effect and make you part of the color scheme with your clothes.

Munsell Color Space

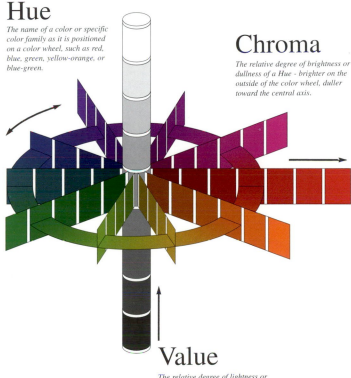

Hue
The name of a color or specific color family as it is positioned on a color wheel, such as red, blue, green, yellow-orange, or blue-green.

Chroma
The relative degree of brightness or dullness of a Hue - brighter on the outside of the color wheel, duller toward the central axis.

Value
The relative degree of lightness or darkness of a hue, progressing from white/light at the top to black/dark at the bottom of the central axis.

Color Figure 41 Three Dimensions of Color
Every color reflects a specific hue, value, and intensity contributing to the ultimate effect of the color.

Color Figure 42 Ellen's cluster pieces in representative outfits.

Color Figure 43 Wendy's cluster pieces in representative outfits.

Color Figure 44 Susan's cluster pieces in representative outfits.

1
Silk
Shirtblouse
In 26 colors
$99

1 Madeleine's signature shirtblouse of sensuous sueded silk. Genuine Mother-of-Pearl buttons. Tailored collar and breast pockets with flaps. Rounded side slits; back yoke with inverted pleat. Cuffs, shoulder pads. Hand wash. Sizes S(6–8), M(10–12), L(14–16), XL(18–20).

White (1), winter white (2), brown (3), rose (4), rush green (5), powder (6), cinnamon (7), frost green (8), dark green (9).
#4576 . . . $99

Light grey (1), grey (2), charcoal (3), greige (4), dove (5), royal (6), putty (7), brown (8).
#4746 . . . $99

Peach (1), coral (2), burgundy (3), yellow (4), olive (5), mint (6), dusty blue (7), navy (8), taupe (9).
#4326 . . . $99

Color Figure 45 Color Via Catalog
Catalog color choices are often large and varied in terms of hue, value, and intensity.

Instructions:

- Carefully cut this page out of the book.
- Cut out each color scale only when you are ready to use it.

- When ready, cut the individual color chips apart and mix them around.
- Rearrange color chips on the appropriate page for Exercises 5-4, 5-5, and 5-6.

EXERCISE 5-4

Warm ⟶ Getting Cooler

Cool ⟶ Getting Warmer

EXERCISE 5-5

Warm Hue/High Value–Light ⟶ Getting Darker

Cool Hue/High Value–Light ⟶ Getting Darker

EXERCISE 5-6

Warm Hue/Low Intensity–Dull ⟶ Getting Brighter

Cool Hue/Low Intensity–Dull ⟶ Getting Brighter

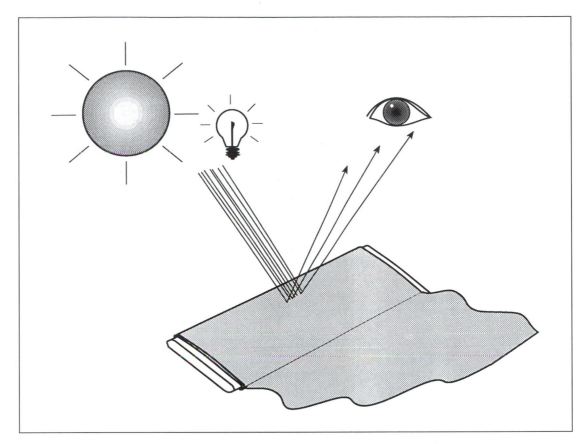

Figure 5–1. Light waves from the sun or a light bulb shine on an object, such as fabric. Light waves not absorbed by pigment in the fabric are reflected and stimulate the eye to experience the sensation of color.

in terms of dimensions. Each sensation that we experience and loosely call "color" is a combination of three dimensions, or characteristics, of color — hue, value, and intensity. Every color has a characteristic hue, value, and intensity. Differences in these characteristic dimensions account for the differences we see in colors.

Each dimension of color makes specific contributions to appearance. To understand and control the effects of color, it helps to learn the terms commonly used to describe color. It is essential to become aware of the dimensions of color. It is important to train your eye to recognize each of the dimensions universally used by artists, designers, painters, art educators, and others who work with color. (See Figure 5–2, and Tables 5-1 and 5-2 throughout the chapter.)

Hue

Hue refers to the name of a color or specific color family, such as yellow, orange, red, violet (purple), blue, or green. There are three kinds of hues — primary, secondary, and tertiary. They are positioned equidistantly around the color wheel.

Primary hues cannot be obtained by mixing other hues, but all other colors can be formed or created by mixing them. The primary hues in pigment (paint, ink, or dyes) are red, yellow, and blue. (The primary hues in light are different from those in pigment, as is the way they mix. This is a separate study in itself, important for those working with light.)

Secondary hues in pigment are generally described as green, orange, and violet. They result from the mixture of two primary hues in equal amounts.

- Orange results from mixing red and yellow.
- Green results from mixing yellow and blue.
- Violet (purple) results from mixing blue and red.

Tertiary hues, or intermediate hues, lie between a primary and a secondary hue. They result from a mixture of the primary and secondary hue on either side, in equal amounts. Their names are hyphenated and begin with the primary color to identify the mixture.

- Yellow-orange results from mixing yellow and orange.
- Yellow-green results from mixing yellow and green.
- Blue-green results from mixing blue and green.
- Blue-violet results from mixing blue and violet (purple).
- Red-violet results from mixing red and violet (purple).
- Red-orange results from mixing red and orange.

Hues can be changed from one to another by adding varying amounts of a neighboring hue. You can create an almost infinite number of hues as you move gradually around a color wheel.

Hue also refers to a color's relative degree of warmness or coolness, a physically measurable phenomenon.

Color Wheel

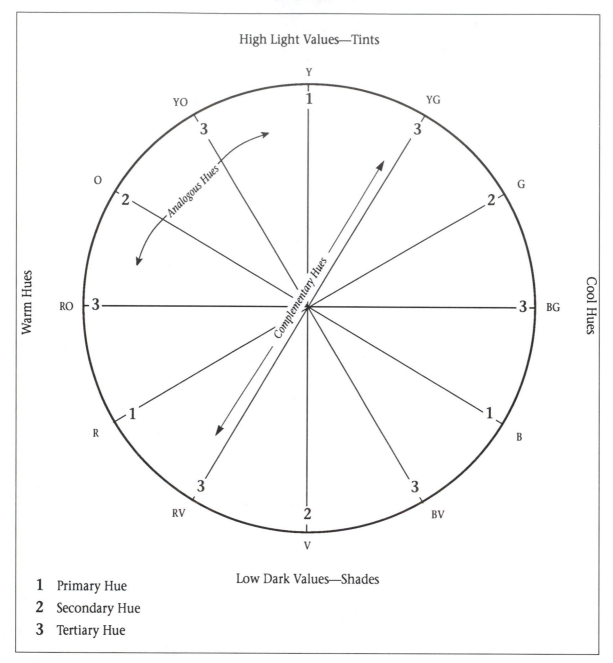

High Light Values—Tints

Warm Hues

Cool Hues

Low Dark Values—Shades

1 Primary Hue
2 Secondary Hue
3 Tertiary Hue

Figure 5–2.

Warm hues include red, orange, and yellow. They are generally positioned on the left half of the color wheel.

- Warm hues are associated with the sun or with fire.
- Warm hues reflect more light.
- Warm hues have an exciting, stimulating effect on the body and the psyche. (See Table 5–3 throughout this chapter.)
- Warm hues have longer wavelengths and appear to advance, thus causing shapes to appear closer, somewhat larger and more emphatic. (See Color Figure 4.)
- Warm hues tend to make us feel more comfortable in cold weather.

- Mixing yellow or orange into any hue will cause it to become visually warmer. In this mix of color, the main hue is in the second position — as in yellow-red or orange-blue.

For example, red is considered a warm hue, but may appear even warmer with the addition of orange (brick red, an orange-red). Green is considered cool, but may appear warmer with the addition of yellow (lime or olive, both yellow-greens).

Cool hues include green, blue, and violet. They are generally positioned on the right side of the color wheel.

- Cool hues are associated with the sky and water.
- Cool hues absorb more light.

Table 5–1 Dimensions of Color

		Message (Psychological Effect)		Illusion (Physical Effect)		Some Color Names	
Hue	**Warm**	Stimulating Exciting Energetic Happy Courage	Youthful Powerful	Stimulating Exciting Loud Advancing Closer	Larger Heavier weight Emphasize	Red Orange Yellow Coral Fuschia Terra Cotta	Hot Pink Cream Canary Brick Wheat Strawberry
	Cool	Calming Soothing Peaceful Mature Serene	Aloof Reserved	Calming Quiet Soothing Receding Further away	Smaller Lighter weight Minimize	Blue Green Purple Lavender Mauve Blueberry	Aquamarine Peacock Celery Wedgwood Seafoam Azure
Value	**Light**	Stimulating Fresh Delicate Youthful Open		Louder Advancing Closer Larger Lighter weight	Cooler Emphasize	Sky blue Mint green Lilac Banana Peach Eggshell	Melon Aqua Shell pink Ivory Sand Almond
	Dark	Calm Soothing Sophisticated Mature Closed Depressing		Calming Soothing Receding Further away Smaller	Solid Heavier weight Warmer Minimize	Navy blue Hunter green Teal Charcoal Black Mustard gold	Rust Kelly green Aubergine Plum purple Wine Brown
Intensity	**Bright**	Bold Dramatic Youthful Energetic Tension	Cheerful Happy	Stimulating Exciting Loud Advancing Closer	Larger Heavier weight Emphasize	Shocking pink Fuschia Tangerine Lime green Kelly green Saffron	Chartreuse Peacock Sapphire Royal Orchid Poppy
	Dull	Subtle Serious Somber Serene Sophisticated	Depressing Fatigue Mature	Calm Quiet Soothing Receding Further away	Smaller Lighter weight Minimize	Ash blue or gray Dusty rose Peach Dusk blue Taupe Burnt Orange	Slate blue Lavender haze Rose beige Cocoa brown Olive Moss

- Cool hues have a calming, soothing effect on the body and the psyche.
- Cool hues have shorter wavelengths and appear to recede, thus causing shapes to appear further away, somewhat smaller and less emphatic. (See Color Figure 4.)
- Cool hues tend to make us feel more comfortable in hot weather.

- Mixing blue or green into any hue will cause it to appear cooler. In this mix of color, the main hue is in the second position — blue-green or blue-yellow.

For example, a warm red will appear cooler with the addition of blue (burgundy, a blue-red). A cool green will appear even cooler with the addition of blue (turquoise or aqua, both blue-greens).

Table 5–2 Psycho-Physical Effect of Color

Characteristics of Color	Effects
Warm hues Light values Bright intensities Strong contrasts	Youthful Exciting Advancing Enlarge Emphasize
Cool hues Dark values Dull intensities Weak contrasts	Mature Calming Receding Reduce Minimize

Analogous hues contain a hue in common. They lie next to one another on the color wheel.

For example, blue and blue-green are analogous hues, and each contains blue as the common hue. Analogous hues red-orange, orange, and yellow-orange each contain orange as the common hue.

Complementary hues are most opposite or contrasting in character, one being warm and the other being cool. They lie directly across from, or opposite, one another.

For example, blue and orange are complementary colors; as is red and green, yellow and violet (purple), red-violet and yellow-green, and so forth.

- When seen next to one another, complementary hues appear brighter, stronger, more intense.
- Complementary hues combine to dull one another and to make gray. Stated another way, any hue can be dulled or neutralized to the point of becoming gray or brownish when you mix it with its complement.

Achromatic colors include white, gray, and black. They are "without pigment" or "without hue" and considered neutral colors. They are sometimes displayed in the center of a color wheel, or just below. Gray results from a mix of white and black, or from a mix of complementary colors. With the addition of a small amount of yellow or blue even the neutral colors black, white, or gray can become warmer or cooler.

For example, with yellow added to gray, it appears warmer and may be called taupe or creamy gray. With blue added to gray, it appears cooler and may be called steel blue gray or silver gray.

Value

Value refers to the relative degree of lightness or darkness of a hue. White is generally positioned at the top of a value scale, gray in the middle, and black at the bottom. (See Color Figure 15.) Each pure hue has a natural or normal value, just as it appears on the color wheel. Yellow is naturally light and violet is naturally darker.

Light, high values include yellow-orange, yellow, and yellow-green. They are positioned at the top of the color wheel — in natural value order.

Tints are high value colors, above or lighter than natural — white has been added to the hue, reflecting more light.

For example, green becomes mint when white is added and is called a tint. Other tints include pink, peach, and lilac.

- Tints have a more stimulating effect on the body and the psyche. They can work to lift your moods.
- Tints reflect the light and appear to advance (see Color Figure 16), thus causing shapes to appear closer, somewhat larger, and less compact. They don't define the silhouette, unless the surrounding background is dark.

Medium values include orange, red-orange, red, blue, blue-green, and green. They are positioned in the middle area of the color wheel — in natural value order.

Dark, low values include red-violet, violet, and blue-violet. They are positioned at the bottom of the color wheel — in natural value order.

Shades are low value colors, below or darker than natural — black has been added to the hue, absorbing more light.

Table 5–3 General Perception of Color

	Message/Function	Characteristic Dimensions of Color	Some Color Names	
Weather	To feel and appear warmer	Warmer hues Darker values Brighter intensities Stronger color contrasts	Coat colors in: Cinnamon rust Burgundy Brown Brick Terra cotta	Garnet Curry Maple Mustard (and warmer cool hues)
	To feel and appear cooler	Cooler hues Lighter values Duller, softer intensities Close color contrasts	Baby blue Turquoise Aqua Lavender Soft mint	Pearl gray Lilac Seafoam green (and cooler warm hues)
Occasion/Activity	To feel and appear casual/informal (casual business)	Warmer hues Light to medium values Medium to bright intensities Strong contrasts	Red Melon Lemon Salmon Coral	Copper Daffodil Hot pink (and warmer cool hues)
	To feel and appear dress-businesslike (formal business)	Cooler hues Medium to darker values Dull, muted to medium intensities Strong color contrasts, subtle	Forest green Wine Navy blue Flannel gray Raisin Aubergine	Charcoal French blue Olive (All wardrobe neutrals)
	To feel and appear dressy/formal	Any hue, value, intensity, or degree of contrast	All around the color wheel, plus White Black	
Values	To save time	Darker values	Navy blue Brown Black	
	To save money	Duller intensities	All wardrobe neutrals	
	To impress others	Bright or dull intensities Strong contrasts	Fuschia Royal blue Emerald green	
	To feel comfortable	Cooler hues Darker values Duller intensities	Dusty blue Sage green	Antique turquoise

Table 5–3 General Perception of Color (*continued*)

	Message/ Function	Characteristic Dimensions of Color	Some Color Names	
Personality	To feel and appear refined, ingenue/romantic	Warm to cool hues Lighter values Dull, muted to medium intensities including pastels Close contrasts, subtle	Shell pink Lavender Misty rose Orchid	Blue Peach All pastels
	To feel and appear happy, youthful, gamin/sportive	Warmer hues Light to dark values Medium to bright intensities Strong contrasts, bold	Coral Red Khaki Ivory Brown	Camel Cinnamon Brick (and warmer cool hues)
	To feel and appear dramatic/exotic	Warm to cool hues Dark values, deep Bright intensities, rich Strong contrasts, bold	Magenta Fuschia Emerald green Royal blue	Regal purple Sapphire Amethyst
	To feel and appear mature, serious, somber, classic	Cool hues Dark values Dull intensities	Navy blue Taupe Charcoal Aubergine	Maroon Gray Black
Figure/Body Build	To maintain or decrease attention and apparent size — to appear taller and slimmer	Cooler hues Darker values Duller intensities Close contrasts	Cornflower Navy blue Khaki (and duller, darker warm hues)	Grape Charcoal Mauve
	To increase attention and apparent size — to appear shorter and heavier	Warmer hues Lighter values Brigher intensities Strong contrasts	Shocking pink Canary Pumpkin (and intense, lighter cool hues)	Tangerine Poppy Raspberry

For example, green becomes jade when black is added and is called a shade. Other shades include rust, teal, olive, and burgundy.

- Shades have a quieting influence on the body and the psyche.
- Shades absorb light and appear to recede, thus causing shapes to appear further away, somewhat smaller, but more compact. They define the silhouette, unless the surrounding background is light. (See Color Figure 16.)

Intensity

Intensity, saturation, or chroma, refers to the relative degree of brightness or dullness of a hue. Royal blue is bright and slate blue is comparatively dull. All hues on the color wheel are seen at natural or full intensity. They are said to be fully saturated.

Bright, intense, vivid hues are saturated with a heavy concentration of pure clear pigment.

For example, scarlet is a red hue of high intensity and is said to be nearly pure, strong, or fully saturated. Other bright colors include shocking pink, chartreuse, and emerald or kelly green.

- Bright intensities reflect more light.
- Bright intensities are definitely stimulating to the body and the psyche. They are attention getters, but depending on the lighting, the culture, and occasion, too much can overpower the wearer and become hard on the viewers' eyes.

- Bright, intense colors appear to advance, causing shapes to appear closer, larger, and more emphatic. (See Color Figure 26.)
- Bright colors tend to be more difficult to coordinate in a wardrobe.

Dull tones, muted or grayed hues, are less intense or less saturated, containing a relatively lower concentration of clear pigment mixed with gray or its complementary color. Tone is not a word that applies to just any color.

For example, *dusty rose is a tone of red, dulled by green or gray. Other dull or low intensity colors include mauve, cornflower blue, forest green, and taupe.*

- Dull, muted colors absorb more light. As you will learn, however, there is a big difference between dull and dead.
- Dull, low intensities or tones appear softer, conservative, and have a quieting, soothing influence on the body and psyche.
- Because they absorb more light, dull, muted colors appear to recede, thus causing shapes to appear further away, smaller and less emphatic. (See Color Figure 26.)
- To dull or tone down any hue, mix it with its complementary color. Again, any hue can be dulled or neutralized even to the point of becoming gray or brownish when you mix it with its complement.
- Pastels, by traditional definition, are slightly dulled tints.
- Dulled, muted colors, because they combine both warm and cool hues, tend to coordinate well in a wardrobe and with the wearer.

Color Perception

The perception of color is a very personal experience, physically and psychologically. No two people perceive a color in exactly the same way, even within the framework of general perceptions outlined in Table 5–2. You may see color differently than someone else due to a difference in:

- the color of the iris in your eyes, with its varying amount of the pigment melanin, as it absorbs and reflects light waves.
- the shape and color (yellowing) of the lens in your eyes, as it changes with age, and as it absorbs and reflects light waves.
- the functional ability of the photoreceptors in the retina of your eye, as they respond to light waves.
- the functional ability of your optic nerve to transmit information to your brain.
- the functional ability of your brain to interpret that information.
- your cultural and educational background as it influences your interpretation preference and use of color.
- your personal and professional experience as it influences your interpretation, preference, and use of color.

Although individuals with normal color vision may agree in identifying a hue as red, they may disagree over the point at which the red becomes red-orange or blue-red, or about which red is the brightest or dullest.

In many instances, what color an individual notices and considers attractive is simply the result of what he or she has been culturally conditioned, educated, or trained to see, think, and say is attractive.

For example, *Minna was born and raised in Finland where daylight is often short and the skies are cloudy. She tends to prefer soft, muted hues. She does not appreciate strong colors. Maria, born and raised in Puerto Rico, where the skies are more often clear and sunny, prefers bright colors and bold contrasts. She tends not to appreciate muted hues and weak contrasts.*

For example, *Lana learned a color system that taught only certain colors were attractive together or on her. She was taught that black and rust or brown did not harmonize and that she looked unattractive in black. Seeing beautiful clothing combinations in black and cinnamon or nutmeg, she now wants to grow in her understanding and appreciation of color. She finds she has to work very hard, however, to overcome her previous learning and attitudes.*

The light source and the reflective surface can also influence your perception of color.

For example, *ordinary household incandescent or tungsten lighting is strong in yellow, orange, and red wavelengths. Incandescent lighting emits a somewhat warmer light that enhances warm colors and deadens cool colors. Tinted incandescent bulbs allow you to better control their effect and create different moods. Add to those options cool and warm fluorescent lighting, in varying qualities, and you have a wide range of lighting effects on the colors you see.*

After–Image and Eye Fatigue

It is important to recognize that color perception tends to change with exposure to a color. Pure or intense hues are visually tiring. With prolonged viewing of an intense color, the eye becomes fatigued and automatically adapts itself. It automatically imposes an after-image in the complementary hue to rest the eye. (See Color Figure 31.)

For example, after viewing a vivid red circle for a few minutes, and then shifting your gaze to a blank space, you can expect to see a green or blue-green after-image in the same shape. This complementary after-image will visually mix with the hue of any surface, including the skin. Magenta colored clothing can therefore cause the face of the wearer to appear green to the viewer.

An after-image effect may also be seen with exposure to extreme value contrasts. (See Color Figure 21.)

For example, after viewing a black triangle for a few minutes, and then shifting your gaze to a blank space, you can expect to see a white after-image in the same shape. White or very light tints in clothing can make skin appear darker. Black or very dark shades in clothing can make skin appear lighter. Large amounts of black eye-makeup can create after-image impressions on light skin. Skillful makeup application can prevent this effect.

A very bright hue will appear duller and duller, as the eye adapts itself to prolonged viewing. This effect occurs because the after-image hue mixes with the originally bright hue and dulls it. (See Color Figure 33.)

For example, the eye that adapts to bright red or fuchsia will automatically begin to see the red as somewhat duller due to the complementary blue-green after-image that mixes within the eye. This adaptive effect leads to the tendency to select brighter and brighter colors to offset the effect of eye fatigue. As the viewer grows gradually accustomed to bright hues, she or he requires brighter and brighter hues to maintain the same apparent intensity. To an unadapted viewer, however, the color still appears normally bright — and possibly too bright for the person or the occasion.

Colors in Contrast

Colors are seldom seen alone. Colors appear to change as they are seen in combination with other colors — personal coloring, other clothing, cosmetic colors, and against surrounding background colors. You can expect colors to have an altering effect on one another — to change in contrast to one another. This phenomenon is known as **simultaneous contrast**, and the color changes are generally predictable. (See color figures for examples of simultaneous contrast.)

- Warm colors can make cool colors appear cooler.
- Cool colors can make warm colors appear warmer.
- Complementary colors emphasize the apparent warmness or coolness of the other.

This reveals the relative aspect of color, as hues tend to "push apart" in predictably opposite directions around the color wheel.

For example, red and orange will appear warmer next to a cool blue-green. Yellow-green will appear cooler next to yellow-orange. Blue-green eyes may appear more blue when green clothing or eye shadow is worn. Blue-green eyes may appear more green when blue clothing or eye shadow is worn. Brown eye shadow makes blue eyes look bluer by complementary contrast, and a blue sweater makes blonde or brown hair appear richer or stronger.

- Light colors can make medium to dark colors appear darker.
- Dark colors can make medium to light colors appear lighter.

This demonstrates the relative aspect of color, as values "push apart" in the opposite direction of lighter or darker — white or black, up or down on the value scale.

For example, yellow will make yellow-green look darker, and green will make yellow-green appear lighter. Facial skin will appear lighter next to dark-colored clothing or when dark eyeliner and mascara are worn. Skin may appear darker next to light-colored clothing.

- Bright colors can make medium to dull colors appear duller.
- Dull, muted colors can make medium to bright colors appear brighter.

Again, this points out the relative aspect of color, as intensities "push apart" in opposite directions across the intensity scale.

For example, medium blue eyes will appear brighter when a slightly duller blue sweater or eye shadow is worn, and vice versa. Medium intensity blue eyes will appear duller when a vivid, bright blue shirt or eye shadow is worn.

The size of a colored area has marked influence on the way the color will be perceived. The larger the colored area, the more consistent the color will appear. The smaller the area, the more easily it appears to change.

For example, the small area of eye color is most easily influenced by surrounding colors and appears to change quickly in hue, value, and intensity. In small amounts, small color differences such as blue-gray and blue-green

---

> **TIP**
> ☞
> **FROM THE PROS**
>
> **The many factors influencing color perception account for the predictably different results you can expect from personal color analysis.** You can receive as many different results as you have analyses. It is wise to remain objective in color judgments and response to color.

may become indistinguishable. Blue-gray may appear blue-green when combined with other colors in a print dress, and blue-green eye shadow and liner may be used to influence blue-gray eyes to appear more blue-green.

This automatic physical response to color is called **optical mixing**. It occurs when small colored areas, such as a print, check, or stripe, are closely placed. (See Color Figure 12.) Each colored area tends to take on the color of the neighbor, and they visually blend within the eye. The eye is unable to separate or distinguish between the small areas of color, and they become optically mixed. The effect is increased with distance. It accounts for the advice to stand several feet away from a patterned piece of fabric, allowing you to see what colors your eye automatically blends together. In some cases, a color can be lost from view completely.

Another effect you can expect to experience is called **irradiation**, or **spreading**. Irradiation is predictable when extremely contrasting colors are placed close to one another. In this situation, a bright, warm hue of longer wavelengths appears to spread, or overlap, onto an equally bright, but cool hue of shorter wavelengths. Extremely light values with more light reflected appear to spread onto very dark values with few light rays reflected. This effect is very disturbing, as colors appear to jump or crawl across the surface. (See Color Figures 22 and 32.)

Creative Color Schemes

Hues, values, and intensities from all around the color wheel can be creatively combined and worn by all individuals. You only have to look around you. The combinations are endless, limited only by the bounds of your imagination.

Interest, unity, and color harmony in design, however, are easier to achieve with fewer colors. You can't plan or put together a wardrobe that includes all color families in all intensities all at once, or they're going to clash and fight with one another and with you.

Some individuals are able to use a random mix of colors successfully. However, they usually have an innate sense or talent for working with color. If you don't feel similarly endowed, it may help to decide on a specific group of colors, a color scheme, as a guideline for coordinating a cluster of clothes. A color scheme simplifies your planning and your shopping. It saves you money on clothes that don't coordinate. A color scheme makes daily decisions about what to wear faster and easier.

Interest and harmony are easier to achieve in an outfit or a cluster when:

- The color scheme includes a balanced variety of warm and cool hues, light and dark values, and bright and dull intensities.
- One wardrobe neutral is somewhat lighter than the other.
- Accent colors are comparatively the lightest, darkest, or brightest colors in the outfit or cluster.

- Accent colors are used in smaller amounts or in fewer clothing pieces.

You will want to avoid a color scheme in all warm or all cool colors, all light or all dark values, and all bright or all dull intensities. Your own moods, and the occasions in your life, demand more variety and versatility. Variety within a beautiful color scheme is what you're after. Choose from several creative color schemes. (See Figure 5–3 throughout the following sections.)

Monochromatic color schemes present the harmony of one hue. *Mono* is a prefix meaning "one." Hence, one chromatic hue. The achromatic colors black, white, and gray may or may not be considered part of a monochromatic color scheme. (See accentuated neutral color schemes.)

For example, a monochromatic color scheme based on red might include tints of pink and shades of scarlet and crimson. Based on violet, it might include tints of lavender and amethyst and shades of grape.

- Monochromatic color schemes depend on varying values and intensities of one hue for contrast and interest.
- Monochromatic color schemes are generally considered to be calming in psychological effect, but depending on the hue, and if carried out in extremes of light and dark value contrast, or extremely bright intensities, they can be exciting.
- Monochromatic color schemes are most effective if the hue repeats, or is in complementary contrast, to your hair, eye, or skin coloration, making you part of the color scheme with your clothes.

To increase interest and prevent potential boredom with a repetitious monochromatic color scheme, rely on the following:

- A variety of interesting and harmonious clothing style lines.
- A variety of interesting and harmonious clothing textures.
- A variety of solid color and patterned pieces — print, stripe, or plaid.
- A face framing hairstyle, also with interesting style lines and textural effects.
- Makeup to add contrast. Blush provides warm cheek color and brightens your eyes. Eye shadow, eyeliner, and/or mascara provide dark-light contrast on light skin.

Analogous color schemes present the harmony of two, three, or four hues that lie next to one another on the color wheel. All hues have one hue in common.

For example, an analogous color scheme containing yellow as the common hue might include tints and shades of yellow-green, yellow, yellow-orange, orange, and red-orange.

- Analogous color schemes may or may not vary in the degree of warmness or coolness, lightness or darkness, brightness or dullness.

Creative Color Schemes

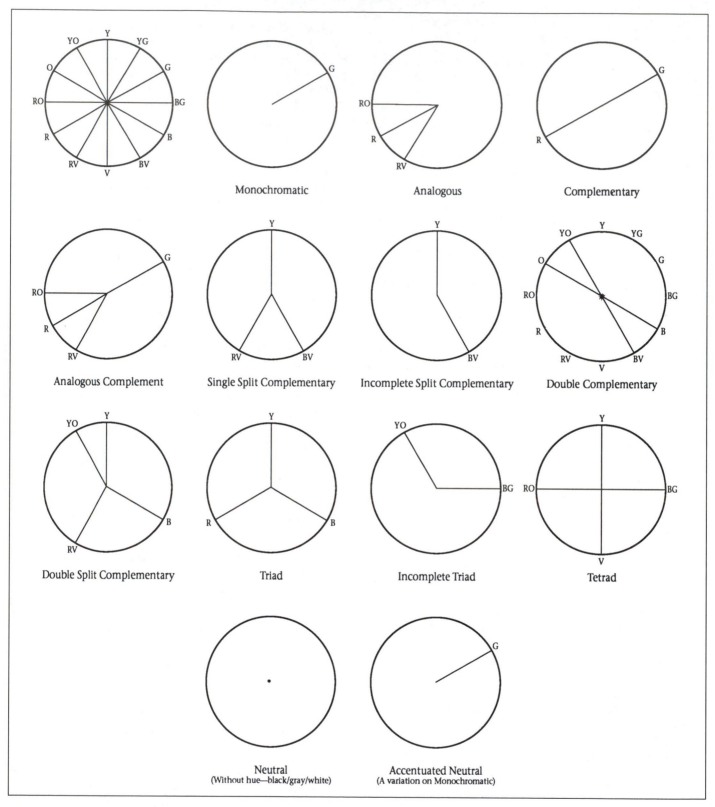

Figure 5–3.

- Analogous color schemes carry an emotional quality associated with the dominant colors, warm or cool. They can be calming or exciting, depending on the degree of contrast in hue, value, and/or intensity.

- Analogous color schemes are most effective if one of the hues repeats some aspect of your personal coloring — your hair, eye, or skin coloration, making you part of the color scheme with your clothes.

Complementary color schemes present the harmony of two hues that lie opposite one another on the color wheel.

For example, complementary color schemes include tints and shades of blue and orange, red-orange and blue-green, red and green, red-violet and yellow-green.

- Complementary color schemes, by their very nature, combine both warm and cool hues, and often, lighter and darker values.
- Complementary color schemes can be very stimulating due to their opposite visual characteristics. By dulling the intensity, or varying the value, of one or both hues, a more calming effect may be achieved. Blending the complementary hues into a fabric weave or print may further reduce the stimulating effects of complementary color schemes.
- Complementary color schemes are among the most versatile and flattering, containing hues that both repeat and provide complementary contrast to personal coloring.

There are several near-complementary color schemes. These color schemes include: analogous complementary; incomplete split complementary; single split complementary; double complementary; double split complementary.

- Each near-complementary color scheme includes both warm and cool hues, lighter and darker values. They are more common and easier to wear than a strictly complementary color scheme because the color combinations are less extreme or bold.
- In each near-complementary color scheme, the hues may be varied in value or intensity for an infinite variety of combinations and effects.
- In each near-complementary color scheme, you will immediately become part of the color scheme if you repeat some aspect of your personal coloring in the clothes and cosmetics, thus achieving greater harmony in your total appearance.

Triad describes a color scheme that presents the harmony of three colors spaced equidistant from one another around the color wheel.

For example, tints and shades of the primary hues red, yellow, and blue create a triad, as do the secondary hues orange, green, and violet. Each set of tertiary hues does also.

- Triadic color schemes combine both warm and cool hues, lighter and darker values.
- Triadic color schemes can be very stimulating due to their visual characteristics. By dulling the intensity, or varying the value of the hues, more calming effects may be achieved. Blending the complementary hues into a fabric weave or print may further reduce the stimulating effects of complementary color schemes.
- Triadic color schemes are among the most versatile and flattering, containing hues that can both repeat and provide complementary contrast to personal coloring.

Incomplete triad color schemes are a variation on the triadic color scheme, with similar characteristics.

Tetrad describes a color scheme that presents the harmony of four colors spaced equal-distance from one another around the color wheel.

Characteristics are similar to the triad and near-complementary color schemes.

For example, tints and shades of yellow, blue-green, violet, and red-orange form a tetrad; as do tints and shades of yellow-green, blue, red-violet, and orange. These color schemes tend to be more pleasing if colors are used in unequal amounts.

Neutral color schemes present the harmony of one, two, or three achromatic neutrals — black, white, and gray.

For example, a neutral color scheme might include only black, all white, or gray alone. It might feature black with white, gray with white, or black and gray.

- Neutral color schemes may or may not vary in the degree of warmness or coolness, lightness or darkness, brightness or dullness.
- Neutral color schemes vary in mood and effect, depending on the degree of light and dark value contrast.
- Neutral color schemes are most effective if the degree of lightness or darkness in your hair and/or skin coloring is repeated in the lightness or darkness of the clothing, making you part of the color scheme with your clothes.

Accentuated neutral color schemes present the harmony of any one chromatic hue in combination with one or more achromatically neutral colors.

For example, an accentuated neutral color scheme might include red or teal with black, red with black and white or gray, rust with gray, and so forth.

- Accentuated neutral color schemes may or may not feature black, white, or gray in varying degrees of warmness or coolness, lightness or darkness, brightness or dullness.
- Accentuated neutral color schemes may feature one hue as a brighter accent color only.
- Accentuated neutral color schemes may rely on one hue as the dominant color and rely on black, white, and/or gray as accent colors.
- Accentuated neutral color schemes are often most effective when the chromatic hue repeats a hue in your personal coloring.

Where to Look for a Wonderful Color Scheme

Where do you start in coming up with a beautiful color scheme? Start with a wonderful pattern of colors — in a print, stripe, or plaid — to inspire you with a color scheme you will want to plan and coordinate a cluster around. Ideally, one or more of the colors in the print, stripe, or plaid that you select repeats some aspect of your personal coloring. Ideally, one or more of the colors in the pattern is also a wardrobe neutral you can use for basic clothing pieces, with other colors coming into the cluster as accents.

Start now to be on the lookout for a pattern of colors that you love, feel like you could wear forever, and that reflects you the way you want to be seen.

Color and the Principles of Design

Large areas of color can become tiresome. Large areas of bright color can even become bothersome. The "law of areas" is a time-tested guideline that states large areas of color are more pleasing if balanced in combination with proportionally small areas of another color. Exceptions might be seen in evening wear and active sports apparel, or involve cultural or racial customs and tradition.

A color scheme of predominantly warm hues can be balanced and given added interest by introducing a small amount of cool hue.

For example, rust, tan, and brown may be livened by the addition of a small amount of blue in the arrangement. Brown eye shadow and mascara may appear more glamorous for evening occasions with the addition of teal blue-green eyeliner.

A color scheme of predominantly cool hues can achieve an exciting sense of balance and is given added interest by the addition of a warm hue.

For example, forest green and navy blue can be livened with a small quantity of cinnamon rust or white in the color scheme.

A color scheme of light values may appear more interesting with the addition of a darker accent color, and vice versa.

For example, a color scheme of peach and mint green can achieve an exciting balance with rust or hunter green added. Black and charcoal can become more interesting and visually balanced with a little yellow.

Dominant colors draw attention to themselves and therefore emphasize the area where they are placed.

Strong contrasts of hue, value, and/or intensity draw attention to and emphasize the point or place where colors come together. They interrupt eye movement and may cause the figure to appear larger, heavier, and/or somewhat shorter, depending on where that point is located on the body. Use them only in places where you want to draw attention and to emphasize.

While taller women can usually carry more color contrast than short women, everyone can benefit by some contrast at the collar, neckline, shoulders, or in the center front to draw attention into the center and upward toward the face. It is essential to evaluate the selection of hues, values, and intensities in relation to one another and to your purpose.

5.

Become more aware of personal coloring and how it can relate to clothing selection and coordination.

❧

Individuals possess an infinite variety of personal coloring patterns. Many people have a combination of apparently warm- and cool-based hues. Most people lie somewhere between those extremes, with differences so subtle they seldom need to limit their selection of clothing or cosmetic colors. It helps to become aware of the vast and rich range of human coloration and the subtle changes within it.

Remember, all color, including personal coloring, is relative and may appear to change with changes in lighting, background colors, clothing, and cosmetics. Personal coloring can be expected to actually change with age, diet, exposure to the environment, and health. Skin and hair can become, for example, lighter, darker, redder, or yellower.

Personal Color Evaluation

Evaluate your personal coloring with your hair exposed, without makeup, and in a good light — preferably day-

---

T I P
❧
FROM THE PROS

When matching solid colors, make sure they are balanced, or "color keyed" in the same degree of warmness or coolness, such as reddish-navy blue paired with a matching reddish-navy blue and not a greenish-navy blue. If unmatched, color differences become noticeable as colors "push apart" and clash with one another. However, when you move beyond matching or similar colors, to analogous, near-complementary and complementary colors, the color keys can be mixed harmoniously. It is often difficult to color match fabrics of the same weight and similar texture. You will find that differences in fabric texture can make color matching easier.

T I P
❧
FROM THE PROS

Keep in mind that because all of the elements of design are interrelated, **the ultimate effect of any color is influenced by the other elements** of design — the lines, shapes, textures, and patterns in the clothes. This influence is what makes so many "fashion rules" unreliable or invalid. The rule appears to work in one outfit, but not in another because the lines, the fabric, the pattern, or the combination of clothes caused the effect to be different than expected. As you study Chapters 3–7, learning what the predictable effects of each element are, you will be better equipped to evaluate the total effect of any given garment or outfit.

---

light or under a balanced white light. Begin with the hue of your hair.

Hair Color: Because it covers a relatively large area, hair is an important personal body color to consider in relation to clothing and cosmetic colors. Also, it is readily seen and remembered by others. The dominant hue of your hair and its highlights are relatively apparent and easy to identify.

Natural hair color is a variation of red, orange, and yellow hues — most likely a combination of several hues. Hair may, or may not, appear predominantly warmer or cooler.

Hair that appears warmer in hue, with red, red-orange, and/or golden highlights, is traditionally described as:

golden blonde	honey blonde
strawberry blonde	titian red
rusty red	auburn
chestnut brown	brownette (medium brown)
brunette (dark brown)	umber black
creamy white	golden gray

Hair that appears cooler in hue, with blue, green, or silver highlights, is traditionally described as:

platinum blonde	flaxen blonde
ash blonde	brick red
taupe	soft brown
blue black	raven black
white	silver gray
blue gray	

Hair color described as "salt and pepper" combines obvious amounts of gray, white, and medium to dark brown hair. Its warm or cool appearance depends on the amounts of each, which vary among individuals.

Hair color value is traditionally described as light, medium, or dark.

For example, pale flaxen blonde hair is very light in value, an ash blonde is medium value, a brunette is dark, and umber black is very dark in value. "Salt and pepper" colored hair combines a variety of values.

Hair color intensity, compared to bright clothing color, is only moderately bright to very dull. Nonetheless, hair is traditionally described as bright, medium, or dull.

For example, platinum blonde or titian red hair is relatively bright, a brownette is medium, and ash blonde is duller.

Eye Color: The hue of eyes is fairly easy to determine, although it is easily influenced by surrounding colors and may appear to change.

Eyes that appear warmer in hue are traditionally described as:

amber	russet
brown	hazel brown
olive green	umber black

Warm colored eyes may have brown, amber, rust, olive, or gold rims, lines, or flecks in them.

Eyes that appear cooler in hue are traditionally described as:

blue	blue green
turquoise	green
violet	blue violet
blue black	blue gray

Cool colored eyes may have white or gray rims, lines, or flecks in them.

Eye color value is traditionally described as light, medium, or dark.

For example, blue, green, and violet eyes are generally considered light to medium in value. Brown eyes range from medium to dark. Gray eyes run from light to dark.

Eye color intensity, compared to bright clothing color, is only moderately bright to dull. Even so, eyes are traditionally described as bright, medium, or dull.

For example, intense brown eyes are often described as being black. Blue eyes may appear a bold, bright blue or blue green, but may range to a dull blue gray, or just plain gray.

Skin Color: Skin coloration is the most difficult for most individuals to identify, since the actual hue is less intense and the gradations are so very close. You will remember that a hue may appear relatively warm next to one color and relatively cool next to another. This is nowhere more evident than with skin coloration. Skin may appear warmer in one situation and immediately cooler in another.

In evaluating skin color, it helps to become aware of the several pigments that influence apparent coloration.

- Melanin: Virtually everyone has some aspect of orange in his or her skin. This ranges from orange-red to orange-yellow and is determined by the pigment melanin present in the surface layers of the skin.

- Carotene: Skin coloration is further influenced by the yellow pigment, carotene. Your diet can increase the carotene content in the skin.

- Hemoglobin: Physical health, physical activity, and emotional reactions influence blood circulation and visible blue or red pigmentation. The intensity of visible color depends on the concentration of surface blood vessels and the oxygen-rich (red oxyhemoglobin) or oxygen-poor (blue reduced hemoglobin) state of the blood vessels below the surface. The dilution or absence of melanin influences the intensity of red or blue in skin coloration.

Observe the hue of your skin on your forehead or temples. Skin color can vary too much over the nose and cheeks, and around the mouth and chin. Notice surface overtones on the forward areas of your face — forehead, cheeks, nose, and chin. Look for undertones visible in the recessed areas of your face — under your eyes, around the base of your nose, and in the indentation of your chin.

Skin that appears warmer in hue has more melanin, with less blue complementary color showing through. Gradations in warm skin are traditionally described as:

ivory	creamy
peach	tan
golden beige	copper toned
red orange	olive
ebony	dark brown
umber black	

Overtones on warm skin appear more peach to orange. Undertones in warm skin appear a dull mustard yellow, brown, and/or greenish.

Skin that appears cooler in hue has less melanin, with more blue complementary color showing through. Gradations in cool skin are traditionally described as:

white	porcelain
translucent	fair
pink	rosy
red	pale beige
rose beige	mahogany
bluish brown	blue black

Overtones on cool skin appear pink to red. Undertones in cool skin appear blue and/or violet.

Skin color value is easy to determine, and is traditionally described as light, medium, or dark. There is a range within each category, and exposure to the sun can darken skin.

Skin color intensity, compared to bright clothing color, is only moderately bright to dull. Even so, skin can appear warmer and brighter, or cooler and duller. Blue undertones, the complementary color to orange, create a softer, dulling effect on orange-red and orange-yellow overtones.

Special considerations in skin coloration include blemishes, scars, birthmarks, white patches without pigmentation, prominent moles, and an inclination to blush easily. If present, you may choose to avoid repeating and therefore emphasizing those colors in clothing near the face.

Personal Color Selection

By way of review, you can expect to look terrific wearing colors that repeat your hair, eyes, and cheek coloration, and in some variety of tints and shades. You can also expect that colors you've had positive experiences with in your life will be some of your favorite colors. They may or may not be one and the same. Beyond those, you may need some helpful guidelines.

Artistic compositions are both pleasing and interesting when they include well-proportioned contrasts in warm and cool hues, light and dark values, bright and dull intensities. (See Color Figures 25 through 46.) Because you are part of the artistic composition you create with your clothes, you need to be aware of contrast present in your personal coloring. Ask yourself the following specific questions and circle your answers.

1. Is there a variety of hues in my hair, eye, and skin coloring — or are they basically one hue (orange melanin in hair, eyes, and skin)? If you identify one hue in your hair and another in your eyes or skin, you can rightly answer "yes," you do have hue contrast in your personal coloring. If not, the answer is "No."

For example, Liz has blonde hair, blue eyes, and fair skin. She has two hues in her personal coloring. She does have some hue contrast. Tory has brown hair, brown eyes, and brown skin. She does not have any hue contrast. (The white of the eyes and teeth are not generally enough to be considered a hue contrast.) Judith has brown hair, green eyes, and cool skin. She has hue contrast. Della has white hair, blue eyes, and warm skin. She has hue contrast. How about you?

1. I do have warm/cool hue contrast.   Yes   No

2. Is there a variety of light and dark value between your hair and skin — or are they both dark, or both light? If your skin is light and your hair is dark you do have value contrast; answer "Yes." If your hair, skin, and eyes are all light, all medium, or all dark, you would say you do not have value contrast and your answer is "No."

For example, Liz has blonde hair, medium blue eyes, and light skin. She does not have much value contrast. Her coloring is comparatively light. Tory has dark hair, dark eyes, and dark skin. She does not have much value contrast. Her coloring is all dark. Judith has dark hair, medium green eyes, and light skin. She does have value contrast. Della has white hair, medium blue eyes, and slightly darker skin. She has some value contrast — not a lot, but some. How about you?

2. I have light/dark value contrast.   Yes   No

3. Is there some brightness in my personal coloring, or are the colors soft and subdued? If you can see lots of shiny highlights in your hair, your eyes sparkle, or your cheeks are full of natural color, you can feel confident your personal coloring is bright. If your hair is softly muted, your eyes are relatively grayer, or your cheeks show no warm overtones, your personal coloring is subdued or less intense.

For example, Liz has shiny, bright blonde hair, vivid blue eyes, and rosy cheek color; Liz has stronger, brighter looking coloring. Tory has intense brown-black hair, sparkling brown eyes, and strong warm skin coloring; she has brightness in her personal coloring. Della has shiny, intense, white hair you can't miss; she has some intense personal coloring. Karen has ash blonde hair, soft blue-green eyes, and fair skin. She does not have very much intensity in her personal coloring. How about you?

3a. I have bright/dull intensity in my personal coloring.   Yes   No

You can create an attractive, interesting, and memorable appearance when you present a harmonious variety of warm and cool hues, light and dark values, bright and dull intensities. You can use your clothes and cosmetics to provide needed hue, value, and/or intensity contrasts near your face. Ask yourself the following specific questions, and circle your answer.

3b. Do I need to add some hue contrast? Yes   No

Little hue contrast indicates the need for new hues in clothing, and possibly makeup, to supply that characteristic of color missing from your personal coloring. If you answered "No" to question number 1, you can now answer "Yes," I do need to add some hue contrast in my clothing and/or cosmetics to create an interesting and attractive appearance.

For example, Liz has hue contrast in her personal coloring already. She doesn't need to add new colors in her clothing, unless she chooses to. She can also choose to emphasize the hues she already has by simply repeating those colors in her clothing, or with complementary contrast colors in her clothing.

Tory's personal coloring is all brown — darker values of orange. She looks fantastic when she adds new colors in her clothing — royal blue (the complementary color to orange), fuchsia, yellow, green, red, and so forth. If she chooses to simply repeat her own personal coloring, with clothes in dark brown, light brown, tan, and/or ivory, she is smart to choose interesting style lines and textures to add more interest to her entire appearance. In addition, she may choose to introduce new hues with her eye shadow, blush, and lip color.

3c. Do I need to add some value contrast? Yes   No

Little value contrast between the hair and skin narrows the range of values you can wear attractively. While hue contrast may be enough, even stunning, you also have the option of wearing clothing and makeup lighter or darker than you are to provide value contrast. If you answered "No" to question number 2, and you do want to

create an attractive, interesting, and memorable appearance, your answer to this question is "Yes, I can benefit by adding some value contrast to my appearance."

For example, Liz has relatively light personal coloring. She can benefit by wearing a color, or colors, somewhat darker or lighter than she is. Even blue chambray fabric is darker than her hair or her skin, and yellow is lighter. If Liz chooses to wear a very dark color that appears to overpower her coloring or drains color from her face, such as navy blue or charcoal, she can restore the value balance by combining a lighter color in the outfit — such as yellow, pink, blue, lavender, and so forth. A lighter blouse color to frame her face works perfectly. If she chooses to wear a lot of white, which may reflect light onto her face and appear to "wash out" her own coloring, she can do the reverse, and combine a somewhat darker color in the outfit.

Tory's personal coloring is predominantly dark in value. She is smart to use her clothing to introduce some value contrast into her appearance. That's easy, because every hue comes in values lighter than she is. However, if she chooses to wear an equally dark hunter green, she can include a lighter color near her face for contrast. She might choose a shirt, scarf, or third layer piece of clothing to introduce this needed color.

3d. Do I need to add some intensity into my personal coloring?   Yes   No

Little intensity in personal coloring indicates the use of somewhat brighter clothing colors, or simply complementary colors, to add interest to personal coloring. If you answered "Yes" to question number 3, your answer now will be "No, not really. Not unless I choose to really play it up." Della's hair is definitely bright; Liz's hair is quite bright, as is Tory's. If your answer was "No," your answer now is "Yes, I can add some intensity to my appearance to give me a little more visual life."

For example, with ash blonde hair, Karen's total appearance will become brighter when she wears teal blue-green or black, and the sheen of gold jewelry. Teal is the complementary hue to her hair color and brings out gold highlights. Both colors are stronger than her personal coloring. Again, if the colors appear to overwhelm Karen's personal coloring, she can balance the effect by introducing a somewhat duller color to the outfit, particularly near her face.

Take care not to overpower personal coloring with clothing or makeup colors that are too intense.

For example, a bright blue eye shadow may overpower and dull blue eyes. A blue eye shadow of the same intensity will repeat and emphasize blue eyes, and a somewhat duller blue eye shadow will cause blue eyes to appear even brighter and bluer by contrast.

Only in extreme cases will hair or skin coloration rule out your freedom to wear a broad range of colors. Those extremes include a lot of yellow (sallow), blue (ashen), red (ruddy), and yellow-green (jaundiced). If you discover a noticeable amount of any of these colors in your skin, and you feel they are not pleasing, you will want to avoid direct repetition and complementary contrast. You can expect them to emphasize these skin colors. Violet (purple), orange, green, and red-violet are the respective complementary hues to watch out for in large quantities.

Wear Any Color You Need or Want to Wear

If you like a particular color, or have positive memories concerning it, consider wearing it. The key is colors in combination. With a working knowledge of how colors affect one another, you can learn to control the effects. Consider the quantity of the color and its placement on your body. Accent colors can be placed to focus attention where you want it. Your choice of colors is also influenced by the occasion and the people you will be with.

For example, if a woman likes shocking pink, she might wisely choose to wear only a little to the office, on a pin or scarf, worn up near her face. For a Saturday picnic with friends and family, she might choose a skirt with a pink ruffle that directs attention to her great legs.

In a clothing store or department, try on new colors that interest you. Or go to a fabric store and hold fabrics, in colors you want to try, up near your face. If the hue is so warm (orange or yellow) that it obviously clashes with your face coloring, choose a slightly cooler version — or try pairing it with a cooler clothing color up near your face.

For example, if a russet sweater appears to clash with relatively pink skin, try pairing it with burgundy and blue in a print blouse or scarf. (The color scheme is an analogous complement.)

If the hue of the clothing is so cool (blue or violet) it obviously clashes with your coloring, choose a slightly warmer version — or try pairing it with a warmer clothing color.

For example, if blue-violet makes you look positively blue blooded, choose a more red-violet hue or coordinate the blue-violet with a rich brown and camel. (This creates a complementary color scheme.)

If the value of the color is so light, and reflects so much light that it washes you out, choose a darker version of the color — or pair the light color with a darker clothing color to absorb some of the light and provide better balance in dark/light contrast. Makeup, skillfully applied, may accomplish this purpose.

For example, counter the reflective effect of ice blue or pale pink by pairing them with slate blue or burgundy respectively, or with hunter green instead. (These color schemes include monochromatic blues or reds, analogous blue and green, and complementary red with green.)

If the value of the clothing is so dark it absorbs light and seems to drain color from your face making you appear pale, choose a lighter version of the color — or pair it with a lighter color to reflect more light and provide better bal-

ance in dark/light contrast. Makeup, skillfully applied, may accomplish this purpose.

For example, a navy blue or charcoal gray suit may appear too dark, too stark. If that's the case, wear it with a soft pink or peach shirt. Pearls or metal jewelry add light to the outfit as well. Blush brings a little color to your cheeks. (These color schemes range from an incomplete triad, to complementary, to an accentuated neutral.)

If the intensity of the clothing color is so bright that it overpowers and dulls your personal coloring, and you become dull in comparison, choose a slightly duller version of the color — or use it in a smaller quantity, paired with a larger amount of subdued color. Makeup, skillfully applied, can brighten your personal coloring, allowing you to wear brighter clothing colors more attractively.

For example, if emerald green appears too bright on you, pair it with a piece of clothing the color of your hair, or with a wonderful patterned piece of clothing that includes green and your hair color in it — such as emerald green with tan, burgundy, blue, and black on a blonde, or green with silver and black on a woman with salt and pepper gray hair. Lipstick can repeat burgundy in the pattern. Mascara can be used to darken and intensify the impact of your eyes. (Color schemes include a double complement and an accentuated neutral.)

If a clothing color is so dull that, on you, it seems to lack luster, causing you to appear harsh or drab and lifeless as well, choose a brighter version of the color — or pair it with a brighter clothing color to liven your looks or to blend more closely with your own stronger coloring.

For example, a dull, drab sage or seafoam green comes alive when paired with reds, rusts, and/or gold.

If you've decided a particular color does very little for you in large amounts but is present in small amounts in a print, plaid, or a stripe, don't worry about it. It won't even be seen from a few feet away. Then remember, color is a relative element of design, altered by other colors around it. Very likely, the color appears quite different among several colors than it does alone.

Rely on complementary hues to work to your advantage, enhancing your appearance, emphasizing your own individuality, and creating a more memorable appearance.

For example, blue, worn by a brunette with blue eyes repeats the color of her eyes and calls attention to them. At the same time, the blue is a complementary hue to her brown hair and will therefore emphasize the hair's warm highlights by complementary contrast. It might also provide dark/light contrast with her skin and hair.

Russet, worn by a green-eyed strawberry blonde with ivory skin, is a similar, yet darker, version of the hair and skin color. It repeats warm highlights in the hair. At the same time, it can provide value contrast with hair and skin, as well as near-complementary hue contrast with her green eyes.

When selecting solid colors or combinations of colors, ask yourself, "What is the artistic relationship of my clothes and cosmetics to my personal coloring?"

For example, taupe (grayed-brown), when worn by a woman with ash blonde hair, will repeat the hue and the value of the hair, while providing some value contrast with the skin. To make her appearance more interesting and appealing, she might introduce a cooler hue such as turquoise or teal in a blouse or accessory near her face. Or she could apply blue-green eye shadow or liner. The blue-green hue provides interesting hue contrast with both hair and skin.

Color Draping

To help you recognize colors that do repeat or contrast attractively with your personal coloring, color draping can be an informative, optional experience. Color draping is not a new exercise. It has been practiced for decades in college clothing selection classes following a unit on basic color theory, without typecasting. With an understanding of how color works, you can better assess the apparent effects of colors on your hair, eyes, and skin, and plan for the attractive and most effective use of colors you choose to include in your wardrobe.

As you observe each separate color drape on yourself in the mirror, ask yourself the following questions:

1. Does the color make my skin look more healthy or vibrant?
2. Does the color intensify and bring out the color of my eyes?
3. Does the color bring out my hair color, making it appear rich in color and intensifying the highlights?
4. How does the color relate to my personal coloring?
5. Does the color make me feel good about myself?

You may not be able to answer "Yes" to all these questions, in which case you will want to consider your purpose and color selection for the upcoming occasion.

For example, you probably won't care if your clothing color does not emphasize your eye color if you are speaking to an audience twenty feet away from you. They won't see your eye color anyway. This might, however, be an important consideration if you are going to dinner with someone who will be sitting just across the table from you — and you want all attention on you.

A color draping experience can show you a vast array of colors you can wear without concern.

- Virtually everyone can wear medium value and medium intensity colors.
- It is essential that you not influence other people's color perceptions and evaluations by telling them what you see or think before they draw their own conclusions. And vice versa, do not let others tell you what they see and want you to see as well —

what they think and want you to think. Research shows that descriptive words can precondition color perception and evaluation. Color drapes arranged in so-called seasonal or color-keyed groupings likewise precondition and skew response.

- Pay close attention to degrees of difference in warmness and coolness as you attempt to repeat personal coloring or match clothing pieces.
- Remain aware of your option to combine warm and cool colors, shifting their apparent degree of warmness or coolness in one direction or another.
- Discover those few, not-so-terrific, or "worst" colors that obviously clash with, overpower, or appear to drain your personal coloring. These are colors you will want to avoid wearing in large amounts of solid color near your face — colors you may choose not to wear, or choose to wear in complementary combinations only.
- Discover, or reaffirm your confidence in, those few "best" colors that obviously repeat or provide complementary contrast with your coloring.
- Discover that vast range of colors you can wear attractively.

6.

Select clothing in colors that meet your individual needs or purposes — appropriate for your life–style, personal style, and fabric.

- Choose colors with characteristics appropriate for the mood, occasion, or activity. (See Tables 5–1 and 5–3.)
- Choose colors with characteristics that reflect the values of the wearer — what she or he believes to be valuable or important. (See Tables 5–1 and 5–3.)
- Choose colors with characteristics that are compatible with, or that reflect, the wearer's personality. (See Tables 5–1 and 5–3.)

- Choose colors with characteristics that flatter your face and figure. (See Tables 5–1 and 5–3.)
- Choose colors with characteristics that complement the surface characteristics of the garment fabric. (See Table 5–3.)
- Choose colors that will fit in well and coordinate with the existing wardrobe. (See Chapters 9 and 10.)

7.

Coordinate or combine colors, as well as basic and costume styles, to achieve greater variety, interest, and individuality.

In addition to color, the following discussion may acknowledge lines, shape, fabric, and pattern in the clothes, as these elements of design are interrelated and influence your choice of clothes to be combined in any one outfit.

Harmony among Colors

In combining colors in clothing, your goal is to **maintain a consistent theme or mood, occasion, and personality**, while achieving an interesting and harmonious balance among them — balance between warm and cool hues, light and dark values or bright and dull, in a variety of style lines, shapes, and textures. (See Tables 5–4 and 5–5.)

Women not satisfied with their wardrobe often combine clothes with colors that clash, conflict, or communicate contradictory traits. Depending on the person wearing them, colors that conflict may appear too severe, strict, and stern, or too bold and brassy. The wearer may feel psychologically uncomfortable in the clothing and observers may notice the conflict.

For example, some women love to see pink and fuchsia in the garden, but feel too much like a doll wearing them. They are psychologically more comfortable in shrimp, coral, brick, and red.

A Style of Your Own

Experiment a little and discover which colors are most in harmony with you, the places you go, and what you do there. As you experiment, you will discover colors you like to wear so much that they become part of your personal style — colors so specifically associated with you that they trigger an image of you in the minds of the people who know you.

Dominant/Subordinate Colors

When combining colors, **one color must be dominant and all others subordinate by descending degrees**. The mood, theme, or personality communicated by one color must be most obvious and most important — dominant. Different colors can be introduced into the design, but they must be done so to a lesser degree — they must attract less attention. This requires a delicate balance, but you can do it.

Two equally bright colors (or colors in a print) used in equal or nearly equal amounts compete for attention because there is too much repetition of bright or intense color. A relatively large amount of dull color, used with an equally large amount of bright color, can also be disturbing because there is too much contrast. You can introduce contrast into an outfit by simply varying the hues, values, and/or intensities, or by varying the amounts of the colors used according to the law of areas.

For example, Wendy has a beautiful hand-knit sweater in many colors, including cranberry red, orange, blue, and olive green. Paired with a cranberry red skirt, the large quantity of strong color in the skirt fights with the strong red and orange in the sweater. Paired with a duller navy blue denim skirt, however, colors in the sweater are dominant and the skirt becomes subordinate background color.

For another example, bright orange, yellow, and blue could appear harmonious if orange is used in a jacket, yellow in a shirt beneath, and blue in a short skirt or walking shorts. The orange jacket is dominant, the blue skirt is subordinate to the jacket, and the yellow shirt is subordinate to both skirt and jacket in terms of quantity and attention to color.

You can counter the serious formality of dark colored clothing by introducing some lighter, brighter colors (and soft or shiny textures).

For example, visualize a pink sport style shirt (in pima cotton or silky fabric) combined with a navy blue suit. Add pearl earrings rimmed in gold, and a gold necklace or bracelet — or both. The total look of the outfit is still dominantly businesslike, with navy blue the dominant hue, pink being subordinate, and both gold and pearl white being sub-subordinate.

This flexible and creative way of combining colors opens up endless possibilities for greater individuality and subtle communication. Colors can be combined to reflect a woman in any way she wants to feel or be seen. This applies to men as well.

Table 5–4 Image Makers and Breakers in Color

Image Makers In Color	Image Breakers In Color
• Harmonious color scheme • Clothing colors relate well to your personal coloring — emphasize positive personal coloring • Great color, great style • Creative use of color in clothes • Clothing colors appropriate for the occasion • Makeup coordinates with personal coloring and with the clothes • Subtle makeup, artfully applied, with natural-looking effects • Natural-looking nail polish color in clear, cream, soft coral, rose, and red coordinated with clothes	• Clashing, conflicting colors • Clothing colors do not relate well to your personal coloring — emphasize negative personal coloring • Great color, lousy style • Color cloned according to a stereotype • Gaudy, garish, overly bright colors in a professional setting • Makeup does not coordinate or relate to personal coloring or clothing colors • Excessive, harsh makeup, poorly applied, attracting attention to itself • Gaudy, attention-getting nail polish color in burgundy, brown, navy blue, purple, or black

Table 5–5 Image Makers and Breakers in Color Cosmetics

Image Makers In Color Cosmetics	Image Breakers In Color Cosmetics
• Smoothly blended, without lines • Colors coordinated with skin coloration • Muted soft blue, green, teal, or plum eyeshadow • Muted rose or brick shadow • Eyeshadow blended to brow bone • Dark brown eyeliner and mascara • Upper and under-eye liner; tapered line • Blush well blended on and just under the cheekbone • Lipcolor in natural hues of pink, peach, rose, and red	• Hard edges on obvious lines of color, smeared colors • Obvious foundation or contouring colors, white undereye concealing cream, white highlight, bright or dark blush • Bright, light blue, aqua, green, or violet eye shadow • Pink, red, or yellow eyeshadow • Eyeshadow applied up to the eyebrow • Black eyeliner or mascara on light skin • Under-eye liner only; thick line • Circles or streaks of cheek blush, applied too low or near the nose • Shocking pink, orange brown, burgundy, or white lip color

Makeup, Makedown, Makeover

I've always maintained that, without a bit of makeup, I'm as plain as a "mud fence." I was in a hurry one Saturday and decided I couldn't take time to put on my makeup. I was feeling good about life in general, so I headed out on errands as my very plain, unpainted self.

Minutes later, in a local department store, I was confronted by a former student who looked to be seven feet tall. "Mrs. Rasband," he loudly exclaimed for the whole store to hear. "It's really you! How marvelous! You really are as plain as you said you were!"

I smiled at smug-looking shoppers, thought beautiful thoughts, reminded myself that beauty comes from within, and beat a hasty retreat!

On days when I'm going to be out in the world, I find it's smart to take a little time to put on makeup. There's a real difference in the way I look with makeup, as well as how I feel, and in the way others respond to me.

The process of making up has a logical order about it, so you can learn to do much of it quickly and by habit. Don't feel you have to follow a set number of steps rigidly, or that you must use all of your makeup all of the time. You may choose to use more on a special occasion — to create greater visual presence or to appear more glamorous. You may choose to use less and appear casual for active sports or an at-home occasion. You have options.

Basic makeup procedures include using moisturizer/protectant on your clean face, before applying any actual makeup. This step seals in moisture and provides a barrier film to protect your skin from the environment. A light lotion will do nicely for day and makes a marvelous makeup base.

Wait a few minutes and then, as a general rule, start your makeup applications at the top of your face and work down to avoid smearing.

1. **Foundation** makeup, while not essential, is applied first. Foundation evens out skin coloration and can change apparent skin color. Skillfully applied, it can camouflage blemishes. Some foundations provide protection from the sun. Choose foundation to match your skin coloration, dot it onto your face, and blend smoothly in an up and outward direction. When using foundation, less is always best.

2. **Under-eye concealing cream** camouflages undertones and evens out skin color, as it moisturizes the under-eye area. Light skinned women are advised to choose concealing cream a tint lighter to camouflage dark areas. Avoid ghostly white concealing creams. Blend smoothly, in an up and outward direction.

3. **Powder** sets foundation makeup, evens out skin coloration, camouflages minor blemishes, and softens the appearance of makeup by eliminating any shine. It is a natural-looking alternative in place of foundation. Choose loose, translucent powder to match your skin. Press or brush on lightly, using a cotton ball or cosmetic brush. Smooth and blend powder with a cotton ball or brush, in a down and outward direction to avoid brushing facial hair up.

4. **Eyebrow pencil** adds color to harmonize brow and hair coloration, fills in brows, and can correct eyebrow shape and length. It, too, can create illusions about face and eye shape. Choose the color to coordinate with brows and hair color. Brush brows in an up and outward direction to smooth and shape. Fill in sparse areas with delicate pencil strokes, in the direction of hair growth. Taper to nothing at the outer end of the brow. Rebrush. Avoid thick, heavy application.

5. **Eye shadow** adds both hue and value contrast. It emphasizes your eyes and creates illusions about eye and face shape. Cream types are easier to blend and they moisturize your eyelids. Choose the color to coordinate with eyes and clothing colors. Apply to the eyelid and below the brow bone. Blend smoothly in an upward and outward direction, diminishing to nothing just below the brow bone. Lightly powder the area to set shadow and prevent creasing.

6. **Eyeliner** adds value contrast along the edge of the eyelid and emphasizes the eyes, creating the illusion of larger eyes. Choose the color to coordinate with hair, eyes, and/or clothing colors. Draw a smooth line along the edge of the upper eyelid and slightly into the upper eyelashes. Taper to nothing toward the center or the inner corner of the eye. Repeat on the lower eyelid. If needed, blend the line to soften the effect. Avoid underlining the lower lid only, as it creates an unbalanced effect. Avoid joining upper and lower lines at the outer corners.

7. **Mascara** adds value contrast on light-skinned women. It visually thickens and lengthens eyelashes on all women. It emphasizes the eyes, while softening the appearance of eyeliner. Choose the color to complement personal coloring. Tilt your head back and stroke color onto the top of upper lashes. Look straight forward and stroke color in an upward direction, on the underside of your upper lashes. Tilt your head down and stroke lower lashes in a downward direction. Stroke individual upper and lower lashes with the tip of the brush. Separate lashes and remove any clumps of mascara.

8. **Blush** adds warm color to the cheeks and imparts a healthy glow to your whole face. It draws attention to your eyes, emphasizes eye color, and creates illusions about facial contours. Choose the color to coordinate with skin, lip color, and clothing color. Using a soft brush, apply blush in an upward and outward direction over your cheekbone. Blend smoothly with the brush or a dry sponge. Avoid applying too close to the nose or jaw. Avoid circles or streaks of blush.

9. **Lipliner** adds hue and value contrast. It defines and corrects the lip line and/or size, while it emphasizes lips. Choose lipliner in the same or slightly darker shade as lipstick color. Trace the outline of your lips, reshaping only if necessary for better balance and proportion.

10. **Lipstick** adds hue and value contrast to emphasize the lips, as it moisturizes lips. Choose a color to coordinate with skin, blush, and clothing color. Apply lipstick to the area inside the lipliner, stroking from center to corners. Avoid an uneven or smeared line.

To maintain beautiful skin, remove your makeup nightly and cleanse your face. When you're over forty you'll be glad you did!

Review Main Points

The element color provides you with unlimited potential for creative wardrobing. It provides interest and harmony. Wardrobe neutrals are dulled or muted tones of many hues, as well as black, white, or gray. They combine beautifully with a wide range of other colors. Accent colors add interest to your outfit and your wardrobe. Build the bulk of your wardrobe around neutral colors. Gradually acquire needed or wanted accent colors. Each characteristic dimension of color contributes to the total effect of the clothing. Colors can be manipulated to communicate messages, feelings, and moods, and to create a variety of illusions about the body. Because clothing colors interact with one another and with the wearer, their dimensions need to be compatible with one another and with the wearer, the time and place, and the fabric they are made of. In combining different colors, one color must be dominant, and all others subordinate, by degrees. Combining colors, in interesting and harmonious ways, is one of the keys to putting together an interesting, versatile, and fashionable wardrobe.

Review Questions

1. How can you recognize a wardrobe neutral? _____
_____.

2. What makes a color an accent color? _____
_____.

3. Build the bulk of your wardrobe around _____ colors.

4. You can expect colors that _____ your personal coloring to flatter you and enhance your appearance.

5. Describe what is meant by, "Become part of the color scheme with your clothes." _____
_____.

6. The dimensions of color include _____, _____, and _____.

7. Value refers to the _____ or _____ of a color.

8. Cool colors have the effect of _____ the body and emotions.

9. What happens in the process of simultaneous contrast in colors? _____
_____.

10. Complementary color schemes combine_____ colors from the _____ sides of the color wheel.

11. List four colors you can expect to work well as wardrobe neutrals.
_____   _____
_____   _____

12. Which of the following words does not belong in the group? Circle the word.
charcoal   fuchsia   chartreuse   tangerine

13. Match the following characteristics of color to the appropriate mood or message it communicates.

_____ bright

_____ warm

_____ light

_____ dark

a. active, exciting, stimulating

b. gentle, feminine, happy

c. strong, decisive, formal

d. sporty, casual, fun

14. To keep your cool in hot weather, select clothing colors that are

_____ and _____.

15. How can you find, or decide on, a color scheme to use in coordinating a

cluster of clothes? _____

Discussion Questions

#1 Identify and discuss colors that you associate with fond memories. What was the occasion of the memory? What feelings come back as you remember the occurrence?

Notes: _____

_____

_____

#2 Discuss the illusory effects of the color in clothes your fellow students are wearing. What feelings or personality traits are communicated by the various lines? What occasions, moods, or themes are represented by the colors?

Notes: _____

_____

_____

#3 What types of color schemes are represented by the clothing your fellow students are wearing?

Notes: _____

_____

_____

#4 Which class members have a variety of hues in their personal coloring, and which have a oneness of personal coloring? Which have a variety of values in their personal coloring, and which do not?

Notes: _____

_____

_____

Exercise 5-1   Color Recognition

Name_____

Look at what you are wearing.

• Identify and list clothing colors and checkmark which colors are a wardrobe neutral or accent color.
• Identify the hue, value, and intensity of each item.
• Work with a classmate and identify as above.

You – Clothing Color	Wardrobe Neutral	Accent Color	Hue (Warm/Cool)	Value (Light/Medium/Dark)	Intensity (Bright/Medium/Dull)

Classmate – Clothing Color	Wardrobe Neutral	Accent Color	Hue (Warm/Cool)	Value (Light/Medium/Dark)	Intensity (Bright/Medium/Dull)

Exercise 5–2   Color Preference

Name_____

Look in your closet, selecting five to ten favorite pieces of clothing, and five to ten less favorite pieces of clothing.

- In the appropriate section — favorite/less favorite — identify the clothing color.
- Place a checkmark in the appropriate column to identify the hue — warm or cool.
- Identify the value — light, medium, or dark.

- Identify the intensity — bright, medium, or dull.
- Identify which colors are a wardrobe neutral or accent color.
- Total the number of colors identified in each column.
- Analyze how these characteristics have influenced your preferences.

Clothing Color	Hue		Value			Intensity			Wardrobe Neutral	Accent Color
Favorite Clothes	Warm	Cool	Light	Medium	Dark	Bright	Medium	Dull		
TOTALS										

Clothing Color	Hue		Value			Intensity			Wardrobe Neutral	Accent Color
Less Favorite Clothes	Warm	Cool	Light	Medium	Dark	Bright	Medium	Dull		
TOTALS										

Conclusions:

Exercise 5–3   Local Store Experience

Look in a local clothing or fabric store for colors you have never worn before. In front of a full-length mirror, experience the look and effect of these colors on you.

Fabric Store Experience:

• To see how the color might look on you, drape it on your body to simulate a piece of clothing.
• Notice and note how the color makes you look and what it appears to communicate.

Clothing Store Experience:

• If possible, to see how the clothing will look on you, try it on.
• Notice and note how the garment looks and fits on your body.
• Notice and note what the colors appear to communicate.

Exercise 5–4   Hue Scale Sensitivity

Name _____

- Locate color chips for this exercise.
- Cut out the hue scales.
- Cut the individual color chips apart.
- Arrange color chips on the appropriate scale below.

Warm Hue ⟶ **Getting Cooler**

Cool Hue ⟶ **Getting Warmer**

Exercise 5–5 Value Scale Sensitivity

Name _____

- Locate color chips for this exercise.
- Cut out the value scales.
- Cut the individual color chips apart.
- Arrange color chips on the appropriate scale below.

Tint   *Shade*

Warm Hue
High Value – Light   ────────────────▶ **Getting Darker**

Tint   *Shade*

Cool Hue
High Value – Light   ────────────────▶ **Getting Darker**

• Locate color chips for this exercise.
• Cut out the intensity scales.
• Cut the individual color chips apart.
• Arrange color chips on the appropriate scale below.

Tone   *Pure Hue*

Warm Hue
Low Intensity – Dull ——————→ **Getting Brighter**

Tone   *Pure Hue*

Cool Hue
Low Intensity – Dull ——————→ **Getting Brighter**

Exercise 5–7   Wardrobe Neutral/Accent Color Recognition

Name_____

- Collect three pictures of clothing in wardrobe neutral colors.
- Mount and label.
- Identify the hue, value, and intensity of each garment.

- Collect three pictures of clothing in accent colors.
- Mount and label.
- Identify the hue, value, and intensity of the clothing.

Exercise 5–8 Preferred Color Characteristics

Name _____

Plot your preferred color characteristics or traits on a continuum between opposites.

Special Note: When it comes to black and white, western or American culture does not adhere to traditional oriental yin-yang symbolism.

Receding — Yin   **Advancing — Yang**

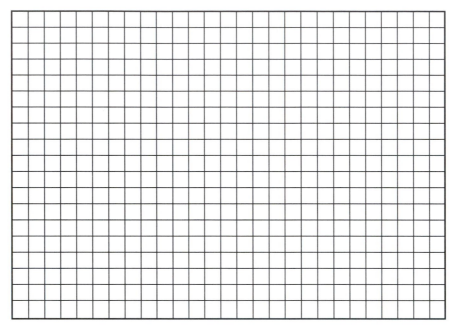

Cool	Warm
Dark shades	Light tints
Dull tones	Bright, intense
Close contrasts	Strong contrasts
Blue	Red
Green	Orange
Violet purple	Yellow
Pastels	Jewel colors
Blue-green	Yellow-green
Blue-violet	Yellow-orange
Red-violet	Red-orange

Exercise 5–9 Color Coordination

Name _____

Find pictures of clothing pieces, in colors you would like to combine into an outfit for yourself. Don't worry about lines, shapes, textures, or pattern now. Look for colors you believe will flatter you. Look for colors that combine harmoniously. Mount and identify accordingly. Write a paragraph explaining the reasons for your selections.

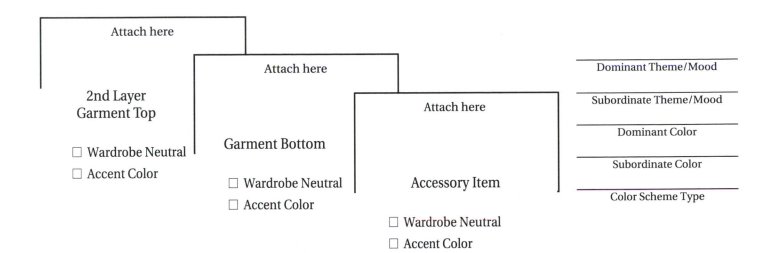

Attach here

2nd Layer
Garment Top

☐ Wardrobe Neutral
☐ Accent Color

Attach here

Garment Bottom

☐ Wardrobe Neutral
☐ Accent Color

Attach here

Accessory Item

☐ Wardrobe Neutral
☐ Accent Color

Dominant Theme/Mood

Subordinate Theme/Mood

Dominant Color

Subordinate Color

Color Scheme Type

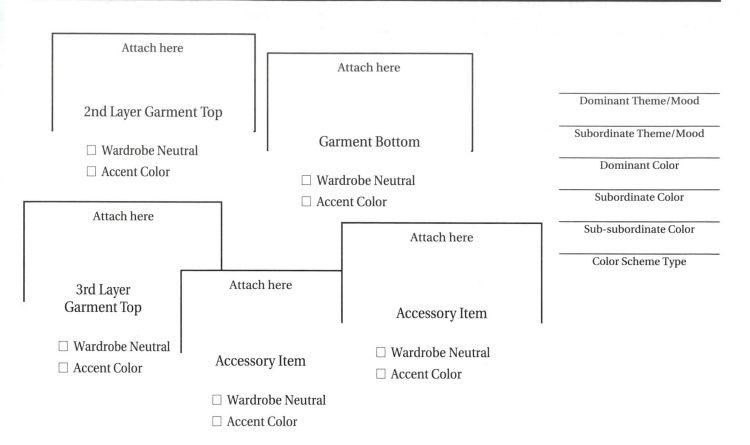

Attach here

2nd Layer Garment Top

☐ Wardrobe Neutral
☐ Accent Color

Attach here

Garment Bottom

☐ Wardrobe Neutral
☐ Accent Color

_____
Dominant Theme/Mood

_____
Subordinate Theme/Mood

_____
Dominant Color

_____
Subordinate Color

_____
Sub-subordinate Color

_____
Color Scheme Type

Attach here

3rd Layer
Garment Top

☐ Wardrobe Neutral
☐ Accent Color

Attach here

Accessory Item

☐ Wardrobe Neutral
☐ Accent Color

Attach here

Accessory Item

☐ Wardrobe Neutral
☐ Accent Color

Exercise 5–10 Personal Style Evaluation, Part 3

Name _____

Objectively identify factors that influence your personal style.

What is your racial origin?

☐ Caucasian   ☐ Oriental   ☐ Negroid

☐ Hispanic   ☐ East Indian   ☐ American Indian

☐ Other _____

What is your approximate hair color?

☐ Platinum blonde   ☐ Lt. flaxen blonde   ☐ Lt. golden blonde   ☐ Dk. ash blonde

☐ Lt. golden/honey blonde   ☐ Red blonde

☐ Soft red   ☐ Bright titian red   ☐ Dark rust-red   ☐ Dk. brick red

☐ Light brown   ☐ Medium brown   ☐ Dark brown   ☐ Auburn red-brown

☐ Blue-black   ☐ Umber-black   ☐ Creamy white   ☐ Blue-white

☐ Lt. creamy gray   ☐ Dk. golden gray   ☐ Silvery gray   ☐ Charcoal gray

☐ Salt and pepper

What is your approximate eye color?

☐ Lt.-Med. blue   ☐ Dark blue   ☐ Blue-gray   ☐ Gray

☐ Blue-green   ☐ Olive green   ☐ Hazel blue   ☐ Hazel green

☐ Violet   ☐ Amber-brown   ☐ Lt.-Med. brown   ☐ Dark brown

How do you describe your skin coloration?

☐ Fair/Porcelain   ☐ Pink   ☐ Rose-beige   ☐ Blue-black

☐ Ivory/Creamy   ☐ Peach   ☐ Golden-beige   ☐ Umber-black

☐ Ruddy-red   ☐ Copper/tanned   ☐ Golden-grown   ☐ Olive

☐ Pink warm cheek coloration — overtones   ☐ Peach warm cheek coloration — overtones

☐ Little to no warm cheek coloration

☐ Blue undertones   ☐ Green undertones   ☐ Violet undertones

☐ Freckles   ☐ White patches   ☐ Birthmark   ☐ Blemished

☐ Pitting   ☐ Scar   ☐ Dry   ☐ Oily

Which statement best describes your general personal coloring type?

- ☐ Light hair; light skin; dark brown eyes.
- ☐ Light hair; light skin; light to medium brown eyes.
- ☐ Light hair; light skin; blue, green, violet, or hazel eyes.
- ☐ Brown, red, or black hair; light skin; brown eyes.
- ☐ Brown, red, or black hair; light skin; blue, green, violet, or hazel eyes.
- ☐ Brown hair; dark skin; brown eyes.
- ☐ Gray or "salt and pepper" hair, light or dark skin, brown or gray eyes.
- ☐ Gray or "salt and pepper" hair; light or dark skin; blue, green, or violet eyes.
- ☐ White hair, light skin, and any eye color.
- ☐ White hair, dark skin, and any eye color.

Chapter

6

Fabric Selection and Coordination

Learning Objectives

Your goal in completing this chapter is to be able to:

- Differentiate between all-season fabrics and seasonal fabrics.
- Appreciate the value of classic patterns in a wardrobe.
- Explain the difference between fibers and fabric.
- Recognize a fiber's generic name and its trade name.
- Identify the individual characteristics of specific fibers.
- Describe how yarns are formed.
- Recognize common types of weaves.
- Understand and explain the functions of texture.
- Predict the effect of fiber, yarn, and fabric characteristics on garment performance, mood, and message.
- List fabric finishes that enhance garment performance.
- Discuss the purpose and advantages of layering clothes.
- Select clothing fabrics to meet your needs.
- Coordinate and combine two or more textures harmoniously.

Preview Main Points

1. Rely on all-season fabrics, light- to medium-weight woven and knit fabrics that you can wear at least three seasons or about nine months of the year.

2. Acquire seasonal clothing in lightweight fabrics for warm weather and heavyweight fabrics for cold weather gradually, as needed and as can be afforded.

3. Layering is the key to making all-season clothes work. Layering provides maximum versatility and insulating effect.

4. Knowing about fibers and fabrics, as an element design, will help you make wise consumer decisions about clothing selection, coordination, and care.

5. Select clothing fabrics with textural characteristics that meet your individual needs or purposes — appropriate for life-style, personal style, and clothing style.

6. Coordinate or combine two or more fabrics in a garment or an outfit to achieve greater variety, interest, and individuality.

1.

Rely on all–season fabrics, light– to medium–weight woven and knit fabrics that you can wear at least three seasons or about nine months of the year.

When you build the bulk of your wardrobe with all-season fabrics, decision making gets easier, your clothing dollar goes further, and fashion options increase. It keeps more clothes in use, rather than in storage.

All–Season Fabric Weight and Texture

Fabric weight and texture are keys to comfort and versatility. (See Table 6–1.)

- Medium-weight, medium-textured fabrics are the most comfortable and versatile for all-season wearability. There are no extremes of light or heavy weight, of smooth or rough textures.
- Medium-weight and medium-textured fabrics do not attract a lot of attention to themselves.
- Medium-weight and medium-textured fabrics make good background textures, easy to combine with either extremes of lighter or heavier, smoother or rougher fabric.
- Everyone can wear medium-weight and medium-textured fabrics attractively.
- People don't get quickly tired of medium-weight and medium-textured fabrics.

Choose all-season fabrics made from the natural fibers and from high-quality blends of natural and man-made fibers. Blends combine the good looks and absorbency of a natural fiber with the easy care properties of a man-made fiber, often at lower cost. High-quality blends contain no more than 35 percent man-made fibers.

Microfibers, a new breed of polyester, is improving the reputation of man-made fibers. (See Figure 6–1.) Microfibers are ultra-fine, finer than silk. They're strong, soft, lightweight, drapable, wrinkle resistant, and water-

Figure 6–1. This microfiber parka is luxuriously lightweight, soft, and warm. *(Courtesy Madeleine Direct)*

resistant. Looking much like silk or rayon, microfibers wash, dry, and wear like cotton. Blended or solo, give them a try.

How to Recognize Fabric Weight

Fabric weight is designated by ounces, ranging from less than one ounce per yard, to nineteen ounces or more per yard. Factors affecting weight include fiber type, yarn twist, fabric weave, and added finishes.

Think of feather weight in terms of thin, delicate lingerie and blouse weight fabric, weighing between one to three ounces.

Light weight compares to relatively thin blouse, skirt, and dress weight fabric, weighing four to six ounces.

Medium weight relates to shirt, skirt, dress, slack, and suit weight fabric, between six to ten ounces. (See Figure 6–2, page 148.) Straight skirts are generally slightly heavier to support their shape, than are gathered, draped, and flared skirts. Higher weights within this group, used in women's wear, are referred to as bottomweights.

Table 6–1 Fiber to Fabric

	Summer Weights Lightweight		All-Season Fabric Light to Medium Weight		Winter Season Heavyweight	

Cotton	Batiste
	Bengaline
	Calico
	Eyelet
	Dotted Swiss
	Feather cord
	Polished
	  cotton
	Seersucker
		Hopsacking
		Madras plaid
		Organdy
		Piqué
		Sateen
		Voile
			Broadcloth
			Chambray
			Chino
			Oxford cloth
			Gingham
			Denim
			Gabardine
			Jersey knits
			Percale
				Pinwale to
				  medium
				  wale
				  corduroy
				Sailcloth
				Terry cloth
				Velour
					Cord
					Knits
					Poplin
					Flannel
					Wide wale
					  corduroy
					Velveteen
					Quilted
					Tapestry
						Homespun
						Suedecloth

Linen	Crash Handkerchief Twill Tweed Washed or sueded linen "Linen" says it all		(Blends of cotton, linen, and silk with polyester, nylon, acetate, or acrylic create new options in all season fabrics.)		(Seldom worn)	
Silk	Broadcloth Chiffon Organza		Broadcloth Crepe Crepe de chine Charmeuse Faille Noil Jersey knits	Satin Shantung Tafetta Tweed Washed or sueded silk	Brocade Foulard Serge Surah Tapestry Velvet	

Wool			Challis
			Cool wool
			Crepe
			Lightweight
			  crepe de
			  chine
			Sheer flannel
			Lightweight
			  cashmere
				Tropical
				  weight
				  gabardine
				Lightweight
				  knits
					Cord
					Doubleknit
					Flannel
					Jersey
					Gabardine
					Serge
					Cashmere
					Melton
						Blanket
						  woolens
						Felt
						Fleece
						Heavy knits
						Tweed
						Velour

Rayon	Chiffon Georgette Organza		Brocade Broadcloth Challis Crepe Crepe de chine Damask	Faille Gabardine Jersey Microfibers Satin Tafetta		

Note: Man-made fibers simulate natural fibers or blend with them to create a corresponding range of fabrics.

Heavyweight fabric compares to pants, suits, outerwear jacket, and thick coat weights at twelve ounces and more. (See Figure 6–3.) Tailored garments require heavyweight fabric to support the shape and conceal seam allowances beneath tailored detailing.

In determining fabric weights, it is not likely you will have occasion to weigh your clothes. It is likely you already have a lot of experience to fall back on, based on the way your own clothing fabrics have performed for you in the past. Realistically, the simplest test is to pick up garments in similar style but different fabrics, compare, and begin to gather more experience. You will quickly get a "feel" for the various weights.

Figure 6–2. Cotton knits vary from light to heavy weight. Dress weight cotton knits are generally medium in weight. *(Courtesy Lands' End)*

Figure 6–3. Add heavyweight fabrics into your wardrobe after you have met your all-season needs. *(Courtesy Madeleine Direct)*

2.

Acquire seasonal clothing in lightweight fabrics for warmer weather and heavyweight fabrics for colder weather gradually, as needed and as can be afforded.

Lightweight fabrics well suited to warmer weather include:

batiste	voile
seersucker	calico
eyelet	all linen fabrics
microfiber broadcloth	

Heavyweight fabrics well suited to colder weather include:

cotton cord	wool flannel
wide-wale corduroy	gabardine
cotton flannel	melton
tapestry	felt
velvet	fleece
serge	tweed

3.

Layering is the key to making all–season clothes work. Layering provides maximum versatility and insulating effect.

Layering

Layer several pieces of clothing for added warmth as the temperature drops — indoors or out. Air trapped between a number of lightweight layers and heated by the body adds to the insulating effect of the clothes. (See Figure 6–4.) The insulating effect or value of clothing can be defined in terms of a unit of measurement called a **clo**. The design and fit of a garment, as well as the number of layers, contribute to **clo** value, potential warmth, and body comfort.

- Layer more for warmth in cold weather. Remove a layer or two during the day if necessary if the temperature rises. Wear less in warm weather.
- Because natural fibers absorb body moisture and allow it to evaporate, it is wise to wear them next to your skin for the most efficient effect.
- Each clothing layer to the outside must be cut or sized larger to fit easily over the others — sweaters, jackets, and coats in particular must be larger to fit over clothing beneath.

Figure 6–4. Layering is easy and effective when you have basic styles to work with. *(Courtesy All Week Long by Eddie Bauer; photographer Richard Warren)*

TIP

FROM THE PROS

Layering allows for creative dressing at its best! Layering brings style, versatility, and exciting interest to a wardrobe.

4.

Knowing about fibers and fabrics, as an element of design, will help you make wise consumer decisions about clothing selection, coordination, and care.

The following section of this chapter concentrates on fabric and texture, the actual medium — the tangible material — clothing is made of. It brings the lines and shapes to life!

Importance and Functions of Fabric and Texture

- Fabric and texture support the structural design of a garment.
- Texture stimulates the senses.
- Texture adds variety and interest to a garment, an outfit, and to your appearance.

- Texture keeps fabrics from looking alike and the observer from becoming bored.
- Fabric texture creates powerful illusions about the size and shape of the body.
- Texture communicates visual meaning, messages, or moods.

Types of Fibers

A **fiber** is the basic structure in fabric — a single, slender, hairlike structure that can be made into threads, yarns, and finally fabrics. There are two types of fibers: natural and man-made.

Natural fibers are made from natural sources — plants, trees, or animals. They include:

Plant Fibers	Animal Fibers
cotton	silk
flax (linen)	wool
ramie	hair fibers

Manmade fibers are made from synthetic sources — primarily or completely from chemicals. They include:

Cellulosic Fibers (derived from wood pulp)	Noncellulosic Fibers
rayon	acrylic
acetate	modacrylic
triacetate	metallic
	nylon
	olefin
	polyester
	spandex
	vinyon

TIP

FROM THE PROS

If in doubt about a fiber content, burn a small snip from a seam allowance or fabric yardage over your bathroom sink. Generally, if it leaves a soft ash and/or smells like burning hair, it is a natural fiber. If the residue is hard and brittle, it is synthetic. Acetate is easy to identify: It will dissolve completely in acetone.

Generic names for fibers refer to a general group of fibers similar in their composition. Cotton, wool, rayon, acrylic, and polyester are generic names. (See Tables 6–2 and 6-3, page 152.)

Trade names, or brand names, are given to manmade fibers produced by a particular manufacturer. A manufacturer registers its trade names with the U.S. Department of Patents and Trademarks. Protected by law, a trade name cannot be legally used for the same type of fiber produced by another manufacturer. Dacron, Lycra, and Orlon are trade names, used in combination with their generic names, such as Orlon® Acrylic and Lycra® Spandex. (See Table 6–3.)

Table 6–2 Natural Fibers — Characteristics, Use, and Types

Generic and Trade Names	Assets Advantages	Liabilities Disadvantages	Some Fabric Varieties	Some Principal Uses
COTTON	Light to heavyweight Versatile Very absorbent Quite strong when wet or dry Washable Can be bleached Dyes well No static build-up	Wrinkles easily unless treated Shrinks unless treated Subject to mildew Ignites readily unless treated Weakened by excess sunlight	Batiste Broadcloth Chambray Chino Corduroy Damask Denim Dotted Swiss Flannel Gabardine Lace Lawn Madras Muslin Organdy Oxford cloth Percale Pique Plisse Pongee Poplin Sailcloth Seersucker Terry Cloth Velour Velvet Velveteen Voile	All types of apparel and household yardage
LINEN *(May be called flax)*	Light, medium, to heavyweight May be soft or somewhat stiff Very absorbent Strong and durable Lint free Natural luster Resists moths and other insects	Shrinks unless treated Wrinkles unless treated Subject to mildew Expensive Ignites and burns readily unless treated Bright, strong colors may run during washing	Cambric Damask Drill cloth Hopsacking "Linen" usually says it all	Dresses Suits Jackets Slacks Toweling Table linens
RAMIE *(China grass or nettle)*	Medium weight Inexpensive Absorbent Lustrous Strong Dyes well Resists shrinking Resists mildew Imitates the look and feel of linen	Somewhat stiff Shrinks Wrinkles easily Ignites and burns readily unless treated	Ramie Often blended with cotton, rayon, or wool	Sweaters Jackets

Table 6–2 Natural Fibers *(continued)*

Generic and Trade Names	Assets Advantages	Liabilities Disadvantages	Some Fabric Varieties	Some Principal Uses

SILK	Lightweight
	Naturally lustrous
	Very luxurious
	Soft
	Drapes well
	Strong
	Absorbent
	Resilient
	Dyes well
	Resists mildew
	Burns slowly
		Expensive
		May water spot
		Damaged by
		  perspiration
		Damaged by excess
		  sunlight
		Colors may change
		  with age, strong
		  soap, or high
		  temperature
		Shrinks somewhat
		Damaged by high
		  heat
			Batiste de Soie
			Brocade
			Chiffon
			Crepe
			Damask
			Foulard
			Marquisette
			Matelassé
			Moiré
			Organza
			Pongee
			Shantung
			Taffeta
			Tulle
			Velvet
			Voile
				Blouses
				Shirts
				Dresses
				Jackets
				Scarves
				Ties
				Hosiery
				Linings
				Drapery
				Upholstery

WOOL	Light to heavyweight
	Absorbent
	Dyes well
	Resilient
	Has fine insulating
	  capacity
	Resists mildew
	Flame resistant
	
	Worsted
	  Long fibers
	  Smooth
	  Firm and durable
	  Strong
	  Holds shape well
	  Tailors well
	
	Woolen
	  Short fibers
	  Soft
	  Wrinkles hang out
	  Available in a
	    variety of weights
		Builds up static
		  electricity
		Attacked by moths
		Damaged by strong
		  soaps and
		  detergents
		Shrinks and felts
		  if washed, unless
		  treated
		Dries slowly
		
		Tends to pill
			Cavalry twill
			Challis
			Crepe
			Felt
			Flannel
			Foulard
			Gabardine
			Tweed
			Voile
			
			Used in nylon,
			polyester, and
			animal hair
			blends
				Apparel of all types
				Blouses
				Shirts
				Sweaters
				Coats and jackets
				Suits
				Socks
				Blankets
				Carpet
				Upholstery

Table 6–3 Man-made Fibers — Characteristics, Use, and Types

Generic and Trade Names	Assets Advantages	Liabilities Disadvantages	Some Fabric Varieties	Some Principal Uses
Cellulosic Fibers				
RAYON *Avicolor* *Avisco* *Avril* *Avron* *Avtex* *Bemberg* *Coloray* *Durvil* *Fiber 40* *Fibro* *Fortisan* *Jetspun* *Zanaire* *Zantrel*	Light to medium weight Highly absorbent Soft and comfortable May be shiny Good drapability Usually dyes well Versatile Economical	Weaker than most fabrics Weaker when wet Shrinks unless treated Damaged by excess sunlight Retains static electricity and clings Ignites readily Wrinkles	Barathea Batiste Bouclé Challis Chiffon Crepe Damask Foulard Faille Gabardine Lace Satin Microfiber fabrics	Lingerie Lining fabrics Apparel of all types Drapery Upholstery Used in cotton and polyester blends Adds luster to cotton
ACETATE *Acele* *Airloft* *Avisco* *Celaperm* *Celebrate* *Chromspun* *Estron* *Loftura*	Lightweight Dries quickly Luxurious feel — silky Able to drape well or retain "crispness" Can be made in various lusters Economical/ inexpensive Moderately absorbent Dyes well Shrink resistant Resists wrinkles Resists moths and mildew Not *easily* damaged by sunlight	Weaker than most other fibers Weaker when wet Weakened by excess sunlight Builds up static electricity May water spot Melts under high heat	Brocade Crepe Double knit Faille Knitted jersey Lace Moiré Satin Taffeta Tricot	Dresses Blouses Knitted sportswear Foundation garments Lingerie Draperies Lining fabrics Sleepwear Drapery Upholstery Quilted products Used in many cotton blends to add smooth touch and more luxurious look
TRIACETATE *Arnel*	Lightweight (A refinement of acetate) Resists shrinkage, wrinkling, and fading Easy care Good pleat retention	May water spot	Faille Flannel Jersey Sharkskin Taffeta Textured knits Tricot Used in blends	Lingerie Sportswear Jersey dresses Pleated garments Sleepwear Linings

Table 6–3 Man-made Fibers (*continued*)

Generic and Trade Names	Assets Advantages	Liabilities Disadvantages	Some Fabric Varieties	Some Principal Uses
Noncellulosic Fibers				
ACRYLIC *Acrilan* *Bi-Loft* *Creslan* *Fi-lana* *Orlon* *Pa-Qel* *Remember* *So-lara* *Zefran* *Zefkrome*	Lightweight Soft, slight, sheen Can be made to be light, and fluffy, similar to wool Generally retains shape Resilient, resists wrinkles Dyes well Good abrasion resistance Dries quickly Resists mildew, moths, sunlight, and chemicals Not easily damaged by sunlight	Is weaker when wet Nonabsorbent Fabric may "pill" Builds up static electricity	Bouclé Double knit Face fabric in bonded fabrics Fleece fabrics Pile fabrics Woollike fabrics	Sweaters and other knitted garments Socks Sports clothes and skiwear Work clothes Blankets Draperies Carpets/upholstery Used in wool blends to add strength, crease resistance, and shrink resistance Added to cotton gives crease resistance, shrink resistance, and makes softer, faster drying, and requires less ironing
ANIDEX	Adds permanent stretch with excellent recovery Improves fit and comfort Resists sunlight Resists oil stains Resists gas fading	Resists bleach	Elasticized fabrics	Hosiery Foundation garments Lingerie Sportswear Skiwear
MODACRYLIC *Acrilan* *Dynel* *Elura* *Kanekalon* *Orlan* *Teklan*	Lightweight Luxurious feel Soft and warm Somewhat elastic yet resilient Flame resistant Dries quickly Lustrous Nonallergenic fur substitute Dyes well Resists mildew	Fibers soften when heated Nonabsorbent Retains static electricity	Fleece fabrics Knit-pile fabrics Assorted nonwoven fabrics Fake furs	Deep pile coats, trims, linings Blankets, carpets Fleece Fake furs Wigs and hairpieces

Table 6–3 Man-made Fibers *(continued)*

Generic and Trade Names	Assets Advantages	Liabilities Disadvantages	Some Fabric Varieties	Some Principal Uses
NYLON *Antron* *Blue "C"* *Cantrece* *Caprolan* *Celanese* *Crepeset* *Cumaloft* *Enka* *Enkalure* *Hydrofil* *Patina* *Qiana* *Ultron* *Zafran*	Light to medium weight Exceptionally strong Elastic Resists wrinkles Resists abrasion Resists shrinkage Smooth Dries quickly Dyes well Resilient/elastic Lustrous Easy care, washable Generally resists moths and mildew	Nonabsorbent White will turn gray with wash and wear Scavenger for color, may need to be washed separately Builds up static electricity Fades in sunlight May feel moist and clammy in warm, humid weather Damaged by heat	Jersey knits Lace Net Tulle Chiffon Voile Stretch fabrics Used in cotton and wool blends Microfiber fabrics	Lingerie Hosiery Foundation garments Evening wear Costumes Sweaters and knit shirts Slacks Dresses Jackets Ski and snow wear Curtains Bedspreads Carpet Drapery Upholstery Adds strength, pleat retention, spot resistance, shrink resistance to wool, rayon, cotton, or acetate and makes them faster drying and need less ironing
POLYESTER *Arlin* *Ceylon* *Dacron* *Encron* *Fortrel* *Golden Touch* *Kodel* *KodOfill* *Trevira* *Ultra Touch* *Vycron*	Strong Crisp and resilient Resists wrinkles Retains heatset pleats and creases Dyes well, colorfast Abrasion resistant Resists most chemicals, moths, mildew, sunlight, and perspiration Easy care, washable Various degrees of luster Dries quickly	Retains static electricity Fabric may "pill" Nonabsorbent May feel clammy and uncomfortable in warm, humid weather Heat shrinks with repeated washings and drying Knits stretch with repeated wearings Oil stains readily and holds the stain	Crepe Doubleknits Gabardine Jersey knits Pique Microfiber fabrics Used in cotton, rayon, and wool blends	Lining fabrics Apparel of all types, particularly knits Household goods Fiberfill Adds strength, crease resistance, and shrink resistance to cotton and wool
SPANDEX *Agilon* *Duraspun* *Lycra* *Spandelle* *Vyrene*	Lightweight Resists body oils Strong and durable Resists abrasion Supple Highly elastic Good stretch and recovery	Damaged by heat	Elasticized fabrics Nonrubber elastic fiber used in blends	Foundation garments Hosiery Swimwear Ski pants Athletic uniforms Stretch lace

Types of Thread or Yarn

A **thread or yarn** consists of a single fiber or several fibers spun or twisted into continuous strands for making into fabric. There are two main types of yarn. Type I yarns such as woolen are made from short, rough fibers. They are softer, fuzzier, and weaker. Type II yarns such as worsted are made from long, smooth fibers. They are firmer, smoother, and stronger.

Tightly twisted threads and yarns are firmer, crisper, stronger, heavier, and appear relatively duller. Fabrics made from them generally last longer. They may shrink. They may shed soil, but soil tends to show more readily. Crepe is a fabric made from tightly twisted yarns.

Loosely twisted threads and yarns are soft, weak, light, and appear relatively shiny. Fabrics made from them generally wear out faster. They may pill or become fuzzy on the surface. They tend to pick up soil more readily, but do not show the soil readily. Flannel is a fabric made from loosely twisted yarns.

How Fabric Is Formed

Fabric is another word for cloth. The two most common types of fabric are formed by weaving or knitting. **Woven fabrics** are made (fabricated) by interlacing two or more yarns, one over and under another, at right angles to each other. (See Table 6–4.) **Knitted fabrics** are made (fabricated) by interlooping one or more yarns together, into a series of interlocking loops. (See Table 6–5.)

Basic weaves include the plain weave, twill weave, satin weave, and pile weaves. (See Table 6–4.) **Basic knits** include weft knits and warp knits. (See Table 6–5.) **Tightly woven and tightly knitted fabrics** are generally stronger, firmer, heavier, and longer-lasting. Gabardine and serge are tightly woven fabrics. **Loosely woven and loosely knitted fabrics** are generally softer, weaker, lighter, snag more easily, and are not long-lasting. Flannel is a loosely woven fabric.

Fabrics can also be formed (fabricated) by crocheting, braiding, netting, quilting, bonding, laminating, and felting.

T I P
FROM THE PROS

Don't confuse fibers with fabrics when considering selection and use. Fashion advice often runs "linen, serge, gabardine, rayon and challis" all into the same reference. This is confusing to the many people who don't know that linen and rayon are fibers, while serge, gabardine and challis are fabrics — fabrications from fibers. Linen doesn't come in serge, gabardine, or challis fabric, but gabardine is a fabric that can be made of cotton, wool, or polyester fibers, and challis is a fabric commonly made of wool, rayon, or acetate fibers.

Types of Finishes

A fabric **finish** is any special treatment to a fabric that changes its characteristic texture or improves its performance — temporarily or permanently.

Finishes can create many specific surface effects by adding:

shine	glaze
crinkle	fuzzy nap
print	stripe
embossing	wavy moire pattern
smoothness	firmness
softness	
a broken in or "not quite new" look	

Finishes can make a fabric more:

absorbent	shrink-resistant
crease-resistant	wrinkle-resistant
stain-resistant	mildew-resistant
moth-resistant	anti-cling
water-repellent	waterproof
flame-retardent	

Texture

Texture refers to the surface character of the fabric — the look, feel, and hang or drape of the fabric. The fiber, yarn, weave, and finish combine to create a fabric's texture.

Textural characteristics range between extreme opposites, with words that describe those extremes. (See Figure 6–7.) A few sets include:

Figure 6–7. Lightweight, crisp fabric is necessary if fabric is intended to stand away from the body.

Table 6–4 Basic Weaves

Type of Weave	Method of Fabrication	Characteristic/Texture	Some Fabric Names
Plain Weave (*simplest weave*)	A crosswise *filling* yarn passes over and under a lengthwise *warp* yarn. Yarns may be woven tightly or loosely. No right or wrong sides to the fabric, unless finished or printed so. Ribbed and basket weaves are variations of the plain weave.	Widest range of textural characteristics Light to heavyweight Sheer to opaque Fragile to sturdy/strong Pliable to firm Smooth to rough Dull to shiny Fine to coarse	Broadcloth, Canvas, Challis, Chambray, Crepe, Duck, Dress linen, Gingham, Homespun, Monks cloth, Muslin, Organdy Oxford cloth, Percale, Pongee, Seersucker, Shantung, Taffeta, Voile
Twill Weave (*most durable weave*)	A crosswise *filling* yarn passes over and under one or more lengthwise *warp* yarns. In each successive row, the *filling* yarn passes under the *warp* yarn on the right or left of the previous *filling* yarn, creating a characteristic raised diagonal ridge or wale on the right side of the fabric.	Medium to heavyweight Firm Relatively tight or compact Strong and durable Visible diagonal lines	Calvary cord, Chino, Covert, Denim, Drill, Flannel, Foulard, Gabardine, Herringbone, Serge, Sharkskin Surah, Tweed, Whipcord
Satin Weave	Either a crosswise *filling* or a lengthwise *warp* yarn passes or "floats" over four to eight yarns at a time. The long floats are visible on the right side of the fabric, and snag easily. Dobby and Jacquard weaves are figured variations of the satin weave.	Generally shiny, lustrous surface Smooth Firm, yet pliable	*True satin weaves:* Satin Sateen *Figured weaves:* Brocade Damask Pique Tapestry

Table 6–4 Basic Weaves (*continued*)

Type of Weave	Method of Fabrication	Characteristic/Texture	Some Fabric Names
Pile Weave 	A third set of either crosswise *filling* or lengthwise *warp* yarns (pile yarns) are woven into the basic plain, twill, or satin weave, to form loops in the right side of the fabric. The loops may remain uncut or be cut. Pile can be woven in stripes or cut at different heights to create a sculptured effect. Cut or uncut, the pile yarns give fabric a third dimension.	Soft Thick Pliable Bulky Some luster or light reflection Smooth to ridged	*Cut Pile:* Chenille Corduroy Fake furs Plush Velour Velvet Velveteen *Uncut Pile:* Terry cloth Mohair Novelty fabrics

light — heavy
dull — shiny
sheer — opaque
smooth — rough
soft — hard
silky — scratchy

pliable — firm
fine — coarse
thin — thick
flat — bulky
delicate — sturdy
crisp — limp

Each fabric has its own unique combination of textural characteristics. They may be similar or they may contrast with each other. Change any textural characteristic, and you may change the impression or message the garment conveys. (See Table 6–6, page 159.)

For example, a skirt or dress can appear businesslike in a dull-surface wool or rayon gabardine. It can also look festive in shiny silk or silky-looking polyester.

For example, a cotton blazer can appear inexpensive and casual. The same style blazer in a plush wool flannel can look dressier and more expensive but invitingly approachable. Still the same style blazer, made up in linen, can appear more dressy, expensive, authoritative and reflect self-confidence — all because linen has some luster and is firmer, crisper, stiffer. A velvet blazer looks the most dressy, even luxurious, due to softness, depth, and delicate sheen.

Fabrics with interesting textural characteristics — such as crepe, crinkle-cloth, corduroy, and velvet — can add interest and enhance the most simple clothing styles or one-color outfit. (See Figure 6–8, page 162.) Top stitching or decorative trim can add even more textural interest, contrast, or variety. Attention is drawn to areas of textural contrast, so place the contrast only in areas you want to emphasize.

Fabrics with different characteristics can cause the same style garment to appear very different in the way it looks, hangs, and fits and in the illusions it creates about the figure.

For example, furry and fuzzy fabrics appear duller in color than do flat or smooth fabrics. This effect will influence visual weight added to a figure by furry or fuzzy texture.

For example, a flared, shirt-style dress may cling to your figure if made of jersey knit. The same style may add bulk and unnecessary weight and warmth if made of thick wool flannel. But the same shirt-style dress may look terrific in a sporty fine-wale corduroy. Tubular and angular styles require medium weight, firm fabrics that hold the shape of the garment. Thick, bulky, rough, and heavy fabrics conceal the body shape beneath, but they do increase visual size and weight.

Illusions in Fabric and Texture

An illusion is a false perception or interpretation of something we see — something that deceives our eye when we look at it. An illusion makes something look quite different than it really is. Regardless of the facts, and according to our mind's eye, we tend to believe the illusion. Fabrics can be manipulated, arranged, and layered to create illusions. (See Table 6–6.)

Table 6–5 Basic Knits

Type of Knit	Method of Fabrication	Characteristic/Texture	Some Fabric Names
Weft or Filling Knit	Made with only one yarn. Can be hand or machine knit. Stretch in both the lengthwise and crosswise direction. Plain, purl, rib knit and double knit variations of the weft knits. All except double knits run easily.	Light to heavyweight Flat to pebbled Can be sheer Soft Stable to stretchy Ribbed to cable ridges	Jersey
Warp Knits	Made with several sets of yarns placed side by side. The multiple yarns interlock. Machine knit. Tricots and raschel knits are variations of the warp knit. Usually resists runs.	Light to heavyweight Strong Soft Less stretch Lacy	Tricot Jersey
Pile Knits	A yarn or yarns are knitted into the basic knit to form extra, free-standing loops on the right side of the fabric. Loops may be cut or uncut.	Nubby to ridged Closed to open and lacy	Stretch terry cloth Stretch velour Stretch fleece

Table 6–6 General Perception of Fabrics

	Message/Function	Fabric Characteristics		Some Fabric Names	
Weather	To feel and appear cooler	Lightweight (tropical weight) Thin or sheer Flat Smooth	Absorbent Silky Loosely woven	Batiste Broadcloth Calico Cool wool Dimity Eyelet Featherweight challis	Gauze Gingham Microfiber broadcloth Seersucker Voile
	To feel and appear warmer	Medium to heavyweight Soft Thick Lofty Bulky	Good insulating properties Rough Tightly woven	Boiled wool Camel hair Cotton cord Wide-wale corduroy Fake furs Felt	Flannel Fleece Gabardine Melton Serge Tweed
Occasion/Activity	To feel and appear casual/informal (casual business)	Similar textures Light to heavyweight Soft Dull Opaque Rough	Durable Nubby Stretch knits	Burlap Cable knits Camel hair Canvas Chambray Corduroy Denim Flannel Knits Leather	Madras Pigskin Poplin Sailcloth Seersucker Suede Terry cloth Ticking Tweed Velour
	To feel and appear dress-business-like (formal business)	Similar textures Dull Opaque Firm Crisp to firm	Sturdy Fine, compact Smooth to semi-smooth	Broadcloth Cashmere Firm knit Doubleknit	Flannel Gabardine Serge
	To feel and appear dressy/formal	Contrasting textures Light to medium weight Dull to lustrous, shiny Translucent Transparent Metallic Smooth Silky	Airy Soft Sheer Fluid to crisp Clingy	Brocade Charmeuse Chiffon Crepe de chine Faille Georgette Lace Lamé Marquisette Moiré	Organdy Organza Peau de soie Satin Sateen Taffeta Velvet Velveteen Baronet satin Metallic

Table 6–6 General Perception of Fabrics *(continued)*

	Message/Function	Fabric Characteristics		Some Fabric Names	
Values	To save time	Easy care Wash and wear	Quick dry No iron	Knits Crepe Silk noil	Permanent press finishes Crinkle cloth
	To appear beautiful	Silky Lustrous	Supple Soft	Brocade Challis	Satin Charmeuse
	To impress others	Expensive Special care	Luxurious	Cashmere Crash Suede	Tapestry Satin
	To be comfortable	Soft Smooth	Absorbent	Knits Velour Suedecloth	Corduroy Camel hair
	To save money	Low cost Durable Versatile	Readily available Wash and wear	Denim Chambray Knits Chino	Twill Gingham Gabardine Broadcloth

Personality	To feel and appear refined, ingenue/romantic/ feminine	Similar textures
		Light to medium
		    weight
		Soft
		Thin
		Delicate
		Smooth
		Fluid, flowing
			Transparent to
			    opaque
			Dull to shiny
			Filmy
			Drapable
				Angora
				Batiste
				Cashmere
				Challis
				Chiffon
				Dimity
				Dotted Swiss
				Eyelet
				Challis
				Chintz
				Crepe
					Georgette
					Lace
					Mohair
					Napped wools
					Organdy
					Organza
					Patent leather
					Suede
					Tulle
					Velvet
					Voile

	To feel and appear gamin/sportive/tailored	Medium to
		    heavyweight
		Pliable to firm
		Durable
		Smooth to rough
		Ribbed, cabled,
		    nubby
		Bulky
		Coarse
		Uneven
		Opaque
			Duller
			Lofty
			Stretch knits
				Boiled wool
				Boucle
				Cable knits
				Camel hair
				Canvas
				Chambray
				Corduroy
				Crinkle cloth
				Crocheted lace
				Denim
				Double knits
				Flannel
				Gauge
				Hopsacking
				Leather
				Linenlike
					Gabardine
					Oxford cloth
					Pique
					Raw silk
					Ribbed knits
					Seersucker
					Shantung
					Suede
					Suedecloth
					Sweatshirting
					Tussah
					Tweed
					Twill
					Velveteen
					Whipcord
					Popcorn knits

	To feel and appear dramatic/exotic	Contrasting textures Dull to shiny Opaque Glittery Hard Stiff	Smooth to rough Firm Clingy	Antique satin Brocade Crushed velvet Faille Fur Gabardine Jersey Linen Lamé	Leather Metallics Raw silk Satin Serge Sharkskin Taffeta Tissue suede
	To feel and appear mature, serious, somber, classic	Similar textures Dull Opaque Firm Crisp to firm	Sturdy Fine, compact Smooth to semi- smooth	Broadcloth Cashmere Firm knit Double knit	Flannel Gabardine Serge

Table 6–6 General Perception of Fabrics (*continued*)

	Message/Function	Fabric Characteristics		Some Fabric Names	
Figure/Body Build	To maintain or decrease attention and apparent size — to appear taller and slimmer	Light to medium weight Dull Opaque Thin Flat	Flat, smooth Firm Hard finish	Batiste Broadcloth Chino Crepe Denim Gabardine	
	To increase attention and apparent size — to appear shorter and heavier	Heavier weight Shiny, satiny Transparent Soft Thick Bulky Rough and flimsy Limp to crisp, stiff Lacy Sheer	Loopy Shaggy Furry Fuzzy Clingy Stretchy Tweedy Napped Nubby Bonded	Bulky knits Chintz Fake fur Flannel Homespun Organdy Quilted fabrics Satin Seersucker	Taffeta Tweed Velour Velvet Medium wale corduroy Widewale corduroy
Facial Features	Can drain and dull color Emphasize facial blemishes by contrast	Flat Smooth Shiny Light reflecting		Satin Tafetta	
	Emphasize facial blemishes by repetition	Nubby Bumpy		Shantung Bengaline Tweed	Waffle cloth Seersucker Antique satin
	Can add color	Dull Muted Light absorbing Nubby Rough		Flannel Corduroy Silk noil Velvet Linen	
Garment Style	Fabric holds the shape well, including bonded knit Few seams — straight tubular, tailored, A-line	Light to heavyweight Firm to stiff Crisp Thicker		Brocade Heavy linen Heavy gabardine Kid leather Organdy	Serge Sailcloth Ottoman Heavy slipper satin Taffeta
	Moderate drape Some gathers and folds	Medium weight Medium body Medium thickness Somewhat pliable		Cotton jersey Challis Lamé Lightweight gabardine Lightweight linen	Wave flannel Lightweight wool crepe Velvet Velveteen Wool jersey
	Fabric folds easily, many folds and gathers, and drapes well Falls loosely, flows gracefully Many seams, curved	Light to medium weight Fluid, very pliable Thinner Flat Soft		Batiste Broadcloth Chiffon Chiffon velvet	Silk crepe Georgette Silk jersey Voile

Figure 6–8. The fluffy texture of this sweater adds interest to the monochromatic outfit. *(Courtesy Madeleine Direct)*

Figure 6–9. A thick, heavy, fur collar demands a tall figure to carry it off without becoming overwhelmed. *(Courtesy Madeleine Direct)*

A general goal in using clothing as a resource is to select and arrange fabrics and textures in ways that enhance the body — in ways that make the figure appear more nearly ideal. Fabrics can be used in ways that emphasize the most attractive lines and shapes of the body, and camouflage or counter those body lines and shapes you consider less attractive, in effect minimizing or eliminating them.

Fabric and the Principles of Design

Select fabric textures that are proportionally in scale with your figure. (See Figure 6–9.)

Thick, bulky, heavy fabrics on a small figure will overpower the person because of the extreme contrast in size and weight. Moderation is the guideword.

Textures can be used to divert attention away from a particular figure variation and toward a more flattering area of emphasis.

For example, a small amount of smooth, shiny fabric can be used as piping on a bodice neckline or yoke to draw attention away from prominent hip bones, "knock" knees, or long arms.

Layering your clothing works wonders to camouflage and visually balance an asymmetrical figure. Not only do the layers smooth out the figure, but attention goes to the texture rather than to the body. Again, clothing is dominant and the body subordinate.

> **T I P**
> ☞
> **F R O M   T H E   P R O S**
>
> Don't forget that because all of the elements of design are interrelated, **the ultimate effect of any texture is influenced by the other elements** of design — the lines, shapes, colors, and patterns in the clothes. This influence makes many "fashion rules" unreliable. The rule appears to work in one outfit, but not in another because the lines, colors, patterns, or the combination of clothes causes the effect to be different than expected.

5.

Select clothing fabrics with textural characteristics that meet your individual needs or purposes — appropriate for life-style, personal style, and clothing style.

- Choose fabrics with textural characteristics appropriate for the environment and the weather or season of the year.
- Choose fabrics with characteristics appropriate for the mood, occasion, or activity. (See Figure 6–10.)
- Choose fabrics with textural characteristics that reflect the values of the wearer — what she or he believes to be valuable or important.
- Choose fabrics with textural characteristics that are compatible with, or that reflect, the wearer's personality. (See Figure 6–11.)
- Choose fabrics with textural characteristics that flatter the figure.

Query Box

Fabric is like a second skin.
Which fabrics would you like to try?
Which would work for you?

silk broadcloth	cotton knit
wool crepe	polyester gabardine
cotton corduroy	wool flannel
linen	orlon fleece
rayon challis	silk chiffon
cotton gabardine	cotton-poly oxford cloth
wool tweed	suede
acetate faille	cotton chambray
nylon knit	silk taffeta
cotton seersucker	cool wool
camel hair	cotton velour

Figure 6–10. A soft, warm, quilted fabric, highlighted with metallic threads, sets the moods for luxurious lounging on a mid-winter evening. *(Courtesy Madeleine Direct)*

While you look for fabrics in weights and textures that lend themselves to the style of the garment, you must also consider their effect on the figure — in terms of your purpose and goals.

You can expect firm, stiff, taut fabrics to repeat and reinforce the angularity of the body (and the apparent

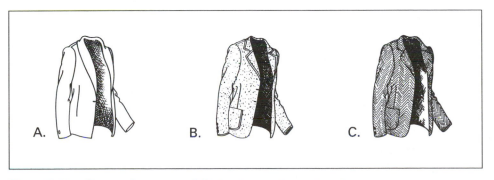

Figure 6–11. Texture determines differing degrees in sportive character.

assertiveness of the person). Soft, pliable, draped, fluid fabrics, however, counter body angularity, adding graceful softness to fill out the figure and create a few desirable curves.

Predictably, soft, pliable, draped, fluid fabrics repeat and reinforce body curves, may cling to the body, and focus attention on the body. On the other hand, firm, taut fabrics cut with straight lines counter body roundness and firm up body contours, causing the figure to appear slimmer (and more straight-forward or assertive).

TIP
FROM THE PROS

To determine the potential effects of a fabric or texture on your figure, try a "fit and fall test." Before buying fabric, stand about five to eight feet in front of a full-length mirror. Drape the fabric over your body in the same line and amount as the finished garment might drape or fall. Evaluate the visual effect on your figure. Before purchasing a garment, try it on and proceed with the "blink test."

Figure 6–12. Soft, pliable fabric is ideal for a draped design. Attention goes to the fold lines. *(Courtesy Madeleine Direct)*

- Choose fabrics with textural characteristics that flatter the face.

Fabric texture relates directly to facial skin texture and hair texture.

For example, rough textured fabric worn near the face can repeat and emphasize a rough skin condition or scarring. Slightly smoother texture might be a better choice. Curly hair, paired with a curly mohair sweater or jacket, can be a matter of too many curls, as both fight for attention. Set off your curls with smoother fabric in the clothes. (More on this situation under Dominant and Subordinate Textures later in this chapter.)

- Choose fabrics with textural characteristics that look, feel, and hang appropriately for the style of the garment. (See Figure 6–12.)
- Choose fabrics that will fit in well and coordinate with the existing wardrobe.

If you are unsure about the appropriateness or effect of the fabrics you wear and the image you project, study Table 6–6. As you discover pictures of fabrics that interest you, add them to your style file for future reminders.

6.

Coordinate or combine two or more fabric textures in a garment or an outfit to achieve greater variety, interest, and individuality.

Harmony of Mood and Occasion

To appear harmonious, **combine two or more textures in terms of the mood, occasion, personality traits, and values you want to communicate.** Textures may be similar to or may contrast with each other.

Similar textures are relatively easy to combine. Smooth textures tend to appear controlled, formal, cool, and aloof. You can combine smooth textures with smooth textures and achieve a harmonious mix of textures. The end, however, can be too repetitious — everything can look the same to the point of appearing monotonous or boring.

Contrast in textures can be more interesting, effective, and appealing, communicating subtle differences of mood, occasion, and personality.

For example, tulle, satin, and sequins are associated with dressy, festive, or glamorous occasions, yet the difference in their surface textures adds interest to the whole outfit. The same is true in the combination of denim, flannel, and cowhide, with silver buttons and belt buckle. All textures work together as they communicate dress for the casual, rugged, western outdoors.

Law of Areas

In combining textures, your goal is to achieve an interesting balance between smooth/shiny and rough/dull — between repetition and contrast. This usually requires uneven amounts of fabric texture and the law of areas. (See Figure 6–13.)

The **law of proportional areas** asserts that a small amount or area of advancing texture can balance a large amount or area of receding textures.

For example, a small amount of bright and shiny sequins on a shiny satin bodice is balanced by a large amount of dull-surface tulle making up the long, full, bouffant evening gown.

This flexible and creative way of dressing opens up the possibilities for greater individuality.

A Style of Your Own

Depending on the person wearing them, certain fabrics may be too firm, stiff, and severe, or too limp and lifeless in comparison to the person and his or her preferences. The person may feel psychologically uncomfortable in the clothing, and observers may notice this.

For example, a suit of corduroy may be too bulky for the woman who prefers lightweight, flat, smooth fabrics. A costume fabric called "eyelash," with stiff-standing, lash-like plastic hairs, may conflict with the personality of a generally reserved and refined woman, causing her to feel and/or appear uncomfortably overdone, frivolous, and silly.

So experiment a little and discover which fabrics are most in harmony with you, the places you go, and what you do there. As you experiment, you may discover fabrics you like so much that they become part of your personal style, something that is uniquely you. (See Table 6–7.)

Figure 6–13. A small amount of metallic contrasts marvelously with sumptuous angora. Dark/light value contrast adds to the dramatic effect.

Table 6–7 Image Makers and Breakers in Fabric

Image Makers In Fabric	Image Breakers In Fabric
• Interesting and harmonious mix of varied textured fabrics	• Monochromatic mix of flat fabrics or conflicting mix of textured fabrics
• Opaque, solid fabrics	• Mesh, fishnet, or transparent fabrics on all but "costume" occasions
• Quality weave or knit	• Poor quality weave or knit
• Fabrics that retain their shape	• Saggy, baggy, or limp fabrics that lose their shape
• Fabrics that retain original texture	• Snagged or "pilled" fabric surface
• Fabrics that flow over the figure without clinging — or worn with noncling slip	• Clingy fabric

Warm Up to Cooler Weather

It's cold in the morning and hot in the afternoon. It's warm one day and cool to cold the next. It's time to layer your clothes. Layering is also the answer to dressing for an under- or over-heated office.

For all-season wearability, separates, in basic, classic styles are the most versatile clothes year-round. Trendy, fad items made up in all-season fabrics allow you more wearing before the item becomes outdated. Consider the following examples of all-season dressing:

A classic cotton polo shirt can go it alone in warm weather or be worn layered under another shirt, sweater, or jacket in cool weather. Layer all four when it gets downright frigid. For dressier looks, layer over a silk blouse when it's cool and let it shine on its own when the air is warm.

Corduroy shirts can double as jackets. Tailored sport shirts with long sleeves are more versatile than those with short sleeves. You can roll up the sleeves when the temperature rises or slip one on over a cotton-knit turtleneck when it drops. Top it all with a sweater or a sporty down vest for still more warmth.

Tunics and vests in all their varieties add warmth as well as interest to your wardrobe. Consider cotton, silk, or wool knit sweater vests, woven cloth vests, and suede or leather vests in cardigan or pullover styles.

Unlined cardigan jackets in longer lengths work well in summer or winter. Cardigan sweaters are indispensable and come in silk, cotton, rayon, wool, or cotton/silk, wool/silk blends. Wear a cardigan tucked in. Wear it belted over a skirt or slacks. Wear it loose-hanging like a jacket layered over a blouse or dress. Toss it over your shoulders for an easy evening wrap. A cardigan is a warm yet fresh looking alternative to a blazer in early spring.

A lightweight knit suit can be comfortable worn alone in summer; it works well with a short-sleeve blouse in fall and spring, but will carry you through the winter paired with a long-sleeved shirt or blouse.

In the cool of a spring or fall morning, you can layer a cotton sweater under the jacket of a lightweight suit. Remove the sweater and leave it in the office before you go to lunch. If it's still warm outdoors when time to go home, tie the sweater around your shoulders and carry the jacket. For grayer days, choose a lightweight classic raincoat with zip-out lining to give you the option of added warmth.

Enjoy comfortable year-round wear from a cotton/poly broadcloth shirt and gabardine skirt. They go it alone in summer paired with canvas espadrille shoes. During spring and fall, top them with an unlined, raw silk, cardigan jacket and switch to leather pumps.

Come winter, layer a heavier, wool knit sweater vest over the shirt and wear the raw silk jacket over all. While the raw silk jacket is not actually heavier than the sweater vest, it appears to be heavier because it is very loosely styled with gathers that fall from a fitted yoke. Leather boots complete the winter outfit.

On cold winter days, or when traveling to a cold climate, consider adding an additional layer of lightweight cotton, silk, or wool underwear. It layers beautifully under the dressiest of clothes. Available in specialty lingerie and sporting goods stores, the underwear can also be ordered from catalog companies.

Dominant and Subordinate Textures

In all cases, one fabric must be dominant in any garment. Similarly, when combining two or more fabrics with different textures, **one texture must be dominant and all others must be subordinate by descending degrees** — one texture must appear most important and all others appear less important or attract less attention to themselves.

Rough textures seem relaxed, casual, warm, and friendly. However, one must be careful combining rough with rough. Two equally rough textures can compete for attention — too much repetition of the same degree of roughness, hence, competition.

For example, a rough raw silk and a rough silk tweed both have surfaces with nubby slubs on the surfaces of the fabrics, in about the same size. These slubs attract attention — all of them, everywhere at once. It's too much. It is better to have one of the fabrics smoother than the other.

A dull, rough texture combined with a very smooth and shiny texture can also be disturbing — too much contrast.

For example, silk paired with corduroy, or chiffon mixed with terry cloth, for example, are seldom combined in an outfit because the contrast in weight, surface texture, and mood are too different — again, too much contrast.

A very rough texture, combined with a slightly rough texture and still another slightly smooth texture is usually harmonious because the rough texture is dominant and all others are subordinate by descending degrees. The rough texture attracts the most attention, and each of the others attracts less.

For example, and for this reason, medium-textured fabrics are the most versatile — they are more easily combined than are extremely smooth or extremely rough-textured fabrics. A medium-textured flannel suit pairs easily with a smooth silk blouse and a nubby sweater knit vest.

For example, wearing a string of shiny pearls on a smooth satin blouse, topped with a soft, fuzzy angora sweater and paired with suede trousers, is an example of combining different textures we associate with a similarly feminine, dressy mood, unexpectedly offset with sportive suede. The dominant texture is the fuzzy angora sweater. The texture in the trousers claims less attention, the blouse claims still less attention, and the necklace claims even less than the blouse. It's all a matter of degree.

The way you layer a combination of clothing textures determines their all-season wearability, comfort, and attractiveness. A combination of textures generally appears more harmonious when each layer to the outside is slightly heavier in actual weight — or appears to be heavier due to fuller styling — than the layer underneath.

For example, first layer clothing, underwear, is generally the most lightweight. Second layer clothing generally includes a slightly heavier shirt, blouse, or tunic, and slacks or skirt, possibly a dress instead. Third layer clothing consists of sweaters, vests, jackets, and coats — each slightly heavier in weight. Use them much like accessories to change the looks of second layer clothes. A tunic, jumper, or dress becomes a third layer when worn over a shirt or blouse. Fourth layer clothes can include a sweater over a vest, a jacket over a sweater or a coat over a jacket. Obviously, you can build to five or more layers if the shirt, blouse, vest, sweater, jacket, and coat increase slightly in size and in actual or visual weight.

Achieving harmony between fabric weight at the hem and the weight of shoes, both visual and actual, causes difficulty for many women. Wearing a skirt or pants made of lightweight fabric generally calls for visually lighter weight shoes. Thinner soles and higher heels appear most compatible. Wearing a skirt or pants made of heavier fabric with heavier shoes creates visual harmony. Thicker soles and/or lower heels appear to balance heavier fabric at the hem. Boots often make an attractive choice.

Fabrics make the difference between clothes you love to wear and clothes that hang unloved and unworn in your closet. The logic of investing in an all-season wardrobe is gaining increased attention. It makes sense. Knowing about fibers, yarns, weaves, and fabrics will help you make wise clothing decisions — leading to better performance, longer wear-life, and increased satisfaction with your wardrobe.

Review Main Points

Natural and man-made fibers are made into yarns and then into fabrics. Fibers, yarns, and weaves determine the texture of the fabric. Build the bulk of your wardrobe around medium-weight, medium-textured, all-season fabrics. Gradually acquire needed seasonal clothing in lightweight or heavyweight fabrics. Layer your clothing to get the most versatility and insulating effect. Because fabric textures interact with one another and with the wearer, they need to be compatible with one another and with the wearer, the time, and the place. In combining, one fabric must be dominant and any other subordinate. Combining fabric textures in interesting and harmonious ways is one of the keys to putting together an interesting, versatile, and fashionable wardrobe.

Review Questions

1. All-season fabrics can be worn about _____ months of the year.

2. Fabric _____ is a key to comfort and wardrobe versatility.

3. _____, _____, and _____ are examples of medium-weight, all-season fabrics.

4. Define a fiber. _____
   _____.
   _____

5. Name two types of fibers. _____ and _____.

6. Antron® is the _____ name of a fiber.

7. You can expect clothes made from tightly twisted yarns to last _____ than clothes made from loosely twisted yarns.

8. What is the difference between fiber and fabric? _____
   _____
   _____

9. Which of the following names does not belong in the group? Circle the word.
   crepe   denim   rayon   jersey

10. List four finishes that will change the performance of a fabric.

_____   _____

_____   _____

11. When we speak of how a fabric appears or feels, we are referring to its

_____.

12. Match the following fabrics to the appropriate textural characteristic.

_____ velveteen   a. rough

_____ linen   b. firm

_____ tweed   c. crisp

_____ gabardine   d. soft

13. Which of the following fabrics does not belong in the group? Circle the word.

georgette   satin   charmeuse   chambray

14. When combining two or more fabrics with different textures, one fabric must

be _____ and all others must be _____.

15. When layering clothing, each layer to the outside must be slightly larger and

_____ than the layer beneath.

Discussion Questions

#1 Share an experience in which you may have felt physically miserable in your clothing — too hot, too cold, damp, itchy. What could you have done to avoid such an experience? What would have been a better choice of fiber or fabric?

Notes: _____

_____

_____

#2 Discuss feelings and behavior, experienced or expected, when wearing sweat-shirting, T-shirting, and denim, as compared to wearing a silky fabric, satin, taffeta, or velvet.

Notes: _____

_____

_____

#3 Look back at Table 6–6. If you were hired for a summer job at an ice cream parlor (or a hospital), what fabrics would lend themselves to work clothes? Why? What fabrics would be appropriate for a job interview at an investment office? Why?

Notes: _____

_____

_____

Exercise 6–1   Fiber and Fabric Recognition

Name _____

Look at what you are wearing.
• Identify the fibers in each item of clothing.
• Identify the type of weave or knit.
• Identify the fabric name.
• Work with a neighboring classmate and identify as above.

You – Clothing Item	Fiber	Weave or Knit	Fabric Name

Classmate – Clothing Item	Fiber	Weave or Knit	Fabric Name

Exercise 6–2   Fiber and Fabric Preference

Name _____

Look in your closet, selecting five to ten favorite pieces of clothing, and five to ten less favorite pieces of clothing.

- In the appropriate section — favorite/less favorite — identify clothing item and fiber content.
- Place a check mark in the appropriate column to identify fiber type.
- Identify fabric name.
- Place a check mark in the appropriate column to identify

- seasonal fabric type.
- Describe the fabric's characteristics.
- Total the number of fiber types and seasonal fabric types.
- Analyze how these characteristics have influenced your preferences.

	Clothing Item	Fiber Content	Natural	Man made	Blend	Fabric Name	Cold Weather	All-Season	Warm Weather	Characteristics
Favorite Clothes										
	TOTALS					TOTALS				
	Clothing Item	Fiber Content	Natural	Man made	Blend	Fabric Name	Cold Weather	All-Season	Warm Weather	Characteristics
Less Favorite Clothes										
	TOTALS					TOTALS				

Conclusions:

Exercise 6–3   Local Store Experience

Look in a local clothing or fabric store for fibers and fabrics you have never worn before. In front of a full-length mirror, experience the look and the feel of these fabrics and/or clothes.

• To see how the fabric might look on you, drape it on your body to simulate a piece of clothing.

• Notice and note how the fabric folds or gathers in your hands.

• Do the gathers fall softly down or stand away from your body?

• If possible, to see how the clothing will look on you, try it on.

• Notice and note how the garment hangs and feels on your body.

Summarize your experience and conclusions with ready-to-wear fabrics and yardage:

Exercise 6–4 Fiber and Fabric Recognition

Name _____

Find a fabric sample for each of the following categories. Mount and label accordingly.

Lightweight

Attach here

_____
Fiber Type

_____
Weave/Knit Type

_____
Fabric Name

Medium Weight

Attach here

_____
Fiber Type

_____
Weave/Knit Type

_____
Fabric Name

Heavyweight

Attach here

_____
Fiber Type

_____
Weave/Knit Type

_____
Fabric Name

Crisp

Attach here

_____
Fiber Type

_____
Weave/Knit Type

_____
Fabric Name

Soft-Pliable

Attach here

_____
Fiber Type

_____
Weave/Knit Type

_____
Fabric Name

Firm

Attach here

_____
Fiber Type

_____
Weave/Knit Type

_____
Fabric Name

Casual-Informal

Attach here

_____
Fiber Type

_____
Weave/Knit Type

_____
Fabric Name

Dress-Business

Attach here

_____
Fiber Type

_____
Weave/Knit Type

_____
Fabric Name

Dressy-Formal

Attach here

_____
Fiber Type

_____
Weave/Knit Type

_____
Fabric Name

Exercise 6–5　Fabric Coordination

Name _____

Find fabric samples or pictures of fabrics you would like to combine harmoniously in a warmer weather outfit, an all-season outfit, and a colder weather outfit. Mount and label accordingly. Write a paragraph explaining the reasons for your selections.

Warmer Weather

Attach here

1. Dominant Texture

_____
Fiber Type

_____
Weave/Knit Type

_____
Fabric Name

Attach here

2. Subordinate Texture

_____
Fiber Type

_____
Weave/Knit Type

_____
Fabric Name

Attach here

3. Sub-subordinate Texture

_____
Fiber Type

_____
Weave/Knit Type

_____
Fabric Name

All-Season

Attach here

1. Dominant Texture

_____
Fiber Type

_____
Weave/Knit Type

_____
Fabric Name

Attach here

2. Subordinate Texture

_____
Fiber Type

_____
Weave/Knit Type

_____
Fabric Name

Attach here

3. Sub-subordinate Texture

_____
Fiber Type

_____
Weave/Knit Type

_____
Fabric Name

Colder Weather

Attach here

1. Dominant Texture

_____
Fiber Type

_____
Weave/Knit Type

_____
Fabric Name

Attach here

2. Subordinate Texture

_____
Fiber Type

_____
Weave/Knit Type

_____
Fabric Name

Attach here

3. Sub-subordinate Texture

_____
Fiber Type

_____
Weave/Knit Type

_____
Fabric Name

Attach here

4. Sub-sub-subordinate Texture

_____
Fiber Type

_____
Weave/Knit Type

_____
Fabric Name

Preferred Fabric Traits and Textures

Name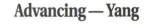

Plot your preferred fabric characteristics or traits on a continuum between opposites.

Receding — Yin   **Advancing — Yang**

Fluid, pliable	Firm, stiff
Lightweight	Heavyweight
Fine	Coarse
Flat, smooth	Rough, nubby
Soft	Hard
Thin	Thick
Shiny	Dull

Exercise 6–7 Writing to Learn about Fabrics

Name _____

Imagine you are writing a two-page article for a consumer fashion magazine or a newspaper.

- Choose a fashion fabric you want to write about — possibly a fabric you've never worn before.
- Research your topic. Sources include books, magazine and newspaper articles, and interviews with fashion professionals — in person or by telephone, and your own experience — past or new.
- Include information about typical fiber, method of fabrication, characteristics, illusory effects, uses, fashionability, cost, and care.

Chapter 7

Pattern Selection and Coordination

Learning Objectives

Your goal in completing this chapter is to be able to:

- Differentiate between classic patterns and trendy patterns.
- Appreciate the value of classic patterns in a wardrobe.
- Understand and explain the functions of patterns.
- Identify the sources of inspiration for patterns.
- Identify the types of motifs used in patterns.
- Describe the ways patterns are arranged on fabric.
- Explain how patterns are formed or introduced into fabric.
- Be aware of additional characteristics that influence a pattern design.
- Predict the effect of a particular pattern on garment performance, mood, and message, and on the figure.
- Recognize good and poor quality patterns.
- Select fabric patterns to meet your needs.
- Coordinate and combine two or more patterns harmoniously.

Preview Main Points

1. Rely on solid colors and classic patterns, in small to medium scale prints, stripes, and plaids.

2. Acquire an occasional trendy pattern for added interest, as needed and as is affordable.

3. Knowing about pattern as an element of design will help you make wise consumer decisions about clothing selection and coordination.

4. Select patterns that meet your individual needs or purposes — appropriate for your life-style, personal style, and for the fabric.

5. Coordinate or combine patterns in an outfit to achieve greater variety, interest, and individuality.

1.

Rely on solid colors and classic patterns, in small- to medium-scale prints, stripes, and plaids.

Plain, solid color fabrics provide a foundation for your wardrobe and combine easily with other solid colors, but don't stop there. You can count on classic patterns — in print, stripe, and plaid designs on clothing — to add the interest and variety needed to enliven what might otherwise become a dull wardrobe composed entirely of solid colors.

Classic Patterns

- Classic patterns are a key to flexibility, versatility, and individuality in a wardrobe.
- Classic patterns are always in good taste and do not detract from you.
- Classic patterns expand the range of moods and feelings reflected by your clothing — prints offer self-expression, fun, sophistication, and style.
- Classic patterns retain their fashionability, and therefore their wearability, for years.
- Virtually everyone can afford to buy classic patterns; style is not a matter of money.

This is not to suggest that you build a wardrobe consisting entirely of patterned fabrics. You'd lose all flexibility and get tired or frustrated with this approach faster than you would a wardrobe composed of all solids. Moderation makes good sense.

Plan to work with lots of solid-colored clothing pieces and a few terrific patterned pieces. It's easy to work with patterned fabrics when you choose patterns that include one or more colors from a cluster of clothes. Better yet, choose a wonderful pattern to inspire the color scheme for an entire cluster. There are thousands of wonderful patterns to choose from.

TIP

FROM THE PROS

Be on the lookout for patterns that you love, that feel like you could wear them forever, and that seem to reflect you well. In a sense, the difficulty of determining a color scheme is already done for you. The colors to be combined are already present in the pattern on the fabric. Make that pattern uniquely yours as you develop and refine your own personal style.

Query Box

Which of these classic patterns have you tried? Which might you like to try?

Scotch plaid	pin dots
Glen plaid	polka dots
windowpane plaid	coin dots
Glen check	pinstripes
houndstooth check	chalk stripes
tattersall check	herringbone
gingham check	tweed
paisley	foulard
medallion	calico florals

How to Recognize Classic Patterns

If the pattern looks familiar, and seems to be always available and in style, then it is most likely a classic pattern. (See Table 7–1.) Figures in the pattern are smaller in scale — small to medium, but not large. Classic patterns are more often rendered in wardrobe neutrals, allowing them to combine easily with a wide range of other clothing colors. Many classic patterns are traditional menswear patterns redefined and recolored suitably for women's fashions. Classic patterns are needed most by people who want to get many looks and years of service from a cluster of clothing — along with those employed in formal, conservative, or public, and service-oriented businesses — also by people in leadership positions.

2.

Acquire an occasional trendy pattern for added interest, as needed and as is affordable.

Like costume and trendy clothing styles, trendy patterns are extreme in some aspect of design, associated with specific occasions, or come and go quickly. (See Table 7–2.)

How to Recognize Trendy Patterns

A trendy pattern — print, stripe, or plaid — is usually:

- Distinctive in lines or shapes.
- Larger in scale.
- Bold in color — either bright, or in strong contrasts of warm and cool hues, light and dark values.
- Limiting in the places it can be worn appropriately or comfortably.

Table 7–1 Classic Patterns

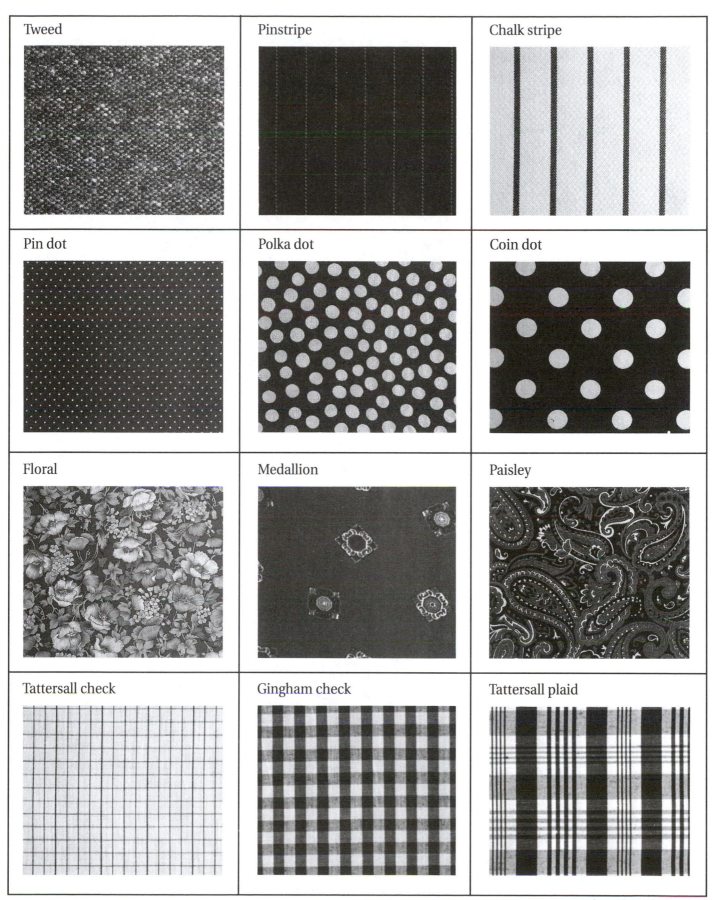

Tweed	Pinstripe	Chalk stripe
Pin dot	Polka dot	Coin dot
Floral	Medallion	Paisley
Tattersall check	Gingham check	Tattersall plaid

(Photos by Mike Nielson)

Table 7–2 Trendy Patterns

(Photos by Mike Nielson)

"Undulating piano keys in black, white, and chartreuse" adequately describes a bold and short-lived, trendy print. The latest cartoon character to sweep the country is bound to make a lot of people uncomfortable if emblazoned across their chests. Balloons two feet in diameter don't lend themselves to anybody's body. Such are the characteristics of a trendy pattern, some poorly designed from the outset.

TIP

FROM THE PROS

Trendy patterns are a wonderful vehicle for updating your wardrobe with minimal expense. One trendy printed garment or accessory can revitalize your entire basic cluster or wardrobe. It's fine to have one or a few, but not a whole closet full. Classic patterns are what build more workable wardrobes.

More trendy patterns can be included in wardrobes of people who work in creative businesses, such as art, music, theater, interior design, and fashion. More extreme patterns are often more acceptable for those with an active social calendar.

3.

Knowing about pattern as an element of design will help you make wise consumer decisions about clothing selection and coordination.

Technically speaking, pattern is not a separate element of design. Pattern is a combination of several design elements — lines and shapes in colors, arranged in or on textural material. Each element is totally interrelated when you look at a pattern design. Because patterns have their own visual effects, and because you can manipulate or change the character of a pattern and its effects, it seems appropriate to treat pattern as a specific element — to work with it and make it work for you.

Importance and Functions of Pattern

- Patterns add interest to plain surface fabrics, to simple styling, and to your entire wardrobe.
- Patterns help coordinate two or more solid colored items — "pulls" them together into a harmonious color scheme.

Table 7–3 Pattern Sources

Nature	Man-made	Combination

- Patterns help coordinate you with the clothing, as they repeat a color present in your personal coloring, making you part of the total color scheme.
- Patterns can create a point or area of emphasis.
- Patterns affect the body and the psyche — the way you think, feel, and act.
- Patterns camouflage and create powerful illusions about the size, shape, and weight of the body.
- Patterns provide lines, colors, and visual texture to distract attention away from the body.
- Patterns communicate visual meaning, messages, or moods.
- Your choice in patterns becomes a visible expression of personal style and individuality.

So Nice to Sew On

Some patterns can make sewing easy, such as an all-over print that does not require any matching or careful positioning. The pattern is the focus of the garment, allowing you to choose a simple design that is easy to sew. Intricate design details actually get lost in the pattern. There's no point going to a lot of work if they don't contribute to the design. The pattern draws attention to itself and obscures any sewing imperfections — great for the beginner, or the sewer who's in a hurry. Tackle more complicated patterns, including plaids, when you have more time and experience.

Sources of Inspiration

Patterns feature repeated shapes or figures in their design, called motifs. A single shape might be a flower, a fish, a flute, a pinstripe, or a polka dot. Designers get their ideas for motifs from the world around them — specifically from two sources: objects or occurrences in nature, and man-made objects or events. Any given pattern might contain motifs from one or a combination of both sources. (See Table 7–3.)

Nature is the most frequent source of design ideas. Flowers and leaves are most popular, due to their infinite variety and pleasing psychological associations. Small animals, birds, fish, and seashells follow in popularity. Less specific motifs include marbles, waves, clouds, and sunsets. Inspiration might come from a scent or flavor found in nature, leading to the creation of quite original motifs.

Man-made objects provide an endless variety of design motifs, some pleasing, some not so pleasing. Household items are popular subjects. Geometric motifs take shape from man-made objects. And again, creative ideas might spring from a man-made scent or flavor. Man-made symbols that represent an idea, an object (a teapot), a location (garden tools), an organization (Girl Scout logo), a holiday (Christmas trees), a cultural group (motorcycle insignia), or country (flags), provide additional inspiration for design motifs.

Types of Pattern Motifs

Designers interpret, render, or present their sources or objects of inspiration in four ways, identified as (1) realistic or naturalistic, (2) stylized, (3) geometric, or (4) abstract. Any given pattern might contain one or more motifs, interpreted in one or more ways. (See Table 7–4.)

Realistic or naturalistic patterns imitate or duplicate natural or man-made objects in a photographic manner — as they actually look. There is little imagination on the part of the designer. The clear reality of the motif is obvious and runs the risk of becoming monotonous. With every detail intact, the pattern is distracting. You tend to concentrate on the design, rather than the wearer.

For example, strawberries that look as if they are growing in a garden, toys that belong in the nursery, animal and reptile skins, and animals on the farm typify realistic patterns.

Stylized patterns are the designers' conventionalized impression or interpretation of natural or man-made objects. (See Figure 7–1.) They reflect imagination rather than imitation. The designer has creatively changed the shape, the color, or possibly the proportions. The artist has simplified the detail, flattened three dimensions to two, altered reality, and added something of his or her own, yet the objects are still recognizable.

For example, a paisley motif is a simplified, stylized leaf form. A fleur-de-lis is a French variation of a lily.

Geometric patterns are the result of imagination that conforms to the strict use of lines and recognized geometric shapes based on mathematical formulas and traditional woven fabrics. (See Figure 7–2, page 184.)

For example, stripes, checks, plaids, polka dots and circles, squares, rectangles, triangles, diamonds, chevrons, and stars fit in this category. Scallops, a line of connecting semi-circles, and African tribal prints also qualify.

Abstract patterns arise from the artist's imagination and appear as a blur or splashes of color and unrealistic, free-form, or flowing lines and shapes, with the possible suggestion of texture. (See Figure 7–3, page 184.) They do not represent anything natural or man-made. This type of pattern offers total freedom of expression, an option appealing to many contemporary designers. Less traditional or less familiar to most people, abstract patterns

Figure 7–1. Stylized flowers are the most popular type of motif. *(Courtesy All Week Long by Eddie Bauer; photographer David Martinez)*

can be strange and unacceptable to many. Such patterns are often impossible to match at seams.

Arrangement of Motifs on Fabric

Every pattern consists of motifs arranged in some way on the fabric. To be practical, the arrangement must have a place to start over, or begin again, both lengthwise and crosswise. The distance between the places where a pattern begins, and then begins again, is called a "repeat." Knowing what this distance is allows a fashion designer or home sewer to plan for enough fabric to make a garment. Patterns with large and bold motifs or large repeats take up more fabric. Thus they are more costly to produce and more difficult to position on the body. Smaller and more subtle motifs are less frustrating to work with in clothing.

Table 7–4 Types of Motifs

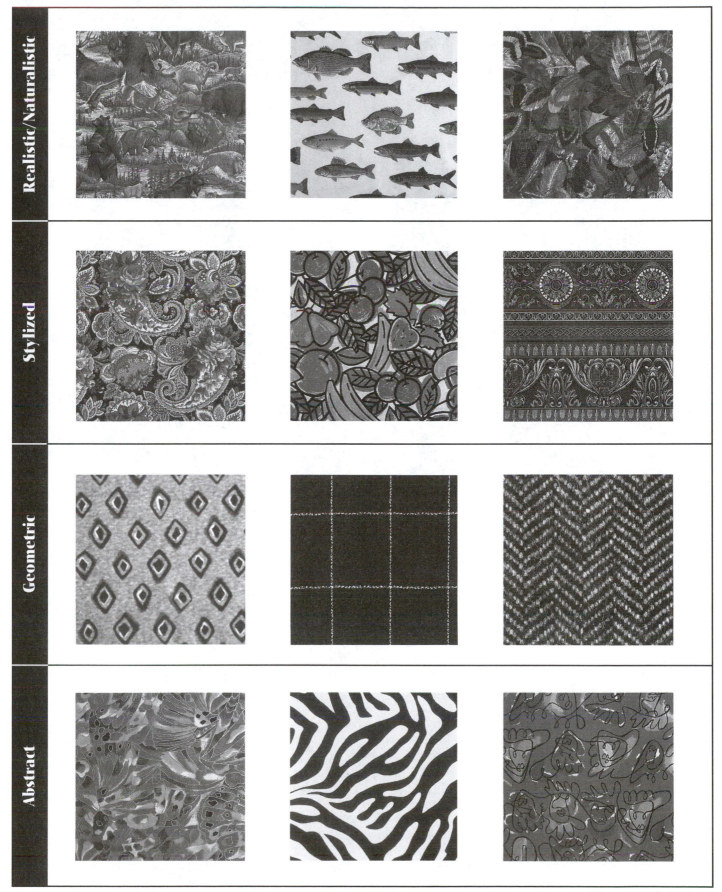

(*Photos by Mike Nielson*)

Figure 7–2. The process of knitting lends itself to the creation of geometric shapes. *(Courtesy Eddie Bauer; photographer G. Remington)*

Figure 7–3. The pattern on this wearable art piece places a stylized cat within abstract streaks and splashes of color. *(Courtesy Roberta Glidden)*

Typically, a motif can be arranged in at least nine different ways: (1) all-over arrangements, (2) four-way, (3) two-way, (4) one-way, (5) border, (6) panel, (7) scarf, (8) spaced or single, and (9) novelty arrangements. (See Table 7–5.)

All-over arrangements appear the same from any direction you look at them. They have a methodical, formal, regular rhythm, leading easily from one motif to another. Because they take up the least amount of fabric and require little to no matching, all-over patterns are the easiest, most common, and least costly to use.

Four-way arrangements appear the same from four directions, given a quarter or 90° turn. They include polka dots, gingham checks, and balanced checks or plaids — those with a design the same from all four sides. Rhythm is regular. With motifs arranged in rows, garment pattern pieces require matching on corresponding seams for a pleasing appearance. Matching can be done in either the lengthwise or crosswise direction, making it less difficult.

Two-way arrangements appear the same from only two directions, given a half or 180° turn. Seen from one end or the other, motifs are either stripes or arranged in stripes, and appear the same on each side of the stripes.

Geometric patterns in dots, checks, stripes, and plaids are often two-way. If motifs have an obvious top or bottom, such as people or trees, their logical position may alternate — one upright, one upside down — thus appearing correct from two directions.

One-way arrangements appear right-side-up from one direction only. Having a recognizable top and bottom, words, numbers, functional objects such as teapots, trees, and people are examples of one-way motifs. They are meant to be seen in their logical position on the body and not upside down. All clothing pieces must be positioned in the same direction on the fabric, making matching difficult. Unbalanced plaids and stripes are particularly difficult to match. Because matching takes careful planning, requires more fabric, and results in higher cost, one-way patterns are used less often.

Border arrangements, or border prints, appear right-side-up from only one selvage edge of the fabric. Dominant motifs in the pattern create a specific border along that edge. Subordinate motifs may create another, smaller or less important border along the opposite selvage edge, and may be scattered across the mid-section of the fabric. (See

Table 7–5 Pattern Arrangements

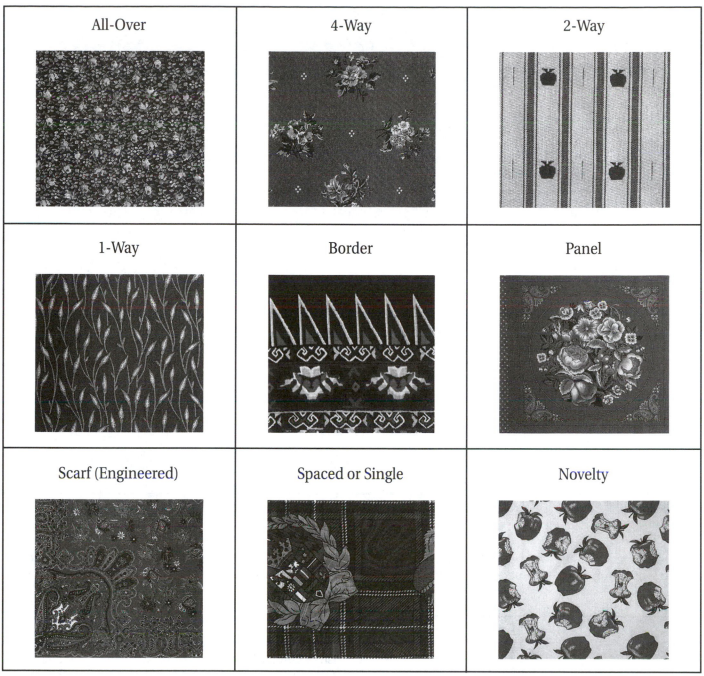

All-Over	4-Way	2-Way
1-Way	Border	Panel
Scarf (Engineered)	Spaced or Single	Novelty

(Photos by Mike Nielson)

Figure 7–4.) In clothing design, a border of appropriate width is traditionally placed along the hem edge of skirts, jackets, sleeves, and pockets, on collars and around armscyes or armholes. The border attracts attention to itself and to that area of the body. It reinforces the direction of the print — more often horizontal.

Panel arrangements have one direction only, and are large but narrow. They reinforce the vertical direction and are intended to be used in one length without repeating. Clothing design is often planned around the use of this type of print. Hand-painted designs on long, loose-fitting caftans and gowns are typical.

Scarf or bandanna arrangements form a square — small, medium, and large squares to fill the size of a scarf. The pattern's change in direction at the corners limits use yet allows creative placement in clothing design.

Spaced arrangements appear as single motifs widely spaced or separated from other motifs. (See Figure 7–5, page 187.) If there is a repeat, it is a large one. Spaced arrangements create a staccato, often spotty, rhythm. A dominant motif can be positioned to emphasize one spot or area of the garment and/or body.

Novelty arrangements follow no specific or repeating pattern (see apple motif in Table 7–3), but feature

Shoulder

Waist

Hip

Hip

Hem

Cuff/Collar

Figure 7–4.

irregularly spaced motifs — or a combination of both. Like spaced motifs, they can create interesting points of emphasis.

TIP

FROM THE PROS

The background area, or negative space, behind the motifs **is as important as the motifs in the foreground**. The quantity and shape of the background should be interesting and pleasingly proportioned in itself. The arrangement is more interesting if the background is either smaller or larger than the motif.

How Patterns Are Formed

Patterns are introduced (1) into the fabric while it is being made, or (2) onto the fabric after it is finished.

Patterns in fabric are formed with threads or yarns that have been dyed before weaving or knitting them into the fabric. The many different weaves produce different patterned effects. Weaving and knitting introduce more tints, shades, and tones into a pattern than printing does. Lace, crochet, and macramé are additional methods of fabrication that produce patterns.

Patterns on fabric are applied onto the surface of finished fabric with dyes by printing, painting, and spraying techniques, or with needlework by appliqué, embroidery, cutwork, and quilting techniques. They may be applied all over the fabric before it is cut, or onto a single section after it is cut, even constructed, allowing the pattern to conform to the shape and structure of the garment. Printing a pattern produces sharp edges and contrasts in color.

Additional characteristics — relating to each of the other elements of design — affect the appearance, psychological mood, and message of any pattern, as well as the physical illusions. They include:

- Angular, geometric, shaped motifs, compared to rounded motifs.
- Small-scale motifs, compared to large-scale motifs. (See Figure 7–6, page 188.)

Figure 7–5. Man-made objects inspired the motifs in this spaced arrangement. *(Courtesy All Week Long by Eddie Bauer; photographer David Martinez)*

- Close or compactly spaced motifs with little ground or background color visible, as compared to widely spaced motifs with a lot of background showing. In the latter case, the background color is generally dominant.
- Close value contrasts, compared to strong value contrasts.
- Soft, muted, or dulled hues, compared to strong, bold, or intense hues.
- Conservative and formal as compared to creative and informal, casual or exotic.
- Delicate, gentle, ladylike, and romantic — yin, compared to sturdy, forceful, businesslike, and dramatic — yang.

Predictably, patterns become more bold or striking as they increase in size, spacing, value contrast, and intensity of hues. It helps to determine potential effects by describing a pattern — to yourself or someone else — in terms of its specific characteristics.

For example, small-scale motifs, closely spaced in an all-over woven arrangement, with close value contrasts in soft and muted hues will create a calm and quieting effect.

It is not likely to add visual size or weight to the figure, nor to overwhelm the figure.

The combination of characteristics determines the overall character of the pattern. Change even one characteristic and you change the effect.

For example, if you combine light and dark values, in a printed design with large, unbroken shapes, the pattern will be very sharp and bold, attracting a lot of attention. Take the very same design, but reduce the value contrast to include all medium-value hues. The effect will be much softer, more gentle, and relaxed.

Working with an endless variety of motifs and manipulating the characteristics, designers have unlimited opportunity to create new and exciting patterns. To determine the dominant colors, lines, and shapes in a pattern, try the "squint test." Viewed through half-shut eyes, subordinate details — lines, shapes, and colors — in the pattern fade and the dominant ones become more obvious.

Illusions in Patterns

An illusion is a false perception or interpretation of something we see — something that deceives our eye when we look at it. An illusion makes something look quite different than it really is. Regardless of the facts, and according to our mind's eye, we tend to believe the illusion. Patterns can be created and arranged to create illusions.

Colors mix in the eye. What is an obvious combination of two or more hues or values up close appears to blend from a distance, creating the illusion of a solid color, which appears to be a different color altogether. (See Color Figure 12.)

For example, when seen from a short distance away, blue and green can mix in the eye and appear teal-blue-green. A black-and-white check looses its sharpness and appears a dull gray from a few steps away. Red and white appear pink. Multi-colored tweeds often appear to be one solid color a few steps away. A navy blue and yellow patterned blouse blends into green and appears to clash with a solid navy suit when you see them together from fifteen feet away. Red flowers and green leaves on a plum-colored background mix in the eye to appear olive green, combining beautifully with an olive-colored skirt and plum-colored vest.

T I P

☞

F R O M   T H E   P R O S

To determine if the texture creates a visible pattern, stand about three to five feet away from the fabric, garment, or figure wearing the pattern — in front of a full-length mirror if you're wearing the pattern. Distance improves your perspective. Look for an obvious striped or repetitive effect. Then move back to about ten feet, and finally to twenty. At each distance evaluate the appearance of the pattern and its effect on the appearance of the garment. Look also to see if an all-over pattern creates a directional stripe. (See Figure 7–7, page 189.)

Pattern Scale

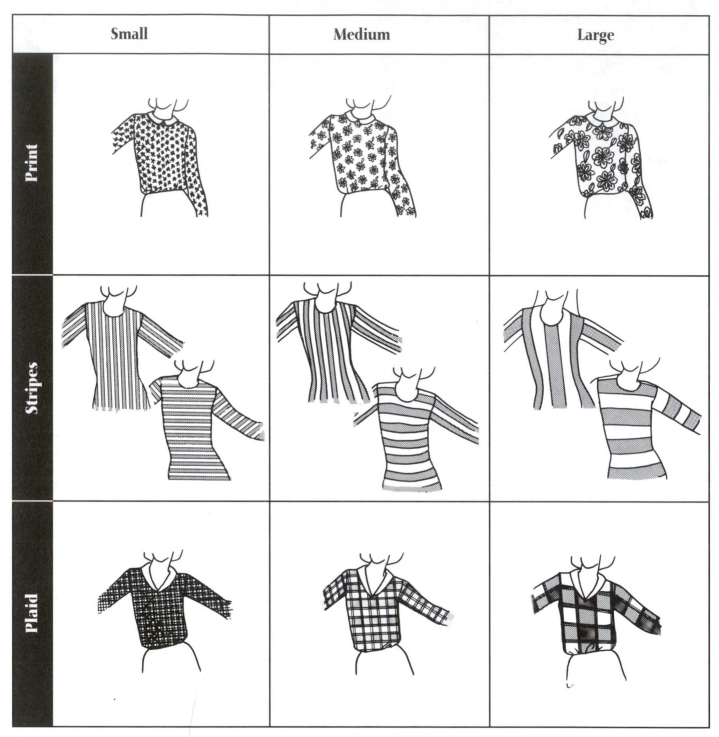

	Small	Medium	Large
Print			
Stripes			
Plaid			

Figure 7–6.

A fabric weave or surface texture often gives the appearance of a pattern, or vice versa, the fabric pattern creates a definite visual texture. In all cases, either the pattern, the surface texture, or the light reflection factor must be dominant.

For example, corduroy creates textural stripes. Gabardine forms a diagonal twill; so does denim. A vertical cable-knit creates stripes in a sweater. A jacquard weave can introduce beautiful textured flowers on cotton, linen, or *silk. A pronounced basket weave suggests small checks, and a tweed contains slub yarns resembling small dots.*

A general goal in using clothing as a resource is to select and locate patterns in ways that enhance the body — in ways that make the figure appear more nearly ideal. Patterns can be used in ways that highlight and emphasize the most attractive areas of the body and can camouflage or counter those body areas considered less attractive, in effect minimizing or eliminating them.

Figure 7–7. Seen from some distance, lighter colored motifs in the all-over pattern on the dress create the effect of diagonal lines. *(Courtesy All Week Long by Eddie Bauer; photographer David Martinez)*

Pattern and the Principles of Design

Balance. Working with a spaced pattern, in this case a single grouping of related motifs, consider carefully its placement on the figure. Placed too high, too low, or too far to one side, it may cause the figure to appear off-balance. There must be enough empty space below, above, or to the opposite side to balance the visual weight of the pattern.

A symmetrical, geometric stripe or plaid may show up an asymmetrical figure variation, such as uneven (high or low) shoulders, bust, waist, or hip. Lines in the pattern will lie at different levels as they cross the body.

A boldly patterned skirt can balance the appearance of a large bust area, while a patterned scarf, shirt yoke, or bodice can work to balance larger hips and legs.

Proportion and scale. To appear harmonious, the size of a pattern needs to be in proportion and scale for the body. Compare the size of clothing patterns (motifs alone, motifs in a grouping, and motifs with background space) to the size of the body — and remember, size is relative. What appears medium on one person may appear small or large in relation to someone else. (See Figure 7–6.)

In general, small- to medium-sized patterns appear in scale with a smaller body. Small- and medium-sized patterns work well on a medium-sized body. Somewhat larger scale patterns may work on occasion, as long as they are not so large they begin to overwhelm. Small, widely spaced motifs cause a large figure to appear even larger, as the eye travels further between motifs. Medium- to large-scale patterns, moderately spaced, are harmonious on a comparatively larger body. There is sufficient body frame to spread the pattern over and to carry it off in grand style.

For example, *Heather is four feet eleven inches tall, with small bone structure. She wears small-scale patterns well but prefers more assertive, medium-scale patterns for professional situations. Karen is taller, with large bone structure. Small-scale patterns appear insipid on Karen. By contrast, they only serve to make Karen appear even larger. Medium- to large-scale patterns are more harmonious with Karen's body build.*

Notice where breaks between a solid color and a pattern are positioned, or between two patterns. Determine if the breaks are in harmony with the body proportions or contribute to more pleasing proportions. A short figure broken into too many horizontal sections tends to appear shorter and heavier. Vertical sections tend to visually lengthen the figure.

Emphasis. Patterns, or the dominant motifs within a pattern, and pattern breaks draw attention to themselves and therefore emphasize the area where they are placed. Use them only in places where you want to draw attention and to emphasize.

For example, *placing a dominant pattern or motif on the bust, waist, stomach, hip, or buttocks, generally draws negative attention to that body area. This is particularly negative in effect in professional and leadership roles — or any occasion when attention on the body is not effective in the accomplishment of goals.*

Criteria for Quality Patterns

In picking out a pattern for an outfit or as inspiration for a whole cluster of clothes, evaluate the characteristics of the pattern. Decide if it is a high-quality pattern or a poor one before you buy it. There is a wide range in the quality of patterns. Many are adequate, some are exceptionally beautiful, and others are ugly, and seem to violate all principles of good design. In general, the beauty and quality of a pattern depends on the individual motifs within the pattern and on their relationship to each other. Granted, what you believe to be beautiful or ugly is very individual, influenced by cultural and educational background. The following general guidelines, however, apply in most cases, and relate directly to the principles of design. Combined with objective observation, they can help you discriminate between a good and a poor quality pattern.

The subject matter, or theme, for motifs in a quality pattern is pleasing.

For example, geometric, abstract, and flowered patterns are easily suitable motifs on fabric. Table legs, tennis shoes, turnips, or toads are not the most pleasing shapes or objects with which to adorn your clothes. They can be distracting, even disturbing. Faces and words distract attention.

Individual motifs look like they belong together and communicate the same theme or message.

For example, romantic roses and bows work well together. If the bows are a sporty plaid, however, the yin roses may not work with the yang bows at all. Larger argyle diamond shapes on a sporty sweater, paired with smaller diamond shapes on coordinated pants make visual sense together. Seashells and sailing rope work well together. (See Figure 7–8.)

The subject matter is stylized, rather than realistic or photographic.

For example, plants that look like they're still on the vine, or animals still in the zoo, may look fun but they work best on children's clothes, quilts, or crafts. If you choose to wear them, save them for fun, casual, costume occasions.

Embroidered motifs on a jacket may be leaves and flowers, but the artist or designer has used imagination and creativity to simplify and change the way they look. The effect could be a beautiful blend of strong yet feminine lines, carried out in crewel stitch embroidery.

Faces in a pattern are difficult to wear because they are distracting and generally conflict with your face.

There is well-balanced, harmonious variety in the size, shape, and color of the motifs.

For example, two or more floral motifs of the same size, printed in dull colors, become monotonous. Printed in bright colors, they fight for attention. Very large daisies will completely overpower comparatively small daisy motifs. Better to combine large motifs with medium or medium with small so the difference is not so great.

The color scheme, such as red-yellow-blue or ivory-tan-rust-sage, includes some contrast in hue, value, and intensity to help the viewer distinguish between different parts of the pattern.

There is a pleasing relationship between the motifs and the background of a quality pattern.

For example, consider a print with small-scale paisley motifs and polka dots. Spaced too far apart, the paisley motifs look more like amoebas floating amid a sea of dots. There is no relationship between the two, and the background space is too large and is uninteresting. Floral motifs spaced too close together make the background space look crowded. Stylized flowers on an oriental jacket, however, drift delicately across the background, leading the eye from one motif to the next.

A quality pattern looks flat and stable — with motifs arranged in an orderly, rhythmic manner.

Figure 7–8. Seashells and sailing rope appear to belong together. *(Courtesy Clifford and Wills)*

Figure 7–9. White roses appear to rise up off the background, creating a three-dimensional effect.

For example, bright pink, aqua, and white roses appear to rise up three-dimensionally, or jump off a black background. The pattern appears jumpy, jerky, and you feel pulled back and forth between motifs. Orange and purple stripes appear to vibrate due to a spreading effect between the colors. Pass up any patterns that appear to jump, wave, wiggle, or vibrate. (See Figure 7–9.)

4.

Select patterns that meet your individual needs or purposes – appropriate for your life–style, personal style, and for the fabric.

Choose patterns with characteristics appropriate for the mood, occasion, or activity. (See Table 7–6.)

For example, wearing a brightly colored pattern, reminiscent of the sixties, can undermine your credibility and your influence in business or community meetings. On the other hand, a businesslike glen-plaid or pinstripe can put a damper on a romantic evening out. Consider where you're going and select a pattern that communicates the mood and feelings you want to convey.

Choose patterns with characteristics that reflect your values.

For example, a small-scale pattern can communicate modesty, a bold pattern a bid for attention. A single pattern centered on a T-shirt, featuring a crude slogan or cartoon, may communicate a message quite the opposite of what the wearer really thinks, feels, or believes. The mistaken message may attract negative attention.

Choose patterns with characteristics that are compatible with, or that reflect, your age and personality.

For example, cats, rabbits, pigs, and teddy bears may be delightful on children's clothing, but not on core clothing pieces for adult women. A severe looking pinstripe or a bold geometric pattern is fine for a woman with an assertive nature and strong visual presence, but they can overwhelm, intimidate, or conflict with a softer, gentler personality and appearance.

Choose patterns with characteristics that flatter your face and figure. (See Table 7–6.)

For example, tiny motifs or polka dots can emphasize freckles more than you might like. A small, busy pattern with rounded lines and shapes can clash with the curlicues of permed hair, rather than blend harmoniously. And con-

sider this: Shapes in a pattern can conflict with the shape of your glasses. If a pattern appears too busy in comparison to your face, glasses, or hair, wear a solid color between your face and the pattern.

Large-scale patterns can overpower a child or small-figured woman, while tiny prints can get lost on a large figure. Petite women need to scale down their plaids in proportion to their figure. Larger women can carry most medium- to larger-sized patterns, but only in loose-fitting styles. Circle dots the size of dinner plates won't work for anyone. Printed in bright colors, the after-image appears to bounce all around the fabric.

Medium-scale plaids, and some larger plaids, can be terrific on a larger figure. Just make sure the garment fits loosely enough so that none of the plaid gets pulled out of line over body contours. Plaid straight skirts cut straight on grain look huge, but plaid, flared skirts cut on the bias work beautifully on a large woman. They hang in soft ripples or folds all around the body. For broad shoulders, plaid on the bias also works well.

A large-scale floral, in an all-over swirling design, on a billowing formal dress may overwhelm the wearer. A bodice of solid color may be needed to stabilize the skirt and save the dress.

You will discover you can easily wear patterns with stronger value contrast if you have stronger value contrast in your personal coloring, if you have dark hair and dark skin, or bright white hair. If your coloring has little value contrast, select your patterns to provide some value contrast. This works best if one of the colors in the print repeats your personal hair, eye, or skin color — making you part of the color scheme with the pattern.

Choose patterns with characteristics that look, feel, and hang appropriately for the fabric and style of the garment. (See Table 7–6.)

For example, an intricate pattern gets lost in the threads of terrycloth or fleece. Detailed patterns demand a smooth surface fabric to show up. A bold, assertive pattern may or may not conflict with a delicate, sheer fabric. It's important to check out the effect.

The sportive character of a horse-and-rider or pheasant print could conflict with the character of a frilly, ruffle-neck, or puff-sleeve blouse. It works much better in equally sportive or man-tailored pieces of clothing.

A large-scale motif won't fit on a collar or sleeve, or if widely spaced, it will be lost. The entire motif should be seen on the bodice or skirt, rather than frustrating the viewer with incomplete motifs. If not, choose a smaller motif.

When using animal motifs, numbers, or faces, plan for the location of seams and hem edges. You can't cut through the middle of a cow or a face without some psychological discomfort.

Choose patterns that will fit in well and coordinate with the existing wardrobe. (See Chapters 9 and 10.)

Table 7–6 General Perception of Patterns

	Message/Function	Characteristics	
Occasion/Activity	To feel and appear casual/informal (casual business)	Small, medium, large — Brighter colors More contrast Embroidery Tie dye, batik Med. to wide stripes Horizontal stripes Multi-colored stripes	Calico prints Plaids Stripes Argyle Checks Tweed Herringbone
	To feel and appear dress-businesslike (formal business)	Smaller Weaving Printing Vertical stripes Less contrast Darker colors Duller colors	Geometrics Paisley Foulard Houndstooth checks Pinstripes Glen plaid Windowpane plaid
	To feel and appear dressy/formal	Medium to larger scale Bright Stronger color contrasts	Paisley Panel prints
Personality	To feel and appear refined, ingenue/romantic	Monochromatic Tiny, small Naturalistic Border prints Embroidery Lace Flowing abstracts	Flowers Hearts Scrolls Polka dots Paisley
	To feel and appear sporty/sportive	Small to med. to large — Brighter colors More contrast Embroidery Tie dye, batik Med. to wide stripes Horizontal stripes Multi-colored stripes	Buffalo checks Animal prints Geometric plaids, checks, and herringbone
	To feel and appear dramatic/exotic	Strong contrasts in hue and value Zigzag stripes Large, bold, sharp edges Dino checks (dinosaur)	Widely spaced and single figure motifs — large pictures Abstract patterns Ethnic Plaid on the bias Animal prints
	To feel and appear mature, serious, somber, classic	Small-scale patterns Cool Dull Close contrasts	Close spaced

Table 7–6 General Perception of Patterns (*continued*)

	Message/Function	Characteristics	
Figure/Body Build	To maintain or decrease attention and apparent size — to appear taller and slimmer	Border prints on collar horizontally on the shoulder yoke or vertically along the CF Closer value contrast Dominant vertical lines or vertical eye movement or direction Closer spread Plaid cut on the bias diagonal	Geometric patterns All-over pattern Small to medium patterns (small is too much contrast to large person) Vertical stripes Herringbone Pin stripes Fine wale corduroy
	To increase attention and apparent size — to appear shorter, larger, and heavier	Dominant horizontal lines or horizontal eye movement or direction Plaid cut on grain Large patterns Rounded, circular motifs Strong hue and value contrasts Widely spaced	Horizontal Border print at waist or hip Border print at hem or sleeve cuff Dots Circles Horizontal stripes
Garment Style	Few seams — Tubular, tailored, A-line Simple style, little to no shaping	Medium to large More detail, complex pattern Geometrics	
	Moderate drape Some gathers	Medium-scale patterns	
	Fabric folds to many gathers, and drapes well Falls loosely, gracefully Many seams, curves Complex style	Single pattern, less detail Smaller pattern obscures the seams and detail (larger pattern if gathered in to appear smaller and seams hidden under folds)	Smocked, shirred, gathers Seams cut into the pattern, distort the pattern

For example, the shapes and colors in a print or plaid may be terrific, but if they don't harmonize with the shapes and colors in your wardrobe, you won't get much wear out of your purchase. If you have two pieces of solid-colored clothing that don't work well together, find a patterned piece of clothing containing the same two colors. Use it to visually coordinate the two pieces of clothing.

As suggested at the beginning of this chapter, find a pat- tern to inspire the color scheme of an entire cluster of clothes that works for you. Take your color cues from the pattern and begin to build for your future.

Pieces to Buy Patterned

In beginning wardrobe building, select only a few second-layer pieces in patterns — blouses, shirts, and dresses. In the beginning, third-layer sweaters, jackets, and coats need to be solid in color, so they combine easily with both solid colors and patterns. You can expect to wear a solid-colored jacket (third layer) or suit with a patterned shirt longer than you will wear a completely patterned jacket or suit. A subtle tweed jacket is a good exception to that guideline, and there may be others. Similarly, don't buy a patterned coat (third or fourth layer) until after you have a solid-colored coat.

For example, Ellen already owned a black basic coat to wear over virtually everything she owned. That gave her freedom to choose a bold patterned jacket in colors to wear with her solid-colored clothes.

In most cases, buy patterned belts, shoes, handbags, scarves, or gloves only after you have solid-colored ones you can wear with solid-color *and* patterned clothing pieces. The exception is a patterned accessory piece that may have inspired your cluster color scheme in the first place. After you have your basic accessories, you can branch out.

For example, in a cluster of clothes planned around khaki tan, poppy, and hunter green, accessories with strongly patterned clothes are basically simple and subordinate to the pattern. Having acquired basic clothing pieces, shoes, and boots in those colors, a pair of fabric flats can be added in a tapestry print that looks fantastic with solid-colored clothes in the cluster.

5.

Coordinate or combine patterns to achieve greater variety, interest, and individuality.

Harmony among Patterns

Combining and coordinating patterns is a little trickier than combining textures or colors. Patterns involve the coordination of lines and shapes in colors on textures — all at once. But when a mix is done well, it adds an element of sophistication or surprise well worth the effort. These are the guidelines.

To appear harmonious, **coordinate or combine two or more patterns in terms of the activity, occasion, mood, values, and personality traits they communicate**. They should be similar or related in subject matter.

To appear harmonious, **coordinate the colors in the patterns**. Colors must look as if they belong together — as if they are part of a single color scheme, **sharing one or more colors in common**. To carry well from a distance, one hue in a pattern must noticeably outweigh the others. It must be dominant.

Combining flowers with flowers, or geometrics with geometrics, is relatively easy. Combining flowers with geo-

metric dots and stripes can be more interesting and work beautifully if the patterns are related in scale and the patterns have colors in common.

For example, imagine a long, cotton, lounging dress made with several patterns — small yellow flowers on black; delicate yellow, blue, and red flowers with yellow stems and dots on black; and yellow stripes on black. Motifs in each pattern are small or narrow, and yellow is the dominant hue in each pattern.

Women who combine clothes with patterns that clash, conflict, or communicate contradictory traits look cluttered.

For example, the look of a red-flowered blouse and a brown plaid skirt just do not combine well. The red and brown, as well as the particular flower and plaid, do not relate to one another in any way. Each piece communicates a different feeling, an opposing mood. If circumstances allow, the blouse and the skirt each need to be paired with another garment, in either a solid color or related pattern.

A Style of Your Own

Depending on the person wearing them, the patterns that conflict may appear too severe, strict, and stern; too fussy, frilly, and frivolous; or too bold and brassy. The person may feel psychologically uncomfortable in the clothing, and observers may notice this.

For example, a gentle, fun-loving, young woman may feel overwhelmed by the serious nature of a pinstripe skirted suit paired with a chalk-stripe shirt. She might look terrific in the suit as far as others are concerned, but she may feel too stiff, stuffy, and strict. She might prefer and feel psychologically more comfortable in a floral print blouse paired with a solid-colored suit, or in a small-scale, all-over print shirt paired with a textural striped corduroy suit.

So experiment a little and discover which patterns are most in harmony with you, your personality, the places you go, and what you do there. You may find you have a personal preference for artistically styled floral or leaf prints — maybe a vintage paisley, geometric prints, stripes, and plaids — maybe a scotch plaid, or unusual and abstract prints. You may discover you prefer quiet patterns with curved lines and wispy shapes in soft and muted colors — possibly hand painted, or you may prefer bold patterns with straight lines and precise shapes in strong colors and contrasts. Whatever your choice, the patterns you wear should say something specific to you and about you — something that marks your personal style.

Dominant/Subordinate Patterns

In all cases, one pattern must be dominant in the garment or outfit. **One pattern** (occasion, mood, or personality) **must be dominant and all others subordinate by descending degrees**. Stated another way, the mood, theme, or personality communicated by one pattern must be most obvious and most important. Different patterns can be introduced into the design, but they must be done so to a lesser degree — they must attract less attention.

Two or three equally sized and equally spaced patterns worn together will compete for attention and be too repetitious and busy. Equally small-scale dots, stripes, checks, and plaids or prints in a shirt, slacks, and jacket invite disaster. On the other hand, a tiny, insipid pattern paired with a large-scale, bold pattern becomes jarring to the eye — too much contrast.

The "grunge" look of the early 1990s combined virtually any pattern with any other pattern or patterns available. Many teens adopted the look precisely because it was disturbing to the eye.

Some contrast in graduated sizes is desirable. A small-scale pattern, paired with a medium-scale pattern, is much more pleasing to the eye — some contrast, but not too much. A single, large motif or larger grouping of motifs mixes well with a pattern of medium-scale motifs.

For example, *visualize a single-theme pattern hand painted on a T-shirt, paired with a tiered skirt, each tier sporting a bold but small- to medium-scale floral print. The larger pattern on the T-shirt is dominant, while those in the skirt are subordinate.*

Three patterns, one smaller in scale, combined with a comparatively medium-scale pattern, and a larger-scale pattern, can appear harmonious because the largest pattern is dominant and all others are subordinate by degrees. Stated another way, select only one strong pattern, then a softer, more subtle pattern, and finally a fairly neutral piece. A pencil stripe, paired with a faint plaid, and finally a solid color or textured fabric will do nicely. Fabric and fashion designers rely on this technique. Capitalizing on the "grunge" look, Perry Ellis put together his own interpretation, making it work harmoniously. *Sew News* put an equally tamed version of "grunge" on the cover of the August 1993 issue. It was beautifully done, with each pattern subordinate by degrees.

IMAGES

More on Mixed-and-Matched Patterns

Forget the idea that patterns are too hard to work with. Forget the old "rule" about never mixing patterns, or two at most. Forget the "rule" that says all patterns must be the same size, along with its opposite, no two patterns should be the same size. When it comes to visual design in dress, "always and never" rules never work. What follows are guidelines to help you break outdated rules with style. A harmonious effect is possible when:

- The patterns or motifs are related in subject, communicating one theme, mood, occasion, or set of personality traits.
- The patterns have at least one color or color family in common — or similar degrees of lightness and darkness. Colors must look as if they belong together. Imagine a textured tweed coat worn over a striped silk shirt, paired with a dominant windowpane skirt, all in monochromatic shades of brown, tan, and ivory.
- The same pattern in the same colors is used in different sizes, with one size dominant. Imagine small polka dots and coin-sized dots both in pastel peach and white. The larger dots are dominant.
- The same pattern in the same size is used in reversed or different color schemes, with one color scheme dominant. Imagine checks in black and white with checks in aqua and black. Or, visualize checks in black on aqua, with checks in aqua on black. The brighter pattern is dominant.
- The same pattern in different sizes is used in different color schemes, with one overall pattern dominant. Men do this all the time. Imagine a charcoal pinstripe suit, a burgundy pencil-stripe shirt, and a rep-stripe tie in charcoal, black, and burgundy. The larger rep-stripe tie is dominant, and its colors pull together the suit and the shirt. Try something similar for yourself — with a tie, or a scarf in place of a tie.
- Different patterns in the same size in the same or related colors, are worn with one pattern dominant. Imagine a herringbone jacket with a paisley print skirt. The busier paisley print is dominant.
- Different patterns in different sizes in the same basic color scheme are worn with one overall pattern dominant. Imagine black-and-white pin-dot crepe pants, paired with a black-and-white pin-stripe crepe blouse, topped with a black-and-white checked jacket and finished with a black, white, and red paisley scarf. The scarf is dominant in pattern, size, and color.

You can state these guidelines in several different ways, but the general guideline remains. One or two of the elements — motif, color, or size — can be different as long as you keep one element the same, and as long as one pattern is dominant. No matter how much the same or different, one pattern must be dominant and all others must be subordinate by degree.

If you're not sure what you're doing, you're smart to start by separating two patterns with a solid color. Try a floral scarf on a solid-colored blouse, paired with a tweed or glen-plaid jacket.

If you like the look, advance to pairing a patterned suit with a patterned shirt. It's safe in a navy blue suit with shrimp-colored pin-dots, paired with a narrow-striped blouse in navy and peach. Add a peach-colored pocket square for flair.

Go the distance with a patterned suit, patterned vest, and patterned blouse. You could try a medium check suit, a small check vest, a stripe shirt, and a large diamond-textured scarf. Or, try a basket-weave jacket, a pinstripe shirt, with a bold, tapestry print vest, and solid-colored slacks. It can make a strong statement.

If you're still uncertain about mixing patterns, play it safe and start with one designer's mixes. Donna Karan, Louis Dell'Olio, Jessica McClintock, Carol Little, Karen Kane, and Gloria Sachs create some of the best mixes you'll find.

For example, imagine a tweed jacket, Donegal sweater, plaid shirt, and paisley skirt. All pieces are rather sportive in mood and occasion. Assume there are rusty reds, blues, and greens in each of the patterns. Sizes range from tiny fabric dots in the tweed jacket, to a small-scale plaid in the shirt, to a medium-sized paisley pattern in the skirt, and to somewhat larger shapes on the otherwise solid-colored sweater. It works!

This flexible and creative way of combining patterns opens up endless possibilities for greater individuality and creativity.

T I P
FROM THE PROS

To test the harmony of the combination, think in terms of sizes, gradations, or amounts — huge, large, medium, small, and tiny. If you can look at the mix of patterns, see repetition of mood and color, and can say to yourself, "This one is small, this one is medium, and this one is comparatively larger," you've probably got a winner.

Review Main Points

The element, pattern, is used to add interest and personal style to your wardrobe. Patterns work to coordinate solid-colored clothes. Classic patterns are small to medium in size and moderate in color and design. Trendy patterns are more often larger and bolder, associated with a particular product, person, place, or occasion. Acquire more classic patterns in your wardrobe and fewer trendy patterns to update your solid-colored clothes. Patterns are inspired by both nature and man-made objects. Motifs are realistic, stylized, geometric, and abstract. Patterns are introduced into or onto fabric by weaving and other methods of fabrication, and by various printing techniques. The arrangement of a pattern on fabric determines its use, layout, and cost. Patterns can be manipulated to communicate messages, feelings, and moods, and to create a variety of illusions about the body. Because patterns interact with one another and with the wearer, they need to be compatible with one another and with the wearer, the time, and the place. In combining different patterns, one must be dominant, and all others subordinate, by degrees. Combining patterns in harmonious ways is one of the keys to putting together an interesting, versatile, and fashionable wardrobe.

Review Questions

1. Classic patterns are usually _____ scale.

2. Costume and trendy patterns are often designed in _____ colors.

3. Patterns add _____ and _____ to your wardrobe.

4. _____ and _____ objects are both sources of inspiration for patterns.

5. List two types of plaids, or two types of checks.

   _____   _____

6. Describe two ways you can use a patterned piece of clothing to your advantage.

   _____

   _____

7. Describe what makes a pattern stylized. _____

_____

_____

8. _____-way pattern arrangements have an obvious top or bottom, and are more difficult to match.

9. Ideally, if one of the colors in a patterned piece of clothing _____ your personal coloring, you will look like part of the color scheme with your clothes.

10. List four characteristics of a pattern that can affect the mood and message of a garment and the illusions it may create.

_____

_____

_____

_____

11. Which of the following words does not belong in the group? Circle the incorrect word.

panel

border

natural

spaced

12. Match the following patterns to the appropriate mood or message they tend to communicate.

_____ plaid   a. active, exciting, happy

_____ calico floral   b. abrupt, sportive, casual

_____ herringbone   c. strong, decisive, formal

_____ medallion   d. gentle, feminine, cute

13. More tints, shades, and tones are introduced into a pattern by _____

_____

_____.

14. A beautiful vest or a boldly patterned scarf can work to visually balance larger hips or thighs and draw attention upward.   True   or   False

15. _____ scale patterns are appropriate for virtually everybody.

16. Large motifs combined with small motifs in the same pattern are likely to appear

_____.

17. Patterns that appear three-dimensional, as if they rise or jump off the surface, are usually _____ quality designs for use in clothes.

18. It's smart to own a solid-colored pair of _____ before you purchase a patterned pair.

19. In combining two or more patterns, each pattern needs to be similar or related in _____.

20. You could combine a large-scale, floral print with a _____

Discussion Questions

#1 Look around you at the patterns class members are wearing. Now that you know something about line, shape, color, and texture, discuss these elements of design, and their influence in the patterns. Discuss possible effects the pattern might have — the message, mood, and occasion the pattern tends to communicate.

Notes: _____

_____

_____

_____

_____

#2 On a designated day, wear to class a favorite patterned piece of clothing, or a patterned accessory. Discuss which colors each person might choose as solids with the print, and to build a cluster with. Invite differing responses from class members, as they reflect the potential for other effects and individuality.

Notes: _____

_____

_____

_____

_____

#3 Discuss reasons why people might advise others not to wear patterned clothing pieces. Discuss ways to overcome the narrowness of this type of advice.

Notes: _____

_____

_____

_____

_____

#4 The same concepts and strategies that apply to women's clothing also apply to men's clothing. Discuss typical and possible pattern combinations in menswear.

Notes: _____

_____

_____

_____

_____

Exercise 7–1   Pattern Recognition

Name_____

Look at what you are wearing.
- Identify, list, and check mark any piece of clothing that features a classic or trendy pattern.
- Identify the type of motif — realistic, stylized, geometric, or abstract — formed in each patterned piece of clothing.
- Identify the type of pattern arrangement — all over, four-way, two-way, one-way, border, panel, or spaced — in each patterned piece.
- Identify the method of introducing each pattern into or onto the fabric — weaving, knitting, printing, painting, or other.
- Work with a classmate and identify as above.

You – Clothing Item	Classic Pattern	Trendy Pattern	Motif (realistic, stylized, geometric, abstract)	Pattern Arrangement (all over, 4-way, 2-way, 1-way, border, panel, or spaced)	Method of Producing (weaving, knitting, printing, painting, other)

Classmate – Clothing Item	Classic Pattern	Trendy Pattern	Motif (realistic, stylized, geometric, abstract)	Pattern Arrangement (all over, 4-way, 2-way, 1-way, border, panel, or spaced)	Method of Producing (weaving, knitting, printing, painting, other)

Look in your closet, selecting three to five favorite patterned pieces of clothing and three to five less favorite patterned pieces of clothing.

- In the appropriate section — favorite/less favorite — place a check mark in the appropriate column to identify the kind of motif — realistic, stylized, geometric, or abstract.
- Place a check mark in the appropriate column to identify the method of introducing the pattern into or onto the fabric — weaving, knitting, printing, painting, or other.

- Describe any special characteristics about these patterns.
- Place a check mark to identify the pattern as classic or trendy.
- Total the number of lines identified in each column.
- Analyze how these characteristics have influenced your preferences.

	Clothing Item	Motif				Pattern Arrangement							Method of Introducing Pattern onto Fabric					Classic Pattern	Trendy Pattern
		realistic	stylized	geomet.	abstract	all-over	4-way	2-way	1-way	border	panel	spaced	weaving	knitting	printing	painting	other		
Favorite Clothes																			
	TOTALS																		
Less Favorite Clothes		realistic	stylized	geomet.	abstract	all-over	4-way	2-way	1-way	border	panel	spaced	weaving	knitting	printing	painting	other	Classic Pattern	Trendy Pattern
	TOTALS																		

Conclusions:

Exercise 7–3   Local Store Experience

Name _____

Go to a fabric store. Look through several pattern catalogs. To appeal to a wider range of people, pattern envelopes feature two to three different versions or personal types of the same pattern design. Usually one version is more yin and/or yang than the other. Usually one version is more tailored, one is softly tailored, and one is untailored. Often, it is a matter of color, fabric, and design detail. Yin and yang characteristics are selected in different combinations. Look in a local clothing and/or fabric store for patterns you have never worn before. In front of a full-length mirror, experiment with the look and the feel of these patterns in relation to you. Do you wear the pattern, or does the pattern wear you?

Fabric Store Experience

• To see how a pattern might look on you, drape the fabric on your body to simulate a piece of clothing. Notice and record how the patterns make you look and what they appear to communicate. Evaluate the possible effects on the pattern from the lighting.

• Practice pairing a patterned fabric with several solid color fabrics and evaluate the effects. If possible, secure fabric swatches for your most pleasing combination in Exercise 7–5.

Clothing Store Experience

• Hold the garment up to you. Notice and record how the patterns make you look and what they appear to communicate. If possible, to see how the clothing will look on you, try the garment on. Notice and record how the patterns look on you and make you look. Notice and record what the patterns appear to communicate. Evaluate possible effects on the pattern from the lighting.

Exercise 7–4 Classic/Trendy Pattern Recognition

Name _____

- Collect five or six pictures of garments featuring classic patterns.
- Mount.
- Label.

- Collect four or five pictures of garments featuring trendy patterns.
- Mount.
- Label.

Exercise 7–5   Pattern Coordination

Name _____

Find pictures of clothing pieces in patterns you would like to combine into an outfit for yourself. Don't worry about style and color now. Look for patterns that can be expected to flatter your figure. Look for patterns you can combine harmoniously. Mount and identify accordingly. Write a paragraph explaining reasons for your choices.

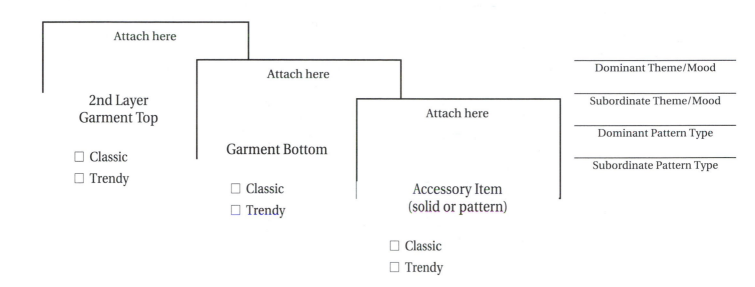

Attach here

2nd Layer Garment Top

☐ Classic
☐ Trendy

Attach here

Garment Bottom

☐ Classic
☐ Trendy

Attach here

Accessory Item (solid or pattern)

☐ Classic
☐ Trendy

Dominant Theme/Mood _____
Subordinate Theme/Mood _____
Dominant Pattern Type _____
Subordinate Pattern Type _____

Attach here

2nd Layer Garment Top

☐ Classic
☐ Trendy

Attach here

Garment Bottom

☐ Classic
☐ Trendy

Dominant Theme/Mood _____
Subordinate Theme/Mood _____
Dominant Pattern Type _____
Subordinate Pattern Type _____
Sub-subordinate Pattern Type _____

Attach here

3rd Layer Garment Top

☐ Classic
☐ Trendy

Attach here

Accessory Item (solid color or patterned)

☐ Classic
☐ Trendy

Attach here

Accessory Item

☐ Classic
☐ Trendy

Exercise 7–6   Preferred Pattern Characteristics

Name _____

Plot your preferred pattern characteristics or traits on a continuum between opposites.

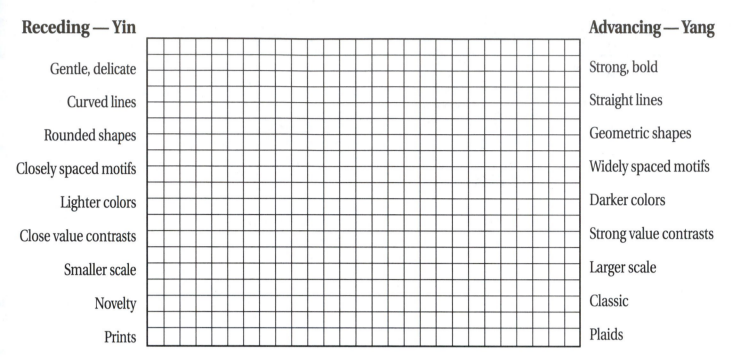

Receding — Yin   **Advancing — Yang**

Gentle, delicate — Strong, bold

Curved lines — Straight lines

Rounded shapes — Geometric shapes

Closely spaced motifs — Widely spaced motifs

Lighter colors — Darker colors

Close value contrasts — Strong value contrasts

Smaller scale — Larger scale

Novelty — Classic

Prints — Plaids

Note: With reference to color, the American culture is not consistent with Oriental interpretation, and considers darker colors to be more assertive, or Yang.

Chapter 8

Personal Style Selection and Coordination

Learning Objectives

Your goal in completing this chapter is to be able to:

- Recognize differences between tailored, softly tailored, and untailored.
- Describe the relationship between yin and untailored, yang and tailored.
- Understand the value of yang/tailored and yin/untailored clothing.
- Differentiate between yin/yang physical, personality, and clothing characteristics or traits.
- Recognize characteristics for each yin/yang category.
- Discuss, understand, and appreciate differences in personal style.
- Identify your position and range on a yin/yang continuum.
- Understand how to cross over or borrow opposing clothing traits.
- Select clothing to meet your needs.
- Coordinate and combine yang/tailored with softly tailored or yin/untailored clothing pieces harmoniously.

Preview Main Points

1. Rely on tailored clothes, designed with predominantly straight lines, angular and tubular shapes, dulled and darker colors with stronger value contrast, firmer fabrics, and smaller patterns for occasions when you need to appear more authoritative and capable.

2. Soften the look of tailored-looking clothes with designs that introduce some curved lines and rounded shapes, lighter and brighter colors with less value contrast, more pliable fabrics, and larger patterns for occasions when you need to appear more approachable and friendly.

3. Knowing more about tailored, softly tailored, and untailored design details, as they relate to yin/yang characteristics, will help you make wise consumer decisions about clothing selection and coordination for your personal style.

4. Select clothing designed with the appropriate degree of assertiveness or approachability appropriate to meet your individual needs or purposes — appropriate for your life-style and personal style and goals.

5. Coordinate or combine tailored/yang with softly tailored or untailored/yin clothing pieces for more effective visual communication, greater versatility, interest, and individuality.

1.

Rely on tailored clothes, designed with predominantly straight lines, angular and tubular shapes, dulled and darker colors with stronger value contrast, firmer fabrics, and smaller patterns for occasions when you need to appear more authoritative and capable.

Many basic and classic clothes are commonly referred to as "tailored." But what does tailored mean? What is the most tailored piece of clothing you can think of? A man's business suit is the most tailored apparel most people think of. In your mind, visualize a basic, classic man's suit. It is composed of:

- Straight lines.

For example, the outlines or silhouette lines and closures appear as straight lines. Interior lapel and pocket lines are straight.

- Angular and tubular shapes.

For example, collars and lapels form angles at the points. Pockets form angles at the corners. The suit jacket is designed with a tube around the body and tubes around the arms. Suit trousers are designed with tubes around the legs. Even a woman's straight skirt — the most tailored-looking skirt there is — features straight lines and a tubular shape.

- Dark colors, with strong dark/light value contrast.

For example, the most used suits come in variations of navy blue, gray, brown, and black. Colors other than black and navy blue are dulled. In contrast, the shirt is white, or at least light.

- Firm and smooth fabric.

For example, fabric able to support and hold the angular and tubular shapes of the finest men's suits are made from long threads tightly twisted into yarns, and tightly woven into firm (not stiff) fabrics — worsteds. Additional firmness and body are introduced to the fabric via interfacing and shoulder pads. Shoes, belts, and wallet are generally smooth leather.

- Small to medium geometric patterns, traditionally conservative.

For example, the most often used patterns in menswear include small- to medium-scale checks, plaids, and stripes, which have been popular and accepted for generations.

Psychologically, these lines, shapes, colors, textures, and patterns appear strong and stable, communicating formality, authority, and credibility. All design elements are interrelated and are used to reinforce the more severe

Figure 8-1. This dark wool worsted, pinstripe pantsuit illustrates tailored clothing at its most extreme. *(Courtesy Madeleine Direct)*

effects of one another and hence, the tailored image. (See Figure 8–1.)

You, too, can rely on a tailored appearance to empower you with the feeling and appearance of strength, ability, and authority in leadership and professional situations — in the home, the school, the church, the community, and the workplace.

2.

Soften the look of tailored–looking clothes with designs that introduce some curved lines and rounded shapes, lighter and brighter colors with less value contrast, more pliable fabrics, and larger patterns for occasions when you need to appear more approachable and friendly.

There are endless degrees of difference between clothing that causes you to appear authoritative as compared to those that allow you to appear more approachable. Think in terms of opposites on a continuum between tailored and untailored — authoritative and approachable. Then think of a very tailored, serious-looking woman's suit jacket and straight, below-the-knee-length skirt. In your mind's eye, curve the lines of the jacket lapels, creating a rounded shawl collar. Maybe you'd prefer a little puff at the top of the sleeve, or imagine rounding out the shape of the skirt, just slightly, creating a fuller style, possibly a gathered dirndl or flared style skirt. (See Figure 8–2.)

Any or all of these changes in line and shape — depending on the degree you want or need — will counter or soften the look of a tailored suit. Psychologically, curved or rounded lines and shapes appear softer, more flexible, friendly, and fun, communicating personal warmth, gentleness, and a more sensitive, caring attitude.

You can further counter a tailored look using lighter or brighter colors, less dark/light value contrast, softer, more pliable fabrics, and larger or more feminine patterns. Don't go too far, however, if you need to maintain a softly tailored effect for more casual business and leadership situations. Go further, as you like, for totally casual, social, or at-home situations. Your options for countering include:

- Curved lines.
- Rounded shapes.

Figure 8-2. This pastel cotton broadcloth dress, with gathered waistline and lace-edged collar, illustrates feminine, untailored clothing. *(Courtesy All Week Long by Eddie Bauer; photographer David Martinez)*

- Lighter colors, with less dark/light value contrast.
- Softer, more pliable, and textured fabric.
- Medium to large patterns, with more curved lines and shapes.

It's a matter of degree. There is a world of manipulations available. It's up to you to strike the mix or blend of tailored, softly tailored, and untailored elements to meet your needs. (See Figure 8–3.)

Figure 8-3. Soft color and fabric counter the tailored style lines and shape in the coat and jacket to blend with feminine features and hair. *(Courtesy Madeleine Direct)*

3.

Knowing more about tailored, softly tailored, and untailored design details, as they relate to yin/yang characteristics, will help you make wise consumer decisions about clothing selection and coordination for your personal style.

For the purpose of this discussion the terms *tailored* and *untailored* can be likened to the terms *yin* and *yang* introduced in Chapter 2. You can use both sets of terms to compare opposite characteristics in clothing.

Tailored and *untailored* are words widely used to describe clothing traits. Yet *tailored* and *untailored* do not describe physical bodies, or personality traits. *Yin* and *yang* are words that do lend themselves to describing physical body characteristics, psychological or personality traits, as well as clothing traits. (See Table 2–3, page 33.) In many in-

stances, those traits correspond closely to Western society's expectations regarding tailored and untailored clothing.

Importance and Functions of Yin/Yang Concept

- Describes and classifies physical, personality, and clothing traits.
- Allows comparison based on similarity and differences in traits.
- Assists in discovering, developing, and refining personal style in dress.
- Advances knowledge, understanding, and acceptance of the self and others.
- Becomes a tool for solving image-related problems and in creating the type of appearance necessary to achieve goals.
- Guides the use of clothing as a means of visual communication.
- Guides the creation of powerful illusions about the individual.
- Provides a tool for adding variety and interest to your appearance.

Yin/Yang Continuum

Yang and tailored can be positioned on one end of a continuum (See Figure 8–1.), while yin and untailored can be positioned at the opposite end. (See Figure 8–2.)

Yin/Untailored ....Tailored/Yang

There are many degrees of difference on the continuum between tailored and untailored, between yin and yang. You have some experience in evaluating your physical body, your personality, and your preferred clothing characteristics from doing exercises in previous chapters. Based on that experience, plot your approximate positions on the following yin/yang continuums. (Review yin/yang traits listed in Table 2–3.) Do you think you reflect all yin traits, all yang traits, dominant yin traits, dominant yang traits, or a relatively equal blend of both? Any combination is possible.

There are numerous ways you might need to plot yourself. (See Table 8–1, page 210.) You might plot your body and personality consistently yin, or consistently yang. That makes for easy dressing when you decide to keep clothing traits consistent. Visual and psychological conflict can result when you don't. You might, however, plot your body as yin and your personality traits more yang. Or, you might plot your body as yang and your personality traits more yin. This requires a compromise in clothing traits to present both the body and personality harmoniously.

Be aware of the following points:

Physical Body Characteristics

- These characteristics are most obvious to others.
- Present your physical self attractively and appropriately.

Personality Characteristics

- These characteristics are very important to you.
- Be true to your psychological self — personality and values.

Clothing Characteristics

- These characteristics influence you and others.
- Manipulate these characteristics to satisfy the need to present your physical self appropriately while also being true to your psychological self.

Problems of inconsistency and conflict, or lack of harmony, are common.

For example, visualize a tall, large-boned girl, with a square jaw, broad shoulders, and a long stride to her walk, dressed in a profusion of ruffles, frills, ribbons, and lace. The extremely yin details contrast too much, or fight with the dominant yang figure and manner. Now imagine a homecoming queen wearing a long, flowing gown and heavy, clunky shoes, while singing a romantic ballad. The yang shoes conflict mightily with the yin girl and the gown. Think of a sporty young girl dressing up like a dra-matic high-fashion model or a romantic, sexy-looking siren. The person and the persona don't work with one another. There is obvious lack of harmony within these specific examples.

Establish Your Own Limits

When you determine your positions on the continuum, you can better see yourself in relation to your clothes. Personal style in dress implies limits on the yin/yang continuum — the limits in dress design to which you are willing to go and still look and feel authentic, congruent, or comfortable with yourself in your clothes. It's a matter of deciding if you are comfortable wearing clothing characteristics that are very yin, slightly yin, slightly yang, or very yang. (See Figure 8–4.)

In selecting clothing, it is a matter of saying to yourself, "That's too yin (or yang) for me — for my height, for the way I move, for my personality or my mood, or for the occasion, etc." You can substitute "too tailored" or "too untailored" and make the same point.

For example, Jana is graceful, gentle, and soft-spoken. She feels totally comfortable in a pink and lime floral print blazer made of rayon. The look is softly tailored, not too tailored for Jana. Gina, however, is direct and outspoken. The same jacket looks too pretty, too delicate, too yin for Gina. She feels much more comfortable in an equally strong, red, orange, or black blazer made of linen, wool gabaradine, or wool flannel. The total look is comparatively tailored.

When you say to yourself, "That's me," you're responding to the similarity of the clothing traits and yourself — in whatever unique blend you might be. When someone else says, "That's you," they are reacting to the harmony they see between you and the clothes. For many people, recognizing this correlation is enough. They are fully able to find the clothes they need and want to wear. Others want or need to go further.

Yin-Yang Continuum

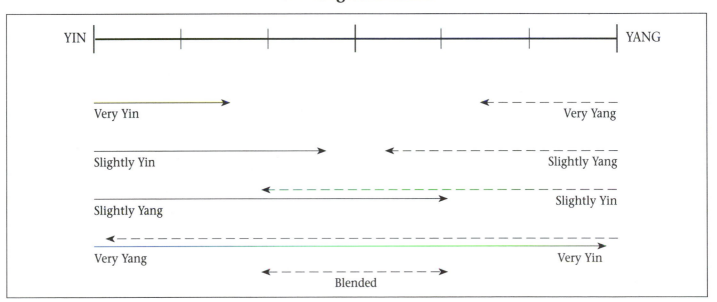

Figure 8-4.

Table 8-1 Descriptive Characteristics Which May Reflect Opposites (Examples)

EXAMPLE A

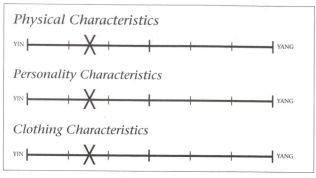

Consistent Traits — Natural harmony

EXAMPLE B

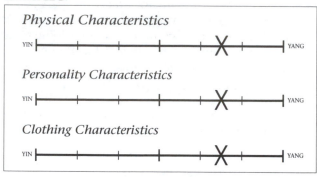

Consistent Traits — Natural harmony

EXAMPLE C

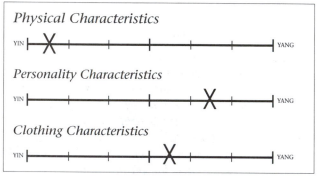

Inconsistent Traits — Clothing compromise to present physical self well, yet express personality

EXAMPLE D

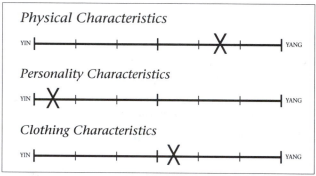

Inconsistent Traits — Clothing compromise to present physical self well, yet express personality

EXAMPLE E

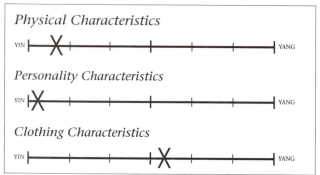

Inconsistent traits, possibly due to professional role requirement. Feminine yin and yang compromise.

EXAMPLE F

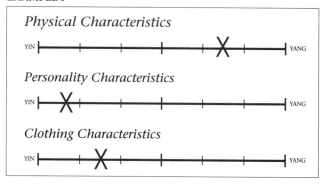

Inconsistent Traits — Clothing characteristics will not present physical body well. Lack of harmony results.

EXAMPLE G

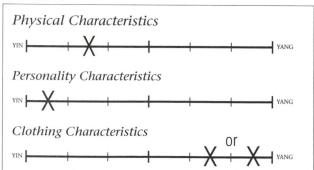

Conflict between opposing traits is apparent. Personality and appearance are not congruent.

EXAMPLE H

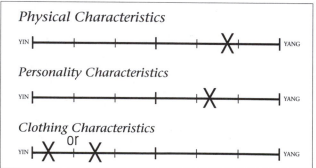

Conflict between opposing traits is apparent. Personality and appearance are not congruent.

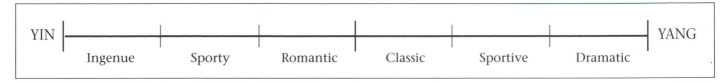

YIN							YANG
	Ingenue	Sporty	Romantic	Classic	Sportive	Dramatic	

Figure 8-5.

Yin/Yang Personal Style Categories

In her work, Bell Northrup divided the yin/yang continuum into six sections, categories, or types. She gave each section along the continuum a descriptive name to simplify communication. She identified many body traits, personality traits, and clothing traits stereotypically characteristic for each category or type.

You will remember that personal style in dress involves "the usual clothes you choose to wear, and the way you usually choose to wear them — how you consistently put the clothes together to meet your needs, in ways uniquely you." Northrup identified the typical clothing women in each category — or personal style type — usually choose. Each category is unique in terms of the clothes needed by the body and the personality traits characteristic for that category or type. The six categories include (1) ingenue, (2) sporty, (3) romantic, (4) classic, (5) sportive, and (6) dramatic. (See Figure 8–5.)

The names and words Northrup used may not be the best words available, nor the names or words you might have used. This is to be expected, particularly with such subjective topics as the body, personality, and clothing. Yin/yang charts in this book have been updated and expanded in the effort to assist understanding and application. Even this effort does not resolve all conflicts in name or word usage.

For example, take the word "submissive," generally included as a stereotypical yin characteristic. Keep in mind, all characteristics are "apparent" traits — what appears to be, not necessarily what actually is. Real life provides us with endless numbers of visually yin women possessing wonderfully soft-spoken, gentle manners who are incredibly strong. These women are capable of great accomplishments. Depending on their roles and response from others, they may choose to modify typical yin clothing, introducing some yang design traits to better communicate their strengths and abilities.

The focus of this discussion is on yin/yang categories and how they can relate to you and to your selection of tailored, softly tailored, and untailored clothing. (See Tables 8–2 through 8–5, pages 212 through 218, 220 through 223.)

This discussion and accompanying tables are not meant to be exhaustive nor absolute, but to represent a portion of continually evolving thought on this subject. They are intended to help you evaluate apparent harmony between your face and figure, your personality, and your clothing selection and coordination. They are suggested outlines much like recipes or formulas for achieving harmony in personal style — something almost easier to sense than to describe. Each recipe or formula, however, must be adapted to reflect and meet your unique and individual needs and goals.

Some people take a negative view of the six yin/yang categories or types. It is interesting, however, to consider what Mark L. Knapp wrote in his text, *Non-Verbal Communication in Human Interaction.* "Is it not plausible that, if so many people have the same conception (mental image), a stereotype may be the result of a distillation of ages of social experience . . . stereotypes may be more accurate than we wish to admit."

If we recognize that yin/yang stereotypical traits are potential stimuli for communication and response (See Figures 8–6 and 8–7, page 213.), then we can assume that if the traits (characteristics, cues, clues, symbols) are present

Figure 8-6. Soft, pliable fabric and a softly rounded cowl neckline in the blouse blend with the physical traits of the woman to communicate a romantic personal style. *(Courtesy Madeleine Direct)*

Table 8–2 Physical and Personality Traits Representing the Opposites of Yin and Yang in Women

	Yin	Yang
Height	Shorter (5'4" and under) Petite	Taller (5'8" and over)
Build	Small-boned, curved, delicate, narrow or sloping shoulders	Large-boned, angular, sturdy, broad or square shoulders
Posture	Graceful, tilted head with chin lowered, ballet posture	Erect, back on heels, head held high with chin raised
Head and Facial Contour	Heart-shaped, rounded; straight or receding chin	Long, square; straight or protruding jaw; high cheekbones, flat cheeks
Features	Smaller, rounded	Larger, angular
Eyes	Round, wide open, wide apart	Oval, slanting, close together
Eyebrows	Delicate, arched	Straight, angular, heavy
Nose	Shorter, turned up, delicate	Longer, larger, straight
Mouth	Smaller, heart-shaped	Larger, flat curves
Skin	Fine-textured	Slightly coarse-textured
Coloring	Lighter, little contrast; blonde to light brown hair, fair skin; blue, green eyes	Darker, strong dark/light contrast; dark, bleached, or red hair; medium to dark skin; brown eyes
Hairstyle	Natural, fluffy, soft curls	Controlled, straight, smooth, wavy, coarse-textured

	Yin	Yang
Personality, Manner, Expression	Receptive, dependent, friendly, informal, coy, naïve, impulsive, gentle, warm, idealistic, ladylike, unsophisticated, desiring to follow and to please	Assertive, independent, reserved, formal, dignified, poised, deliberate, forceful, cool, realistic, businesslike, sophisticated, desiring to lead and protect
Voice	Higher, softer	Lower, louder
Gestures and Walk	Graceful, impulsive, airy, gentle, light	Purposeful, deliberate, controlled, firm, decisive, long vigorous stride
Age	Youthful, appears younger, or elderly	Mature, appears older

Adapted from charts published in *Art and Fashion in Clothing Selection* by Harriet T. McJimsey.

in our own clothing and appearance, they will be perceived as such and responded to in predictable ways — in which case we become that stereotype or close thereto. Whatever the case, which characteristics or traits do you possess, reflect, or communicate? Are they associated with any particular yin/yang stereotypical category? Is it a type you want to reflect or be remembered as? Will those traits help you in achieving your goals? If not, what are your alternatives? Are there personal traits you could benefit from by developing? Are there clothing traits you could adopt that might foster this development? This is food for thought and action.

TIP
FROM THE PROS

While Northrup's categories are workable, she did not provide well for individuals with a specifically artistic and creative personal style. Emily Cho and Neila Fisher in their book *It's You,* and Alyce Parsons and Diane Parente in their book *Universal Style,* include discussions of an "arty" or "creative" personal style you may appreciate. These references also introduce another category, "sexy-alluring." This category, as a consistent personal style of dress, can lead to negative attention, in the home, school, community, and workplace.

Figure 8-7. A dramatic stance combines with bold shapes and shiny lamé fabric for a generally dramatic appearance. *(Courtesy Madeleine Direct)*

Table 8–3 Costume in Relation to Yin and Yang

	Yin	Yang
Line Type	Curved, rounded, broken or interrupted lines	Straight, angular, restrained curves, long, unbroken lines
Line Direction	Horizontal and upward movement of line	Vertical, diagonal, and downward movement of line
Silhouette Shape	Rounded, bouffant, bell, flared triangle, hourglass	Tubular, rectangular, A-line Wedge — inverted triangle, draped, pleated
Color	Lighter, closer value contrasts Clear to softly grayed intensities and pastels Cool and cool-warm hues	Darker, strong value contrasts Dull and bright intensified Warm and warm-cool hues
Texture	Pliable, smooth, crisp, transparent, sheer, fine, lightweight, soft; organdy, net, taffeta, soft sheer woolens, crisp cottons, chiffon	Firm, rough, rich, shiny, luxurious, opaque, heavy; tweeds, satins, brocades, lamé, gabardine, crepes
Pattern	Smaller scale, flared, rounded, checks	Larger scale, plaid, stripe
Details	Smaller buttons and belts; smocking, gathers, cording, piping, bows, lace; shorter sleeves and jackets	Larger buttons and belts; pleats, bands, braids, ribbon; longer sleeves and jackets
Balance	Symmetrical, except in small detail	Asymmetric or symmetrical
Scale	Small scale; many details; placed high; near collar yoke or midriff waist	Larger scale; few details; placed low; more often found in skirt
Emphasis	At shoulder, neckline, yoke	At waistline, hipline, hem
Rhythm	Interrupted, staccato rhythm as found in buttons that are paired, creating different intervals of spacing	Long, flowing, legato, continuous rhythm as found in long drapery; regular marching rhythm as found in evenly spaced buttons on a dress with a continuous front opening

Material adapted and expanded at Conselle Institute, from charts published in *Art and Fashion in Clothing Selection* by Harriet T. McJimsey

Table 8–4 Yin Personal Style Characteristics

Characteristics		Ingenue	Sporty	Romantic
Figure	Height	Shorter, below average	Shorter, below average	Average
	Build	Small-boned, dainty, delicate, triangular	Small-boned, compact, well coordinated, inverted triangle	Beautiful, curvaceous, hourglass figure, long-legged
	Posture	Graceful, ballet posture, head tilted, appealing, compliant	Erect, perky, hands on hips	Graceful, willowy, relaxed
Head and Face	Contour	Width between eyes, rounded cheeks and chin	Small, rounded cheeks and chin	Oval, triangular, heart-shaped, triangular
	Features	Smaller, dainty, delicate	Smaller, rounded	Average
	Eyes	Large, round, wide apart and open, long-lashed, coy or demure glance	Wide open, wide apart, twinkling, friendly	Large, long-lashed, alluring glance
	Eyebrows	Delicate natural arch	Natural	Arched
	Nose	Dainty, fine boned, upward tilt	Short, turned up, rounded "button end"	Delicate, long, straight, or slightly turned up
	Mouth	Small, heart-shaped, soft, relaxed	Small, rounded	Curved full lips, slightly parted
	Skin	Smooth, fine-textured	Smooth, fine-textured	Smooth, fine-textured
	Hairstyle	Short or long, feather cut, curly	Short, natural, bangs, braids, "ponytail", straight or curly	Long, curly, soft, feminine style
Coloring	Hair	Blonde	Light brown to blonde	Dark, golden blonde, red
	Skin	Pink, light brown	Tanned or freckled	Clear, fair
	Eyes	Blue	Blue, blue-green, green, hazel, brown	Violet, dark blue, brown

Table 8–4 Yin Personal Style Characteristics *(continued)*

	Characteristics	Ingenue	Sporty	Romantic
Expressions	Personality, expression and manner	Positive traits Approachable, receptive, sparkling, demure, shy, gentle, innocent	Approachable, receptive, casual, direct, natural "tomboy," perky, animated, mischievous, laughs easily, unpretentious	Approachable, receptive, flirtatious, charming, warm, responsive, sensuous, unsophisticated
		Negative traits Submissive, naïve, like a doll or little girl, unprofessional	Submissive, naïve, immature, careless	Submissive, naïve, helpless, unprofessional
	Voice	Higher pitch, soft, gentle	Lower pitch, boisterous	Soft
	Walk and gestures	Graceful, dancing, light, airy	Quick, "skipping," free and natural, swinging, awkward	Graceful, languorous
	Age	Ageless	Youthful, or appears young	Youthful, or appears young
Details of Design in Dress	Line	Curved, princess lines	Curved, horizontal	Curved, draped, horizontal
	Shape	Full-rounded, bouffant, bell	Softly rounded, bell	Flared, flowing, full-gathered
	Color	Cool and cool-warm hues, lighter, pale, pastels, pink, mint, aqua	Warm and cool hues, primary colors, med. values, med. to bright intensities, red, white, blue, green, yellow, rust	Warm and cool hues, med. values, med. intensities, black, violet, rose, mauve, apricot
	Fabric/texture	Lighter weight, pliable, silky, dotted swiss, batiste, voile, organdy, angora, crepe	Crisp, pliable, corduroy, woolens, jersey, gingham, quilted, chambray, denim, hand knits, eyelet, seersucker, pique, twill	Pliable, flowing, soft, luxurious, lace, silky, cashmere, challis, chiffon, jersey, crepe, velvet, voille, brocade satin
	Pattern	Floral prints, closely spaced, all over	Smaller scale plaids, checks, polka dots	Rounded prints, floral
	Details	Many, bows, ruffles, shirring, gathers, lace	Quite a few, buttons, pleats, ribbons, smocking, gathers, embroidery, appliqué, pleats	Many, ribbons and bows, gathers, ruffles, jabot, shirring, embroidery

Table 8–4 Yin Personal Style Characteristics *(continued)*

Characteristics		Ingenue	Sporty	Romantic
Clothing	Clothing — general	Dressier, untailored, dresses	Casually tailored, "preppy" unmatched suits	Softly tailored and un-tailored, dresses, fitted
	Brand/designer names	Laura Ashley Jessica McClintock Jennifer Reed	Marisa, Christina, Guess, Esprit, Ralph Lauren, Eddie Bauer, Benetton, Liz Claiborne, Laura Bingotti	Givenchy, Nancy Johnson, Albert Nippon, Geoffrey Beene, Diane Fres, Jane Singer, Lilli Ann, Ungaro
	Neckline	Scoop	Bateau or boat, crew, bib, henley	Scoop, ruffled, sweetheart, portrait
	Collars	Shawl, bowed, Puritan	Peter Pan, sailor, mock turtleneck, Mandarin	Lace, cowl, jabot
	Sleeves	Sleeveless, petal, melon, lantern, juliette	Sleeveless, puff, ruffle, roll-up, Kimono	Butterfly, ball, cape, flounced, bishop
	Blouses/shirts	Camisole	Tank top, polo shirt, cow-boy, middy	Peasant blouse, surplice, prairie
	Skirts	Tea-length, bouffant	Pleated, kilt, A-line, button-down	Dirndl, flared, tiered, sarong
	Dresses	Pinafore, dropwaist	Shifts, jumpers, baby doll, dropwaist	Empire, princess, wrap dress, peasant
	Pants	Flared, short shorts, draped-waist culottes	Pedal pushers, culottes, Bermuda shorts, jeans, knickers, overalls	Harem
	Vests	Shorter weskit	Shorter weskit	Fitted
	Sweaters	Twin set, novelty knit	V-neck, Fair Isle	Cowl neck
	Jackets	Short, box	Shorter, bolero, aviator, blazer	Edwardian, short capes, wrap, hacking
	Coats	Couchman, directoire, polo	Short poncho, duffle sport	Princess, swing, wrap
	Shoes	Sling-back pumps, bowed pumps, Mary Janes, satin pumps	Spectator pumps, penny loafers, sneakers, mocca-sins, saddle oxfords, clogs, topsiders	Dainty flats, ballet slippers, dainty straps, Mary Janes, patent leather
	Hats	Picture hats, veiled hats, slouch, bonnet	Sailor, beret, crew, jockey, cloche, breton, darby	Picture hat, cartwheel

Table 8–4 Yin Personal Style Characteristics *(continued)*

	Characteristics	Ingenue	Sporty	Romantic
Clothing	Handbags	Clutch	Tote, leather pouch, hobo, box	Clutch, fabric pouch
	Belts	Fabric belt, sash	Western, rope, chain	Shaped, sash, Grecian rope, fabric, cord, obi wrap
	Gloves	Shortie, wrist-length	Mittens	Elbow length and above
	Socks/stockings	White, pastel, ankle socks	Ankle socks, knee socks, tights, leggings	Lacy stockings, white, pastel
	Scarfs	Bowed	Cowboy, twisted, knotted	Shawl
Accessories	Jewelry	Delicate, diamonds, pearls, pearl choker, drop earrings	Hand crafted, circle pin, bead earrings	Delicate, dainty, seed pearls, cameo, locket
	Makeup	Strong, but not overdone; fake eyelashes	Minimal, natural	Minimal, soft

Adapted from charts published in *Art and Fashion in Clothing Selection* by Harriet T. McJimsey.

Yin-Yang Comparative Categories

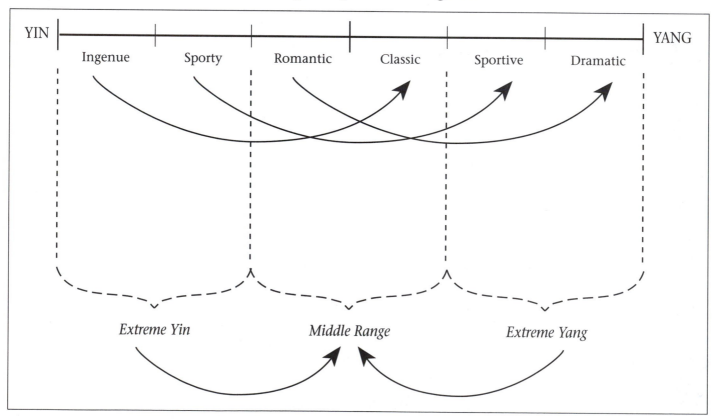

Figure 8-8.

Comparative Yin and Yang

As you read over, study, and compare the characteristics typical for each category (type) — you will gradually come to recognize points about the continuum as a whole, and similarities between the three yin categories (types) and the three yang categories (types). (See Figure 8–8.)

- Ingenue and sporty are the most extreme yin types (untailored).
- Sportive and dramatic are the most extreme yang types (tailored).
- The romantic yin and classic yang are intermediate types, blending characteristics of both yin and yang (softly tailored). Some of these characteristics are assumed to some degree by most people on related occasions.
- Ingenue is the most feminine yin, just as classic is the most feminine yang (relating to movement and personality traits, not sexuality).
- Sporty is the most masculine yin, just as sportive is the most masculine yang (relating to movement and personality traits, not sexuality). (See Figures 8–9 and 8–10.)
- Romantic is the most seldom seen yin, just as dramatic is the most seldom seen yang. People often assume some of these characteristics on evening and costume occasions.

- Characteristics along the continuum progress from relatively youthful to more mature. Classic and sportive individuals are more mature and possibly more reserved than ingenue and sporty types.
- Characteristics along the continuum progress from relatively naïve to more sophisticated. While ingenue and romantic are somewhat similar in their yin traits, romantic types are more sophisticated than ingenue, and dramatic individuals are more sophisticated still.
- Characteristics along the continuum tend to progress from untailored, to less tailored, to softly tailored, to tailored.

A change in occasion or situation often illicits changes in characteristics of mood, behavior, and dress — change roles and you often change clothes to complement or reflect the role. This is not to say you are not being yourself as you move in and out of a particular category. There is more than one "you" inside — more than one "me."

For example, *a woman often feels more youthfully yin while playing with her children and more romantic when out for the evening. She might have the need for a more mature, classic, somewhat yang appearance in a community leadership role, and a decidely more yang, tailored appearance during business hours. Clothing can enhance her feelings and her ability to function in her various roles.*

Figure 8-9. This denim dress typifies an untailored, yin, sporty or gamin design. *(Courtesy All Week Long by Eddie Bauer)*

Figure 8-10. This denim dress typifies a more tailored looking, yang, sportive design. *(Courtesy J. Crew; photographer Otto Stupekoff)*

Table 8–5 Yang Personal Style Characteristics

Characteristics		Classic	Sportive	Dramatic
Figure	Height	Average	Taller, above average	Taller, above average
	Build	Average for height, well-proportioned	Strong, sturdy, broad or square shoulders, possibly muscular or stocky	Current fashion figure, angular, large-boned, long-legged
	Posture	Easily erect, poised	Relaxed and casual, or vigorous and alert; solid, flat-heeled, hands on hips	Fashionable or erect, stiff, elevated chin, weight on heels
Head and Face	Contour	Oval	Long, or broad, square jaw, wide forehead	Long oval, high cheekbones, flat planes in cheeks, length and angularity
	Features	Average	Larger, angular	Larger, angular
	Eyes	Average size, clear, direct gaze	Average size, sparkling, approachable	Deep set, heavy lids, close together, angled or slanted, piercing, direct gaze
	Eyebrows	Smooth arch	Thick, dark, natural	Sharply defined, angular line
	Nose	Straight, well-shaped, average size	Strong, large, blunt, heavy, irregular	Long, pointed, flared nostrils, straight or convex curve in profile
	Mouth	Average	Wide, average, or heavy lips, smiling	Wide, flat curve, thin or heavy lips held firmly
	Skin	Smooth	Slightly more coarse	Slightly more coarse
	Hairstyle	Simple, neat, plain but not severe	Short, casual, unset, large wave	Extremes of fashion, plain, severe, center part with chignon is typical
Coloring	Hair	Light brown, darker blonde, taupe	Dark, brown or auburn	Black, dark brown, auburn, bright bleached blonde
	Skin	Clear, with no sharp contrasts	Tanned, freckled, natural looking	Dark, olive, or cream
	Eyes	Blue or hazel	Dark brown, green, hazel	Black, brown

Table 8–5 Yang Personal Style Characteristics (*continued*)

	Characteristics	Classic	Sportive	Dramatic
Expressions	Personality, expression and manner	Positive traits 　Assertive, gracious, poised, refined, under-stated elegance, con-ventional, sensible	Assertive, free, easy, casual, frank, open, friendly, con-fident, persistent	Assertive, formal, dignified, reserved, haughty, sophis-ticated, exaggerated, tem-peramental, theatrical, aloof, mysterious
		Negative traits 　Boring, unimaginative, too proper	Aggressive, dominant, brusque	Aggressive, intimidating, distant, unnatural, affected, pretentious
	Voice	Well modulated, pleasing	Naturally low pitch, strong, clear	Low, husky, resonant, emphatic, deliberate
	Walk and gestures	Calm, poised, well controlled	Long strides, free swinging, large, easy, relaxed, natural	Decisive, energetic, or slow and purposeful
	Age	Mature	Mature, but friendly and casual at any age	Mature, or appears older than others of same age
Details of Design in Dress	Line	Straight, restrained curves	Straight, angular, vertical	Straight, angular, vertical, diagonal
	Shape	Tubular, rectangular, flared-triangular	Tubular, rectangular, flared-triangular	Tubular, triangular, inverted triangle, bouffant
	Color	Medium value contrasts, navy blue, French blue, gray, white, peach, beige, taupe, cream, mauve	Warm and warm-cool hues, earth tones, primary colors, strong value contrasts, dull to med. intensities, brown, tan, olive, reds, blue, hunter green, ivory, terra cotta	Warm and cool hues, strong value contrast, bright, intense, black, charcoal, violet, purple, royal, white, emerald, gold, fuschia
	Fabric/texture	Smooth, pima-cotton, crepe, jersey, flannel, challis, silky, silk noir	Nubby, rough, shantung, suede, tweeds, gabardine, leather, knits, quilted, linen, denim, raw silk, chambray, handwovens, oxford cloth, twill, gauze, camel hair	Severe to elaborately tex-tured, ornate, glittery, shiny, satin, brocade, velvet, lamé, novelty weaves, cashmere
	Pattern	Small to medium prints, paisley, polka dots, traditional, jacquards	Medium prints, leaf prints, geometrics, checks, paisley, plaids, herringbone, stripes	Large prints, abstract, leop-ard/jungle prints, stripes, widely spaced
	Details	Fewer	Fewer, border, pockets, pleats, epaulettes	Fewer

Table 8–5 Yang Personal Style Characteristics *(continued)*

Characteristics	Classic	Sportive	Dramatic
Clothing — general	Softly tailored, matched suits	Tailored, man-style, sports clothes, unmatched suits	Extremes in style, high fashion, matched and unmatched suits, asymmetrical
Brand/designer names	Georgio Armani, Calvin Klein, Mary McFadden, Talbots, Perry Ellis, Brooks Brothers, Evan Picone	Jill Sander, Liz Claiborne, J.G. Hook, Clifford & Wills, Ellen Tracy, Gloria Sachs, Jones of New York	Lagerfeld, Halston, Claude Montana, Gautlier, Bob Mackie
Necklines	Jewel, keyhole, square	Crew neck, V-neck	Halter deep-V
Collars	Shawl, cowl neck	Convertible, notch, turtle-neck	Reverse
Sleeves	Cap, set-in, smooth	Raglan, push-up, ¾ length, sport shirt, drop-shoulder	Long fitted, trumpet, dolman, batwing
Blouses/shirts	Shell, yoke-style	Camp shirt, safari shirt, sport shirt	Body suit, tunics
Skirts	Straight, A-line, dirndl	Straight, A-line, trouser, stitched-down pleats, pleated	Straight, pegged, six-gore, trumpet
Dresses	Shirt waist, blouse dress	Shifts, shirtwaist, coatdress, sweater dress, halter dress	Sheath, tent, caftan, chemise
Pants	Stove pipe	Pleat-front trouser, safari shorts, split skirt, gauchos, jumpsuit	Palazzo pants, bell, flared
Vests	Fitted	Longer, knit, unfitted	Long to full length
Sweaters	Sweater set	Cardigan, Shetland, turtle-neck, cable knit	Long to full length
Jackets	Chanel, fitted blazer, notched or shovel lapel	Longer, notched lapel, unfitted blazer, safari, car coat	Swing, peaked lapels
Coats	Duster	Longer poncho	Swagger, cape, tuxedo
Shoes	Leather pumps	Fringed loafer, stacked heels, boots, clogs, sandals	High heels, boots
Hats	Pill box, cloche	Fedora, military	Turban, fez, hood, toque

(Row group label, vertical:) Clothing

Table 8–5 Yang Personal Style Characteristics *(continued)*

Characteristics		Classic	Sportive	Dramatic
Clothing	Handbags	Chanel bag, envelop, tailored toe, swagger	Coach, tote, safari, satchel	Envelope
	Belts	1" medium leather	1¼ to 2" wide top-stitched leather, suede	Wide elastic, cummerbund
	Gloves	Slip on	Top-stitched slip on	Gauntlet
	Socks/stockings	Natural sheers	Ribbed socks, tights, leggings	Black sheers, patterned
	Scarf/tie	Jabot, stock tie	Hacking, men's style	Ascot, shawl
Accessories	Jewelry	Conservative, quality, cameo, pearls	Simple, semi-precious, wood, shells, gold stud, hoop earring	Bold, simple or elaborate, ornate, barbaric, geometric, snake, spiral, hoop
	Makeup	Conservative	Minimal or natural	Exaggerated

Adapted from charts published in *Art and Fashion in Clothing Selection* by Harriet T. McJimsey.

Twenty Questions

Understanding your personal style is a matter of knowing yourself. Continue to become more aware of yourself. Ask yourself twenty questions. Then ask twenty more.

1. What physical body characteristics do I possess?
2. What personality traits do I possess?
3. What traits do my favorite clothes possess?
4. What do my clothing traits communicate to me and others?
5. Are my clothing traits congruent, or in harmony, with my body and my personality?
6. Are there any personality traits I'd like to develop, that my clothing might enhance or encourage?
7. Which yin/yang category, or categories, seem to reflect me most nearly — my body, my personality, and the clothes I like best?
8. Which categories seem most foreign to me?
9. Which characteristics, in which categories, are definitely not me?
10. Do I wear more dresses or more separates?
11. Do I wear more skirts or more slacks?
12. Have I really experienced wearing a skirt — and the feelings a skirt allows?
13. Am I missing out on a part of myself that might be nice to experience?
14. Do I use my clothing as a resource or tool to present, express, or reflect the real me?
15. If so, how?
16. If not, how can I use my clothing as a tool to present my physical self well and to be true to my personality (and my values) at the same time?
17. Do I experience any conflicts between the clothes I wear and their appropriateness for my body and my personality (as well as my values)?
18. Do I look and feel authentic and comfortable in my clothes, or do I seem fake or artificial?
19. What characteristics do I borrow from a particular category, on what occasions?
20. What personality or character traits do I want to develop that my clothing might enhance?

The Logic of Yin/Yang

An understanding of the yin/yang concept can be revealing and can provide explanations for why people have certain clothing likes and dislikes, or how clothing can stimulate conflict.

For example, dominant yin women often state they prefer warm-weather clothing, which relies on yin design traits, while they dislike cold-weather clothing, which relies on yang design characteristics. They have to look longer to find winter clothing that blends some yin traits into the design. With this as an influencing factor, a dominant yin woman may dislike living in the North — where personality as well as clothing traits are more yang.

Dominant yang women often state they prefer cold-weather clothing, which relies on yang design characteristics, and they dislike warm-weather clothing, which relies on yin design traits. They have to look longer to find summer clothing that blends some yang traits into the design. Untailored styles they may select tend to be single or basic in design, not frilly or ruffled. With this as a factor, a dominant yang woman may dislike living in the South — where personality as well as clothing traits are more yin.

Dominant yin women, when they become pregnant, have less trouble finding maternity clothing they like — most of which is designed with yin traits.

Dominant yang women, when they become pregnant, have a more difficult time finding maternity clothing they like — little of which is designed with yang characteristics.

A dominant yin mother and yang daughter may disagree, even argue, about clothing choices.

A dominant yang sales associate or personal shopper may have difficulty making a selection or sale with yin customers or clients, because she tries to interest them in the yang styles she prefers.

A woman over forty-five suddenly feels foolish in youthful yin clothing. The teen-age ingenue often grows up to become classic in personal style, while the sporty young woman often grows up to prefer sportive clothing.

A yang student doesn't get along with her yin roommate.

A yang wife doesn't appreciate gifts of yin clothing from her husband.

In each of the preceding cases, substitute the words advancing, assertive, authoritative, and tailored for yang; substitute the words receding, submissive, approachable, and untailored for yin; and you will better understand the reasons behind the difficulties, conflicts, or lack of appreciation.

Understanding and Appreciation

Recognizing yin/yang differences is the first step in resolving difficulties or conflicts related to or stimulated by dress. Too often we reject or separate ourselves from others who are different than we are — our opposites. We tend to be more comfortable with those more like ourselves. When we understand some of the reasoning behind another person's behavior, appearance, and preference in clothing, we are more apt to accept that person. With continued association, we may even come to appreciate that other person for those differences. Opposites can attract, but only when there is an effort to understand, accept, and appreciate.

In the days ahead, be on the lookout for examples of harmony and conflict in appearance, to help you in your awareness, understanding, and application of the yin/yang concept in dress. Evaluate every attractive, appealing, harmonious appearance you can. Examine the details of dress.

Discover how the elements of design have been manipulated. Decide how the clothes seem to relate to the person. Take note of every conflicting appearance you can. Examine the details and try to discover how the elements of design have been used. Try to determine why the details seem unrelated, incongruent, unharmonious.

With increased awareness and experience, you will come to understand your preferred style and details of dress. Find pictures that illustrate your preferred style and add them to your personal style file. The more you understand your preferred style of dress, the more you will use your clothing as a medium of self-expression, and the less you will depend on others to define your dress. The more consistent, stable, and secure you are in your dress, the less concerned you will be about it, and the more you will be able to forget about yourself, allowing you to get on with the activities of your day, and to pursue the goals in your life.

4.

Select clothing designed with the appropriate degree of assertiveness or approachability to meet your individual needs or purposes — appropriate for your life–style and personal style and goals.

Range on the Yin/Yang Continuum

Seldom does a person fit neatly into one yin or yang category, into strictly tailored or untailored clothing. Any attempt to require you to fit into a mold rightly brings criticism. It is a matter of how far on the continuum, or how far into a specific category, a person is willing to go with dress. Again, personal style in dress implies limits on a yin/untailored or yang/tailored continuum. Your consistent and self-imposed limits determine your range — the range within which you look and feel authentic, congruent, or comfortable with yourself in your clothes. Each individual's range differs to some degree. (See Figure 8–11.)

Your clothing selection and personal style generally reflect traits within your range. Again, consciously or unconsciously, people will often recognize the correlation, stating something like, "That (clothing) looks just like you!" Therein lies part of the fun with fashion.

For example, *one young woman explains, "I thoroughly enjoy my clothes. I love the fun of choosing what to wear, of being able to express myself. I like dressing casually sportive for class in the morning, adding an assertive layer for work in the afternoon, removing that layer and adding a single piece of jewelry or a scarf to soften my look for evening, or changing altogether, into something more dressy, more feminine. Dressing can be fun, creative, and expressive. Personal style reflects a difference between me and others."*

Personality Range

(Limits on the Yin-Yang Continuum)

Examples

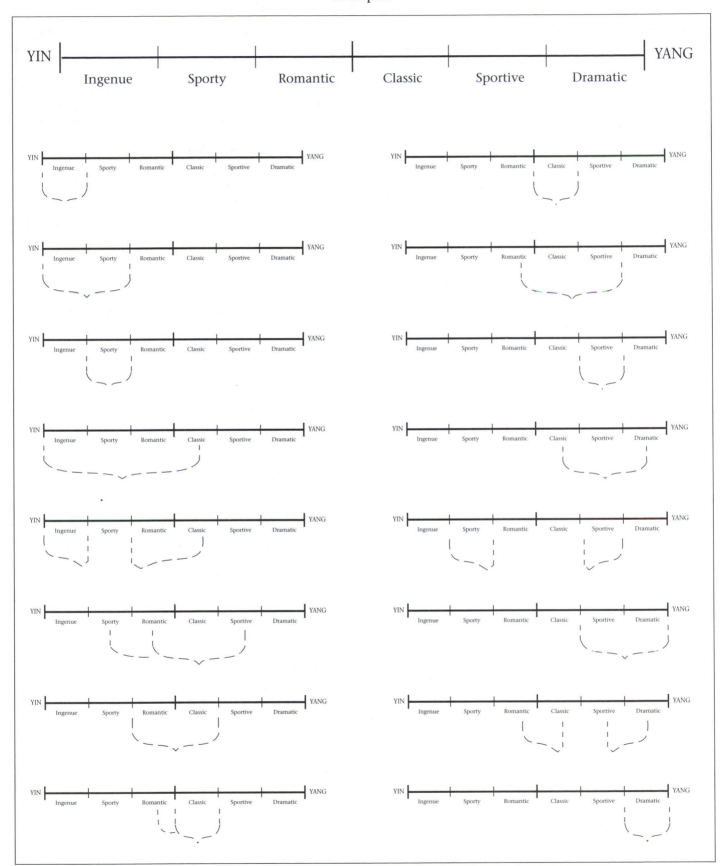

Figure 8-11.

Crossover Characteristics

Individuality in personal style usually includes some crossover, with borrowing and blending of both yin and yang characteristics — what McJimsey discussed as composite types. The person with a wide range on the yin/yang continuum, or the person with sections from both sides, qualify as a composite type; they crossover. They borrow traits to meet different needs for different moods and occasions, roles, and goals.

A specific outfit can be predominantly yin but include something borrowed from the yang side of the continuum. And vice versa, an outfit may be predominantly yang, but include something borrowed from the yin side of the continuum. (See Figure 8–12.) You can take a yin clothing style and present it in a yang manner. Or, you can take a yang clothing style and present a yin variation of it.

For example, visualize a physical yang (tall, large-boned, and brunette) with yin personality traits (soft-spoken, gentle, and sensitive), whose favorite outfit is predominantly yin (a dress, in soft fabric, and floral print) with some borrowed yang characteristics (darker colors and large-scale pattern). The dress might even include lace (yin), but the lace will be flat, heavier, cotton lace (yang version).

For example, visualize a physical yin (shorter, delicate features, and blonde) with yang personality traits (purposeful, direct, and precise), whose favorite outfit is predominantly yang (separates, earthtones, contrasting colors, and firm fabrics) with some borrowed yin characteristics (small-scale patterns and clothing sizes).

When you acknowledge different sides of your own personality, and when you use clothing to express those different sides, you're dealing with yin/yang crossovers. (See Figure 8–13.) When the look doesn't work, you say, "It's not me." When it does work, you declare, "It's me!" We've all had this experience, and it is delightful. You can do it too. (See Figures 8–14 and 8–15, page 228.)

Do It Yourself

In crossing over, or borrowing, it works well to maintain your preferred yin or yang clothing styles, made in fabric weights appropriate for the style and the weather but to select the scale, specific fabrics, colors, patterns, and/or trims from the other yang or yin side of the continuum, to better present your body or reflect your individuality.

In buying ready-to-wear clothing, you may be able to:

- Remove or add some design details.

Personality Crossover and Borrowing

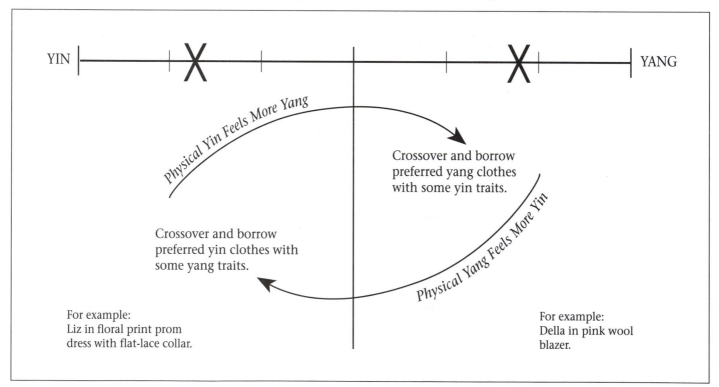

YIN ———————— X ———————— | ———————— X ———————— YANG

Physical Yin Feels More Yang

Crossover and borrow preferred yang clothes with some yin traits.

Crossover and borrow preferred yin clothes with some yang traits.

Physical Yang Feels More Yin

For example:
Liz in floral print prom dress with flat-lace collar.

For example:
Della in pink wool blazer.

Figure 8-12.

Personality Borrowing

Examples

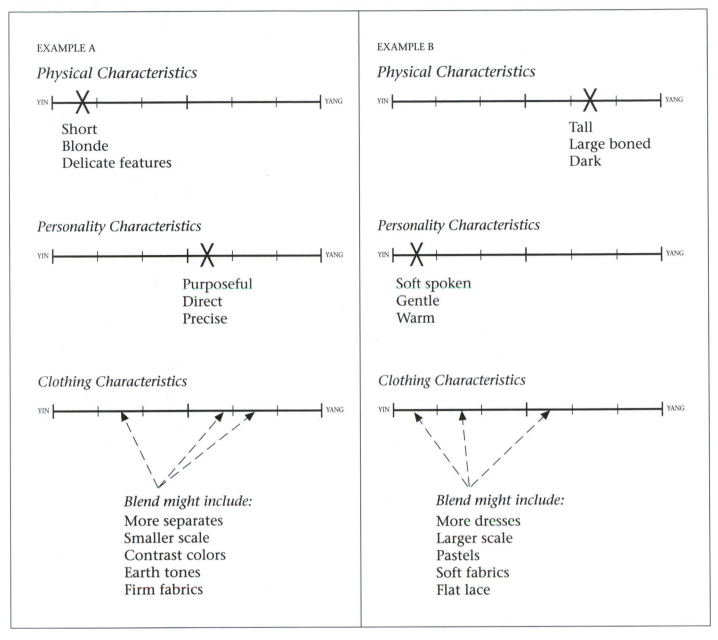

Figure 8-13.

For example, you might remove a bow or epaulettes, add a detachable collar or embroidery, or change the buttons.

- Change the position of division lines.

For example, you might move a pocket up or down, shorten a sleeve, shorten a peplum, shorten or lengthen a hem.

- Change the way you wear the style.

For example, you might choose to wear a collar closed at the throat, appearing more closed and unapproachable. Or you might choose to wear the collar open at the neck, appearing more open and friendly.

- Add an accessory to further counter the effect of the clothing.

For example, add a cameo or a whimsical pin at the neck to counter or soften the effect of the closed collar.

- Add another layer in your preferred yin or yang style.

For example, wear a blazer over a cotton knit polo shirt to counter or dress up the casual effect of the polo shirt.

Sewing Expands Your Options

If you sew, you can deal with the design while it's still on paper. You can change almost anything on a pattern — to some degree — to better meet your needs.

Figure 8-14. This dominant yin chooses a tailored yang blazer, but in a pink plush woolen, well-suited to her personal style. *(Courtesy J. Crew; photographer Mark Abrahams)*

Figure 8-15. This dominant yang selects a feminine, untailored yin dress, but in a darker color with a heavy, flat lace collar in a contrasting color better suited to her personal style. *(Courtesy All Week Long by Eddie Bauer; photographer David Martinez)*

• Change some aspect or detail of the design on the sewing pattern.

For example, you might simply add or omit pockets, cuffs, even a collar; or change the line or size of the pocket, collar, or skirt. You can change the grainline position, or change darts or pleats to gathers or flares, add or reduce fullness, add or omit seamlines, lengthen the sleeve or skirt hem.

• Add, omit, or adapt trim.

For example, add or omit piping in seams you want or don't want to emphasize. Add or omit lace, ruffles, beading, and so forth.

• Select fabric, color, and pattern suited to you.

For example, the style may be perfect, but you can choose softer fabric and a lighter color for a more yin appearance, or choose firmer fabric and a darker color to appear more yang.

5.

Coordinate or combine tailored/yang with softly tailored or untailored/yin clothing pieces for more effective visual communication, greater versatility, interest, and individuality.

Harmony in Dress

By now you have learned that the elements of design can be combined in ways that are never rigidly absolute, seldom regular, yet are always logical. In the search for beauty, interest, and harmony, we strive to combine similarity with variety — repetition with contrast. Nowhere is that more delightfully demonstrated than in the results of combining tailored with untailored clothing, yin with yang characteristics of dress.

In all art forms, including dress, the main parts of the composition must be similar, or our senses would become confused. You don't, however, want everything so much the same that the outfit becomes boringly predictable. It is important, therefore, to introduce some variety — some contrast or difference in one, or some, of the parts. Without variety our senses cannot be fully stimulated. People like a touch of the unexpected — a surprise element to renew interest and attract them to your uniqueness.

Therefore, **coordinate or combine the parts of a garment, or the parts of an outfit, in terms of the activity, occasion, mood, values, and personality traits they communicate**. Make them similar or related in terms of yin/untailored or yang/tailored — having a single, dominant theme. That prepares the way for you to introduce a little variety, a subordinate theme.

Dominance and Subordinance

The concept of dominance and subordinance demands that whatever is dominant appears largest, most important, and attracts the most attention. Whatever is subordinate is smaller, less important, less emphatic, or attracts less to little attention. (See Figure 8–16.) The variety — that which is different — is always present in the smaller amount or area. It introduces a subordinate theme and counters the dominant theme. It can, however, be the focal point of interest.

For example, the dominant theme or mood communicated by a tailored suit is probably business. The dominant theme may be communicated by the tailored style and reinforced by the use of similarly businesslike colors, fabrics, and patterns throughout all areas of the outfit. The complete outfit may, however, feature subordinate feminine detailing to communicate desired approachability and warmth. The subordinate idea may be communicated by a piece of jewelry, a lace jabot, or a lace-edged pocket-square — just enough of the unpredictable to add interest to the look of the outfit. Too much feminine detailing, such as a lace blouse with frilly collar and cuffs, in combination with the otherwise tailored business suit can be expected to conflict with one another and create mixed messages.

Regardless of differing amounts, and in the hierarchy of dominance and subordinance, one thing must be dominant and all other things must be subordinate by degree. That is to say, among a combination of clothing pieces and accessories, **one item must be dominant and all other items must be less dominant or subordinate by degrees.**

For example, a chesterfield box coat is designed with one dominant line type (straight) and line direction (vertical) and a few subordinate lines (curved, diagonal, horizon-

1
Silk suit

Figure 8-16. The body, suit, and bracelet are yang Dramatic. The heart-shaped pendant introduces a touch of unexpected yin femininity, which becomes a focal point when carried out in reflective, heavy metal — totally in harmony with the clothes and with the wearer. *(Courtesy Madeleine Direct)*

tal) in the collar and hem; one dominant color (gray) in the body of the coat and a subordinate contrasting color (navy blue) in the collar; and one dominant fabric (wool melton) in the body of the coat and a subordinate fabric (velvet) in the collar. The coat is dominant yang in design, with subordinate yin characteristics in the collar. The collar is the focal point in an outfit.

You may be confused when you consider the size of an area or the amount of a color, fabric, or pattern in an outfit. What is dominant is not necessarily present in the largest area or amount nor is it always the focal point — although it may be.

For example, the dominant style of the suit discussed previously was decidedly tailored business, yet featured a feminine focal point. Placed in a central or obvious location, a jeweled brooch or lace jabot in a contrasting color or material becomes a focal point. While small, it claims attention precisely because it is different. Being small, its difference does not compete with the larger area of the tailored-business outfit but appears balanced and is a welcome variation on a traditional theme. The lace-edged pocket-square is still smaller and less demanding, sub-subordinate to the lace jabot. It is a look that designer Ralph Lauren parleyed into a multi-million-dollar business.

Another designer, Jessica McClintock, has a way with beautiful, romantic dresses like no one else. During the eighties she touched a chord with women of all ages, supplying Gunne Sax™ dresses with lace and ruffles that appealed to both yin and yang. McClintock's feminine designs featured longer flared skirts on a fitted bodice, often with long fitted or full sleeves, and either a built-up neckline or a lowered neckline. All-over patterns were small to medium, in floral motifs. Colors, however, were generally darker or ivory — more yang. Her dresses were trimmed with ribbon and lace, but ribbon was darker, and lace was often ivory, in medium to heavy weights, often sewn flat to the bodice and down the skirt, or ruffled at the hems only. The combinations of characteristics were irresistible to thousands of women, including yang women who had never owned such a pretty dress before. McClintock was a tremendous success, and while designs have evolved and changed over the years, they continue to sell well.

The application of dominance and subordinance is precisely why Ralph Lauren and Jessica McClintock have been so successful. Both know the importance and impact that blended styles and crossover design characteristics can have. Ralph Lauren put a little yin in his yang, and Jessica McClintock put a little yang in her yin. Their clothing appeals to a wide range of buyers.

Keep in mind, create only one dominant point of attention or emphasis in an outfit — preferably near the face for business or leadership occasions. Emphasis at the wrist, waist, or hem is generally more appropriate for social occasions. Any other points or areas of attention should be subordinate — less important by degrees. The design elements — line, shape, color, texture, and pattern — can be manipulated to create an infinite variety of yin or yang effects. In the final analysis, it is the dominance of each element and a single focal point that is essential. Test your results with the "blink" test. If your attention jumps back and forth from one spot or area to another, then you have elements competing to be dominant — one style fighting with another, one color clashing with another, one fabric conflicting with another, or one accessory. Something has got to be replaced with something less attention getting, something subordinate. If

Figure 8-17. Shirt styling is dominant yang, rendered in a soft knit and paired with a softly pleated chiffon shirt which adds a degree of yin femininity to the total look. *(Courtesy Madeleine Direct)*

your eye travels smoothly throughout the outfit and can focus on one place — one point of greatest contrast — you have very likely succeeded.

A Style of Your Own

This flexible and creative way of combining your clothes opens up endless avenues for greater personal expression, personal development, and personal growth. (See Figure 8–17.) Experiment, discover, and develop looks in harmony with your body, your personality, the places you go, and what you do there. Use it to your advantage.

A Style of Your Own

Style isn't something you buy in a jar and spread all over yourself. Style comes from within. Everyone has the potential for personal style; you may simply need to coax yours out of hiding.

Really think about what you like and what you don't — on other people and in the stores. Build your own style file of favorite looks you find in magazines and catalogs.

If your eye is attracted to rich romantic colors, menswear fabrics, or gorgeous exotic prints, but you think you can't wear them, find a way to wear them. You don't have to drench yourself in them. Incorporating bits and pieces of what you like into your wardrobe is the beginning of personal style.

Take time to experiment with your clothes. That is the very best way to discover what you like, to develop and understand your personal style. That's the way to gain the confidence to stick with what you like, independent of fashion or friends.

Give it a try. First, for a period of one week, put together a different look with your clothes and try to reflect a different part of you each day. Now, don't bother trying out looks you obviously don't like.

If you've always disliked Ivy League "preppy" styles, don't bother with them. And if you're not a flamboyant person, don't try to look the part or you'll only look and feel foolish.

Try expressing your serious self one day. Be your most outgoing, outrageous self the next. And for you, that may not be far. That's fine. It's what works for you. Reflect your more sensitive self another day — warm and caring — and so on throughout your week.

As you go about your days and your business, be very aware of any thoughts about what you're wearing. Be aware of how you feel, how you act, and how others react to you. You'll feel a fantastic surge of self-confidence about your appearance when you can say, "Yes, that works, that's me."

You'll know you achieved some degree of personal style when you can forget yourself and your looks, and when people seem consistently comfortable with you and respond with approval. Their reactions will confirm your growing sense of self.

Next, try achieving at least three different looks with some of your favorite standbys. Don't go overboard as you try out new looks with older clothes. Go slowly, making little changes at a time.

You might try a different accessory, a different color combination, a new look in layering pieces. This can be great fun. It's like putting together a wonderful jigsaw puzzle and getting all the parts to fit.

If you love antique jewelry or vintage hats and stark modern clothes, mix them. Style doesn't require that everything be from the same time period. Your mix is your style.

Have you always worn matched suits? Then switch them around and create an unmatched suit look, pulled together and coordinated by the blouse and other accessories.

Are you a pants person? Try leaving your blouse untucked and beautifully belted. Or top the pants with a tunic for a change of pace. For that matter, try a skirt or dress for a change — maybe a denim skirt.

Are you typically in a dress? Then try wearing a shirt under the dress, with the shirt collar peeking out over the dress collar. Top the dress with a vest or jacket instead. Try a split skirt. You get femininity with the practicality of pants.

Are you always in solid colors? Try a print or plaid for a change, styled, scaled, and colored to your taste. Advance to mixing two patterns with a solid color, all in one outfit.

Do you go overboard on basics? So basic you become boring? Add a costume piece to your closet. A holiday theme sweater could be timely. Instead of wearing a fantastic beaded collar over a basic dress, try it over a classic fringed leather jacket.

Try editing your present look, rather than adding to it. You may be preventing your style from coming through by wearing all the usual accessories — necklace, bracelet, earrings, ring, and a scarf. Try removing a piece or two. Maybe you'll like wearing a pair of fantastic earrings and no other jewelry. Less really can be more.

You don't have to match everything. Jacket and skirt, handbag and shoes, earrings and necklace don't have to be matched sets. A tweed jacket and paisley skirt still produce the look of a suit. Simple gold earrings can mix perfectly with a mother-of-pearl pendant, rimmed in gold.

Don't hesitate to try out the look of these new parts and pieces in the stores before buying. This can save on costly mistakes, both financially and emotionally.

The point of this piece? The learning starts with learning what you like. The looks that work for you!

Review Main Points

Tailored clothing is designed with predominantly straight lines, tubular and angled shapes, dulled and darker colors, with stronger value contrast, firmer fabrics, and smaller patterns. Rely on them for occasions or situations when you need to appear more authoritative and capable. Softly tailored and untailored clothing are designed with curved lines and rounded shapes, lighter and brighter colors, with less value contrast, more pliable fabrics, and larger patterns. Rely on them for occasions or situations when you need to appear more approachable and friendly. Within the yin/yang concept, yin compares to untailored clothing, while yang compares to tailored clothing. Categories that range on a continuum between yin and yang include ingenue, sporty, romantic, classic, sportive, and dramatic. Within each category, physical characteristics or traits, personality traits, and clothing traits are identified. Knowing your range on the yin/yang continuum, you can better select and coordinate the characteristics of your clothing to present your body attractively and appropriately, to reflect your personality accurately, and to help you achieve your goals. Combining your clothing in interesting and harmonious ways is one of the keys to putting together an interesting, versatile, and fashionable wardrobe.

Review Questions

1. Tailored clothes are designed with _____ shapes, while less tailored clothes feature _____ lines.

2. Name two occasions or situations when you could benefit by wearing tailored clothes. _____ _____

3. Yin and _____ generally describe the same or similar clothing traits.

4. Tailored clothing designs communicate _____ and _____.

5. _____ traits are the most obvious to others.

6. List two personality traits characteristic of a dramatic type woman. _____ _____

7. Describe the physical traits characteristic of a sportive type woman. _____ _____

8. Describe clothing traits characteristic of an ingenue. _____ _____

9. It is realistic for people to conform to one yin/yang category.   True   False

10. Characteristics along the yin/yang continuum progress from _____ to more _____.

11. List two pieces of clothing typical for a woman with a sporty personal style. _____ _____

12. Which of the following words does not belong in the group? Circle the word.
    Romantic   Ingenue   Dramatic   Sporty

13. Match the following personal style types to the characteristic traits.

    _____ sporty   a. outgoing, persistent, informal

    _____ sportive   b. practical, timeless, poised

    _____ ingenue   c. forever young, delicate, gentle

    _____ classic   d. bubbly, cute, optimistic

14. It is not surprising to find dominantly _____ women who have difficulty finding summer-weather clothing they like and relate to.

15. Recognizing yin/yang differences is the first step in resolving difficulties or conflicts stimulated by dress.   True   False

16. Describe what is meant by your "range" on a yin/yang continuum. _____ _____

17. Smaller-scale design details and pattern motifs are characteristic of dominant _____ women.

18. The concept of crossover dressing allows you to _____ clothing characteristics from the opposite side of the yin/yang continuum.

19. Describe one way to adapt or change a piece of ready-to-wear clothing to better suit your personal style. _____

_____

20. Describe one piece of clothing you could combine with a blazer jacket to make it more appropriate and in harmony with a romantic or ingenue woman. _____

_____

Discussion Questions

#1 What situations or occasions in your life require, or could benefit from, a tailored image? A softly tailored image? An untailored appearance?

Notes: _____

_____

_____

_____

_____

#2 Identify women [people] in the news and their apparent yin/yang characteristics or types. Discuss how their appearance is received and responded to by the public.

Notes: _____

_____

_____

_____

_____

#3 Going around the classroom, identify ways to make each person's outfit appear more yin. More yang. Having identified several ways, discuss how each person would feel if dressed that way.

Notes: _____

_____

_____

_____

_____

Exercise 8–1   Tailored/Untailored Recognition

Name_____

Look at what you are wearing.

• Identify, list, and check mark any piece of clothing that is tailored, softly tailored, or untailored.
• Identify a personal style type — ingenue, sporty, romantic, classic, sportive, or dramatic — apparent in each piece of clothing.
• Identify any characteristics of line, shape, color, texture, or pattern that lead you to your decision.
• Work with a neighboring classmate and identify as above.

You – Clothing Item	Tailored	Softly Tailored	Untailored	Ingenue	Sporty	Romantic	Classic	Sportive	Dramatic	Characteristics (line, shape, color, texture, pattern)

Classmate – Clothing Item	Tailored	Softly Tailored	Untailored	Ingenue	Sporty	Romantic	Classic	Sportive	Dramatic	Characteristics (line, shape, color, texture, pattern)

Exercise 8-2   Personal Style Preference   Name_____

Look in your closet, selecting five to ten favorite pieces of clothing and five to ten less favorite pieces of clothing.

- In the appropriate section — favorite/less favorite — place a check mark to identify the type of styling — tailored, softly tailored, untailored; ingenue, sporty, romantic, classic, sportive, and dramatic.
- Describe specific characteristics of line, shape, color, texture,

and pattern that influenced your decision.
- Total the number of garments identified in each column.
- Draw some conclusions about how all these characteristics of design have influenced your preferences and personal style.

Clothing Item	Tailored	Softly Tailored	Untailored	Ingenue	Sporty	Romantic	Classic	Sportive	Dramatic	Characteristics (line, shape, color, texture, pattern)
Favorite Clothes										
TOTALS										

Clothing Item	Tailored	Softly Tailored	Untailored	Ingenue	Sporty	Romantic	Classic	Sportive	Dramatic	Characteristics (line, shape, color, texture, pattern)
Less Favorite Clothes										
TOTALS										

Conclusions:

Exercise 8–3   Local Store Experience

Look in a local clothing store for garments that fit the descriptions of tailored, softly tailored, untailored and ingenue, sporty, romantic, classic, sportive, or dramatic. In front of a full-length mirror, experiment with the look of these clothes in relation to you.

Clothing Store Experience:

• Hold the garment up to you.
• Notice and record how the clothes make you look and what they appear to communicate.
• If possible, and to see how the clothing will look on you, try the garments on.
• Notice and record how the clothes look on you.
• Notice and record what the clothes appear to communicate.
• Evaluate the clothing's practicality for your life-style.

Exercise 8–4 Personal Style Recognition

- Collect two pictures of garments or outfits that typify tailored clothing.
- Mount and label.

- Collect two pictures of garments or outfits that typify softly tailored clothing.
- Mount and label.

- Collect two pictures of garments or outfits that typify untailored clothing.
- Mount and label.

- Collect one picture for each yin/yang category — ingenue, sporty, romantic, classic, sportive, and dramatic.
- Mount and label.

Exercise 8–5 Personal Style Coordination

Name _____

Find pictures of clothing pieces in types of styling you would like to combine into an outfit for yourself. Consider the lines, shapes, colors, textures, and patterns. Look for clothes you expect will flatter you. Look for pieces you can combine harmoniously. Write a paragraph explaining the reasons for your choices.

Attach here

2nd Layer
Garment Top

☐ Classic Style
☐ Trend/Fad

Attach here

Garment Bottom

☐ Classic Style
☐ Trend/Fad

Attach here

Accessory Item

☐ Classic Style
☐ Trend/Fad

Attach here

2nd Layer Garment Top

☐ Classic Style
☐ Trend/Fad

Attach here

Garment Bottom

☐ Classic Style
☐ Trend/Fad

Attach here

3rd Layer
Garment Top

☐ Classic Style
☐ Trend/Fad

Attach here

Accessory Item

☐ Classic Style
☐ Trend/Fad

Attach here

Accessory Item

☐ Classic Style
☐ Trend/Fad

Personal & Preferred Characteristics Name_____

Having plotted your physical and personality characteristics, as well as your preferred characteristics, consider each as a group and position yourself in the following Yin-Yang continuums.

Yin..Yang
Physical Body Characteristics

Yin..Yang
Personality Characteristics

Yin..Yang
Clothing Characteristics

Now, determine your range or limits on the following Yin-Yang continuum.

Draw some conclusions regarding your overall position on the continuum in terms of dominant yin or yang and any borrowing or blending of characteristic traits.

Chapter

9

The Cluster Concept

Learning Objectives

Your goal in completing this chapter is to be able to:

- Recognize the value of clustering clothes.
- List the cluster guidelines.
- Explain how to decide on a color scheme for a cluster of clothes.
- Identify suggested pieces in a five-piece and an eight-piece cluster.
- Understand the concept of add-ons.
- Give reasons for making each cluster piece different from the others.
- Relate examples of each cluster guideline.
- Recognize the value of accessories.
- Differentiate between essential and nonessential accessories.
- List types of clothing to include in a complete, expanded wardrobe.
- Complete plansheets for a cluster of clothing.
- Coordinate and combine cluster clothes and accessories.

Preview Main Points

1. Rely on a clothing cluster, a small group of coordinated clothes, including accessories.

2. Rely on the cluster guidelines to put together your clusters.

3. Using cluster plansheets will help you meet your wardrobe goals.

4. Coordinate or combine clothing and accessories for more effective visual communication, greater versatility, interest, and individuality.

1.

Rely on a clothing cluster, a small group of coordinated clothes, including accessories.

You don't need a large quantity of clothing to have a very workable wardrobe. Too many clothes become confusing, time and space consuming, and expensive. What you do need is a simple wardrobe strategy, easy to remember and easy to use.

Early in my career I learned that the easiest, most effective way to build a mix-and-match wardrobe was to put together a small group of coordinated clothes at a time — in a cluster. A cluster is simply a small group, in this case a small group of clothes that work well together — harmoniously. A cluster is open ended, allowing you to add on and adapt as you need to. *Cluster* is a versatile word, working as both a verb and a noun. Clustering is the process, and a cluster is the end result. Clustering is a simple wardrobe strategy.

Importance and Functions

Clustering your clothes is a smart wardrobe strategy.

- Clustering breaks the overwhelming task of wardrobing into smaller, more manageable groups.
- With clusters you get more outfits from fewer clothes, because you coordinate the clothing lines, shapes, colors, fabrics, and patterns.
- Clustering allows you to buy and replace your clothes a piece, or a few, at a time — as fast or slow as your budget allows.
- With clusters you get maximum wear out of older clothes, as you gradually build a new cluster that intermixes with the first.
- Clustering saves you shopping time because you know what you're looking for and whether or not it will work into your existing wardrobe.
- Clustering guarantees mix-and-matchability, and this, in turn, creates a look of quality and good taste.
- Clustering reduces useless impulse purchases that won't work with clothes you already own or into cluster plans.
- Clustering stretches your clothing dollar because you get more outfits from fewer clothes.
- Clustering leads to a more consistent personal style because the style lines and shapes carry through in all the cluster pieces.
- Considering all of the above, clustering simplifies your life!

The Problem

Most women know that a mix-and-match approach to wardrobing has value. Most women know what mix-and-match looks like, or how it works — once it's put together. The problem is, most women don't know how to put it all together — what kind of clothing pieces to look for and buy in the first place to give the results they want. What you need are basic guidelines that yield the same versatile results, while meeting totally different, individual needs.

The Solution

A cost-efficient cluster includes enough clothing for proper spacing between wearing and cleaning, and enough clothing styles for a variety of looks to suit a variety of moods and occasions. To achieve maximum versatility, here are the guidelines.

CLUSTER GUIDELINES

- Find a pattern — a print, stripe, or plaid — to inspire the color scheme of your cluster.
- Plan for five to eight easy pieces of clothing — top and bottom pieces.
- Select pieces that are basic — simple in style lines and shape.
- Select pieces that go together and that will work with at least two other pieces.
- Select pieces that are different from one another — no two pieces are alike.
- Select accessories that go with the clothes.
- Gradually expand your cluster(s) to meet all your wardrobe needs.

2.

Rely on the cluster guidelines to put together your clusters.

- **Find a pattern — a print, stripe, or plaid — to inspire the color scheme of your cluster.**

The most common question asked about wardrobing is, "Where do I start?" Start with a color scheme for the clothes in your cluster. If you don't already have a color scheme in mind, start in your closet, looking for a pattern of colors you really like. Start with the colors in that print, stripe, or plaid as inspiration for the colors in your cluster of clothes. (See Figure 9–1.)

Ideally, one or more of the colors in the print, stripe, or plaid that you select repeats some aspect of your personal coloring — making you part of the color scheme with your clothes. Also, one or more of the colors in the pattern should be a wardrobe neutral you can use for basic clothing pieces, with other colors coming into the cluster as accents — making you part of the color scheme with your clothes.

Figure 9–1. The pattern of colors in the vest inspires colors for a complete cluster. *(Courtesy All Week Long by Eddie Bauer)*

For example, Susan began her first cluster in a color scheme inspired by the colors in a print skirt — in olive green, red-violet, mustard yellow-gold, and black. (See Color Figure 41.) Instead of those colors, you might prefer lemon yellow, lime green, and pink. Choose what works for you.

Start now to be on the lookout for a pattern of colors that you love, feel like you could wear forever, and that reflects you the way you want to be seen.

- **Plan for five to eight easy pieces of clothing — top and bottom pieces.**

Start with a cluster of five coordinated pieces of clothing. The clothes can be brand new or already in your closet, store bought or home sewn, or some of each. It takes about five pieces to give you a variety of looks. Five pieces can add up to eight, nine, or ten different outfits.

Expand to six, seven, eight, or ten pieces. I call these pieces "add-ons" because they're added on to the original five. When you start adding pieces a cluster really comes to life. Eight pieces can be combined to create from twelve to thirty different looks. Gradually, if you like, you can build a twelve- to sixteen-piece cluster that multiplies to create forty-eight to eighty different combinations. From there, the number of outfits increases exponentially with each new piece you add to the cluster.

Five easy pieces might include: two tops, two bottoms, and one vest, sweater, or jacket. Eight easy pieces could consist of: three tops, three bottoms, and one jacket, sweater, or vest. Twelve easy pieces you can count

on can include: five tops, three bottoms, two jackets, and two sweaters or vests.

As a recipe for clustering, it works. But the pieces don't have to be exactly those listed. Clustering is not a cookie-cutter concept. There are no rigid rules outlining exactly what the pieces must be or how many different looks you should get. You can adapt this guideline to any life-style, personal style, or purse. You are the one who picks the pieces that meet your needs and preferences.

For example, Susan started out a five-piece cluster with two shirts, one longer skirt, one pair of pleat-front pants, and a vest. (See Table 9–1.)

Instead of a vest, you might prefer a sweater or a jacket. Instead of a long skirt, you could use a short one, or a split skirt. Instead of pants, you might like a jumpsuit. In an eight-piece cluster, instead of three tops, you might include two tops and one dress. Instead of a one-piece dress, maybe you want a two-piece dress. Instead of a jacket, you might prefer a tunic or a poncho. Choose what works for you.

You might start out with a general, all-season cluster — in fabrics you can wear most of the year.

For example, Susan started with light- to medium-weight fabrics in rayon challis, sueded silk broadcloth, and cotton knit. She added seasonal pieces later — in heavier, winter-weight fabrics suitable for cold weather, including wool gabardine, wool and cotton knit, and wool crepe.

You could choose to start with a specific occasion cluster — a cluster for home, office, evening, or travel — depending

Table 9–1 Five- to Ten-Piece Women's Wardrobe Cluster

Name __Susan__ (Original five-piece cluster)

Life-style __Urban, work, & family__   Personal style __Contemporary classics, relaxed sophistication__

Climate/season of the year __Fall–Winter__   Occasion __Office & town, some social__   Date __—__

ITEM		Wardrobe Neutral Olive	Wardrobe Neutral Black	Accent Colors Gold, Red-violet, Blue, Ivory	Works With	Plans to Acquire	Cost
CLOTHING	Blouse						
	Shirt	Silk camp shirt			Skirt, pants		
	Blouse or shirt			Gold rayon sport shirt	Skirt, pants		
	Skirt	←	Floral print gathered dirndl	→	All tops		
	Pant or skirt	Silk pleat-front pants			All tops		
	Pants						
	One– or two–piece dress						
	Sweater or vest			Red-violet cotton knit vest	Everything		
	Jacket						
	All–occasion coat						
ACCESSORIES	Dress shoe	Leather pumps	Leather pumps	RV suede flats w/ gold trim			
	Casual/ walking shoes		Leather boots				
	Hosiery/socks		Pantyhose (4)	Natural			
	All–occasion handbag		Leather tote				
	Casual/dress handbag	Leather clutch					
	Belt	2" leather		RV suede gold buckle	Everything		
	Scarf/tie						
	Earrings			Mustard & gold RV & brass			
	Necklace						
	Bracelet						
	Gloves						

on what you need most. In fact, it's when you travel that you put cluster concepts to the test.

- **Select pieces that are basic — simple in their style lines and shapes.**

Without much detail or decoration, the look of a basic is easy to change. Five pieces won't be easy to work with if they're costume pieces — clothes so distinctive, so detailed, or so decorated that they clash or conflict and fight for attention. You might like them, but you won't get the versatility you need. So look for basics.

For example, Susan started her first cluster with a basic dirndl skirt, a man-style shirt, vest, camp shirt, and pleat-front pants. The pieces are simple in design, allowing her to change the looks of the pieces. With basics, she has options. She includes a print scarf among her accessories, bringing with it new color and texture. It easily makes the look more interesting, dramatic, and dressy.

With five pieces of basic clothing that coordinate easily, you should get at least six different combinations or outfits. Susan got eight. (See Color Figure 42.) The number of outfits you can put together multiplies with each new piece you add to the cluster.

While you build with basics, you never need to worry about looking the same as anyone else. You wear your basics with a personal touch — adding something of yourself in your particular combination of basic pieces and accessories.

- **Select pieces that go together and that will work with at least two other pieces.**

Too many women buy clothes a single piece at a time or one outfit at a time. A blouse you buy may be beautiful, but if it doesn't go with anything you already own, it's a waste. A blouse and skirt may work together beautifully, but with nothing else. You need more options with each piece of clothing you buy.

In the beginning, while a cluster is small, you can't afford to have singles — pieces that go with only one other piece. Each piece in a cluster needs to work with at least two, and preferably three, other pieces in the cluster, giving you many different combinations.

For example, Susan's red-violet vest goes with the shirts, skirt, and pants in her cluster. The vest adds an interesting layer of color between the jacket and shirt — on its own, or as a part of the color scheme with the scarf. Lip color with this outfit is a similar shade of red-violet, making her more a part of the color scheme with her clothes.

Add-ons include stirrup pants. Worn with the vest, the look is loose over tight, and creates a smooth, flattering, transitional line from shoulder to hip. The number of outfits in the cluster just keeps growing as the pieces intermix. (See Table 9–2.)

Sometimes you walk into a store, see a particular piece of clothing, love it, and just know it's your style. Knowing what's home in your closet, you know whether it will work in with a cluster, or not.

For example, that's exactly what happened to Susan the minute she saw a plaid blazer. Looking and feeling like herself in the blazer, comfortable and beautiful, she bought the blazer, knowing it was exactly the kind of piece to build on.

Anytime you get a new piece of clothing, try it on with clothes you already own.

For example, Susan's new blazer layered over virtually everything in her cluster — even the print skirt. At first, she was reluctant to try it on over the skirt, but when she did, she realized the jacket plaid was medium in scale while the skirt pattern was small scale. With colors in common, the two pieces worked well together. Later in the year, Susan bought a new black skirt, shorter than she had worn for several years. She tried wearing it with a mock turtleneck sweater held over from school days, then layered it with the vest, and with the jacket. Confident the outfit worked, she was comfortable with her look wherever she went.

Designer or brand-name collections often meet the definition of a cluster, with separates designed to coordinate beautifully in many different combinations. It might be nice if you could buy into all of the coordinated pieces at once, but most can't. In addition, purchasing the whole collection leads to a prepackaged look — a look identical to anyone else who also buys the entire collection.

Query Box

Susan is almost a contradiction of traits — creative with common sense, a free spirit with traditional values. She's gentle and reserved in one situation and bubbly, even feisty in another. Susan loves fashion and does not want to appear predictable. She looks for classic styles that are just a little different — that go beyond ordinary. She looks for basics in softer, relaxed shapes combined with bold mixes of color and pattern. The style lines and shapes, the colors, fabrics, and patterns are coordinated to create one theme — to communicate one consistent message of personal style. Call it what you like, one mood or message must be dominant. We would call the theme of Susan's cluster "contemporary casual," "relaxed chic," or "nonchalant sophistication," with clothes for home, creative business, casual entertaining, or evenings out.

What are your personal traits? What design lines, shapes, colors, textures, and patterns would you like to include in a cluster of clothes?

TIP
FROM THE PROS

No name dropping. Don't let yourself or your personal style be ruled by any fashion name. The pieces in your cluster were designed by someone else, but they're yours now. We might recognize something from Sears or Armani, Escada or Fred Meyer, but the way you've selected and put them together is totally you.

Table 9–2 Twelve- to Sixteen-Piece Women's Wardrobe Cluster

Name _Susan_ (Cluster with add-ons and plans to buy)

Life-style _Urban, work, & family_   Personal style _Contemporary classics, relaxed sophistication_

Climate/season of the year _Fall–Winter_   Occasion _Office & town, some social_   Date ———

ITEM	Wardrobe Neutral — Olive	Wardrobe Neutral — Black	Accent Colors — Gold, Red-violet, Blue, Ivory	Works With	Plans to Acquire	Cost
CLOTHING						
Blouse			Ivory rayon crepe	City shorts, plaid blazer, stirrup pant	Specialty store	$89
Shirt	Silk camp shirt			All	own	
Blouse or shirt			Gold rayon sport shirt	All	own	
Blouse or shirt			White cotton soutache braid	All but ivory tops	Discount Outlet Store	$15
Blouse or shirt						
Skirt	←	Floral print gathered dirndl	→	All but ivory tops	own	
Pant	Silk pleat-front pants		Cinnamon gabardine city shorts →	Black & gold tops	Dept. Store	$58
Skirt or pant		Wool crepe short straight skirt		All tops	Catalog	$28
Skirt or pant			Gold cotton knit stirrup pants	Everything	own	
Day dress			RV ✓	All accessories and coats	End of season sale	$52
Dressy dress		✓		?	Holiday gift	——
Pullover sweater or vest		Wool mock turtleneck (old)	RV knit / Ivory knit	All / Gold, cinnamon	own / Catalog Outlet	$38
Cardigan sweater or vest			Red-violet cotton knit vest	All but ivory	own	
Jacket	←	Cinnamon, gold, & black glen plaid double-breasted	→	Everything	own	
Jacket			Blue-violet silk blazer	Print skirt, gold & blacks	Specialty Store	$87
Cloth coat or raincoat	Wool melton double-breasted	Wool melton shawl collar		Everything	Sale / own	$140
ACCESSORIES						
Dress shoes	Leather pumps	Leather pumps				
Casual/walking shoes		Leather boots	RV suede flats w/ gold trim			
Hosiery/socks		Pantyhose (6)	Natural (3)			
All-occasion handbag		Leather tote				
Casual/dress handbag	Leather clutch					
Belt	2" leather		RV suede gold buckle			
Belt		2" leather	Pink – green cord, silky			
Scarf/tie	←	36" square, wool challis floral print	→			
Scarf/tie		Wool fringed muffler		Everything	own	
Earrings			Mustard & gold / RV & brass			
Necklace		Pearls	Pink beads			
Necklace	←	Chain with colored stones	→			
Bracelets/pin			Brass bangle			
Gloves	Leather	Leather				

246 CHAPTER 9

For practical purposes, it's better to select a few pieces from one collection and add other pieces from other collections or brands, building a cluster that reflects your personal style, individuality, and creativity rather than any one designer's. This can reduce your cost, and guarantees that no two clusters end up looking alike.

Sewing offers you another option. Major pattern companies tie into the logic of five easy pieces of coordinated clothing. They design a cluster of five garment patterns in one package. Many feature basic, classic pieces. Make them up in fabric of your choice, and you are, again, guaranteed that your cluster will be like no one else's. Hang on to your favorite patterns that fit and flatter. A simple change of fabric can change the whole look and mood of the garment. The same pattern can be made again and again and look different every time.

- **Select pieces that are different from one another — no two pieces are alike.**

No two pieces in a cluster should be styled exactly alike — at least not until your wardrobe is larger. You might think it would make shopping and dressing easier, but you would be limited and bored in a hurry with two or three of the same thing.

What if you had two or three plaid jackets in a beginning cluster, or three pair of jeans, or three long-sleeve, striped Oxford-cloth shirts? Your looks would be always the same. You would look too predictable, too uniform.

You would feel like you had nothing to wear on another occasion. You might not go places where you could have a wonderful time if you had clothes that contributed to your mood and feelings for the occasion. What's more, similar or identical fashion pieces could go out of style all at once, leaving you wanting to replace more than you can afford in shopping time or money.

Each piece must have merit on its own, making a real contribution to the entire cluster. It should create a different look within any outfit. It should put more life into the cluster and give you more options and outfits. (See Figure 9–2.)

For example, of two tops, one might have short sleeves and the other long sleeves; one might be made of woven fabric, and the other knit; one might be a blouse and the other a shirt. There's a difference you know. A blouse is somewhat dressier or more feminine, while a shirt is more tailored or sportive. Of three bottoms, make one a skirt and one a pant, then make the third whichever you wear most often. Of two skirts, make one shorter and one longer, one pleated and one gathered, one a solid color and one patterned; of two sweaters or vests, make one a pullover and one a cardigan; of two jackets, make one a blazer and the other a wrap style. In place of one top or one bottom, choose a two-piece dress; it'll do double duty. Don't worry about hem length in skirts and pants. A workable cluster can feature several lengths, available for a variety of moods and occasions. The point is to give yourself options.

Figure 9–2. Each piece in this cluster is distinctly diferent in style, color, and texture.
(Courtesy Madeleine Direct)

It isn't just style lines or shapes you should vary. Make each piece different in another element as well — maybe color, maybe texture, or pattern.

For example, *Susan has a variety of garment styles, colors, fabrics, and patterns in her cluster. She has a long-sleeve shirt and a short-sleeve shirt. She has warm colors and cool colors, lighter and darker colors. There are solid colors, prints, and plaids. She has one gathered skirt and one straight skirt. She has loose-fitting pants and form-fitting pants; she has a third-layer vest, a sweater, and a jacket. She's got variety and versatility — and this leads to having fun with fashion. (See Color Figure 42.)*

Separates that serve as suits are a must in any cluster. A matched suit of separates is a practical choice to include, particularly in a beginning cluster. A suit works best for a woman if it includes both skirt and pants, and the jacket doesn't have to be as formal as a notched-collar blazer. Try something softer in style — a blouson or a draw-string jacket. For that matter, a coordinated shirt, with neatly finished hem, doubles as a jacket in a woman's casual-suited outfit. At least one jacket should go with a day dress. Ideally, get a dress that takes you through your day and into evening.

- **Select accessories that go with the clothes.**

An accessory is any item that completes or finishes an outfit and adds polish to the total look.

Contrary to popular advice, accessories are not the most important part of your wardrobe. The most wonderful accessories can go to waste on poor clothing choices, and the most wonderful clothes can be ruined by poor accessory choices. Accessories and the clothes they adorn are equally important. Choose accessories as thoughtfully as you do your clothes. Guidelines concerning basics, classics, all-season fabrics, wardrobe neutrals, and patterns apply to the selection of accessories. Yin/yang concepts apply as well. (See Figure 9–3.)

Figure 9–3. This classic silver jewelry includes a mix of yin sporty and yang sportive styles. *(Courtesy All Week Long by Eddie Bauer)*

Acquire essential accessories in basic, classic styles, wardrobe neutral colors, and classic patterns first. (See Figure 9–4.) They should get your attention and accessory budget first. There are perfect accessories available for every look, at prices that won't put you in debt, and in styles that won't be outdated next year. Essential accessories include: shoes, hosiery, belts, handbags, and briefcases.

Figure 9–4. Basic, classic accessories finish the total look. They work with all pieces in the cluster. *(Courtesy Madeleine Direct)*

Figure 9–5. The look of an assertive black leather jacket is countered slightly by a sporty black beret, bringing a subtle touch of youthful femininity into the personal style. *(Courtesy Clifford & Wills; photographer Val Ostrowski)*

Nonessential accessories come next, after you have the essentials. Acquire nonessential, costume, trendy and seasonal accessories as necessary or desired and as affordable. They include: jewelry, scarves/shawls, hats, handkerchiefs, pocket squares, gloves, hair ornaments, umbrella, detachable collars, cuffs, and dickies.

For example, in the shoe category, three to four pairs of shoes can meet the needs of at-home, business, play or sports, and evening occasions. First, buy basic walking shoes for home and/or business, followed by evening or play shoes — whichever you do most. An all-occasion handbag comes first in that category, followed by specific bags for business, best dress, or casual play. The same logic applies to belts, ties, scarves, gloves, and so forth. Begin with jewelry basic and classic enough to work for day and evening. Eyeglasses and makeup work like accessories. Coordinate them with your cluster as well. (Keep in mind, third-layer clothes — the jackets, sweaters, tunics, and vests — work much like accessories in changing the looks of your second-layer clothes.)

Depending on the climate, culture, and occasion, some nonessential accessories become essential — such as an umbrella, gloves, or a hat in wet or cold climates. Choose all of your accessories with their purpose, power, and potential in mind. Take a moment to think about what each item contributes to the image you want to project. Choose basic accessories in the same general mood and message as your clothes. (See Figure 9–5.)

In a world of standardized style, think of your accessories as details that can give even the most common "assembly line" dress or suit a look of distinction. Your accessories are personality pieces that signal your individuality and personal style.

For example, two identical suits can be made to look totally different on different women with different personal styles. One woman might coordinate a softly styled blouse, scarf, bracelet, and dress heels, with a narrow belt worn over the suit jacket. Another woman might coordinate a turtleneck sweater, necklace, and leather boots, with a large shawl worn over the jacket. Still another might dress up her jacket with a gorgeous jeweled collar. You'd have to look twice to decide if they were, indeed, wearing the same suit.

For another example, see Color Figure 42 and Tables 9–1 and 9–2. Susan chose essential, basic accessories in black to complete her many outfits. Adding on, she got a pair of muted, medium value, olive green shoes and a belt that work with her softly dulled olive green clothing pieces. They are totally classic and good investment pieces, in keeping with her clothing values. And finally, she added a trendy, bright red-violet belt and shoes that pick up color from her print skirt. They're perfect for creative or casual business and social occasions. Attention goes to her feet briefly but comes right back up to the larger quantity of bright color in the shirt and vest, up near her face. Earrings repeat cluster colors and add textural interest. They also draw attention up around her face. They work — and the price is right.

When the pattern in a scarf repeats colors in the clothes, it pulls the pieces together — makes them look more like they belong together. Susan chose a scarf that is medium weight and doesn't lend itself to tying or knotting. Better to drape it or loop it at most. Besides, the pattern in her scarf is worth showing off. She folds it in half, or in a triangle, and simply drapes it over one shoulder, secured at the shoulder with a hat pin. She belts it and gently arranges the folds. The looks are definitely not business as usual. Susan says she's not a "necklace person," but when she finds one she likes, it's a pendant style. Stones in her necklace repeat colors in the cluster. Makeup works like an accessory. Blush and lip color are selected to coordinate and carry out the color scheme. Susan has a cluster with combinations that don't quit — some with simple differences, and some with more obvious changes. Second-, third- and fourth-layer pieces — the shirts and blouses, vests, sweaters, and jackets — are definite look changers. Accessories make for more great looks without adding more clothing pieces.

- **Gradually expand your cluster(s) to meet all your wardrobe needs.**

When you're ready, add pieces to expand and update your cluster.

For example, see Table 9–2. Susan added on the light, fresh look of a white cotton blouse she found at a discount outlet house — at a more affordable price. Soutache braid on the collar added a touch of elegance. City shorts in cinnamon came next, inspired by the colors in her jacket plaid. (See Table 9–6, page 265.) Dressed up with color-toned stockings and high-heel pumps, shorts can have the same impact as a short skirt.

An ivory blouse and sweater added to the cluster made for better dark-light color balance. They featured a wheat motif, out of the ordinary and simple enough to work with the plaid. Susan didn't let their limp appearance on the hanger dampen her interest. If a piece has merit, and you like the idea, then try it on. Maybe all it needs is a figure to fill it out and make it come to life!

Of course a complete wardrobe requires more than five, eight, or even sixteen easy pieces. You can't exercise in a silk blouse or wool slacks. And you aren't likely to use your blazer as a swimsuit cover-up or a nightgown.

Include essential underwear, active sportswear, and sleepwear in a complete, expanded wardrobe. Choose underwear, limited occasion clothes, and seasonal clothing that works within your cluster. (See Table 9–3.)

Limited occasion and seasonal clothes might include a holiday sweater, a full-length formal for gala events, religious apparel, skiwear, or swimwear and cover-up.

Ideally, a basic coat works with all the pieces in a cluster. Start with a cloth coat. The style needs to be full enough to fit comfortably over sweaters and jackets, and long enough to cover your skirts.

For example, Susan chose heavyweight wool, necessary for cold winters, but corduroy or cotton twill are options for all-season weights. Susan has a choice of wardrobe neutral colors — olive or black. Both are basic, classic styles and lend themselves to a variety of looks. She can later add leather and/or fur if her life-style includes places to wear them.

Renew your interest in older clothes or clusters by simply adding a new color.

For example, Susan looks beautiful in blue-violet. Take some of the older pieces in a new color direction. Susan can build on the blue-violet in her print skirt. The large amount of blue-violet in the blazer emphasizes the small amount of the same color in the skirt.

Query Box

Susan can also bring in red or shrimp. She looks terrific in either of those colors, and they're beautiful with olive and black. What color would you add on?

If you like, and when you're ready, you can choose to plan and acquire an entirely new cluster. Lift one or more colors from the original cluster, and combine it with two or more new colors in a new cluster group. The new clothes will coordinate with some of the clothes in the cluster you already own.

For example, lift olive and/or magenta from Susan's cluster and add pieces in navy blue, shrimp, and white. Each of the new colors combines beautifully with olive and magenta. Shrimp and white also work with black, which is already in Susan's cluster.

With time, it's possible to have one expanded all-purpose cluster — twelve, sixteen, or twenty pieces that meet all your wardrobe needs — casual, business, or leadership, and dressy day or evening. It might include dresses, in a multi-colored print or solid color, dresses that work with accessories you already own. Keep in mind that what one person considers casual city or weekend clothes may be very similar to what someone else living in a small town or rural area needs in the way of business clothes.

Every all-purpose cluster has got to have *all* the essentials for daily life — with the exception of grubby-clothes

Table 9–3 Women's Expanded Wardrobe

Name _____

Life-style _____ Personal style _____

Climate/season of the year _____ Occasion _____ Date _____

ITEM		Wardrobe Neutral	Wardrobe Neutral	Accent Colors	Works With	Plans to Acquire	Cost
UNDERWEAR	Full–length slip (1–2)						
	Half slip (1–3)						
	Camisole						
	Panties (8–12)						
	Bras (4)						
	Other						
SLEEPWEAR	Nightgown/ PJ's (2–3)						
	Robe						
	Slippers						
	Other						
ACTIVE SPORTSWEAR	Parka/ windbreaker						
	Boots						
	Hat						
	Gloves						
	Swimsuit						
	Cover–up						
	Exercise clothes						
	Exercise clothes						
	Exercise shoes						
	Jeans						
	Shorts						
	Bermuda shorts						
	Other						
	Other						

occasions. You probably don't need to plan for grubby clothes — clothes to clean the bathroom and garage in, or to plant the garden in. We all get those just by wearing most of the life out of casual cluster pieces. Older shirts and slacks, possibly from a phased-out cluster, meet those needs just fine.

It's possible, if you prefer, to have several smaller clusters, used for different segments of your life — an at-home cluster, a business cluster, an evening cluster, a hot-weather cluster, and so on. Depending on destination, a cluster can make the transition to travel. With clusters, you're always prepared for even last-minute travel arrangements.

A cluster begins with what is essential. As you expand your cluster beyond twelve or sixteen pieces, feel free to include an "ego" item — something you absolutely love and can really use but that doesn't necessarily go with much of anything else. An ego item is something that lifts you above the everyday you. Exercise your creativity within a cluster, and once you've got a cluster, or two or three, you can move beyond the basics.

At some point, you might choose to phase out a cluster you no longer need or have become tired of wearing. Simply wear out those clothes and don't replace them. Whatever your decisions, you never need to start from scratch again. Instead, you can change, update, and add on to what you already own as you create a truly versatile, workable wardrobe — one that works for you, whatever your needs.

For example, Diane is in the process of updating a favorite cluster. Diane is a quadriplegic and demands the same variety of good looks in her clothes as any young woman does. (See Figure 9–6.) Her clothes help her carry out her roles as schoolteacher, public speaker, and wife. Diane's cluster began with a paisley print two-piece dress in turquoise, bur-gundy, black, and white. The tea-length skirt covers her thin legs beautifully. Pants have extra length and are cut higher at the waist in back for better fit in a sitting position. Diane likes the look of loose-fitting tops, bloused over the waist to camouflage her tummy that lacks muscle tone. A wide belt holds her blouse in place and also helps to control her tummy. Best-dress occasions call for ankle-strap shoes. Pumps fall off. Necklace and earrings serve to draw attention up to her face, but tiny clasps and posts are impossible to handle. She chooses an over-the-head necklace and clip-on earrings.

3.

Using cluster plansheets will help you meet your wardrobe goals.

🌿

Plan and chart a cluster of coordinated clothes on paper before you begin to shop. Cluster plansheets can help you to:

- Visualize what you hope to accomplish, and save you from making common mistakes.
- See at a glance what clothes and accessories you already own and what you need or want to add.
- Compare the categories of clothes and accessories for balanced variety in style, color, and fabric.
- Evaluate the mix and matchability of clothing pieces and accessories.
- Save shopping time and money.
- Pack for travel, saving time and preventing items from being left home.

The time it takes to fill out plansheets gets shorter with each experience. After a few times, many women are able to visualize a cluster plan without putting it all on paper.

Wardrobe Cluster Plansheets

Five- to ten-piece and twelve- to sixteen-piece cluster plansheets are provided, as well as a dress-option cluster plansheet. (See Table 9–4.) These allow you to plan for initial and expanded cluster groups of clothing. Feel free to photocopy as many plansheets as you need or want for your personal or family use. (Photocopying for resale is prohibited by law.)

Step 1. Identify cluster guide words.

- Fill in blanks at the top of the plansheet with descriptive words about yourself, your life-style, your personal clothing style, the climate or season of the year, and the occasion(s) the cluster is planned for.

Step 2. Identify cluster colors.

- Study column headings at the top of the cluster chart.
- Write your choice of cluster colors in the spaces provided on the chart.

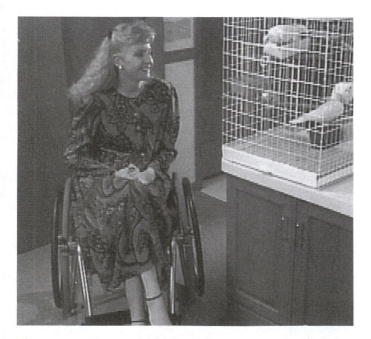

Figure 9–6. Diane, a quadriplegic, demands a variety of good looks in her clothes, suited to the many occasions in her life.

Table 9–4 Twelve-Piece Women's Wardrobe Cluster — Dress Option

Name _____

Life-style _____ Personal style _____

Climate/season of the year _____ Occasion _____ Date _____

ITEM	Wardrobe Neutral	Wardrobe Neutral	Accent Colors	Works With	Plans to Acquire	Cost
CLOTHING						
Blouse						
Shirt						
Blouse or shirt						
Sweater or vest						
Skirt						
Pants						
Dress						
Dress						
Dress						
Dress or jumper						
Jacket						
Jacket						
All–occasion coat						
ACCESSORIES						
Dress shoes						
Casual/walking shoes						
Hosiery/socks						
All–occasion handbag						
Casual/dress handbag						
Belt						
Belt						
Scarf/tie						
Scarf/tie						
Earrings						
Necklace						
Necklace						
Bracelets/pin						
Gloves						

Remember, you can't work with all colors at once and expect to achieve good mix-and-match versatility. So plan your cluster around two or three wardrobe neutrals with accent colors added for variety. Remember that some of the wardrobe neutrals include:

Black	White	Gray
Navy blue	Plum	Mauve
Burgundy	Brown	Rust
Taupe	Camel	Tan
Beige	Cream	Ecru/ivory
Olive	Hunter/forest	Teal

Remember, a few bright colors — such as red, royal blue, emerald green, and gold — can function in place of wardrobe neutrals as core or pivot pieces *if* the brighter, bolder effects are what you want, and *if* it doesn't matter that these colors may not intermix easily with colors in other clusters. Beyond that, bright colors usually function as accent colors. Within a specific cluster, any color used in a single piece of clothing only can be considered an accent color for that cluster.

Remember, you are part of the color scheme with your clothes. Choose a variety of warm and cool hues, light and dark values, bright and dull intensities that will repeat and/or contrast attractively with your hair, eyes, and skin coloration. Consider a favorite darker value color, a lighter value color, with contrasting accent colors. Notice the words darker and lighter. That doesn't mean you have to go all the way to navy blue or black, ivory or white, but you can use colors just darker and lighter than the others. Accent colors will likely be a range of darker to lighter colors. For maximum visual interest, you should be able to say to yourself, "I have comparatively dark, medium, and light colors included in my cluster." For maximum visual interest and communication potential, make one or more of the hues warmer, and one or more hues cooler.

Remember, if you have difficulty deciding on a color scheme, build on colors of favorite clothes you already own. If you're starting from scratch, find a piece of fabric or ready-to-wear clothing in a print, stripe, or plaid that you absolutely love and feel you could wear forever. Use colors present in the pattern as colors in your cluster.

Step 3. Fill in spaces.

- Study Tables 9–1 through 9–4. Become familiar with clothing and accessory pieces listed at the left of the cluster chart.

Note: Garment tops are listed before garment bottoms, and second-layer garments before third-layer garments, in their relative position on your body. Accessories are in positions in terms of essential general use.

- Fill in spaces beneath the appropriate color column with clothing already owned or included in the cluster.

Note: All items in the first and second columns are the color listed at the top, unless otherwise specified. It may work in some cluster plans to identify a lighter or darker

version of the wardrobe neutral color — such as listing "light blue" under a navy blue column.

Note: Under accent colors, because there are generally more than one, you must identify the specific color from those listed at the top of the column.

Note: An arrow bridging two or three color columns identifies the several colors present in a print, stripe, or plaid item.

- Identify the clothing fiber, fabric, and style name or description, using words that are meaningful to you. There is no one right way to fill in a plansheet. Whatever words you use should bring to mind an image of the clothing piece, suggesting approximates in shape, occasion, or mood, cost, and care.

Note: These plansheets allow you a great deal of flexibility. If you need or want an additional clothing piece in one of your colors, simply fill in that additional space. If you have a few more garments than spaces allowed altogether, you can simply divide one space into two. Draw a horizontal or diagonal dividing line across the space. For more garments than all spaces allowed, it's likely you have a second cluster included that needs to be charted on another plansheet — noting that pieces of each cluster intermix.

Step 4. Continue filling in spaces.

- Fill in appropriate remaining spaces with new garments and accessories you plan to acquire. Use a bright colored pen or pencil to differentiate between clothes already owned and new clothes. Include where and when you plan to acquire these items and the approximate price you expect to pay.

Step 5. Test for balanced variety with mix and match-ability.

- Check to see that you have some or several pieces — depending on cluster size — in each column under each specific color.

Note: You want to achieve a balanced variety of warm and cool hues, light and dark values, bright and dull intensities. If you don't have this balance, consider switching the color of a planned-for item or adding a piece(s) in that color to the cluster.

- Using words meaningful to you in the column headed "Works With," note the ability of the clothes and accessories to be paired or mixed with one another.

Note: For maximum versatility, you need most items to go with everything in the cluster, including accessories. However, saying "most" allows you to have an accent color that goes with one or a few pieces only, depending on the size of the cluster.

Note: With experience and increased skill, many people are able to visualize a complete cluster in their minds, making minimal notes on cluster plansheets for quick reference only.

Coordinated Outfits Plansheet

Once you put together an outfit that really works, you'll want to wear it again. The problem is that too many people can't remember what went into the outfit — especially when they're in a hurry. Save yourself time and frustrating attempts to remember, with the coordinated outfits plansheets. (See Table 9–5.)

- List the pieces combined in any given outfit.

Note: You might want to start with the simplest combination and progress to more complex layered looks. Use as many plansheets as you need to list the many outfits in a cluster. You might even put a little star beside its number on outfits you like best. Make the chart work for you!

Note: The list of items also serves to remind you of other pieces you could try putting together.

- Tape your plansheets to the inside of your closet door for quick and easy reference. If you prefer, put them inside a plastic bag and hook the bag over a hanger to hang handy in your closet.

Shopping List Plansheet

You can't keep everything in your head, and chances are, you can't get every clothing item you need or want exactly when you want it. A shopping list gets it off your mind and into your purchase plans. (See Table 9–6, page 265.)

- List items you need to acquire to make your cluster more complete and versatile, taking information from your cluster plansheets.
- List what you plan to coordinate or wear with the item.
- Check mark or write in "Yes," if you need to take the coordinate piece shopping with you for matching or fitting purposes.
- Keep this list handy in your closet, or fold and carry it in your handbag for future reference.

4.

Coordinate or combine clothing and accessories for more effective visual communication, greater versatility, interest, and individuality.

The art of accessorizing is one of the most challenging yet creative phases of wardrobe planning or cluster planning. For maximum versatility, **all clothing and accessory pieces in an initial cluster must look like they belong together**. They must be coordinated or blended in terms of style lines and shapes, colors, fabrics, or textures, and patterns to create the essential balance, pleasing proportion, interest, and harmony with the outfit, the occasion, and with the wearer — suited to your life-style and personal style. While selecting accessories to buy or put with your outfit of the day, learn to mix and match in your mind the clothes you already own. Then select those pieces that will coordinate with many different outfits to give you the versatility you need. (See Table 9–7, page 266.) When in doubt about what goes with what, make a switch or don't wear it.

For example, imagine summer shoes or sandals with a winter skirt, and a summer skirt with heavy winter shoes. They don't belong together, so switch them around. Imagine a sportive print scarf at the neck and a wide, jeweled belt at the waist. Not only do they compete for attention, but they communicate different moods. Take one off. Visualize a casual canvas tote bag paired with an elegant silk evening dress, or a sporty tweed blazer with brass buttons, paired with a dressy rhinestone necklace and satin slingback pumps. They just don't work together. The tote bag and jacket communicate one mood and message, the dress, shoes, and jewelry another. Take off the rhinestone necklace and change the shoes to leather loafers, pumps, or boots. Switch the big canvas tote bag to a smaller, dressier, clutch bag.

Keep in mind when combining clothes and accessories that attention goes to points or areas of contrast in line, shape, color, texture, or pattern — contrast in size and detail. Strong or equal points of contrast between clothes and accessories compete for attention. The look becomes too busy, too spotty. Accessories work more efficiently when the clothing is simple, basic in style lines and shapes, and the colors are more neutral. The clothing then serves as a background for interesting detail and brighter color in accessories. If you build the bulk of your wardrobe clusters around basic styles and colors, you can indulge yourself in spirited accessories as much as you like.

These points work in reverse as well. The most efficient, versatile accessories are basic and in wardrobe neutral colors. So here's another way to approach selection. Select essential accessories in basic, classic styles, smooth textures, dulled colors, and simple patterns. Add on nonessential or costume accessories after you have the essentials.

Color Harmony with Accessories

While there are many ways to achieve color harmony between clothes and accessories, the easiest way is to choose an accessory in a color that repeats a clothing color.

- Repeat the lightest, darkest, or brightest clothing color. This gives you lots of freedom in choice, depending on where you want to focus attention.

For example, in a pant outfit printed with hunter green, yellow-gold, and brown, you can choose any one color, or all. Yellow-gold is the lightest, brown is the darkest, and hunter green appears brightest of the three. If the occasion is strictly social, you won't mind attention going to your feet with a pair of great yellow-gold shoes. If you want attention focused near your face, go with hunter green or brown shoes and yellow-gold in a necklace and/or scarf. If hunter green is a solid color at the hem, you might prefer to choose hunter green for shoes, carrying the color down to lengthen your look and avoid attention on your feet.

(text continued on page 268)

Table 9–5 Women's Coordinated Outfits — Susan

Cluster Colors: Wardrobe neutral ____Olive____ Wardrobe neutral ____Black____

Accent colors ____Red-violet,____ , ____Gold,____ ____Blue,____ , ____Ivory____

ITEM	# 1	# 2	# 3	# 4	# 5
Blouse, shirt, or dress	Gold rayon sport shirt	Olive silk camp shirt	Olive silk camp shirt	Olive silk camp / Black shell	Gold rayon sport shirt
Skirt or pant	Multi-colored floral print gathered dirndl	Olive silk pleat front	Olive silk pleat front	Multi-colored floral print gathered dirndl	Multi-colored floral print gathered dirndl
Sweater					
Vest	Red-violet cotton knit			Red-violet cotton knit	Red-violet cotton knit
Jacket					
Coat					
Shoes	Red-violet suede flats	Olive leather pumps	Olive leather pumps	Black leather pumps	Red-violet suede flats
Hosiery	Black sheer	Natural sheer	Natural sheer	Black sheer	Black sheer
Bag					
Belt	RV suede gold buckle	Olive 2" leather	Olive 2" leather	Olive 2" leather	RV suede gold buckle
Scarf or tie			36" square floral print multi-colored		
Earrings	RV & brass	RV & brass	RV & brass	RV & brass	RV & brass
Necklace					
Bracelet					
Gloves					

Table 9–5 Women's Coordinated Outfits — Susan (continued)

Cluster Colors: Wardrobe neutral ___Olive___ Wardrobe neutral ___Black___
Accent colors ___Red-violet,___ , ___Gold,___ ___Blue,___ , ___Ivory___

ITEM	# 6	# 7	# 8	# 9	# 10
Blouse, shirt, or dress	Gold rayon sport shirt	Gold rayon sport shirt	Gold rayon sport shirt	Gold rayon sport shirt	Gold rayon sport shirt
Skirt or pant	Gold cotton-knit stirrups	Gold cotton-knit stirrups	Black wool crepe short str.	Black wool crepe short	Olive silk pleat front
Sweater					
Vest					Red-violet cotton knit
Jacket		Cinnamon/gold & black glen plaid		Cinnamon/gold & black glen plaid	Cinnamon/gold & black glen plaid
Coat					
Shoes	Black leather pumps	Black leather pumps	Black pumps	Black pumps	Black pumps
Hosiery	Black sheer	Black sheer	Black sheer	Black sheer	Black sheer
Bag					
Belt	Black 2" leather		Black 2" leather		
Scarf or tie					
Earrings	Mustard & gold	Mustard & gold	Mustard & gold	Mustard & gold	RV & brass
Necklace					
Bracelet					
Gloves					

Table 9–5 Women's Coordinated Outfits — Susan *(continued)*

Cluster Colors: Wardrobe neutral ___Olive___   Wardrobe neutral ___Black___

Accent colors ___Red-violet,___ , ___Gold,___ ___Blue,___ , ___Ivory___

ITEM	# 11	# 12	# 13	# 14	# 15
Blouse, shirt, or dress	Gold rayon sport shirt	Gold rayon sport shirt	black shell/ olive silk camp/ gold rayon sport	black shell/ olive silk camp	Gold rayon sport shirt
Skirt or pant	Gold cotton-knit stirrups	Gold cotton-knit stirrups	Gold stirrups	Gold stirrups	Gold stirrups
Sweater	Red-violet pullover				
Vest		Red-violet cotton knit		Red-violet cotton knit	
Jacket					Cinnamon/gold & black glen plaid
Coat					
Shoes	Red-violet suede flats	Black pumps	Black pumps	Olive pumps	Black pumps
Hosiery	Natural sheer	Black sheer	Black sheer	Natural sheer	Black sheer
Bag					
Belt		Black 2" leather	Olive 2" leather	Olive 2" leather	
Scarf or tie					
Earrings	RV & brass	RV & brass	Mustard & gold	RV & brass	Mustard & gold
Necklace					
Bracelet					
Gloves					

Table 9–5 Women's Coordinated Outfits — Susan *(continued)*

Cluster Colors: Wardrobe neutral _____Olive_____ Wardrobe neutral _____Black_____

Accent colors _____Red-violet,_____ , __Gold,__ __Blue,__ , __Ivory_____

ITEM	# 16	# 17	# 18	# 19	# 20
Blouse, shirt, or dress	Olive silk sport shirt			Gold rayon sport shirt	Gold rayon sport shirt
Skirt or pant	Gold stirrups	Multi-floral print gathered dirndl	Floral print gathered dirndl	Floral print gathered dirndl	Black wool/crepe str. short skirt
Sweater		black wool mock turtleneck	black wool mock turtleneck		
Vest			Red-violet cotton knit		
Jacket				Cinnamon/gold/ black glen plaid	
Coat					
Shoes	Olive pumps	Black pumps	Black pumps	Red-violet suede flats	Black pumps
Hosiery	Natural sheer	Black sheer	Black sheer	Black sheer	Black sheer
Bag					
Belt	Olive 2" leather	Black 2" leather	Black 2" leather		Black 2" leather
Scarf or tie					
Earrings	RV & brass	RV & brass	RV & brass	RV & brass	Mustard & gold
Necklace					
Bracelet					
Gloves					

Table 9–5 Women's Coordinated Outfits — Susan *(continued)*

Cluster Colors: Wardrobe neutral _____ Olive _____ Wardrobe neutral _____ Black _____

Accent colors _____ Red-violet, _____ , Gold, _____ Blue, _____ , Ivory _____

ITEM	# 21	# 22	# 23	# 24	# 25
Blouse, shirt, or dress			Gold rayon sport shirt	Gold rayon sport shirt	Black shell Olive silk camp Gold rayon sport
Skirt or pant	Black wool/crepe str. short skirt	Black short skirt	Olive silk front pleat	Olive silk front pleat	Gold stirrups
Sweater	black wool mock turtleneck	black wool mock turtleneck			
Vest			Red-violet cotton knit	Red-violet cotton knit	Red-violet cotton knit
Jacket		Cinnamon/gold/ black glen plaid	Cinnamon/gold/ black glen plaid	Cinnamon/gold/ black glen plaid	
Coat					
Shoes	Black pumps	Black pumps	Olive pumps	Olive pumps	Black or olive pumps
Hosiery	Black sheer	Black sheer	Natural sheer	Natural sheer	Natural or black
Bag					
Belt	Black 2" leather				Olive 2" leather
Scarf or tie				36" square floral print multi-colored	
Earrings	Mustard & gold	Mustard & gold	RV & brass	RV & brass	RV & brass
Necklace					
Bracelet					
Gloves					

Table 9–5 Women's Coordinated Outfits — Susan *(continued)*

Cluster Colors: Wardrobe neutral _____Olive_____ Wardrobe neutral _____Black_____

Accent colors _____Red-violet,_____ , _Gold,_ ___Blue,___ , _Ivory_

ITEM	# 26	# 27	# 28	# 29	# 30
Blouse, shirt, or dress		Gold rayon sport shirt	Gold rayon sport shirt		Gold rayon sport shirt
Skirt or pant	Gold stirrups	Multi floral print dirndl	Black wool str. short skirt	Black wool short skirt	Gold stirrups
Sweater	Black wool mock turtleneck			Black wool mock turtleneck	Black wool mock turtleneck
Vest					
Jacket	Cinnamon/black glen plaid	Cinnamon/black glen plaid	Cinnamon/black glen plaid	Cinnamon/black glen plaid	Cinnamon/black glen plaid
Coat					
Shoes	Black pumps	Black pumps or RV suede flats	Black pumps	Black pumps	Black pumps
Hosiery	Black sheer	Black sheer	Black sheer	Black sheer	Black sheer
Bag					
Belt	Black 2" leather				Olive 2" leather
Scarf or tie		36" square floral print multi-colored	36" square floral print multi-colored	36" square floral print multi-colored	36" square floral print multi-colored
Earrings	Mustard & gold	Mustard & gold	Mustard & gold	RV & brass	RV & brass
Necklace					
Bracelet					
Gloves					

Table 9–5 Women's Coordinated Outfits — Susan *(continued)*

Cluster Colors: Wardrobe neutral   __Olive__   Wardrobe neutral __Black__

            Accent colors   __Red-violet,__ , __Gold,__   __Blue,__   , __Ivory__

ITEM	# 31	# 32	# 33	# 34	# 35
Blouse, shirt, or dress				Gold rayon sport / Olive silk camp	Gold rayon sport shirt
Skirt or pant	Gold stirrups	Black wool str. short skirt	Black wool short skirt	Olive silk front pleat	Gold stirrups
Sweater	RV cotton pullover	Black wool mock turtleneck	Black mock turtleneck / RV cotton pullover		Black wool mock turtleneck
Vest					
Jacket				Cinnamon/black glen plaid	Cinnamon/black glen plaid
Coat					
Shoes	RV suede flats	Black pumps	Black pumps	Olive pumps	Black pumps
Hosiery	Black sheer	Black	Black	Natural	Black
Bag					
Belt		Black 2" leather	Black 2" leather	Olive 2" leather	Black 2" leather
Scarf or tie					Black wool fringed muffler
Earrings	RV & brass	RV & brass	RV & brass	RV & brass	Mustard & gold
Necklace	Chain w/ multi-colored stones				
Bracelet					
Gloves					

Table 9–5 Women's Coordinated Outfits — Susan *(continued)*

Cluster Colors: Wardrobe neutral ___Olive___   Wardrobe neutral ___Black___
Accent colors ___Red-violet,___ , ___Gold,___   ___Blue,___ , ___Ivory___

ITEM	# 36	# 37	# 38	# 39	# 40
Blouse, shirt, or dress	Gold rayon sport shirt	Gold rayon sport shirt	Olive silk camp shirt	Olive silk camp shirt	Olive silk camp shirt
Skirt or pant	*(can't see) Gold stirrups	Multi-colored floral print dirndl	Olive silk front pleat pants	Multi-colored floral print dirndl	Multi-colored floral print dirndl
Sweater	Black wool mock turtleneck				
Vest			RV cotton knit	RV cotton knit	
Jacket	Cinnamon/black glen plaid				
Coat					
Shoes	Black pumps	RV suede flats	Olive pumps	Olive pumps	RV suede flats
Hosiery	Black	Black	Natural	Natural	Black
Bag					
Belt	Black 2" leather	RV suede w/ gold buckle	Olive 2" leather	Olive 2" leather	RV suede w/ gold buckle
Scarf or tie	36" square floral print				
Earrings	RV & brass	RV & brass	RV & brass	Mustard & gold	RV & brass
Necklace					
Bracelet					
Gloves					

Table 9–5 Women's Coordinated Outfits — Susan (continued)

Cluster Colors: Wardrobe neutral ___Olive___ Wardrobe neutral ___Black___

Accent colors ___Red-violet,___ , _Gold,_ _Blue,_ , _Ivory_

ITEM	# 41	# 42	# 43	# 44	#
Blouse, shirt, or dress		Olive silk camp shirt		Olive silk camp shirt	
Skirt or pant	Olive silk front pleat pants	Black wool short skirt	Olive silk front pleat pants	Olive silk front pleat pants	
Sweater	Black wool mock turtleneck		Black wool mock turtleneck		
Vest				RV cotton knit	
Jacket			Cinnamon/black glen plaid	Cinnamon/black glen plaid	
Coat					
Shoes	Black pumps	Black pumps	Black pumps	Black pumps	
Hosiery	Black	Black	Black	Black	
Bag					
Belt	Black 2" leather	Black 2" leather	Olive 2" leather		
Scarf or tie		36" square floral print			
Earrings	Mustard & gold	Mustard & gold	Mustard & gold	Mustard & gold	
Necklace	Multi-chain w/ colored stones				
Bracelet					
Gloves					

Table 9–6 Shopping List — Susan

	What I need:	To coordinate with:	Take along shopping:
Clothing	Blue-violet blazer	Print skirt	Yes skirt
	White cotton blouse	Black skirt	No
	Ivory shirt or sweater	Blacks, plaid blazer	No
	City shorts	Plaid blazer jacket	Yes jacket
	Olive wool coat	Everything	Yes challis scarf
Accessories	New lipstick—basic	All	
	Replace olive heels	Olive clothes and print shirt	No

Table 9–7 Susan's Week-at-a-Glance

Life-style:	City, suburb, married, two children
Personal style:	Contemporary classics, relaxed sophistication
Career:	Part-time consultant
Climate/season:	Fall into winter

	Time	Activity	Outfit

Monday	A.M.
	8:00
	8:30–12:30
	
	P.M.
	12:30
	
	6:30
		Children to school, carpool – MWF a.m.
		Work at home. No meetings.
		
		↓
		
		Grocery shopping
		Errands
		
		↓
		
		Dinner party for husband's boss
			Gold rayon sport shirt
			Red-violet (RV) cotton-knit vest
			Gold cotton-knit stirrups
			RV suede belt
			RV suede flats
			
			Remove gold stirrups
			Add multi-floral print skirt,
			    black nylons
			        RV & brass earrings

Tuesday	A.M.
	10:00
	
	P.M.
	12:00–2:00
	
	3:00
	
	6:00
		Planning meeting with subdivision community safety organization.
		
		↓
		Lunch with PTA Committee
		
		↓
		
		Pick up children from school, carpool, T–Th p.m.
		
		Dinner at home with family
		Homework & games with children
			Gold rayon sport shirt
			Cinnamon/black glen plaid jacket
			Black wool crepe skirt
			Black nylons
			Black pumps
			Mustard & gold earrings
			
			Remove black skirt, nylons, pumps,
			    & plaid jacket
			Add gold stirrups
			    RV suede flats

Wednesday	A.M. 8:00 10:30 P.M. 12:00–4:00 7:00	Children to school, carpool Parent/Teacher Conference Work at home Meet husband & his clients for dinner	Olive silk camp shirt RV cotton-knit vest Multi-floral print skirt RV suede belt Black nylons RV suede flats RV & brass round earrings Remove RV vest & belt Add gold rayon sport shirt Glen-plaid jacket

Table 9–7 Susan's Week-at-a-Glance (*continued*)

	Time	Activity	Outfit
Thursday	A.M. 10:00–12:00	Tutor at elementary school	Olive silk camp shirt Olive silk pleat pants Olive 2" leather belt
	P.M. 3:00 4:00	Pick up children from school, carpool Take children to gymnastics	Olive pumps Natural nylons Mustard & gold earrings
	7:00	PTA Carnival — work booth	Add gold rayon sport shirt over olive silk camp Glen-plaid jacket
Friday	A.M. 8:00 8:30-12:30 P.M. 2:30	Children to school, carpool Work at home. No meetings Dentist appointment	RV pullover sweater Gold stirrups Chain necklace with colored stones RV suede flats

	7:30	Dinner & movie with husband	Remove RV sweater
			    Suede flats
			    Chain necklace
			Add gold rayon shirt
			    Black 2" leather belt
			    Black leather pumps
			    Black nylons

Saturday	A.M. 11:00 P.M. 3:30–5:30	Errands Haircut Shopping in town Museum excursion with children	Black mock turtleneck Gold stirrup pants Glen-plaid jacket, belted Black 2" leather belt Black pumps Black nylons Black wool fringed muffler
	7:00	Barbecue with neighbors in subdivision	Remove glen-plaid jacket Black wool muffler
Sunday	A.M. 10:00 11:00	Brunch Church	Gold rayon sport shirt Glen-plaid jacket Multi-floral print skirt Mustard & gold earrings RV suede flats Black nylons
	P.M. 1:00	Visit relatives Drive in country	Remove glen-plaid jacket
	7:00	At home — plan for coming week Phone calls	Remove floral print skirt Add gold stirrups

(text continued from page 255)

Repeat the color of skirt or pants in a scarf or jewelry near your face and draw attention up. Any of these works.

- When you repeat a clothing color in accessories, that color becomes more important; it becomes readily more noticeable in the clothes. Make sure it's a color you want to make more important or dominant.

For example, even a small amount of teal blue-green in a print or an outfit becomes more noticeable when earrings, belt, and/or bag are teal blue-green. It can be a great way to emphasize beautiful blue-green eyes.

You don't have to hunt up all your accessories of the same color. It can look like you tried too hard and may end up looking monotonous.

- If you do decide to wear all accessories in the same color, select them in some variety of shades or textures for needed interest.

For example, Susan chose red-violet suede in a belt and shoes. She chose earrings in smooth stone and metal, with metals matched — brass with brass, gold with gold.

- If you opt for different colors, generally two or more accessories should be in the same color and be fairly closely grouped, rather than jumping from head to toe.

For example, you might choose to wear a coral-colored hat and scarf with tan shoes and handbag. Repeating coral in hat and shoes can appear too spotty or jumpy.

Dominant/Subordinate Points

In all cases, create **only one dominant point of attention or emphasis in an outfit** — at the neck, waist, hem, and so forth. (See Figure 9–7.) For business and leadership, keep attention up near your face. **All other points or areas of attention must be subordinate — less important by degrees.**

For example, imagine a pinkish-brown dress with small black polka dots, made of lightweight rayon. Visualize the style with a small pointed collar buttoned at the neck, short sleeves, a narrow self-fabric belt at the waist, and a longer full-flared skirt that ripples nicely around the legs. Black is the accent color in the dress, perfect for basic black leather flats or pumps and handbag. The dress can be worn alone, or layered with a black micro-fiber blazer for a very sportive and slightly sophisticated look — although still quite plain. So bring on the added accessories.

Starting with a small gold pinky ring, mentally move up the arm to a relatively medium-sized gold and copper bracelet. Copper has an essence of pink to it — perfect with the soft pinkish-brown in the dress. Both gold and copper metals add a little bright shine to the otherwise dull-surfaced dress. Moving up from the bracelet, you notice a large, heavy but lacy, copper pin at the neck, vintage in style. It's a very personal piece. The dual-colored bracelet

Figure 9–7. This unique triple belt counters vertical clothing lines and creates a dominant point of interest in the upper hip area. *(Courtesy Madeleine Direct)*

serves as a bridge between the gold ring and copper pin. With the ring small, the bracelet flat and medium, and the pin heavy and large, the pin becomes the dominant focal point. Earrings are smaller still, smaller than the ring, and therefore sub-subordinate to all the other jewelry. One more tiny touch of femininity. Tuck a black and copper lace pocket square in the pocket of the black jacket. All you see is a touch of coppery lace. It is elegant, and it works. You can count through all the accessory pieces in terms of size, moving from very small earrings to the comparatively large pin at the neck. You are not even concerned with shoes, belt, or bag, which are relatively plain in style and black or matching print; they go virtually unnoticed in comparison to the jewelry. It's a great piece of wearable art!

Try putting together a look of your own with clothes you already own. Practice the blink test to determine the dominant point or area of interest. It's up to you to make that

The Importance and Function of Accessories

- Accessories finish or complete an outfit.

For example, a skirt or pants with belt loops but no belt looks incomplete, like you didn't finish getting dressed.

- Accessories pull together, coordinate, or unify the look of your outfit.

For example, coordinate the look of rust-colored slacks and a white blouse with a brown, rust, black, and white print tie or scarf. A rust and white striped sport belt would do the job as well.

- Accessories can add needed interest, variety, and individuality to an outfit, and provide an important spark to your personal style.

For example, a wonderful handwoven hemp belt, possibly with a hint of gold metallic thread and a gold buckle may add just the needed textural touch to give variety and interest to an otherwise plain-looking outfit.

You want and need visual variety, but don't go overboard to the point of creating conflict or chaos.

For example, a very businesslike, stiff, straight-lined, rectangular shaped yang handbag conflicts with the softly rounded yin lines of a full, flared chiffon skirt and open-toe evening shoes. Textures of the same weight in different weaves, however, work out well. Imagine teaming bulkier clothing fabrics with opaque, ribbed, or textured stockings. With soft, silky fabrics, wear sheer stockings.

You want to create a look of individuality and personal style, but don't stick with the same accessory every day and night. Some variety makes you less predictable, more interesting and attractive.

For example, a double strand of large pearls may be a particular woman's signature piece, but they may not be all that attractive around her neck, and it certainly gets old and boring after a year or more.

- Accessories can change the look, mood, or message of basic garments, expanding the number of different-looking outfits — dress the clothes up or down, from casual to business, day to evening, and change the look of

clothes from summer to winter.

For example, soften the look of a serious business suit or dress with a touch of lace — in a jabot at the neck or on a pocket square tucked into a breast pocket. Go from day to evening with a jeweled or beaded collar worn over your basic jacket or dress. To make the transition from warm to cooler weather wearing the same basic, cotton knit wrap dress, change your shoes and jewelry. A shell necklace, sandals, and canvas espadrilles signal summer; silver chains, and shoes with socks or tights work in winter.

- Accessories can lead or draw attention to the area where they are placed — to a dominant point of emphasis, and away from a less desirable area.

For example, a gold chain at the neck calls attention away from proportionally larger tummy, hips, or thighs, and up to the neck and face. An eye-catching or low-slung belt only defeats your purpose. Shoes in a contrasting color call attention to themselves. Unless you continue the color upward, or

repeat the color in a larger amount higher on the figure, attention will stay down on the shoes. You decide. Karen often ties a printed silk scarf around the shoulders of her business suit to hold attention up around her face, even when she's seated behind her desk.

- Accessories can update the look of your time-tested classic clothes.

For example, a shawl in the latest fashion color can update the look of a coat. Shoes in the latest style can make your straight skirt look current. A popular new piece of jewelry or trendsetting belt can make an older sweater or jacket look like new again.

- Accessories can upgrade lesser quality clothing, or downgrade even the finest of clothes and your entire appearance.

For example, a snagged or wrinkled scarf, plastic-looking belts, shoes with broken stitching, and tarnished silver jewelry ruin the look of the clothes they accessorize. Get the best quality you can find and afford, then take care of them to upgrade your total look.

point or place appropriate for the occasion and your purpose or goal. If your face disappears, you've got too much attention on the clothes and accessories. Try again; you can do it.

Planned Coordination Is the Key

If you have a closet full of clothes that won't intermix, chances are you are not satisfied with your wardrobe. Planned coordination is the key to making a small cluster of clothes work. Many people buy what they want on impulse or out of frustration. Little to no discipline, thought, or planning goes into putting together the wardrobe. The parts come together without working.

Cluster planning gives you needed discipline and direction. It simplifies your life, providing you with a core of clothes that work together beautifully and effortlessly; clothes that take you the places you need to go; clothes that give you the confidence of always looking terrific. Take the fear out of fashion and wardrobe planning by learning to create a cluster of coordinated clothes.

Review Main Points

A cluster is a small group of coordinated clothes, including accessories. Clustering is a wardrobe strategy designed to guide you in selecting clothing to meet all your wardrobe needs. Cluster guidelines instruct you to find a print, stripe, or plaid to inspire the color scheme of a cluster. Plan for five to eight, top and bottom, pieces of clothing. Select pieces that are basic in style lines and shape. Select pieces that go together, working with at least two other pieces. Select pieces that are distinctly different from one another. Select accessories to go with the clothes. Gradually expand your cluster(s) to meet all your wardrobe needs. Plansheets allow you to plan, evaluate, and review a cluster of clothes. They can help you save time, money, and frustration. Combining coordinated clothing and accessories in interesting and harmonious ways is a key to putting together an effective, versatile, and fashionable cluster of clothes.

Review Questions

1. A cluster is a _____.

2. Give two important functions of clustering.

   _____

   _____

3. Write five of the seven cluster guidelines.

   _____.

   _____.

   _____.

   _____.

   _____.

4. A favorite _____ can provide you with a color scheme for a cluster.

5. Clothes in a five-piece cluster include _____ tops, _____ bottoms, and _____.

6. A packaged set of sewing patterns and _____ _____ often meet the definition of a cluster.

7. Explain the concept of add-ons. _____

   _____

8. Explain why each cluster piece should be different from the others.

   _____.

   _____.

9. Name two categories of accessories. _____ and _____.

10. Which of the following words does not belong in the group? Circle the word.

    jewelry   hosiery   belts   shoes

11. List four kinds or groups of non- or less-essential accessories.

_____ _____

_____ _____

12. A complete, expanded wardrobe includes _____ and

_____.

13. In charting your cluster plans, it is smart to include items you _____

and items you plan to _____.

14. For maximum versatility and harmony, both clothing and accessories in a

cluster need to look like they _____ _____.

15. When combining clothing with accessories, one point or area must be

_____ and all others must be _____.

Discussion Questions

#1 In past years, what efforts have you made, or experiences have you had, in
planning a wardrobe?

Notes: _____

_____

_____

_____

#2 Explain and discuss the meaning behind each cluster guideline. Give examples.

Notes: _____

_____

_____

#3 Discuss clothing pieces you might need or want to have in a cluster for a
teenager; in a cluster for a new graduate; in a cluster for an elderly woman.

Notes: _____

_____

_____

_____

#4 If you were putting plans on paper, what information would you need to
include?

Notes: _____

_____

_____

Look at what you are wearing.

• List the pieces of clothing you are wearing.
• From memory, list other pieces of clothing at home that combine well with these clothes.
• From memory, list accessories that combine well with these clothes.

	Clothing Item	**Coordinating Clothing Pieces**	**Accessories**
1.			
2.			
3.			

Exercise 9–2   Cluster Coordination

Name _____

Look in your closet.

• Select and describe one favorite patterned piece of clothing — print, stripe, or plaid.

• Working with colors in the patterned piece of clothing, try to find four more pieces from your wardrobe that go well with it. Most will be solid colors, but combine another patterned piece if you have one that works harmoniously. List them.

• List accessories that combine well with these five pieces. You may have few.

• If possible, expand this group to include eight pieces of clothing, and any additional accessories you can think of that work with these additional pieces. List all. You may not have many.

Favorite Patterned Item	4 Coordinated Clothing Pieces	Accessories
	Tops: Bottoms:	Shoes: Stockings: Belts: Scarves: Jewelry:
	3 Add-on Pieces	**Accessories**
	Tops: Bottoms:	Shoes: Stockings: Belts: Scarves: Jewelry:

Exercise 9–3 Brand and Designer Clusters

Name _____

Look in a local clothing store (outlet, discount, chain, department, or specialty store).

• Locate brand-name or designer collections (clusters) of coordinated clothes.
• Count the number of tops and bottoms in four different collections (clusters).
• Count the number of pieces in four different collections (clusters).
• Count the number of solid color pieces and patterned pieces in these collections (clusters).
• Among the four, what is the average number of pieces, solid color pieces, and patterned pieces of clothing?
• Evaluate the versatility and success of the collections (clusters), in terms of the occasions they appear to be designed for — casual, business, or dressy occasions.

Brand or Designer Name	# of Tops	# of Bottoms	# of Pieces	# Solid Color Pieces	# of Patterned Pieces	Evaluation Comments
#1 Totals						
#2 Totals						
#3 Totals						
#4 Totals						
Totals (add all)						
Average (÷ 4)						

Exercise 9–4   Magazine Clusters

Name_____

Find pictures of cluster groups of coordinated clothes published in magazines and/or catalogs.

• Count the number of tops and bottoms in four different collections (clusters).
• Count the number of pieces in four different collections (clusters).
• Count the number of solid color pieces, and patterned pieces in these collections (clusters).
• Among the four, what is the average number of pieces, solid color pieces, and patterned pieces of clothing?
• Evaluate the versatility and success of the collections (clusters), in terms of the occasions they appear to be designed for — casual, business, or dressy occasions.
• Attach pages to exercise page.

Collection/ Cluster	# of Tops	# of Bottoms	# of Pieces	# Solid Color Pieces	# of Patterned Pieces	Evaluation Comments
#1 Totals						
#2 Totals						
#3 Totals						
#4 Totals						
Totals (add all)						
Average (÷ 4)						

Exercise 9–5   Video Cluster

Name _____

- Review and refer to companion videotape #2 Part A, the section featuring Ellen.
- List the pieces in Ellen's cluster.
- Using instructions for cluster plansheets provided in this chapter, fill in the appropriate spaces on a five- to ten-piece cluster plan-sheet with clothes you listed in Ellen's cluster. For examples, see Tables 9–1 and 9–2 featuring Susan's cluster.
- Using the coordinated outfits plansheets, list pieces in every outfit combination you can think of.
- Using the shopping list, fill in with items Ellen might plan to add on to her cluster. Include some of your own ideas.

Five– to Ten–Piece Women's Wardrobe Cluster

Name _____

Life-style _____ Personal style _____

Climate/season of the year _____ Occasion _____ Date _____

ITEM		Wardrobe Neutral	Wardrobe Neutral	Accent Colors	Works With	Plans to Acquire	Cost
CLOTHING	Blouse						
	Shirt						
	Blouse or shirt						
	Skirt						
	Pant or skirt						
	Pants						
	One– or two–piece dress						
	Sweater or vest						
	Jacket						
	All–occasion coat						
ACCESSORIES	Dress shoe						
	Casual/walking shoes						
	Hosiery/socks						
	All–occasion handbag						
	Casual/dress handbag						
	Belt						
	Scarf/tie						
	Earrings						
	Necklace						
	Bracelet						
	Gloves						

Women's Coordinated Outfits

Cluster Colors: Wardrobe neutral _____   Wardrobe neutral _____

Accent colors _____ , _____ , _____

ITEM	#____	#____	#____	#____	#____
Blouse, shirt, or dress					
Skirt or pant					
Sweater					
Vest					
Jacket					
Coat					
Shoes					
Hosiery					
Bag					
Belt					
Scarf or tie					
Earrings					
Necklace					
Bracelet					
Gloves					

Women's Coordinated Outfits (*continued*)

Cluster Colors: Wardrobe neutral _____ Wardrobe neutral _____

Accent colors _____ , _____ , _____

ITEM	#____	#____	#____	#____	#____
Blouse, shirt, or dress					
Skirt or pant					
Sweater					
Vest					
Jacket					
Coat					
Shoes					
Hosiery					
Bag					
Belt					
Scarf or tie					
Earrings					
Necklace					
Bracelet					
Gloves					

Women's Coordinated Outfits (*continued*)

Cluster Colors: Wardrobe neutral _____ Wardrobe neutral _____

Accent colors _____ , _____ , _____

ITEM	#____	#____	#____	#____	#____
Blouse, shirt, or dress					
Skirt or pant					
Sweater					
Vest					
Jacket					
Coat					
Shoes					
Hosiery					
Bag					
Belt					
Scarf or tie					
Earrings					
Necklace					
Bracelet					
Gloves					

Women's Coordinated Outfits (continued)

Cluster Colors: Wardrobe neutral _____ Wardrobe neutral _____

Accent colors _____ , _____ , _____

ITEM	#____	#____	#____	#____	#____
Blouse, shirt, or dress					
Skirt or pant					
Sweater					
Vest					
Jacket					
Coat					
Shoes					
Hosiery					
Bag					
Belt					
Scarf or tie					
Earrings					
Necklace					
Bracelet					
Gloves					

Shopping List

	What I need:	To coordinate with:	Take along shopping:
Clothing			
Accessories			

Chapter

10

Wardrobe Evaluation

Learning Objectives

Your goal in completing this chapter is to be able to:

- Understand the difference between a wardrobe inventory and a wardrobe evaluation.
- Understand and appreciate the value of a wardrobe evaluation.
- Prepare for a wardrobe evaluation session.
- Identify clothing you like, dislike, or never wear.
- List the characteristics of clothes you like, dislike, or never wear.
- Discover and understand the reasons behind your clothing likes, dislikes, and decisions not to wear certain items.
- Determine clothing items to discard.
- Discard clothing in appropriate and responsible ways.
- Inventory remaining clothing.
- Plan for needed clothing items.
- Cluster your own clothes.

Preview Main Points

1. Rely on a periodic wardrobe evaluation session.
2. Prepare for a wardrobe evaluation project in advance.
3. Sort your clothes, including accessories, into three groups; those you like, dislike, or never wear.
4. Discard clothes that don't meet your needs.
5. Inventory all remaining clothes, including accessories.
6. Rely on a private, at-home fashion show.
7. Cluster your own clothing.

1.

Rely on a periodic wardrobe evaluation session.

Before revamping your entire wardrobe, take time to evaluate your wardrobe. Wardrobing is a continuous process involving three phases: (1) evaluation, (2) discarding of nonfunctional pieces, and (3) the accumulation of new pieces. (See Figure 10–1.) Planning takes place, and may be revised, within all three phases.

Taking inventory is a vital and integral part of good business management. You've got to know what you have to work with — to identify what's there. It makes sense to apply the same process to wardrobe and image management. But you need to do more than simply inventory what's there; you must decide how well what's in your closet works for you — how well it meets your needs and preferences. That is wardrobe evaluation. You must know what works, what doesn't, and why. Then weed out what doesn't work. Next, organize what's left, and finally, discover how the clothes work together, coordinate, or combine. You will find that wardrobe evaluation is a sound strategy.

The Project

Most people read about doing it. Some people talk about doing it. Few people actually do it. Those who do it every year or two know that it pays off. Fall and spring are logical times to evaluate and organize a wardrobe, when the weather's changing, and so are the styles of new clothes in the stores. It's better to carry out this project at the beginning of the season when your clothes look fresh, instead of at the end when you tend to be tired of them. While now may not be the best time to evaluate your wardrobe, it fits into the logical sequence of your learning as you work through this book.

Importance and Function

Come into the project with an objective attitude. Don't think about the size of the job. Think of all the benefits instead. A periodic wardrobe evaluation and closet clean-out helps you to:

- Identify your clothing needs.
- Clearly define your likes and dislikes — define your personal style.
- Make better use of the clothing you already own.
- Decide what you need to add to or discard from your wardrobe.
- Avoid making mistakes on future clothing purchases.
- Eliminate the "guilt" you feel every time you open the closet door and are faced with unworn, wasted clothes.
- Get ready in good spirits and on time — you're not hit by a shoe box when you reach for something else.
- Save time and energy in shopping, sorting, dressing, cleaning, pressing, repairing, and replacing.
- Save money on inappropriate or unneeded clothing, cleaning, pressing, repairing, and replacing.
- Create and maintain an attractive, healthy self-image — knowing that your clothes enhance your appearance.

Think of the functions of wardrobe evaluation as rewards. Experiencing any of these rewards makes the time and effort worthwhile. In addition, you come into the project with an edge over most people. You already know the difference between basic and costume clothes. You can recognize most classics and trends. You know what wardrobe neutrals are. You can identify both fibers and fabrics. You can judge the quality of a pattern. You've already looked through your clothes several times. By now you have a thorough knowledge of the clothes you own. (See Figures 10–2a and b.) This project, when you actually begin, will go faster and be easier than you might expect.

2.

Prepare for a wardrobe evaluation project in advance.

The only way to get into this project is all the way! Half-hearted measures won't work. Begin with a firm resolve to succeed.

Wardrobing Cycle

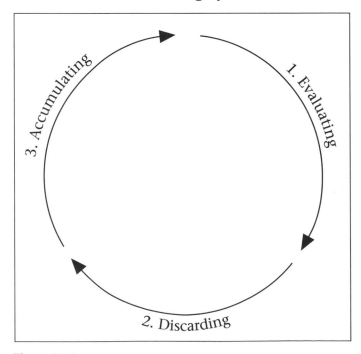

Figure 10–1.

Figure 10–2a & b. Basic, classic, casual separates have a place in every wardrobe. Look for, or plan for, an appropriate balance between casual and dressier clothes. *(Fig. 10–2a courtesy Land's End; Fig. 10–2b courtesy Clifford & Wills; photographer Val Ostrowski)*

The Days Before

Allow yourself plenty of time. Choose a time when you can be alone and nothing will interfere. For most people, evaluating and organizing a wardrobe takes several hours to all day — all weekend if you have many clothes to sort through. That's not surprising when you consider it took years to accumulate your wardrobe in the first place. If it seems too long, take heart in knowing that you'll never have to spend this much time and effort on your wardrobe or closet again. Once done, it's faster and easier the next time.

Invite a friend to help if you like, but only if you're sure your friend can be nonjudgmental, has an objective eye, and a terrific clothes sense. Too often a friend is unable to get beyond personal taste and preference to help you enough. While not meaning to, a friend may try to rush you or engage in irrelevant conversation. But if company is the only way you can get into the project, by all means, invite a friend to help. Offer to return the favor another day.

Supplies

To save time, prepare for the big day ahead of time. Gather supplies you'll need the evening before.

- An extra lamp or two if your room is not well lighted.
- A plain-colored bedsheet, preferably white, to cover the bed if the spread is brightly colored or patterned.
- Medium and medium-large, sturdy, cardboard boxes or shopping bags to use in sorting some of the clothes.
- A few small boxes for small accessory items.
- Zipper-type plastic bags in assorted sizes for sorting accessories.
- A big garbage bag to carry away what doesn't work.
- Note-taking materials, including large and small pads of paper, pens and pencils in red, blue, and black. A small "Post-it" note pad will come in handy too.
- A portable clothes rack for keeping messy piles of clothes off the bed and floor — and for clearing your mind. A clothes rack provides you with an easy view and more access to all your clothes. A broomstick handle, shower curtain rod, or chinning bar suspended between two chairs make workable substitutes.
- A camera and film, preferably Polaroid, is an ideal way to record your best looks for future reference. If you don't have one, maybe you can borrow one.

- A full-length mirror for evaluating outfits. If you don't have one, try to borrow, rent, or buy one. It's something you're going to want sooner or later. Consider it now. It doesn't have to be expensive.
- Something to drink. If it's going to be a long session, plan for a snack or a lunch break with a brisk walk about mid-day to revive your enthusiasm.

The Big Day

Setting aside a whole day for any project makes it a big deal. Think of this project as an adventure you're doing to discover things about yourself and your clothes you never knew. Who knows, you may even run into a long-lost treasure, a real fashion find in the back of your closet. Evaluating your wardrobe is actually less work and more fun than you might imagine.

After breakfast, make final preparations.

- Make your bed and keep it clear of any clutter. You're going to use that space. If needed, cover the bed with the plain-colored sheet.
- Clear the floor of unnecessary clutter.
- Rearrange any chairs in the room, if helpful. You can use them to hold clothes during the evaluation.
- Place the boxes or bags in a convenient place to use later on.
- Set up the lamps, racks, or mirror you've brought in to use.
- Turn on some music, but nothing distracting. It should simply serve as background music to make the time more pleasant.
- Comb and arrange your hair. Put on your usual makeup. You won't feel or look as attractive in the clothes, and possibly won't even like the clothes, if you look less than terrific.

Closet Commentary: Your Closet Tells All

If your clothes make a statement about you — your personality, values, interests, and so forth — then your closet is going to tell the whole story!

- Open your closet and drawers. Before doing anything else, stop and look at their contents as though you were seeing them for the first time.
- Study the arrangement of their contents. How much order do you see? How much control over your life and your image does the arrangement — or lack of arrangement — suggest?
- Notice the clothes hanging in the middle of the closet — or heaped in the middle of the floor. Chances are, they are the clothes you wear most often and reflect the activities or occasions in your life. What activities do the clothes suggest?

For example, *I often see extremes of dress in a client's closet. I see super-grubby clothes at one extreme and super-dressy clothes at the other, with nothing in between*

to wear to work, to the shopping mall, to a nice restaurant, to church, or to a concert. The owner is set for dirty work and dancing, but little else. On the other hand, maybe all I see are the in-betweens, with nothing at either end of the continuum to relax or work around the house and yard in. There's nothing to wear for a special event. The owner appears forever trapped in an office or community image. I prefer to see clothes in a closet that say, "In these I can tackle a dirty job. In these I can really relax. In these I'm ready for business. And in these I'm ready to play." A closet should hold clothes, ranging from grubby to dressy, for all the occasions in your life, and in the degree that works for you and your life-style. On a continuum, what is business dress for one woman can be dressy evening for another.

- Look at the clothes in the back or to the sides of your closet. Chances are, these are clothes you wear least often, if ever. Do any reflect a waste of time and money, lost dreams or an accumulation of clothes from your past?
- Look at the types of garments. How many shirts or blouses do you have? How many skirts or slacks? Do you have twenty T-shirts and no blouses? Are there six party dresses and nothing to wear to work, now that you're ready to get a job?
- Look at the colors and the fabrics. Are they similar, or is there some variety? What feeling do you get from the colors? What feeling from the fabrics?
- Notice the condition of the clothes. Are they lopsided on the hangers, pulling garments out of shape? Are they smashed together, adding to the wrinkles?
- Can you see everything?
- Can you reach everything?
- Ask yourself, "What kind of person owns this wardrobe?" Do the contents of your closet and drawers reflect the person you are, the person you want to be, and the person you want others to see?

Closets are fascinating places, revealing much about the person whose clothes they hold. Consistency, or harmony, between you and your clothes is what you're looking for in wardrobe evaluation.

3.

Sort your clothes, including accessories, into three groups: clothes you like, dislike, or never wear.

Your task is now to remove everything from your closet, drawers, and wherever else they may be. *Everything.* (See Figure 10–3.) Remove the clothes and accessories right down to the last stray sock. I suggest you start with the hanging clothes first. Remove the garments one by one and sort them into three groups.

Figure 10–3. Remove everything from your closet and drawers. *(Courtesy Heidi Neslen)*

The Clothes Sort

Group 1 Clothes you love or like and wear often go in the first group.

Group 2 Clothes you don't particularly like and may dislike, but must wear anyway because they're what you have, make up the second group.

Group 3 Clothes you never wear, regardless of whether you like them or not, belong in the third group.

Hold up each item and ask yourself, "Do I really like this? Do I wear it fairly often or not?" Then put the item in the appropriate group, whether it's on a rack you brought in just for this purpose, on the bed, or over a chair. Proceed quickly. Don't get stalled on any item.

With clothes sorted into groups of like, dislike, and never wear, some people are ready to quit. They don't want to look further or think longer. They argue, "I know if I like it or I don't. I'll keep what I like and pitch what I don't." But remember, it's not enough to simply know what you like and what you don't. You need to know *why*. You need to zero in on the reasons behind good and poor choices. This is the most interesting and helpful part of an evaluation session. Make some notes as you go.

Group One: Why Do You Like These Clothes?

Start with the first group and try to discover why you like them, why the clothes work for you — why they are favorites. Try the clothes on if you need to but consider each garment carefully. You may be surprised, even delighted, at what you learn about yourself. Hint: It's easier to figure out why you like something than why you don't. Start there first.

Look for similarities in styles, colors, and fabrics. Are there more dresses, suits, pants, or skirts in this group? Are the colors mostly light or dark, bright or muted? Are the fabrics mostly woven or knits? Both? Make some notes. It helps. Find out how the clothes fit. Think about how they make you feel when you wear them. Think about how effectively you're able to function when wearing them. What do the clothes say about you? Is it what you want them to say?

If you have difficulty in being objective about the look and messages conveyed by your clothes, you may want to ask for another opinion. Ask a friend, a professional colleague, or a family member. The nonverbal message may come across loud and clear to someone else who is less familiar with the clothes. You will discover you have certain preferences for certain types of lines, shapes, and styles.

For example, maybe you're a person who prefers simple straighter lines as compared to curved lines and fullness. Maybe A-line and flared skirts always fit. You may prefer certain colors or color families, tints, shades, or tones of color. Maybe the colors accurately express or reflect your personality and typical moods. Maybe you're a woman who prefers floral prints instead of solid colors or plaids.

The variety of "maybes" is endless, but whatever the case, try to discover why you have these preferences. Record your answers. Some answers are fairly obvious.

For example, maybe you like these clothes because you receive frequent compliments on how nice you look in them, due to the flattering fit, colors, or lines. Maybe you have a preference for certain items because they fit your life-style. Pants are preferred by one first-grade teacher for the obvious reason that she is down on the floor with the kids during her day. A-line and flared skirts always fit in the "like" group of another woman. Why? Because her figure is fuller around the hips and bottom. A-line and flared styles put more width where it needs to be, allowing the fabric to fit easily and attractively over the area.

For another example, maybe the clothes you like are styles you can wear for a variety of occasions. In speaking about a shirtwaist dress, one woman realized, "This dress has always been a favorite. It fits well and I'm comfortable in it. But it's particularly good for me because I don't have a lot of money to spend on clothes. I can change the way this dress looks and wear it looking casual or dressy — whatever I need."

Some answers take more thought.

For example, one client noticed more dresses, lightweight fabrics, and prints in her group of most-liked clothes. She told me, "I think I prefer dresses because they make me feel feminine. The fabrics are lightweight, and I get a 'floaty' feeling from the movement of the skirt and sleeves. Prints? I must admit, I think I like to wear prints because they are very busy. People tend to notice the print more than they notice my figure, and I feel more comfortable — less self-conscious. But these prints are bouncy and fun, kind of like me, and I like that." Here is a young woman who is gaining a real understanding of herself and therefore her clothing preferences.

For another example, a former student stated, "I like wool separates and sweaters best." Why? "Nothing in-born about it," she reasoned. "I grew up in the Northwest. The weather is cool and somewhat damp most of the time. Everyone wore a lot of wool and knits. I always carried a jacket. Because wool is more expensive and lasts a long time, my mother taught me to select the more simple, classic styles in suits and separates, styles that would last a long time and give me my money's worth. That's what I learned and that's what I like to this day."

Don't panic if you discover you love seemingly contradictory opposites.

For example, one woman had mostly sportive styles in her preferred group of clothes. She was confused by several favorite, more feminine dresses and blouses. Thinking about it, she realized all the styles and fabrics were consistently sportive or tailored, and it was only colors and smaller design details that were noticeably feminine — just enough to reflect the feminine side of her personality but not so much as to conflict with the sportive, tailored styles. She now recognizes that it's precisely this mix of design elements that makes her wardrobe uniquely hers.

The variety of "maybes" is endless in terms of the discoveries you might make about yourself. You may now begin to see that the clothes you love and wear often are the clothes that agree with the activities you engage in — with the way you live. You may begin to see that these clothes agree with the person you feel you are — with your values, personality traits, and the various facets of yourself. (See Figure 10–4.) Make more notes about why you like the clothes in group one. Compare your notes with choices and decisions you made for exercises in previous chapters.

Don't expect to come up with pat answers for every garment or learn every little thing about yourself in one session. Wardrobe evaluation is an on-going process. As you mature, change, and experiment, you will gradually come to know yourself and your resulting clothing preferences. And as you change your roles or responsibilities, you can expect your needs and preferences to change also.

Different Degrees of Yin and Yang in Personal Style

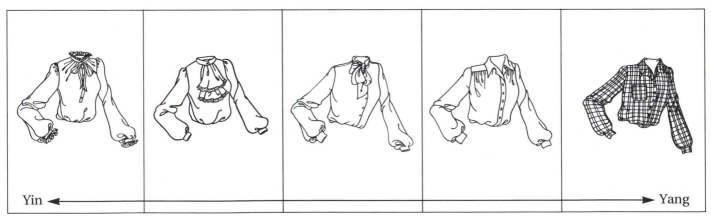

Yin ◄──────────────────────────────────► Yang

Figure 10–4.

With this in mind, take a long and hard look at your older clothes — clothes three or more years old. Are they still appropriate for the person you are today? If not, they are candidates for the "out" box to be discussed later.

When evaluation of this group is complete, set them aside for now. Many items will be the basis for your future wardrobe plans. Remember why you like these clothes and how good you feel wearing them. Resolve to never again wear anything that doesn't give you that wonderful feeling. These are characteristics or traits that you value. They identify your personal style. These preferences will guide your future wardrobe plans and purchases.

Group Two: Why Don't You Like These Clothes?

Go on to the second group. Ask yourself why you don't like the clothes in this group. Make note of your answers and don't be surprised if some are exactly the opposite of your answers concerning the clothes in group one. Again, the variety of "maybes" is endless.

For example, *if you are one who prefers simple, tailored styles, the disliked clothes may be too fussy and frilly for you. If you like warm, light colors and soft textures, maybe the disliked clothes are predominantly dark and rough. Maybe you feel out of place, inappropriate, or unattractive in these clothes. Maybe that's because they don't fit well. Maybe the colors or styles are just too bold for you. Maybe that knit fabric is full of snagged threads and has bagged out in the knees and seat. Maybe that off-white shirt is just plain yellow now.*

You may begin to see disagreement between the activities you engage in, between the person you feel you are, and the traits communicated by the clothes in this group. The clothing traits may be contrary to what you said you are like or what you prefer in clothing design. The clothes may not be consistent with your life-style or your personal style. Knowing this can help you understand why you dislike the clothes in this second group.

For example, *maybe you're a quiet, reserved individual. It makes sense that bright colors and extreme styles are just too bold and overpowering for you. They attract too much attention. Maybe you're a stickler for detail and value good quality clothes — it's the way you were brought up. It's no wonder you don't like fabrics that sag or bag. Maybe you have an eye for color and are therefore more sensitive to the discoloration of that off-white shirt — the one that yellowed with age. Maybe you have sensitive skin and, while the color is great, the fabric is just too rough and scratchy.*

You might say about something in this group, "It's just not me," meaning you bought a garment suited to someone else. Don't stop there. Figure out why it isn't "you."

For example, *as one woman put it, "I see myself as being quite feminine, gentle, and sort of soft — yet fun loving and spontaneous too. It's no wonder I never liked this jacket Mom gave me. It would look great on her, but the style is too severe, the lines too straight, the fabric too firm. It's too controlled for me. I feel uncomfortable wearing it."*

You'll find that when you understand yourself, it's easier to understand the preferences of others. It's easier to accept and even appreciate another's personal style without feeling you have to adopt that style yourself.

If you feel out of place in some of the clothes in group two, chances are they really aren't appropriate for the places you need or want to go.

For example, *maybe you live a casual life-style and these clothes are too dressy or formal. Maybe you own three sets of sweats and never move a muscle. Maybe you have a new job that requires a new image. One client's closet contained "week-ends only" clothes — jeans, T-shirts, and sweats that didn't work at the office — clothes that didn't reflect the new professional image.*

Perhaps the clothes in this group look dreadfully out of date, and you feel trapped in the past when you wear them. Or perhaps you've discovered the clothes aren't coordinated. The colors clash with one another, the fabrics and patterns fight for attention and can't be mixed harmoniously for a variety of looks and occasions.

Any one of these discoveries can be the reason why you dislike the clothes in this group. Becoming aware of the reason is the first step in avoiding the problem in the future.

Interestingly, you may discover that the reason you don't like something is just silly — totally unrelated to you or imposed by someone else. When that happens, you may be able to overcome your former dislike and gain a new wardrobe option.

For example, *I once worked with a young man who had an intense dislike for the color red. He refused to wear red and didn't want anyone else to wear it either. After a lot of thought, he realized he didn't have a good reason to dislike red. Making a phone call home, he learned it was really his mother who didn't like red. Red clothes emphasized the red in her face resulting from a chronic allergy. As a youngster he'd heard her complain about how she hated red. He internalized the dislike but forgot the source. Armed with this new information, he was able to "let go" of his negative attitude, admit that his wife really did look nice wearing red, and finally enjoy wearing a red tie himself.*

If you feel unattractive in some of the clothes in group two, decide if it's due to the lines, the shape, the color, the fabric, or fit. Don't bother trying on something you hate if you're sure of the reason and know you're not going to keep it. If unsure, by all means, try it on.

For example, *maybe the style doesn't flatter your figure because the sleeves attract attention to your larger waist. Maybe the buttons are too big in proportion to your height and size. Maybe your weight has changed enough so the clothes don't fit. Maybe the color looked great on you in the store but looks absolutely awful under florescent office lights.*

There are many "maybes," but once you discover why something doesn't work for you, resolve never to buy it again.

Group Three: Why Don't You Wear These Clothes?

Move onto the third group, those wardrobe orphans — clothes that hang unloved, unwanted, and unworn in the back of your closet. They may be perfectly good clothes you feel you should wear. Chances are you feel guilty about them. In some cases, you may dislike the style, the color, or fabric so much you simply refuse to wear them. No wonder you feel you don't have anything to wear! Find out why.

It's possible that you actually like some of these clothes, but for some reason you can't wear them. Do some checking. Do any of these clothes need cleaning, pressing, or repair?

For example, maybe your time is limited and some of the fabrics wrinkle easily, demanding more care than you're willing or able to give. So they hang there, never ready to wear. Maybe they cost too much to clean. Maybe you have a dress with a belt that doesn't buckle or a shirt with a button missing from the cuff. Maybe a zipper is broken and needs replacing. Maybe the skirt hem you caught your heel in could use a stitch.

Again, the "maybes" are endless.

For example, maybe you like straight skirts, but they're too confining and seldom fit well enough to wear. Maybe some of these fabrics are too warm for your climate or too delicate and easy to ruin. Maybe some of the clothes are just plain worn out, but you haven't been able to bring yourself to part with them. Maybe some of the clothes in this group don't go with anything else in your wardrobe. Maybe you no longer have any place to wear them — like fancy evening or party clothes when you now live in the country. Maybe you've allowed the fashion world to sell you clothes for a life-style you don't live in the first place — you certainly don't need expensive business suits if all your work is in your home.

Is there anything you can or want to do to return these clothes to active service?

For example, perhaps you can wear a light or lively color in combination with a drab or dark color and put new life into the way you look wearing it. Perhaps you are willing to spend the time to line the skirt made of scratchy fabric or to pay someone to do it for you. Consider cleaning, pressing, or mending the garment, replacing a button or zipper, altering for better fit or simple remodeling. It's cheaper than buying new clothes. But, in some cases, new clothes might be just the solution to update the look of the old.

Now is the time to start a shopping list of new items to add to your wardrobe. (See Table 9–6, page 265.) Now is the time to make yourself a note and pin-mark any new seam or hemline. Now is the time to label boxes or bags "wash," "dry clean," "repair," "alter," and "remodel" if that's what you plan to do. Then place selected items in the appropriate containers. Nothing goes back into the closet dirty or needing attention.

Sleepwear and Underwear

If you haven't already included sleepwear and underwear or lingerie in your evaluation, do so now. Be just as committed to deciding what works, what doesn't and why, as you were with your outerwear. Be just as firm with yourself when it comes to discarding sleepwear that doesn't fit properly or looks totally tacky. Discolored slips, limp bras, and panties with over-stretched elastic demand to be replaced as soon as possible. List new items you need for every day and special occasion clothes.

Accessories

Get out all your accessories — belts, shoes, bags, scarves, jewelry, and anything else that serves to complete the look of an outfit. Sort them into three groups, just as you did with your clothes. Consider the style, shape, color, and material of each item. Determine how well they fit, reflect your ideal image, and coordinate with your clothes. (See Figure 10–5.) Decide if the condition they're in has anything to do with how well you like them. All of the concerns that applied to your clothes apply to accessories too. Be a stickler for details as you evaluate each item. Be equally firm as you assign things to the "out" box.

Belts. Do you have belts with broken or hanging threads? Belts that won't buckle? Toss them into the box labeled "repair" or "out." Are your belts in or out of style? Belts that need cleaning or polishing belong in a box labeled "clean/polish."

Shoes. Do you have shoes in styles and heel heights you need for the various activities in your life — shoes for active sports, casual, dress-business, and evening occasions? If not, add what's really needed to your shopping list. Shoes or boots that need a new heel go in the "repair" box. Tight-fitting shoes that make you miserable get tossed in the "out" box.

Stockings and hosiery. Do you have colored stockings with nothing to match? Or could you use a fashionable new shade or two? You're never going to mend socks with holes in the toe or heel. Don't let them take up space any longer. Save no more than two pairs of pantyhose with minor runs for wearing with boots or under slacks. Even those shouldn't be so shabby that they make you feel shabby.

Handbags. Are you over-stocked with casual or with business-looking bags? Do you have a canvas bag that's badly stained? Soiled, cracked, or scratched handbags that can no longer hold their shape are ready for the "out" box. Maybe a bag with a broken strap can still be repaired. You decide which box it belongs in.

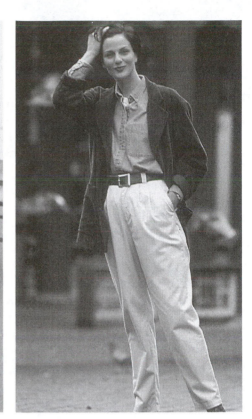

Figure 10–5a, b, c. Casual cluster pieces call for equally casual accessories. Different shoe styles meet a variety of weather needs. *(Courtesy All Week Long by Eddie Bauer; photographer Langley Penoyak)*

Scarves. Keep classic square and oblong scarves. (See Figure 10–6.) Contrary to popular opinion, scarves can look out of date just like anything else. Printed scarves from the sixties and early seventies are easy to spot. Both fabric and pattern appear too stiff with today's clothes. It's time to toss them out, along with scarves that are faded, snagged, or shriveled from years of use.

Jewelry. You will most likely sort through basic and costume pieces, classic and trendy, with a range of dollar values. Get rid of dated pieces, tarnished metal necklaces, and worn-out bracelets or beads. Get rid of single earrings that won't double as a lapel pin.

Umbrellas. An umbrella qualifies as an accessory item. Most people need a basic style in a solid, classic color. Toss any umbrella that can't be cleaned or repaired. An umbrella with a broken rib won't do anything for your image!

4.

Discard clothes that don't meet your needs.

🖎

Now is the time to label an "out" box or bag. It's the natural next step as you are left with clothes in group three that will never work for you. You would get rid of kitchen equipment and garden tools that don't work. You've got to do the same with your clothes.

Figure 10–6. A classic square scarf will deliver years of service, add interest to a basic outfit, and hold attention up around your face. *(Courtesy All Week Long by Eddie Bauer; photographer Rosanne Olson)*

Excuses, Excuses

There are many reasons or excuses you might give that make this task difficult to do. Which of the following sounds most like you?

- "But I might need it some day." You won't.
- "It might come back into style." It won't — at least not exactly the same so that you'll want to wear it again. Details change. The clothes will look dated.
- "I'll get back into it." Size-smaller clothes can be an incentive. They can also put you on a terrible guilt trip and make you feel miserable every time you see them. You don't need that. If you keep the big ones, chances are you will get back into them. You don't need that either. Better to accept your present weight and keep only what fits. If you do decide to hang on to extra sizes, store them out of sight.
- "But it was a gift." Gifts are symbols of love. Keep the love and let go of the symbol.
- "Everyone has one." Don't worry so much about others. Be yourself and true to your own style.
- "It just needs a little fixing and it'll be fine." It's hung there for three years. You know you're never going to fix it. Forget it.
- "But it was so expensive. What a waste if I get rid of it." No matter what the cost, it's money down the drain if you never wear it. Left in your closet it's an additional waste of valuable space.
- "The fabric is still good and the quality is fantastic." Don't be a slave to that one. Good quality alone is not enough if the clothes are dated or dreary.
- "Oh, but it brings back such wonderful memories." Now is not the time to get sentimental over clothes you once enjoyed but are past their prime. Mementos belong in a scrapbook or a storage box, not in your closet.

If it's too traumatic to toss what doesn't work, ask a friend to help you decide — again, it must be a friend who can be objective, someone who knows you, your life-style, and your personal style.

Discard What Doesn't Work

Even if you've already started to discard items you know you don't want, go through each of the groups and make final decisions. This time work backwards. Begin with group three and work your way back to group one. Be absolutely ruthless as you get rid of those clothes that clutter up your closet and your mind. Chances are, you'll toss some of group three, most of group two, and even some things from group one. Here's what goes:

- Clothes too small or too short, no matter how new. This includes jackets that bind in the armpits or elbows, anything that pinches, pulls, or gaps because it's too tight. Such clothes are a constant reminder of your size, making you self-conscious of body bumps and bulges, reinforcing feelings of inferiority with each movement

or glance in the mirror. Such clothes bring negative glances from others. With an objective attitude, you'll be able to toss them into an "out" box or bag.

- Clothes too large or too long. If they don't fit and if they can't be altered easily, into the "out" box no matter how nice.
- Clothes that are uncomfortable. If an item looks terrific in the mirror, but the fabric scratches or rubs a red spot on your skin, it deserves to be dumped.
- Clothes that duplicate something you already have several of — they fill the same need for the same occasion. Too many clothes can be overwhelming and confusing. Pass the extras on to someone else who can make better use of them.
- Clothes with nowhere to wear them make you feel guilty about wasted money. They can make you dissatisfied with a life that doesn't let you wear them. Get rid of them and get on with your life.
- Clothes obviously out of date, no matter how much they cost or how good the fabric still is. It happens all the time. Lapels get wider, shoulders get narrower, armholes get larger, the fit gets looser, trim goes out of style, and so on. They belong in the "out" box.
- Clothes worn out or well on their way, even if you love them. Anything faded, frayed, threadbare, rotten under the arm, with a patent-leather shine on the seat or lining that's turned lacy. They all deserve retirement.
- Clothes that no longer fit your image — your values, personality, or life-style. Clothes that conflict with the accuracy of the image you want to project are not worth keeping. Life goes on, and the way you look is one thing that changes with the changes in your life. If you can't update the look of the clothes, put them in the "out" box.

What to Do with the "Out" Box?

Turn your full attention to the "out" box filled with unwanted clothes. Be ready to label other boxes or bags as you need them. Dispose of these clothes fast, or they'll end up back in your closet. You can dispose of them in the following ways:

Work clothes. Save a few casual clothes and jeans with enough life left in them for yard work and heavy cleaning or painting projects, but don't leave them in your closet. Hang them in a utility area or closet or put them in a box and label it "work clothes."

Copy. If you really can't bear to give up an all-time favorite that still looks fashionable, put it in a special spot with a note that reminds you to "Cut apart and copy the pattern pieces." Then use the pattern pieces to make a brand new garment.

Heirloom quality. If you have an extraordinary piece of clothing, a fashion piece typical of the time, it deserves to be stored away with respect. Consider giving collectors' items to a museum or to a college historic clothing collection for safekeeping. Something less valuable could be great for costume parties a few years from now. (See Figure 10–7.)

Give-aways. Only the best of what's left goes in this box or bag. These are good clothes you think might be appreciated by family or friends. The item may not be "you" but may look perfect on someone else. First choice goes to any friend who helped you with this project.

Swap session. A creative solution is a clothes-swapping party. Plan to invite a group of friends and ask them to bring only their best castoffs. It can be great fun. You might even find something you like for yourself. Or, put a swap box in the basement of your apartment building, condominium, or community center. Label and post one rule: "If you take something, leave something else some time."

Sell. Consider selling usable items at an office, garage, or yard sale, either by yourself or with others. This takes work, and you won't make a lot of money, but you'll make some money, and the clothes will be gone.

Resell. If you're not a salesperson at heart, take nice-looking, usable clothes to a resale or consignment shop. Clothes should be in good repair, clean, and pressed. You split the profit with the shopowner — usually fifty percent of the resale price — who sends you a check when the item is sold. It's smart to call ahead to make arrangements and make sure the shop takes what you have to offer.

Reuse. Remove really good-looking buttons, lace, or trims worth saving to reuse at a later date. Fabric that still has plenty of life in it can be cleaned, taken apart at the seams, pressed flat, and stored to remake into something new.

Children's dress-ups. Kids have great fun dressing up in old clothes. If you don't have children of your own, nieces and nephews or the neighbors' kids will love what you have to spare.

Rags. Soft absorbent fabrics make good dust cloths and car rags.

Donate. What's left in the "out" box goes to a charitable organization of your choice — Good Will, Salvation Army, Deseret Industries, and so forth — to a church or school rummage sale. Some organizations even pick up your discarded items. Don't worry about the fate of these rejects. Someone somewhere needs them. Even if they go for rags or are sold for forty cents overseas, they provide someone else with a job, and the clothes are out of your closet. And getting them out of your closet is the purpose of this whole project. Be sure to estimate or ask your drycleaner to determine the current value of your donated clothes. Their value is tax deductible. Ask the charity organization for an itemized receipt and file it with your tax records.

Evolution of a Wardrobe

Don't be overly concerned if you discarded a lot of clothes or seem to have few left. Take heart, vowing

Figure 10–7. A fun and funky hat may go quickly out of style or no longer fit your personal style. Even then, it makes a great piece for costume parties in years to come. *(Courtesy All Week Long by Eddie Bauer; photographer Geoffrey Bari)*

never to make the same mistakes again. The kind of observation and evaluation you've just completed, coupled with what you've learned about yourself, will help you spot the losers and put your money on a winner every time. What's more, with the mistakes out of your closet and drawers, you're going to have more room for clothes that really work for you.

Remember, wardrobe evaluation and inventory is part of an ongoing process. In years to come, the discovery part of an evaluation session becomes less and less long. Because you know and understand yourself, your clothing needs and preferences, you will weed out less and less. Future sessions will serve as a time to remind yourself of what you have to work with and what you need to replace, update, or add for the first time.

Over the years, you will see your wardrobe slowly change or evolve from one look to another, reflecting changes in your body, your family, your business roles or responsibilities, and your life-style. If you aren't thrilled with your fashion history, now is a good time to make some changes for the better.

5.

Inventory all remaining clothes, including accessories.

❧

Take a closer look at the clothing and accessories you have left. Look at the wearable clothes and accessories lying or hanging about. Notice the types of garments, styles, colors, and fabrics. Is everything casual? Do you need some dressier clothes for other occasions? Are they mostly business clothes? Do you need to add some casual clothes to relax in? How many? Are they all tailored in style or is there too much fluff and frill? Is there a good mix of light, medium, and darker colors? Are most of the fabrics for cold weather or warm? Do you need more variety?

Think back to Exercise 2–1. Is the largest block of time in your day — or the most important block — also the block for which you have the most clothes? If you blocked out the most hours for school, do you have more comparatively casual campus clothes, or too many dressy party clothes? If you blocked out more employment hours, is the bulk of your clothes appropriate for your work? Think about the relation of the pieces to one another and how they will work together. Consider what you need or want to complete your wardrobe. Add to your list.

You may not be able to see immediately what you need. It may be easier to spot what's missing from your wardrobe, or what you have in excess, by taking an actual inventory. An inventory is simply a list of what you have left to work with — of wearable clothes you love and look forward to wearing. You can choose to make a simple list, or you may like the idea of noting particular points about the pieces. You have options.

6.

Rely on a private, at–home fashion show.

❧

With your clothes still out of the closet, and while considering your wardrobe needs and plans, take time to put on your own private fashion show. (If now is impossible, make time another day.) Combine the clothes and accessories into as many outfits as you can think of. It's not enough to just imagine how the outfits will come together. It's not enough to hold up the pieces or lay them out on the bed "scarecrow" fashion. That's a beginning, but not enough. To know if an outfit actually works, you have to try it on — ideally in front of a full-length mirror. The process of coordinating an outfit is visual. Clothing is a visual art form. To evaluate or judge the full effect of an

outfit you have to see it in a full-length mirror. Take your time and work on an outfit until it looks finished and right. No one achieves a look that's right for them without some thought and effort. This activity can be great fun as you mix and match the pieces of your wardrobe and come up with a style of your own.

List Coordinated Outfits

Don't hesitate to make a list of the outfits that work for you. (See Table 9–5, page 256.) You can't keep all those outfits in your head at once. A list will spark your memory when you're in a hurry or not in the mood to fuss about what goes with what. It's an option that works for many people. If you like the idea of using a list, tack or tape it on the inside of your closet door for future reference. If that's not possible, put the list in a gallon-size plastic storage bag, poke it over the hook of a hanger, and hang it in your closet.

Take Pictures

Better yet, or in addition, take a picture of each outfit you want to remember and re-create. Before you change the clothes of one outfit, change the accessories. See if different accessories will change the look of the clothes from casual to dressy, from summer to winter or vice versa. Take more pictures. Polaroid photos are an advantage, allowing you to view the picture immediately and evaluate the success of an outfit more objectively. Often, you'll pick up points you missed in the mirror. When pictures are developed, store them in a box on your closet shelf for quick and easy reference. Plastic zipper bags are perfect for separating pictures into groups of coordinated outfits. Hook or clip the set of pictures right on the hanger of the core item.

Develop a Shopping List

As you write down the components of an attractive outfit, you'll notice what's missing to complete the look and get new ideas for new looks. Add the missing item or items to your shopping list. (See Table 9–6, page 265.) A certain blouse may go well with a particular skirt, but lack something needed to make it look complete or distinctive. That something might be a third layer jacket, sweater, or vest, or a scarf — something to give it clout! Think back on your earlier observations.

For example, if all your skirts are appropriate only for day and business occasions, but you have some lovely blouses, maybe a skirt in a dressy fabric is in order. If all your blouses are tailored for business, maybe a softly styled, lustrous new silk or silklike blouse will carry your suit on into evening and make it worth its investment price. Perhaps a new turtleneck dickie will give a sporty look to your classic shirtwaist dress and a trendy new necklace will take you out to dinner in style. Add your best ideas to your shopping list.

Try putting your clothes together in new ways. Most people get stuck in the rut of wearing something only one or two ways. Creativity is simply a matter of seeing things differently. It is the rearrangement of things into new combinations. The purpose of this activity is to let go of your restraints, relax, and come up with at least five or six different ways to wear a basic piece of clothing — getting several outfits instead of one or two. Lay an item out on the bed and try to find three or four other things to wear with it that you haven't tried before. Then try it on to test the effect.

For example, try wearing a blouse on the outside and belting it like you would belt a cardigan sweater or jacket. Try a scarf at the neck or tuck one in a breast pocket. Try knotting the blouse at the waist. Try layering a shirt with another shirt. One of my favorite new looks came from trying to wear a shirt, with a clean-finished hem, as a jacket over another shirt. Call it a shirt-jacket. Next, I tried a camisole under the shirt-jacket and it worked. So did a turtleneck. Knot both free corners of the shirt-jacket separately and let them hang free for still another effect. Or knot them together in the middle.

You won't be comfortable with all of the looks you can think of. Some won't suit your personality or the image you want to project. Record only the looks that you like.

You'll discover more options if you're willing to mix business suits with unexpected dressy items. There is no rule that says business has to be business eighteen hours a day. A sheer or shimmery top worn under a suit jacket can be very appealing after business hours. Consider breaking up a suit to wear the pieces as separates.

For example, try the suit jacket with other skirts and slacks. Try the jacket over a dress it seems to coordinate with. Try the suit skirt with other jackets, sweaters, or vests. Look in the mirror and make sure the pieces coordinate in style, color, and fabric to communicate one message appropriate for the same mood or occasion. If they don't, try something else.

Take your time. This is not an exercise you can do in a hurry. This may be just the experience you need to recognize or reaffirm your personal style. If you saw something in a magazine or store that caught your interest, now is the time to try it out on yourself.

For example, it was during an at-home fashion show that Chris tried out new combinations she'd seen pictured in her favorite fashion magazine. She practiced how to pair her usual tailored, sportive clothes with pieces slightly more feminine to reflect that part of her personality. It was a valuable learning experience she has applied to herself and with her family ever since.

Don't limit yourself to obvious combinations. Try each top with all bottoms. Try on dressy clothes with casual clothes, and day wear with evening wear in mixes of colors, fabrics, or patterns you've never tried before. Some outfits may look rather odd or the pieces fight with one another for attention. But once in awhile you'll put together something unusual that works surprisingly well. This is when you might discover that a tweed blazer looks wonderfully sophisticated paired with a striped shirt.

If a friend is in on this activity, ask for ideas. She or he may have a different way of looking at things, and may not be bridled by the same influences and biases. She or he may come up with some interesting and exciting ideas and combinations you wouldn't think of, and they may be worth considering.

This exercise will open up a whole new avenue of ideas. Time may not allow you to experiment with all your clothes as much as you want to or need to in one session. That's fine. You can experiment with one basic garment at a time — a skirt, jacket, pants, or a dress — combining it with other clothes and accessories. Record the looks that work on paper or film, or both. With practice, you'll get better at creating new combinations.

7.

Cluster your own clothing.

❧

You will likely see that certain pieces of clothes in harmonious colors and styles work together particularly well and form a group of coordinates. These are *your* clusters. (See Figure 10–8.)

- To make it still easier to review your wardrobe, create new outfits, and determine needed new items, rely on the cluster plansheets. Fill out a plansheet for every cluster of coordinated clothes in your entire wardrobe. You may have several and some clusters may be incomplete or as small as five pieces. Get them all down on paper. Follow instructions provided in Chapter 9.
- Use separate plansheets for seasonal clusters (all-season, spring/summer, fall/winter) and for specific occasional clusters (casual-at home, business, dressy, all-occasion, and so forth).

Figure 10–8. "Scarecrow" and cluster your clothes to help you visualize clothing pieces that work together harmoniously. *(Courtesy Heidi Neslen)*

- A block of blank spaces all the way across a plansheet alerts you to what's needed to complete a workable cluster.

For example, *maybe you're missing a jacket in your first neutral color. Maybe a pair of slacks to pair with your suit jacket and sweater would give you four or more outfits. On the other hand, maybe there's an overload of neutrals and you need some accent colors to add pizzazz to the cluster. If you have five long-sleeve, cotton plaid shirts in a cluster, you could use a dressier, somewhat more feminine blouse or possibly a short-sleeve shirt in another fabric or pattern.*

If you discovered you like wearing skirts more than slacks, you may want to plan for a third skirt instead of a second pair of pants.

For example, *a first-grade teacher wanted to have the option of wearing skirts in addition to pants. To her shopping list she added a longer, loosely styled skirt in a darker color and durable fabric. The skirt gave better balance to her working wardrobe.*

If you discovered that T-shirts are your favorite casual-day and at-home clothes, you might plan to include variations on that idea, such as T-shirt dresses, knit skirts, pants, and tunic tops.

- Whatever the item, record it on the cluster plansheet, along with tentative plans to acquire it and the approximate cost. Include these items on your shopping list. Number or rank the items in terms of priorities, with what you need or want most as number 1 or at the top of the list.

For example, *maybe this season you need a new jacket and that need takes priority over a skirt or slacks. Maybe new shoes belong near the top of the list, before a belt or fifth blouse. Maybe new earrings are just what you want to feel more attractive, and they win out over new underwear. Within reason, it is important to spend your money first on your needs. Add the extra "wants" as affordable. With a little thought and looking, the best buys can satisfy both your needs and your wants.*

- Keep this list in your wallet or handbag to jog your memory when you're shopping. Update the shopping list as needed. A key to staying within a clothing budget is to shop only for what's needed and in the order of need.
- Put each cluster plansheet in a plastic zipper bag to protect it.
- Include snips of fabric from the seam allowance of garments in the cluster, stapled to a note card. Drop any photographs of outfits in the cluster into the bag as well.
- Store the plastic bags in a box or on a hook in your closet, ready to take shopping when needed.
- Update cluster plansheets by adding new purchases.

Pick Up and Put Away

For the sake of the next chapter and because you aren't going to reorganize or remodel your closet right now, take time to vacuum and dust while your closet is empty.

Pick up the bags and boxes. Stash them in a convenient but conspicuous place for delivery to their destinations. Then calendar your time to carry out your decisions to repair, alter, and clean. Remember, nothing goes back in the closet that needs repair or cleaning. Put what's left of your clothes back into the closet — in cluster groups for now.

Early Morning Misery

Seven-year-old Chelsey, just out of bed one morning, was sobbing for no apparent reason. Alarmed, her mother came hurrying in to ask, "Chelsey, what in the world is the matter?"

"Oh-h-h-h," Chelsey wailed, "I just realized, I'll have to put on my clothes every day as long as I live!"

"If only," my daughter used to moan, "I could be dressed and ready to go when I wake up in the morning. It's so hard to be ready on time!" Many a morning she missed her bus. In years since, I met a mom who solved that problem by dressing her child in a clean sweatsuit for bed. He slept soundly and woke up ready to go.

In Seattle last spring, I found myself behind a fellow driving and dressing at the same time. His every maneuver was timed according to the change in the stoplights. He had to be steering with his knees — not a good way to go.

I watched with fascination as his pajamas came off. I followed him right through the lights to the final knot in his tie. He parked his car, combed his hair, climbed out of the car, and went into work.

So what can we do to simplify the morning misery of getting up and getting ready? A little planning can go a long way.

To begin, weed out any clothes you don't need or don't wear. Too many choices only confuse the issue and squash the clothes in the closet.

Organize your closet by categories: blouses and shirts together, slacks together, skirts together, jackets together, and so on, each in its own expected place so it's easy to find without a fuss.

Include as many easy-to-put-on clothing in your wardrobe as possible. For some women, that means one-piece and pullover styles, or clothes with simple front closures. Buttons down the back are too slow. A suit that doesn't require a blouse can speed the process.

When you're in a hurry is when a dress is handy. No extra layers there either. Pants can be quick. Knee-highs are faster than pantyhose. But when you need them, it's nice to have pantyhose on hand in quantity, ready for the morning when you get that inevitable run. Slip-on shoes are faster than straps or shoe laces.

The smartest morning time-saver is to plan the night before. With a mood or message in mind, you can experiment and lay out your clothing the night before.

That includes all accessories with clothes clean, pressed, and in good repair. There just isn't time to fix or press in the morning. Better yet, plan your clothes for the week on the weekend. You're set to get up and go, with time to layer all you like.

Some children and adults may appreciate a Day 1, Day 2, Day 3-type schedule, where particular outfits are repeated every week — or every other week. Fewer decisions may mean fewer frustrations.

Preparing the night before eliminates last-minute changes in the morning that make you late and upset. Try looping your belt into slacks or a skirt the night before. Prepare the purse you need. Better yet, have several ready to go, with duplicate essentials in each bag, waiting only for your wallet.

Hang your clothes on a rack or hook in the bathroom. Wrinkles have a chance to hang out overnight or steam out while you shower.

Knowing what you're going to wear tells you what makeup you'll want to apply. Keep a chiffon scarf handy to protect your hair and makeup when you pull clothing on over your head. There's no time to redo.

A mirror by the door allows you a last-minute look before you leave. You'll feel more at ease and able to forget about yourself and your looks. You can focus on your day knowing you're looking good!

Review Main Points

Rely on a wardrobe evaluation session to identify your clothing needs and the reasons behind your clothing likes and dislikes. Plan and prepare for this project, allowing plenty of time to carry it out. Thoughtfully look over your wardrobe. Sort your clothing into three groups: a group of clothes you like and wear often; a group of clothes you don't particularly like and may even dislike, but must wear anyway; a group of clothes you never wear, regardless of whether you like them or not. Determine your reasons for liking, disliking, or not wearing each clothing piece. Record your answers. Distribute appropriate clothing into containers to wash, dry clean, repair, alter, remodel, or discard. Make plans to follow through. Discard clothes that do not fit, are uncomfortable, or duplicate other clothes. Discard clothes you have nowhere to wear, clothes obviously out of date or worn out, and clothes that no longer fit your image. Inventory specific numbers of garment types and assess your needs. Make a list of those needs. Rely on an at-home fashion show, trying on your clothes in all the combinations you can think of. List the outfits that work well and enhance your appearance. Cluster your clothes, recording the pieces on a plansheet to pretest their harmony and versatility.

Review Questions

1. A wardrobe evaluation requires you to discover _____ you like or dislike particular clothing items.

2. Name two other functions of wardrobe evaluation.

   _____

   _____

3. Explain what a wardrobe inventory is.

   _____

   _____

4. List four items to assemble in your room that will help you in your wardrobe evaluation.

   _____   _____

   _____   _____

5. Explain why you might need to cover your bed with a sheet during a wardrobe

   evaluation session. _____

   _____

   _____

6. List eight characteristics or points to consider in a wardrobe evaluation.

   _____   _____

   _____   _____

   _____   _____

   _____   _____

7. The value of donated clothing is tax deductible.   True   or   False

8. Which of the following words does not belong in the group? Circle the word.
                    stuff   wash   repair   remodel

9. Match the term with its definition.

   _____ Consignment   a. Invite friends to bring their best
                                  castoffs
   _____ Heirloom   b. Used clothes for resale

   _____ Donate   c. extraordinary piece of clothing, a
                                  museum piece
   _____ Swap   d. Salvation Army, Goodwill

10. The activity you spend the most time on during your day should be reflected

    in the _____ group of clothing in your closet.

11. Explain the value of a cluster plansheet. _____

    _____

    _____

Discussion Questions

#1 What do you think the contents of your closet reflect or reveal about you?

Notes: _____

_____

_____

_____

_____

#2 Be prepared to discuss possible influences on your clothing likes and dislikes. How are your likes different than your parents'?

Notes: _____

_____

_____

_____

_____

#3 What agencies or outlets are available in your area for second-hand clothing?

Notes: _____

_____

_____

_____

_____

#4 How has your wardrobe evolved since you were a teenager?

Notes: _____

_____

_____

_____

_____

#5 What do you do to speed the dressing process in the morning?

Notes: _____

_____

_____

_____

_____

Exercise 10–1 Wardrobe Evaluation: Occasions

Name _____

Do like		Don't like
What and why?		What and why?

Do like

What and why?

_____
_____
_____
_____
_____

Casual
Home and
Community

Don't like

What and why?

_____
_____
_____
_____
_____

_____
_____
_____
_____
_____

Business and
Leadership

_____
_____
_____
_____
_____

_____
_____
_____
_____
_____

Dressy Day

_____
_____
_____
_____
_____

_____
_____
_____
_____
_____

Dressy Evening

_____
_____
_____
_____
_____

_____
_____
_____
_____
_____

Active Sports/
Exercises

_____
_____
_____
_____
_____

Exercise 10–2 Wardrobe Evaluation: Elements

Name_____

Do like		**Don't like**
What and why?		What and why?

Do like		**Don't like**
_____	Lines, Type,	_____
_____	and Direction	_____
_____		_____
_____		_____
_____		_____
_____	Shapes/Silhouettes	_____
_____	Type	_____
_____		_____
_____		_____
_____		_____
_____	Colors	_____
_____		_____
_____		_____
_____		_____
_____		_____
_____	Textures	_____
_____	Fabrics	_____
_____		_____
_____		_____
_____		_____
_____	Patterns	_____
_____		_____
_____		_____
_____		_____
_____		_____

Exercise 10–3 Wardrobe Evaluation: Garment Types and Accessories

Name _____

| **Do like** | | **Don't like** |
| What and why? | | What and why? |

Do like

What and why?

Don't like

What and why?

Blouses

Shirts/Tunics

Skirts

Pants

Dresses

Jumpsuits

Do like What and why?		**Don't like** What and why?
_____ _____ _____ _____ _____	Vests	_____ _____ _____ _____ _____
_____ _____ _____ _____	Sweaters	_____ _____ _____ _____
_____ _____ _____ _____ _____	Jackets/Tunics	_____ _____ _____ _____ _____
_____ _____ _____ _____	Coats	_____ _____ _____ _____
_____ _____ _____ _____	Sleepwear	_____ _____ _____ _____
_____ _____ _____ _____	Underwear	_____ _____ _____ _____

Do like		**Don't like**
What and why?		What and why?
	Shoes	
	Hosiery	
	Bags	
	Belts	
	Scarves or Ties	
	Earrings	
	Necklaces	
	Bracelets	
	Gloves	

Exercise 10–4 Wardrobe Inventory

Name _____

Item by Style	Season of Year			Color			Fiber	Fabric	Source		Orig. Cost	Years Service		How Often Worn	Cost per Wearing
	All Season	Spr./ Sum.	Fall/ Winter	Light	Med.	Dark			Ready-to-wear	Custom sewn		Past	Future		

Blouses/Shirts — Casual | Business/Leadership | Dressy

Skirts — Casual | Business/Leadership | Dressy

Dresses — Casual | Business/Leadership | Dressy

Name _____

| Item by Style | Season of Year | | | Color | | | Fiber | Fabric | Source | | Orig. Cost | Years Service | | How Often Worn | Cost per Wearing |
	All Season	Spr./Sum.	Fall/Winter	Light	Med.	Dark			Ready-to-wear	Custom sewn		Past	Future		
Pants/Slacks — Casual															
Business/Leadership															
Dressy															
Vests — Casual															
Business/Leadership															
Dressy															
Sweaters — Casual															
Business/Leadership															
Dressy															

Item by Style		Season of Year			Color			Fiber	Fabric	Source		Orig. Cost	Years Service		How Often Worn	Cost per Wearing
		All Season	Spr./Sum.	Fall/Winter	Light	Med.	Dark			Ready-to-wear	Custom sewn		Past	Future		
Jackets — Casual																
Jackets — Business/Leadership																
Jackets — Dressy																
Coats — Casual																
Coats — Business/Leadership																
Coats — Dressy																
Active Sportswear																

Item by Style	Season of Year			Color			Fiber	Fabric	Source		Orig. Cost	Years Service		How Often Worn	Cost per Wearing
	All Season	Spr./Sum.	Fall/Winter	Light	Med.	Dark			Ready-to-wear	Custom sewn		Past	Future		
Slips/Petticoats Dressy															
Slips/Petticoats Casual															
Bras Dressy															
Bras Casual															
Panties Dressy															
Panties Casual															
Robes															
Sleepwear															
Swimwear															

Item by Style	Season of Year			Color			Fiber	Fabric	Source		Orig. Cost	Years Service		How Often Worn	Cost per Wearing
	All Season	Spr./Sum.	Fall/Winter	Light	Med.	Dark			Ready-to-wear	Custom sewn		Past	Future		

Shoes — Casual, Business/Leadership, Dressy

Hosiery — Casual, Business/Leadership, Dressy

Bags — Casual, Business/Leadership, Dressy

| Item by Style | Season of Year | | | Color | | | Fiber | Fabric | Source | | Orig. Cost | Years Service | | How Often Worn | Cost per Wearing |
	All Season	Spr./ Sum.	Fall/ Winter	Light	Med.	Dark			Ready-to-wear	Custom sewn		Past	Future		
Belts															
Casual															
Business/ Leadership															
Dressy															
Scarves or Ties															
Casual															
Business/ Leadership															
Dressy															
Earrings															
Casual															
Business/ Leadership															
Dressy															

Item by Style	Season of Year			Color			Fiber	Fabric	Source		Orig. Cost	Years Service		How Often Worn	Cost per Wearing
	All Season	Spr./Sum.	Fall/Winter	Light	Med.	Dark			Ready-to-wear	Custom sewn		Past	Future		

Necklaces: Casual / Business/Leadership / Dressy

Bracelets: Casual / Business/Leadership / Dressy

Gloves: Casual / Business/Leadership / Dressy

Exercise 10–5 Personal Cluster Identification

Name _____

- Look at potential cluster groups of clothes in your closet.
- Using instructions for Cluster Plansheets provided in Chapter 9, fill in the appropriate spaces on a five- to ten-piece cluster plansheet with your own clothes.
- Using the coordinated outfits plansheets, list pieces in every outfit combination you can think of.
- Using the shopping list, fill in with items you plan to add on.

Five– to Ten–Piece Women's Wardrobe Cluster

Name _____

Life-style _____ Personal style _____

Climate/season of the year _____ Occasion _____ Date _____

ITEM		Wardrobe Neutral	Wardrobe Neutral	Accent Colors	Works With	Plans to Acquire	Cost
CLOTHING	Blouse						
	Shirt						
	Blouse or shirt						
	Skirt						
	Pant or skirt						
	Pants						
	One– or two–piece dress						
	Sweater or vest						
	Jacket						
	All–occasion coat						
ACCESSORIES	Dress shoe						
	Casual/ walking shoes						
	Hosiery/socks						
	All–occasion handbag						
	Casual/dress handbag						
	Belt						
	Scarf/tie						
	Earrings						
	Necklace						
	Bracelet						
	Gloves						

Twelve– to Sixteen–Piece Women's Wardrobe Cluster

Name _____

Life-style _____ Personal style _____

Climate/season of the year _____ Occasion _____ Date _____

ITEM		Wardrobe Neutral	Wardrobe Neutral	Accent Colors	Works With	Plans to Acquire	Cost
CLOTHING	Blouse						
	Shirt						
	Blouse or shirt						
	Blouse or shirt						
	Blouse or shirt						
	Skirt						
	Pant						
	Skirt or pant						
	Skirt or pant						
	Day dress						
	Dressy dress						
	Pullover sweater or vest						
	Cardigan sweater or vest						
	Jacket						
	Jacket						
	Cloth coat or raincoat						
ACCESSORIES	Dress shoes						
	Casual/walking shoes						
	Hosiery/socks						
	All–occasion handbag						
	Casual/dress handbag						
	Belt						
	Belt						
	Scarf/tie						
	Scarf/tie						
	Earrings						
	Necklace						
	Necklace						
	Bracelets/pin						
	Gloves						

Women's Coordinated Outfits

Cluster Colors: Wardrobe neutral _____ Wardrobe neutral _____

Accent colors _____ , _____ , _____

ITEM	#____	#____	#____	#____	#____
Blouse, shirt, or dress					
Skirt or pant					
Sweater					
Vest					
Jacket					
Coat					
Shoes					
Hosiery					
Bag					
Belt					
Scarf or tie					
Earrings					
Necklace					
Bracelet					
Gloves					

Women's Coordinated Outfits (*continued*)

Cluster Colors: Wardrobe neutral _____ Wardrobe neutral _____

Accent colors _____ , _____ , _____

ITEM	#____	#____	#____	#____	#____
Blouse, shirt, or dress					
Skirt or pant					
Sweater					
Vest					
Jacket					
Coat					
Shoes					
Hosiery					
Bag					
Belt					
Scarf or tie					
Earrings					
Necklace					
Bracelet					
Gloves					

Women's Coordinated Outfits (continued)

Cluster Colors: Wardrobe neutral _____   Wardrobe neutral _____

                Accent colors _____ , _____ , _____

ITEM	#____	#____	#____	#____	#____
Blouse, shirt, or dress					
Skirt or pant					
Sweater					
Vest					
Jacket					
Coat					
Shoes					
Hosiery					
Bag					
Belt					
Scarf or tie					
Earrings					
Necklace					
Bracelet					
Gloves					

Women's Coordinated Outfits (continued)

Cluster Colors: Wardrobe neutral _____ Wardrobe neutral _____

Accent colors _____ , _____ , _____

ITEM	#____	#____	#____	#____	#____
Blouse, shirt, or dress					
Skirt or pant					
Sweater					
Vest					
Jacket					
Coat					
Shoes					
Hosiery					
Bag					
Belt					
Scarf or tie					
Earrings					
Necklace					
Bracelet					
Gloves					

Shopping List

	What I need:	To coordinate with:	Take along shopping:
Clothing			
Accessories			

Exercise 10–6 Wardrobe Problems and Goals

Name _____

What are your current wardrobe problems?

☐ I don't have very much money to spend on clothes.

☐ My wardrobe is too plain, boring, ordinary, safe, predictable.

☐ My clothes are ugly, I don't like them.

☐ My wardrobe is out-of-date.

☐ My clothes don't fit.

☐ I have too many clothes I don't wear.

☐ I don't have enough variety/flexibility in my wardrobe.

☐ My clothes don't go well together — don't mix and match.

☐ My clothes are not orderly, organized, or easy to find.

☐ My clothes take too much time to care for.

☐ I need a few pieces to complete a cluster.

☐ I need appropriate clothes to wear at home.

☐ I need appropriate business clothes for work.

☐ I need some appropriate, special occasion clothing, or evening clothes.

☐ I need a casual-travel cluster of clothes.

☐ I need a business-travel cluster of clothes.

☐ Other _____

What are your wardrobe goals?

☐ Get more clothes for my money.

☐ Get clothes that will last longer.

☐ Get some life into my wardrobe — make it more interesting.

☐ Get some fun and wonderful clothes — beautiful clothes.

☐ Update my wardrobe — look more fashionable.

☐ Get clothes that fit and flatter me.

☐ Weed out clothes that don't work for me.

☐ Build a mix-and-match wardrobe with lots of variety.

☐ Organize my closet so clothes are in order and easy to find.

☐ Build an easy-care wardrobe.

☐ Add a few new pieces to complete a cluster.

☐ Build an at-home cluster of clothes.

☐ Build a cluster of casual-business clothes for work.

☐ Build a cluster of dress-business clothes for work.

☐ Build a cluster of dressier clothes for evening occasions.

☐ Build a cluster of casual-travel clothes.

☐ Build a cluster of business-travel clothes.

☐ Other _____

Chapter

11

Closet Organization and Clothing Care

Learning Objectives

Your goal in completing this chapter is to be able to:

- Recognize the value of proper clothing care.
- Identify the tasks that make up clothing care.
- Understand and explain the functions of closet organization.
- Describe three principles of closet organization.
- Increase your awareness of closet equipment available.
- Explain three ways to group clothing in a closet.
- Organize your own closet.
- List twelve or more ways to increase the wear-life of your clothing.
- Recognize agents of chemical and physical change that damage clothing.
- Discuss locations and containers for long-term clothing storage.
- Choose appropriate cleaning, drying, and pressing procedures.

Preview Main Points

1. Rely on proper clothing care to increase the value of your clothes as a resource.

2. Create and maintain a well-organized closet.

3. Practice good clothes sense to maintain the appearance of your clothing.

4. Be prepared for long-term clothing storage.

1.

Rely on proper clothing care to increase the value of your clothes as a resource.

❧

The wear-life and appearance of your clothes depend on how carefully you:

- Handle and hang or fold your clothes each day.
- Repair your clothing whenever needed.
- Sort, clean, and press your clothes and how often.
- Store limited-occasion and out-of-season clothes.
- Pack your clothes for travel.

These are not favorite tasks for most of us. Nonetheless, the value of your wardrobe depends in large part on the care it receives. Proper clothing care results in longer wear. This, in turn, increases the value of your clothing investment. More than that, the way you care for your clothing influences how others perceive you.

For example, even the most beautiful silk blouse with a ring-around-the-collar is just a dirty shirt. A designer dress with a hem hanging loose looks cheap in quality. An expensive blazer with a button missing is simply a sloppy jacket. Each projects an image of carelessness and lack of attention to detail.

To maintain an attractive and appropriate appearance, you must maintain your clothing. This is part of the clothing management process. With ownership of any resource comes responsibility. You are responsible for the care of your own clothing. This is not a large or difficult job if you do it on a regular basis; however, it requires continuing attention, planning, and organization.

Organization means allowing time and space for clothing care. It demands a routine for clothing-related tasks, such as hemming up a dress, hand-washing a silk blouse, sewing on a button, pressing a skirt, or rearranging your closet. Some tasks are daily, others are weekly, and some may be seasonal or annual.

Both teens and adults admit resenting the time it takes to schedule and carry out routine clothing care. However, the consequences of leaving these tasks undone take a heavy toll in terms of increased stress, lower quality of life, and wasted clothing dollars.

Query Box

Do you hang, fold, and put away your own clothing regularly?

How often do you mend your own clothing?
How often do you wash your own clothing?
How often do you press your own clothing?
Have you helped with family clothing care within the last month?

2.

Create and maintain a well–organized closet.

❧

Closet space, or lack of it, is an age-old problem. Some people are convinced there is no escape from a cluttered closet, but there is. You can organize your closet in such a way that it accommodates your clothes and accessories, and without the project becoming too complicated, elaborate, or expensive.

Closet organization is another action-oriented strategy that logically follows wardrobe evaluation. Logical or not, most people avoid organizing their closets. It's just another one of those projects or essential activities that claim your time and continually nag at you. Closets often get neglected because they're behind closed doors — out of sight, out of mind. "No one will see but me, and I'm busy. Besides, who has a clean closet anyway?"

For some people, a messy closet almost becomes expected, yet their common complaint is that they have "nothing to wear." A quick check often reveals several pieces of clothing dropped carelessly on the closet floor, tossed into a chair, or stuffed into a drawer. A negative attitude about closet organization is an attitude no one can afford to keep.

Importance and Function

Closet organization helps you to:

- Eliminate the "guilt" you feel every time you open the closet door and are faced with a disaster area.
- Simplify and speed the decision of what to wear. See what you have and get what you want when you want it.
- Identify what goes with what and discover new mix-and-match possibilities. You'll use your clothes more efficiently.
- Keep your clothes fresh looking, neatly in shape and lengthen the wear-life of your clothing and accessories.
- Save money. Ruin a piece of clothing and it costs more to replace it.
- Enjoy your living space — closet contents don't spill out and all over your room every time you open the door.
- Bring order to your life, allowing you to enjoy the feeling of satisfaction that comes from being in control of your clothing and your image.

Organizing your wardrobe is actually less work and more fun than you might imagine. It gives you a lift with carry-over for ages to come as you experience the rewards of an organized closet.

A Small Room

A closet is a very small room in which you spend a significant amount of time. Like any room, it's up to you to clean, decorate, and arrange it. If you want to, paint, paper, or redesign the rods and install dividers and shelves. If you plan to make structural changes in your closet, this project will carry over until the changes are complete. If that's going to be awhile, a portable clothes rack will reduce the mess between now and when you can return your clothes to the closet.

Certainly the easiest way to redesign or reconstruct your closet is to hire a qualified carpenter or custom closet building company to do it for you. They are listed in the local yellow pages of your telephone directory. If that doesn't suit your needs, you can redesign and remodel your closet yourself. If structural changes are not needed, you can choose to buy ready-made units that fit into existing space. Whatever the case, decide what needs to be done to expand the available space and use the closet to its fullest potential. If you share your closet, enlist the help and enthusiasm of the other person in completing the project.

Three Principles of Closet Organization

The purpose of a closet isn't just storage, it's display. Just as a store displays its merchandise so you will buy it, your closet should display your clothes so you will wear them. To encourage wearing, work to achieve three principles of closet organization. They include: visibility, reachability, and grouping by categories.

Visibility. Arrange clothes and accessories so they are as visible as possible — so you can see what you have and what works together. You can easily forget what you have and consequently not wear it often, if at all. Get things out of drawers and hang or shelve them in the closet. Once things are out and in view you'll be pleasantly surprised by all the new combinations you'll notice.

Reachability. Common sense tells you to think about how you use your clothes. Arrange clothes and accessories so they are within easy reach. Place the clothes that you wear most often at eye level. Reserve high, low, and back for limited occasion or special occasion items.

Grouping by categories. Arrange clothes and accessories in general groups or categories. Begin by assigning a particular space or place for each garment type — dresses together, shirts and blouses together, jackets together, and so on. Within each type of clothing, arrange garments of similar style for similar occasions, activities, or moods together — shirts in dressy styles and fabrics together, business-like styles and fabrics together, school clothes together, casual styles and fabrics together, and so forth. This often takes on the look of arranging the clothes in clusters — for example, a casual at-home cluster, a business cluster, or an evening cluster. Obviously some clothes work for more than one type of occasion or personal image type.

For example, a lovely silk blouse can hang with business clothes or with evening clothes. Hang a tweed blazer with suit skirts for work and retrieve to wear with jeans during casual after-office hours. Depending on your life-style and personal style, a quality classic T-shirt can work for casual, business, or evening occasions.

Use your cluster plansheets and lists of coordinating outfits to remind yourself of these combinations.

Closet Light

If the light in your closet is weak, get a brighter bulb. If your closet is not light enough to see everything easily, get one or two small lights that work on a battery.

Closet Decor

Light-colored paint or wallpaper makes it easier to see inside.

Small and subtle wallpaper patterns won't overpower the fabrics and patterns of your clothes. Add a rug or carpet if you like.

Hanging Space

The average closet is designed with one long pole or rod the width of the closet, with one long shelf above. This is an inefficient design and leaves a lot of unused space. A new closet design is usually needed to make maximum use of space so clothes can be organized more efficiently.

For an individual with a large closet, a single rod may be sufficient. Additional closet rods, however, can literally double your hanging space. Combine a single and double-layered rod in two-, three-, four-, or five-rod arrangements.

Single-rod solution. This solution may be sufficient for a large, shallow closet used by one person. (See Figure 11–1.)

The single rod is mounted at a height of 60 inches (150 cm) from the floor. If the closet rod is mounted too far forward, leaving space between the closet back wall and the clothes, move the rod back and use the exposed side walls in the front of the closet to mount small shelves or hooks.

Two- or double-rod solution. This solution works in a shallow or walk-in closet and expands the available hanging space. (See Figure 11–2.)

Divide the hanging area into two compartments, usually with a board. Plan to use one-half to two-thirds of the available hanger space for double hanging separates — shirts, skirts, and/or slacks. Allow about one-third to one-half of the space for long hanging clothes — dresses, coats, and robes. Adjust the areas as needed.

Mount a second, shorter rod on the selected side, below the first. You may have to raise the upper rod to a height of 80 inches (200 cm) to accommodate the second rod below at a height of about 40 inches (100 cm) from the floor, or approximately the height of your skirts from the floor.

As alternatives to permanent wall-mounted rods, consider a heavy-duty tension rod or a suspension rod that hangs from the upper rod. Both are easy to install.

Single-Rod Closet Arrangement

Figure 11–1.

Double-Rod Closet Arrangement

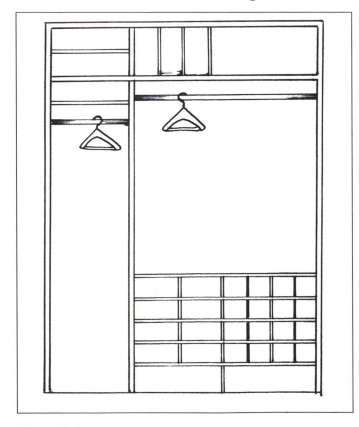

Figure 11–2.

If you have a double closet rod, hang the clothes you wear on the top half of your body on the top rod. Hang the clothes you wear on the bottom half of your body on the lower rod. Viewing them in this natural position will inspire you to coordinate tops and bottoms more effectively and into more combinations.

Alternative solutions. Since there are many different closets to work with, you may have to become creative. Sketch your closet and various ideas that come to mind. For example, you might benefit by a three- four- or five-rod combination. (See Figures 11–3 and 11–4.) If the closet is too shallow to accommodate hangers, you can install rods that run from the back to the front of the closet. These rods attach to the back wall, with support brackets that attach to a shelf above. If you are renting or moving often, you can rely on the heavy-duty tension or suspension rods mentioned earlier.

Open Shelves

Anything that goes in a dresser can go in the closet. Open shelves are just what's needed to get clothes out of the dresser drawers and into your closet in full view. Think about the types of garments you wear most often. You may decide to reduce your hanging space and add more shelves or vice versa. Construct or install shelves above closet rods, down the center of the closet, or at the sides as illustrated in the previous closet design solutions.

Triple-Rod Closet Arrangement

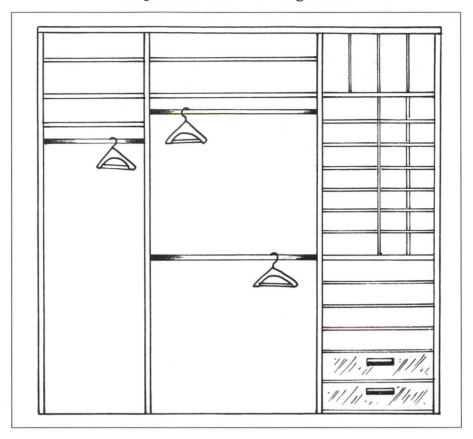

Figure 11–3.

U-Shaped Closet Arrangement

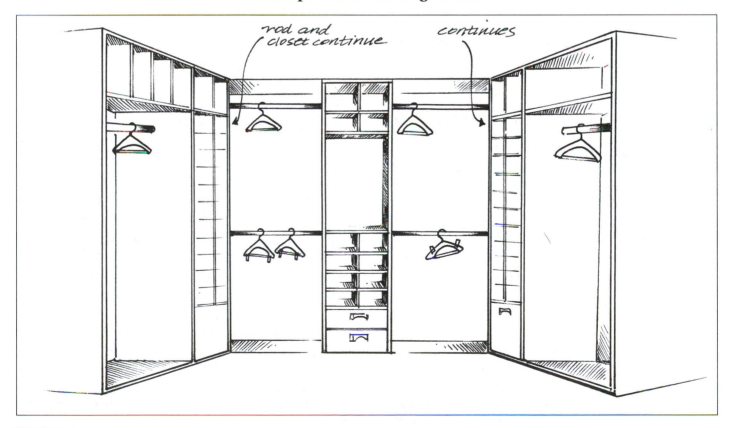

rod and closet continue

continues

Figure 11–4.

- Put items you wear most often on the middle and lower shelves, within easy reach.
- Measure your clothes to determine the correct height, width, and depth for each shelf.
- Allow 6 inches high by 10 inches deep for women's shoes with high heels; allow 4 inches high by 12 inches deep for men's shoes.
- Boots require additional heights up to about 14 inches.
- Sweaters need shelves 14 inches wide by 10 inches deep.

Shelves must be smoothly finished, painted, or covered with shelf paper to protect clothing from snagging. Alternatives to shelves are discussed under the topic "closet accessories."

Closet Walls and Doors

Closet walls and doors are excellent display areas for hanging. If possible, replace folding and sliding doors with "real" doors that open for a full view of the closet and inside door space. Make sure you can close the closet doors without hitting or smashing what is hanging there.

Closet Mirror

You need a full-length mirror to see yourself from head to toe. A full-length mirror can be mounted on one side of a double door. Put a sliding door to good use by mounting a mirror on the outside. It does double duty, making the room appear larger and reflecting your full-length image for evaluating the success of an outfit. If not mounted on a closet door, consider mounting the mirror on another door. Consider also a wall-mounted or free-standing mirror in your bedroom.

Closet Extras

- If space allows, place a laundry bag, basket, or hamper in the closet. If you already have a central laundry shoot or basket, additional closet containers can be used for dry cleaning, personal or special laundry items that require special attention, and items needing repair work.
- In a large, walk-in closet, a pull-down ironing board is handy for quick touch-ups. Include an iron or steamer. Select one that comes equipped with an automatic shut-off device, just in case you're in such a rush you forget to turn it off.
- If you have high shelves, keep a sturdy stool tucked back in a corner of the closet.
- Your closet can also include a shoe brush and shoe horn, cloths for wiping shoe heels, soles, and handbags; a lint remover or masking tape for lint removal; and spot removers (dry and liquid).
- A hanging sachet, pomander ball, or spray freshener is a wonderful way to add fragrance to your closet.

Expanding Beyond the Closet

If your closet space is really limited, consider expanding beyond the closet with selected clothes or accessories. With a little creative thought you can literally decorate your room with these wearable works of art.

- Brass or wooden hat racks and coat trees provide additional hanging space for hats, scarves, casual outerwear, or sweaty exercise clothes.
- Wall shelves lend themselves to clear plastic boxes and baskets for sweaters, socks, and other accessory items.
- Wall mounted boards can be filled with necklaces, bracelets, scarves, ties, or belts on individual pegs, "Shaker" style.
- A jewelry tray on your dresser serves as a place to put the jewelry, watch, or barrettes you've just removed prior to putting them where they belong.
- If there is no closet in your room or you need additional closet space, consider getting an armoire or a free-standing wardrobe.

Closet Equipment

The variety of closet equipment to choose from can be mind-boggling unless you keep two points in mind. Purchase only what will make your clothes visible and not damage them.

Clothes hangers. Clothes hangers come in a variety of shapes and materials. A hanger can preserve or ruin the original shape of a garment. (See Table 11–1.)

Hooks. Mount hooks easily on closet side walls and the back of doors.

Choose from screw-in and self-adhesive hooks. Hooks are great for holding hats, bags, belts, jewelry, robes, pajamas, nightgowns, and lingerie.

Mug racks. Mug racks hang horizontally or vertically on closet side walls and doors. Mug racks are popular solutions for hanging jewelry, belts, small bags, and ribbons.

Pegboards. These are available in all sizes. You can mount a plastic or pressed wood pegboard on the side wall or closet door. Use pegs to hang small accessory items.

Open-wire or plastic grids or shelving. Grids also attach to the side wall or door of closets. Attach hooks or baskets on the grid to hold an array of accessories. Shelves utilize extra wall space.

Towel bars. These are available in kitchen and bath shops or department stores. The bars can be mounted on closet doors or side walls. Smooth-surfaced bars will not snag scarves, ties, sweaters, and other delicate fabrics.

Tie and belt racks or bars. Mount these on the wall or on the back of the door. Use these racks or bars to hang lingerie and leotards as well as ties and belts.

Table 11–1 Types and Uses of Hangers

Types	Uses	Sources	Quality Features	Travel
Wire hangers	Good for most clothes including closely woven skirts, blouses, dresses, light- to medium-weight jackets. For slacks and suits, roll a cardboard tube over the wire.	Buy sturdy wire hangers from dry cleaners or at chain stores.	Wire hangers should not be thin, flimsy, rusty, or rough enough to snag fabric. They should have smooth shoulder slopes. If discolored or bent out of shape, throw them away.	Leave clothes on hangers when packing, so you can hang them immediately.
Wooden hangers	For tailored sport and suit jackets, coats, and heavyweight women's dresses. Women's suit skirts should be hung separately to prevent sagging.	Chain and specialty stores	Hanger size should be right for the suit: men's wider than women's. Shoulder slope should match suit. Must not have rough edges or splinters. Should have curved shape.	Take two or three for suits, heavy dresses.
Specialty hangers	Brass, chrome, and tortoise shell hangers, matching and decorative hangers. For guest and coat closets, to color coordinate.	Catalogs and specialty shops	Specialty hangers can be elegant, expensive. Use if the look is important to you.	Can be used for drip-drying clothes.
Plastic tubular hangers and deluxe vinyl–coated wire	Same as wire hangers.	Chain stores	These hangers are strong and come in many colors. Avoid rough edges that can snag clothes. They hold the shape of clothes only slightly better than wire hangers.	Too bulky to pack in suitcase.
Molded plastic hangers	Best for hooking skirt waist-loops onto hanger.	Usually get from store when purchasing garment.	Molded plastic hangers break easily.	Don't pack in suitcase, too bulky.
Foam–wrapped, molded plastic	Ideal for keeping slippery silk or chiffon blouses and dresses or light- to medium-weight garments on hangers.	Get at store at time of purchase or buy foam from craft store and wrap your own.	These break easily under the weight of heavy clothes.	Pack slippery clothes on hanger and hang on arrival.

Table 11–1 Types and Uses of Hangers *(continued)*

Types	Uses	Sources	Quality Features	Travel
Padded, quilted hangers	Beautiful and soft on the shape of knits, gowns, and party clothes.	Catalogs and specialty stores	Make sure decorative details are soft and colorfast.	Don't take, too bulky for travel.
Skirt hangers (wire, plastic, or wood)	For skirts.	Chain or specialty stores. Sometimes come with purchase.	Metal clamps or clips can leave pressure marks in fabric and suede. Protect with strips of heavy fabric. Wood skirt hangers are best because plastic can break. Most skirt hangers are too narrow to support skirts. Use sturdy wire hanger and three or four clothes pins instead to keep skirts on grain.	Pack skirts attached to hangers if room.
Wooden trouser hangers	For men's trousers, women's slacks, and light- to medium-weight flared skirts.	Catalogs and specialty stores	Hang trousers from either waist or hem, leaves no fold mark. Avoid trouser hangers with swing-out metal bars, which leave crease marks.	Pack trousers on hanger if room.
Multiple-garment hangers	For blouses, shirts, pants, skirts, scarves. Saves space by hanging one garment above the other.	Catalogs, chain, or specialty stores	They save space, but do not display clothes well, are awkward to use, may leave crease marks on pants and clip marks on waistbands. Clothes may slip out. The garment on the bottom may hang on the floor. Use only when cramped for space.	Leave in closet, too bulky for travel.

Over-the-door hangers. Extend your hanging space out into the room. Placed in the bathroom, over-the-door hangers are particularly good for hanging robes, nightgowns, or clothes you plan to wear next.

Clear plastic boxes and bins. Set these on shelves for an easy view, and use them to store lingerie and accessories of all kinds.

Wire or plastic mesh baskets and bins. Mesh containers allow air circulation to keep clothes free from mildew and odor. You'll find mesh baskets in notions departments. Use mesh baskets for foldable clothes and accessories, including umbrellas.

Hat boxes. Look for hat boxes at variety stores and lower-priced chain stores.

Metal shoe rack. Mount a sturdy metal shoe rack on the wall or on the inside of the door for easy access.

Fabric or clear plastic shoe bags. Keep the floor clear with shoe bags hung from the closet rod or from sturdy hooks mounted on the wall or back of the door. Use shoe bag pockets to store rolled up belts, scarves, shoe polish supplies, hangtags, or the extra buttons and yarns that come attached to clothes.

Overhead shoe chests and boxes. Shoe chests or boxes can be placed on upper shelves for added storage.

Floor shoe racks. These work best placed close to the wall and out of the way. Use them for everyday shoes and slippers.

Clear plastic garment bags. Use for storing limited-occasion and out-of-season clothes. Leave the zipper open slightly to allow air to circulate. Opaque bags hide whatever they hold and must be labeled.

Clear plastic clothing bags. The kind you get at the store or the dry cleaners. They can be used for short-term protection, and should be left open or untied at the bottom.

Cloth clothing bags. Cloth covers allow air to circulate around lace, beaded, velvet, leather, and suede garments.

Do-it-yourself. Finish nails or hooks, hammered at two-inch intervals, hold belts and pieces of jewelry. Spaced further apart you can hang handbags and hats.

Small- to medium-sized cardboard boxes stacked on their sides and open to the front are a no-cost option and are especially good as a short-term solution.

It may take several days to get your closet organized and outfitted the way you want it. When it's ready, resolve to make good use of that space and keep it in good working order. See Figures 11–5 and 11–6.

Figure 11–5. Closet clutter before cleanout and organization. *(Courtesy The Closet Organizers)*

Figure 11–6. Orderly closet, easy to access after cleanout and organization. *(Courtesy The Closet Organizers)*

3.

Practice good clothes sense to maintain the appearance of your clothing.

❧

The wear-life of an article of clothing depends on:

- The number of similar items you have on hand at any time.
- How often and how hard the item is worn — or torn.
- The care received in the closet and during cleaning.
- The classic or faddish styling of the garment.

- The strength and quality of fabric and construction.

You can expect heavy and firmly woven fabrics made of tightly twisted yarn to wear longer than lightweight and loosely woven fabrics made of loosely twisted yarn. You can also expect dark-colored fabrics, plaids, and prints to look cleaner longer than light- and solid-colored clothes, as they do not show the soil as readily. Dark colors may, however, fade more noticeably and more quickly than light colors.

Expected Wear–Life or Clothing Life Cycle

If you maintain a small wardrobe composed of one expanded cluster, wearing most pieces at least once a week,

Table 11–2 Wear-life Expectancy Rate (Approximate — depending on wear and care)

Clothing Item	Number Owned	Approximate Years
Blouse/shirt		
Dressy — woven	6	4
Casual — woven	8	3
knit	4	2
Business — woven	6	2
Skirt	6	10
Pants/slacks		
Dressy	2	10
Casual	4	4
Dress		
Dressy	2	8–10
Casual	2	10
Business	3	5
Vest	2	10+
Sweater		
Cotton	4	3
Wool	3	6
Jacket		
Casual	2	4–6
Business	4	3–6
Coat		
All-season cloth	1	4
Winter cloth	1	4–8
Leather	1	4–6
Fur	1	8–15
Bathing suit	1	1

Clothing Item	Number Owned	Approximate Years
Pajama/nightgown		
Lightweight	2	3–4
Flannel, heavy	1	2–33
Robe		
Lightweight	1	4
Quilted, heavy	1	4–6
Underwear		
Panty	8	2
Bra	3	2
Slip	2	3
Belt	4	2
Shoes		
Dressy	2	3–6
Casual	2	1–4
Business	2	2–4
Boots	1	4–6
Stockings		
Socks	8	6 mo.
Pantyhose	4	5 min–5 mo!
Scarf	4	4
Children's clothing		
Sleepwear		1
Play and school		6 mo.–1
Dress clothes		1
Shoes		
Canvas		3–6 mo.
Leather		6 mo.–1

you can expect to gradually wear them out. (See Table 11–2.) It's smart to keep a replacement log to aid in anticipating upcoming clothing needs and planning ahead to take advantage of sales. Such a log can also be used for insurance claims if clothing is ever damaged or lost and you need to determine how much wear was left in the garment. If you maintain a moderate wardrobe — maybe two to four smaller clusters, or one larger expanded cluster — the strongest influence to discard a piece of clothing has very little to do with them wearing out, and everything to do with boredom. In this sense, most clothing goes through a life cycle of its own. The length of this cycle varies from one to many years, depending on your values, interests, and income.

How to Increase Clothing Wear–Life

There are many ways you can maintain the good looks of your clothes, increase their wear-life, and reduce the cost of care for your clothes. Some are the same suggestions your mother used to make, and they center around preventive care. Preventive care means stopping any problems before they start — avoiding situations that can ruin clothes, and setting up situations that protect the clothes.

General Tips

- Before you put on new clothing, check for loose threads, pins, and sticky tags left from manufacturing or packaging.
- Treat delicate fabrics with spray-on fabric protector to repel wet stains such as soup, soda, coffee, or tea.
- Change from your better or delicate clothes to more durable at-home clothes as soon as possible to save wear and tear.
- Dress and undress carefully to prevent tears, rips, and snags.
- Remove shoes before changing clothes.
- Remove belts from belt loops and hang separately.
- Avoid overloading pockets. Remove any items from pockets before you put clothes away.
- Rotate clothing. Between wearings, let clothes rest to allow body moisture and odor to fade, wrinkles to fall out, and the original shape to return.
- Inspect clothes for needed repair, ideally after each wearing, certainly before wearing again, and definitely before dry cleaning or washing. Look for small tears, popped seams, visible linings, falling hems, and loose buttons. (See Table 11–3.)
- Put only wear-ready clothes in your closet, so you'll always know what's available. Clothes that need cleaning or repairing should go in a container kept in a convenient place.
- Hang wrinkled garments in the bathroom while showering or bathing to steam out wrinkles. To maintain sleeve shape while steaming, gently insert rolled towels. Stuff delicate sleeves with tissue or clear plastic bags.

- Save labels and read care tags carefully. Follow their instructions.
- Follow instructions for pressing or ironing. (See Figure 11–7 and Table 11–4, page 333.)

TIP
❧
FROM THE PROS

Test press the heat level from the wrong side, on a hidden area such as a seam allowance, pocket, shirt tail, or hem. If necessary, begin pressing at the lowest temperature and amount of pressure, and gradually increase. One of the kindest favors you can do for yourself is to invest in a commercial steamer. It will save time and money in the long run!

- Turn the iron off, unplug it, drain out any water, and allow it to cool before putting it away.
- Allow freshly pressed or ironed clothes to air-dry completely before wearing or storing away in drawers and closets.

Figure 11–7. Seek out the services of a reliable cleaner. *(Courtesy Heidi Neslen)*

Table 11–3 Common Mending Tasks

Loose or lost snaps, hooks and eyes

Loose or lost buttons

Loose or broken zippers

Ripped seams

Worn or torn knees and elbows

Ripped pockets

Fabric tears

Torn ribbing and lace

Snagged or torn fabric

Dangling belt loops

Snagged or loose hems

Ripped plackets

Ripped pleats

Frayed collars and cuffs

Worn out elastic

Broken lingerie straps

Frayed buttonholes

Loose or frayed linings

Snagged or ripped topstitching

Worn socks and run nylons

Keep Clothes Clean

- Give perfume, lotion, and deodorant time to dry completely before dressing. Wear underarm shields or a lightweight T-shirt or shell to protect clothing from heavy perspiration stains.
- Place a towel around your shoulders before applying powder to your face or using hair spray.
- Place a lightweight scarf over your head before pulling garments on and off to prevent makeup stains.
- Check clothes for stains and spots after each wearing. Many stains can be removed if treated promptly and before washing, dry cleaning, machine heat drying, or ironing the garment. Any of these procedures will set the stain and make it extremely difficult or impossible to remove.
- Brush garments, especially wool, after wearing to remove surface soil and lint. Brush out pockets and cuffs on sleeves and pants. Allow mud to dry before brushing off.
- Remove pills (tiny balls of matted fiber) using a "defuzzer" or razor stroked gently over the surface of the fabric.

- Clean and press clothes when necessary, but don't overdo. It is not usually necessary to clean or press after every wearing. Cleaning and pressing increase the risk of loss of shape, fading and shrinking. The best suit is made to survive only twenty to twenty-five cleanings. If you send a suit to the cleaner every six to eight wearings, you'll wear it out quickly.
- Sort clothes before cleaning according to cleaning method, weight, and/or color to retain original whiteness, brightness, size, shape, and texture.
- Learn and follow correct cleaning and drying procedures. (See Tables 11–4 and 11–5, pages 333 through 338.)

T I P
&
FROM THE PROS

Take clothes out of the dryer just minutes before time is up — while fabric is still warm and slightly damp. Shake out each piece. Lay out and finger press into shape, or hang on plastic or covered hangers to cool and finish drying. Polyester thread used in sewing seams can shrink with heat, causing puckered seams. To stretch the seams, remove clothing while it is slightly damp and gently pull from each end of the seam to stretch the thread and eliminate puckers.

- Dry clean or wash matching pieces of clothing together to prevent fading at different rates.

Store Clothes Properly

- Hang up clothes as soon as you take them off. Clothes that pile up on furniture or the floor lose their shape and wear out fast.
- Don't crowd your closet. Overcrowding causes clothes to wrinkle and become misshapen.
- Before hanging a garment in the closet, remove items from the pockets and belts from belt loops. Hang belts separately.
- Before hanging, button the top button or fastener and zip the zipper.
- Hang each garment individually and straighten the garment on the hanger to preserve its shape.
- Hang damp clothes immediately to preserve their shapes, but don't put them in the closet until they are completely dry.
- Hang smoky-smelling clothes outside the closet until the odor has faded.
- Sew long loops of seam tape to the front and back of the waistline seam of better dresses, a little shorter than bodice length. Hang these loops over the hanger curve to prevent shoulder stretching.
- Place hangers in the same direction, making it easier to get them out.
- Rather than folding skirts, hang them from hanger bars.

Table 11–4 Natural and Man-made Fibers Care

Fiber	Care
Natural Fibers — Cotton	• Preshrink before sewing fabric. • Machine wash in hot water with soap or on delicate cycle of machine. Fabric softener may be used during final rinse. • Chlorine bleach may generally be used on whites; on colored clothes only if specially formulated. • If labeled "do not bleach," never use chlorine bleach. • Machine dry at regular or hot setting. • Remove permanent press items from dryer as soon as cycle is completed and fold or hang immediately. • Press or iron with moderately hot iron. • Press while damp. • Press dark garments on wrong side. • Dry clean if colors run.
Linen	• Machine wash in warm water with mild suds. • Do not twist or wring. • Smooth and let dry on nonrust hangers. • Avoid repeated pressing of sharp creases to prevent fibers from breaking. • Press while damp, on wrong side, with hot iron. • Protect stored linens from mildew. • May be dry cleaned to improve shape retention.
Ramie	• Machine wash in warm water with mild suds. • Do not twist or wring. • Smooth and let dry on nonrust hangers. • Avoid repeated pressing of sharp creases to prevent fibers from breaking. • Press while damp, on wrong side, with hot iron.
Silk	• Usually silk must be dry cleaned. • If labeled "hand washable," use only a mild soap and warm water. • Do not use chlorine bleach or strong soaps and detergent. • Do not wring or twist. • Smooth and let dry on a nonrust hanger. • Press while damp, on wrong side, with warm, not hot, dry iron. • Protect from prolonged exposure to sunlight. • Protect from moths and carpet beetles.

Table 11–4 Natural and Man-made Fibers Care *(continued)*

Fiber	Care
Natural Fibers Wool	• Preshrink fabrics before sewing. • Wool is usually dry cleaned. • If washed, use hand or delicate machine cycle, cold water, mild soap or special wool soap, such as Woolite. • Do not rub, wring, or twist. • Avoid chlorine bleach and strong soaps or detergents. • Smooth out and dry on flat towel. • Press with steam on moderate heat setting, on wrong side of fabric and with press cloth. • Protect against moths and carpet beetles. • Air wool garments frequently. Let stand twenty-four hours between wearings. • Wool may be hung near a steamy tub or shower to remove wrinkles. • "Washable" woolens are good for children's wear, but tailored-style adult clothing tends to lose its shape when washed.

Man-made Fibers Acetate	• Generally acetate should be dry cleaned. If labeled "washable," use the following guidelines:
	  – Do not soak colored fabrics or they may fade.
	  – Wash in mild suds and lukewarm water.
	  – Do not wring or twist.
	  – Smooth or shake out garment and let dry on a nonrust hanger.
	  – Press while damp on wrong side with the lowest setting. Use a press cloth for work done on the right side.
	  – Nail polish and perfumes containing acetone will dissolve fabric.

Acrylic	• Remove oil spots and stains before washing. • Wash delicate items by hand in warm water with soap. Rinse thoroughly in warm water. • Gently squeeze out water; do not wring or twist. • Smooth or shake garment and let dry on nonrust hanger. Knit garments should be dried flat on towel. • When machine washing, use warm water and add a fabric softener during the final rinse cycle once in every four to five washings to reduce static buildup. • Machine dry at low temperature setting. Remove garments from dryer immediately to prevent heat-set wrinkles. • If ironing is required, use a moderately warm iron, never hot.
Anidex	• Machine wash similar to Spandex. • Tumble dry on warm heat or cool.

Table 11–4 Natural and Man-made Fibers Care *(continued)*

Fiber	Care
Man-made Fibers Modacrylic	• Dry cleaning or fur cleaning process is best for deep pile garments. • If washable, machine wash in warm water and add a fabric softener during the final rinse cycle once every four or five washings to reduce static buildup. • If machine dried, use low setting and remove articles immediately after end of cycle. • If ironing is required, use lowest setting. Never use a hot iron or fabric will melt.
Nylon	• Wash delicate items by hand in warm water with soap or detergent. • Rinse thoroughly in warm water and use a fabric softener in the rinse water. • Gently squeeze out water, do not wring or twist. • Smooth or shake out garment and let dry on nonrust hangers. Sweaters and knit items should be dried flat. • Most items made from nylon can be machine washed. Use warm water and add fabric softener to the final rinse cycle once every four to five washings to reduce static buildup. • Bleachable with chlorine bleach, but test for color fastness first. • Machine dry at low temperature setting and remove articles from dryer as soon as cycle is completed to avoid heat-set wrinkles. • If ironing is required, use a moderately warm iron. Never use a hot iron or fabric will melt. • May use a commercial color remover on grayed or yellowed nylon fabric. • Is a "scavenger" for color. It takes on the color from darker clothes during washing and storing. Separate nylon items in washing and in storage bags or containers.
Polyester	• Remove spots before washing with undiluted liquid detergent or spray-stain remover. • Wash delicate items by hand in warm water with soap or detergent. • Rinse thoroughly in warm water. • Use a fabric softener in the rinse cycle to reduce static buildup. • Gently squeeze out water and smooth or shake out garment and let dry on a nonrust hanger. • Most items made from polyester can be machine washed in warm water and soap, with fabric softener used in the rinse cycle. • Machine dry at a low temperature setting and remove items when drying cycle is completed to prevent heat-set wrinkles. • If ironing is desired, use a moderately warm iron. Never use a hot iron or fabric will melt.

Table 11–4 Natural and Man-made Fibers Care *(continued)*

Fiber	Care
Man-made Fibers / Rayon	• Most rayon fabrics wash well with gentle agitation, but some types of fabric and garment construction make dry cleaning advisable. • For washable items, use mild suds in lukewarm water. • Do not soak colored fabrics or fading may occur. • Bleach may generally be used, however, some rayon fabrics are sensitive. Test first. • Gently squeeze suds through fabric and rinse in lukewarm water. • Do not twist or wring fabric. • Smooth or shake out article and dry on nonrust hanger. • Press the article while damp, on the wrong side and with the iron moderately warm. Use a press cloth when pressing on the right side.
Spandex	• Hand or machine wash on delicate cycle in lukewarm water. • Do not use chlorine bleach on any fabric containing Spandex unless directed otherwise. Use an oxygen or sodium perborate type bleach. • Rinse thoroughly. • Drip dry. If machine dried, use low temperature setting. • If ironing is required, use light, quick strokes, on low temperature setting.
Triacetate	• Pleated garments are best hand washed. Most other garments containing 100 percent Triacetate can be machine washed and dried. • Jersey knits need no ironing. Touch up woven garments with steam iron. • Nail polish and perfumes containing acetone will dissolve Triacetate.

Special Occasion Clothes

- Fold stretchy knit and bias-cut dresses at the waist and place them over hanger bars.
- Fold heavy beaded garments with tissue paper to prevent creases and store in a box or drawer.
- Store fragile fabrics (lace, velvet, suede) or fabrics that can snag other garments (sequins, metallics, beads) in clear plastic bags.
- Fabrics that shed (fur, angora, mohair) should not be stored near fabrics that attract loose fibers (velvet, velour, corduroy).

Knits

- Sweaters and knit garments hold their shapes better if they are folded flat on open shelves. Fold the sleeves across the upper chest and bring the bottom up over the sleeves. They tend to stretch when hung.
- Two-piece knit dresses and suits can be folded and laid on a shelf or folded twice and hung over a padded bar, lessening the stretch.

Lingerie and Underwear

- Store by category and by color: panties, bras, full slips, half slips, nighties, and so forth.
- To prevent sliding, store underclothes in clear plastic boxes, plastic coated mesh baskets, and/or drawers.
- Hang nightclothes and underwear for the next day on hooks in the closet.
- Store underwear in or near the bathroom for changing after bathing if it works best for you.

Table 11–5 Clothing Care Label Guidelines

	Label Says	Label Means
Wash	Home launder only	No commercial laundries or dry cleaning. Wash, bleach, dry, and press by ordinary methods, at any temperature without shrinking or fading.
	Washable Machine wash Machine washable	Same as above, unless stated otherwise, at home or in commercial laundry.
	Cold water Cold wash Cold rinse	Use cold tap water or cold setting on machine for cold water only.
	Warm water Warm wash Warm rinse	Use warm tap water or warm setting on machine for water up to 110°.
	Hot water Hot wash Hot rinse	Use hot tap water or hot setting on machine for water up to 130°.
	Machine wash on delicate or gentle	Use delicate or gentle setting on machine, or wash by hand.
	Machine wash on permanent press	Use permanent press setting on machine, or use warm wash, cold rinse, and short spin cycle.
	Machine wash separately	You can expect color to fade. Wash with the same color only.
	No spin	Stop machine before spin cycle or remove item before spin cycle.
	Hand wash	Wash by hand in warm water. Check with dry cleaner before dry cleaning.
	Hand wash only	Do not machine wash or dry clean.
	Hand wash separately	Hand wash alone with same color only.
Bleach	No bleach	Do not bleach. All types of bleach are harmful to the fabric.
	No chlorine bleach Nonchlorine bleach only	Fabric harmed by chlorine bleach. Do not use chlorine bleach. All-fabric, nonchlorine bleach may be used safely.

Table 11–5 Clothing Care Label Guidelines (*continued*)

Label Says	Label Means
Dry — Drip dry	Do not machine or tumble dry. Hang item while wet and let air dry.
Line dry	Hang item while damp and let air dry.
Dry flat	Smooth out the item on flat surface to air dry.
Do not twist, wring, or squeeze	Twisting, wringing, or squeezing will damage fabric. Drip dry or dry flat without wringing or squeezing out water first.
Block to dry	On flat surface smooth and shape item to size while wet to maintain original shape and size. Let air dry.
Tumble dry Machine dry	Dry in machine dryer. Set dryer on specified heat — no heat, low, medium, or high.
Tumble dry — remove promptly	Same as above, but remove from dryer as soon as tumbling stops.
Iron/Press — Permanent press	Item needs no ironing or pressing after washing or drying.
Do not iron	Do not iron or press with heat.
Cool iron	Use iron at lowest, coolest setting. Moderate heat will damage fabric.
Hot iron	Use iron at hot setting. Fabric requires higher heat to remove wrinkles and will not be damaged by heat.
Steam iron	Steam heat is required to remove wrinkles. Iron or press on steam setting.
Iron damp	Dampen item before ironing.
Dry cleaning — No dry clean	Dry cleaning will damage fabric. Follow care instructions provided.
Dry clean only	Washing may damage fabric. Use commercial dry cleaner.
Professionally dry clean only	Self-service dry cleaning may damage fabric. Use professional service.

Socks and Hosiery

- Pair and roll up socks, then stand them in clear plastic boxes on the shelf or store them in shoe boxes, minus the lids.
- Slip knee-high hosiery, pantyhose, tights, and so forth into plastic zipper-type bags. Arrange by style and color in boxes or baskets.
- Save pantyhose with runs in a different zipper-type bag and wear with boots or slacks to save money.

Gloves

- Arrange gloves by color and length in clear plastic boxes or in zipper-type storage bags.

Belts

- Hang coordinating belts on the same hangers as the dresses they match.
- Arrange belts by type (decorative, sporty, business) and color on a belt rack or pegboard, so they are easily seen.
- Fold and store nonhanging belts in clear plastic boxes. To prevent scratching, roll the buckle to the inside.

Shoes

- Apply water and stain repellent to new shoes.
- Put shoes away after they have aired completely, about two hours.
- Retain shoe shape by stuffing the toes with tissue paper or shoe trees. Do not pile shoes on top of one another.
- Brush suede shoes before and after each wearing.
- Store shoes in labeled shoe boxes on shelves. Group shoes according to season, occasion, and color.
- If space is a problem, use hanging canvas shoe bags or back-of-door shoe racks.
- When shoes are not stored on the floor, use the floor space for boots. Stuff boots with cardboard tubes to prevent cracking around the ankles.

Handbags

- Apply water and stain repellent to new handbags.
- Put handbags on a shelf or hang from hooks.
- Stuff soft bags with tissue paper to maintain shapes.
- Put patent leather bags into cloth bags or pillow cases to prevent scratches.

Hats

- Store hats in hatboxes if you have the space. Otherwise, set one hat inside another or stuff the crowns of hats with tissue and hang the hats on hooks on the wall or on a hat rack.

Scarves

- Hang scarves where you can see them and where they can hang without wrinkling, over a rounded hanger bar or towel bar attached to a closet door.

Jewelry

- Store jewelry so that it can be seen. Store precious jewelry apart from costume jewelry in unexpected places to prevent theft.
- Put jewelry in clear plastic divided trays, in a flat fishing tackle box, or in a nail box with clear plastic drawers from the hardware store, so you can see what you have. Small cardboard boxes can be used to divide drawer space for jewelry.
- Store sharp-edged jewelry away from pearls and other smooth jewelry to prevent scratching.
- Hang costume necklaces and bracelets, grouped by occasion and color, on hooks, tie racks, belt racks, or mug racks.
- Use tiny to small zipper-type storage bags to keep earring pairs together.
- Save time pawing through jewelry for special pieces. Put special jewelry in a pint-size, zipper-type storage bag and hook the bag over the hanger of the garment the piece is most often worn with.

4.

Be prepared for long–term clothing storage.

☙

Clothing storage time can range from a few months to several years. While most of your clothing can be worn eight or nine months of the year, some pieces, such as hot or frigid weather wear, is stored for as long as six to eight months. Special event and holiday clothes or costumes may be stored even longer.

You don't want to store away every cool or warm weather item during any season. As soon as you do, the temperature will dip or soar in the direction least expected, leaving you unprepared. Clothes in all-season colors, fibers, and fabrics, such as cottons, silks, and light to medium-weight knits, belong in the bedroom or dressing-room closet all year.

Over the years, you may find yourself storing away fewer clothes as you learn to buy more and more all-season fabrics and gain skill in layering clothes during trans-seasonal and cool-weather periods. There is, however, some value to seasonal storage. You don't get tired of seeing the same clothes all year but welcome the comparative newness of clothing brought back into service for the new season.

Maternity, baby, and children's clothes can be packed away for years. Imagine unpacking baby clothes for a first grandchild, clothes that haven't seen the light of day for twenty years. In excellent condition, they will be well appreciated by the parents. Precious heirloom items with sentimental value, such as wedding dresses, evening gowns, christening or blessing clothes, and priceless fashion pieces are often stored for years and passed down through generations.

Where to Store

Generally speaking, store clothes and fabrics in a dark, cool, dry, dust-free and bug-free place. The agents of chemical and physical change that lead to clothing damage are sunlight, heat, moisture, dust, and insects.

Direct sunlight will cause some fabrics, such as nylon, to deteriorate. Common sense tells you to store clothes in a dark closet or container.

Excessive heat will soften plastic coverings and plastic hangers used in storing and cause them to stick to the clothes. Heat plus moisture will change sulfur dyes, frequently used to create dark-colored cottons, into sulfuric acid that seriously damages fabric. Avoid storing clothes in the attic and near radiators or hot-water pipes.

Moisture, often combined with heat, is the culprit responsible for mold, commonly called mildew, in clothing and fabric. In humid climates or areas, mildew can develop within a day, causing fabric damage and/or discoloration. Mildew thrives on cotton, linen, and rayon. Soil and starch or sizing provides the protein food supply for the mold to grow, even on synthetics.

To prevent mildew, store only clean, dry clothing and fabrics. Store them only in dry areas. Using a dehumidifier or leaving the light on in a closet can eliminate excess moisture in storage areas. Products such as silica gel, activated alumina, or calcium chloride will absorb moisture. These products can be purchased in a hardware or department store. Hang the product in cloth bags or place it in open containers on shelves in the storage area, but don't get it on the clothing.

Dust that collects on any clothing will soil and discolor the fabric, particularly on exposed areas that rest on a hanger, such as the shoulders and collar. Over long periods of time, soil will abrade the fibers away. Hanging clothing must be covered or stored in a container.

Insects thrive on starch, stains, and perspiration. Silverfish love cotton, linen, and rayon. Moths are attracted to wool, hair, fur, and feathers. Earwigs will eat almost anything. Larvae have been known to eat through synthetic fabric fibers to get to natural fibers.

Cedar closets and chests will not kill moths or larvae. Fumes and odor alone may or may not repel moths but do tend to discourage silverfish. Holes will still result if an insect is unknowingly stored in the clothes. Store only clean clothing and fabrics to ensure that they are free of eggs or larvae.

Cedar chips are another option. Put them in the bottom of an old nylon stocking, knot the stocking, and hang it in the closet. A commercial dry cleaner will often mothproof your clothes for a reasonable fee.

Insecticides kill insects and are readily available in liquid, spray, crystal, flake, and ball form or hangable container. Follow the manufacturer's directions. Return clothes to the closet only after the odor of insecticide is gone.

Mothballs, flakes, crystals, and nuggets kill insects. Layer them throughout folded clothing but do not inhale the fumes. Use about one pound of mothballs; place them between layers of tissue paper to prevent them from touching the clothes. Herbal sachets may not keep insects away but mask the unpleasant odor of mothballs.

The combination of spots and stains, perspiration, dust, heat, and moisture often results in offensive odors in clothing. This, in turn, attracts insects. Store only clean, unstarched clothing and fabric.

Additional Storage Points

Discoloration is a problem with long-term storage. White or light-colored cottons, wool, and nylon yellow with age.

Stored clothing can get a musty smell, especially in a damp climate. To make them smell fresh again, add a few drops of witch hazel or a favorite cologne to the water in the steam iron and gently press.

The odor of mothballs can be removed by placing clothes, one garment at a time, in the dryer on no heat for about ten minutes.

Ideally, furs should be professionally stored during warm weather. If you store furs at home, have them professionally cleaned and glazed, then store in a cloth cover or bag.

Shoes, boots and handbags should be cleaned and polished, then stored in cardboard boxes, not plastic containers. Leather, like fur, silk, and down fabrics, requires air circulation.

Specific Storage Locations and Containers

Attics, basements, and garages are notorious for exposing clothes to high heat, moisture, dust, grease, or fumes and bugs. Use these areas only if they are clean, dry, and moderate in temperature. Rely on convenient areas within your home to store unneeded clothing. Heating, cooling, and humidity control systems maintain relatively constant conditions throughout the year.

- Your own closet may be large enough for both warm and cool weather clothes. If so, hang the out-of-season clothes to the far sides or back of the closet.
- A guest-room closet may be the ideal place to store out-of-season clothes.
- Drawers, built into a wall or in a piece of furniture work well. Line them with plastic-coated or acid-free paper.
- Wicker furniture makes attractive and inexpensive storage pieces. You might use a wicker hamper, chest, or foot locker.
- Sturdy cardboard storage boxes are ideal for storage. Cardboard footlockers are made long and low to slide under the bed or behind a couch.

- Trunks and suitcases not in use for travel can be used for storage. Fold clothes neatly into a pillowcase and place them in the travel piece. These bundles are easy to remove when you need the suitcase for a trip.
- Garment bags and footlockers, available in fabric or plastic, hold hanging clothes at the top and a folded item or two on the bottom. The largest bags hang on a portable clothes rack. Open the bag periodically to allow air exchange.
- Cedar chests are effective against moths and other insects only if constructed of cedar heartwood at least ¾-inch (2 cm) thick. Oil from the heartwood kills moth larvae. The odor alone may or may not repel moths but does tend to discourage silverfish. To protect clothing from resin and wood acid, line cedar chests with acid-free paper or muslin sheeting purchased in an art supply or frame shop.
- A dry cleaner will often store clothing, an option worth considering if storage space is simply not available within your home. A small storage fee may be well worth a less-cluttered closet or home and professional care.

Query Box ?

Are you prepared for the everyday care of your clothes? Do you have the following equipment and supplies available to you?

Clothes brush	Spot remover
Lint brush	Prewash spray
Mending kit	Mild soap
Steam iron	Detergent
Ironing board	Mild bleach
Press cloth	Water softener
Shoe polish	Mothballs or crystals

Take care of your clothes and they will take care of you! (See Table 11–6.)

Table 11–6 Image Makers and Breakers in Clothing Care

Image Breakers In Clothing Care	Image Makers In Clothing Care
• Saggy, baggy, out-of-shape clothes	• Clothing that holds its shape
• Lining shows below hem	• Lining out of sight
• Ripped seams or hems	• Seams and hems secure
• Loose, hanging, or missing buttons, snaps, hooks, and eyes	• Buttons, snaps, hooks, and eyes secure
• Dangling belt loops	• Belt loops secure
• Ring-around-the-collar or cuffs	• Collars and cuffs clean
• Makeup on collar or neckline	• Collar and neckline areas clean
• Noticeably dusty, stained, or linty	• Clothing clean
• Noticeably un-ironed or rumpled, overly ironed, flattened, or scorched	• Appropriately ironed or pressed
• Visible cleaners' tag	• Removed tag
• Cracked, overworn belts	• Belt looks good
• Snagged or run stockings	• Stockings free of runs, snags
• Shoes with run-down edges, soles, and heels	• Shoes well-heeled and soled
• Scuffed dress shoes	• Clean, waxed, or polished dress shoes
• Dirty handbags or briefcases	• Clean handbags or briefcases
• Dirty, tattered umbrellas	• Clean umbrellas, in good shape

A Spoonful of Sugar

I need to take my own advice, to plan a monthly time to do my mending on a regular basis. Periodically, my stack of mending reaches a critical height and demands attention. I'm not the only person for whom mending is a bore, a chore, a real pain.

No one says we have to like mending, but it does need to be done if we prefer to use our money for something other than replacement clothing. With some forethought, the task can be made more palatable, even mildly pleasant. Start thinking how great you're going to feel when it's done!

First of all, recruit help.

Literally train the members of your family to inspect their clothes when they take them off. It will save the clothing from falling apart if they go into the wash in damaged condition.

Second, have a convenient and attractive container handy for all clothing that needs mending, perhaps a large basket. Perhaps you could cover a large cardboard box with pretty contact paper. An out-of-sight drawer or a decorative trunk provide other options.

The choice of container is up to you, but clothes needing repair are not the most aesthetically pleasing sight. If you have to look at them piled in a heap every day, you will only grow to detest them even more — just ask me!

Third, establish a specific time for mending clothes. Once a year is not often enough. The time should be regular, but not rigid. As you plan your week, select a time to do it that suits you.

I like to pick out a favorite television show, TV special, or video to "listen" to while I mend. Perhaps you'd prefer to put on a favorite tape or CD.

Maybe the time can be spent visiting with someone in your family or with a friend while you work. Better yet, invite a friend over to mend with you — but not for you. (Misery loves company.)

Parents can turn this time into precious teaching moments with a child. Working together can be satisfying. Who knows, maybe the child will think mending is fun and take over completely.

A friend of mine has to do a lot of telephoning, so she keeps a mending kit near the phone to do hand work while talking. If it works, why not? Whatever the solution, plan the time in such a way as to make it enjoyable for you.

Review Main Points

Proper care and repair will increase the wear-life of your clothing and thereby the value of your clothing investment. To maintain an attractive and appropriate appearance, you must maintain your clothing. This is your responsibility and part of the clothing management process. A well-organized closet simplifies your life, allows you to enjoy your living space, and puts you in charge of your clothing and your image. Three principles of closet organization include the need for visibility, reachability, and grouping of the clothes by categories. Closet equipment is available to make organizing your closet easier and more efficient. The agents of chemical and physical change that lead to clothing damage are sunlight, heat, moisture, dust, and insects. Generally speaking, store clothing and fabric in a dark, cool, dry, dust-free, and bug-free location. Closets, drawers, boxes, chests, trunks, suitcases, and garment bags are appropriate containers to store clothing and fabric in. Inspect your clothes for needed repair and follow through with mending as needed. Inspect your clothing for dirt and stains. Dirt wears out the fibers in clothing fabric. Sorting, stain removal, laundry, dry cleaning, and pressing are essential tasks in the care of clothing. It pays to take care of your clothes.

Review Questions

1. What does "clothing maintainence" mean? _____

_____

2. What are the three principles of closet organization? _____

_____

3. Give a short statement explaining the importance of each principle given in the previous question. _____

_____

4. If you don't have enough closet space for your clothes, what are some things you can do? _____

5. What does it mean to group the clothes in your closet according to garment type? _____

6. What does it mean to group the clothes in your closet according to occasion, activity, or mood? _____

7. Explain the importance of choosing the proper storage method for each article of clothing and give examples. _____

8. Give an example of an article of clothing you may wish to store for several years. How might this garment deteriorate and what can you do to prevent or hinder this deterioration? _____

9. In addition to bugs, what are some things to avoid for long-term clothing storage? _____

10. Why would one want to sort clothes before washing them? How would you sort them? _____

Discussion Questions

#1 Discuss three elements of clothing care and why these are important for your clothes. How often must they be performed and what effect does improper or inadequate care have on others' perceptions of you?

   Notes: _____

#2 Describe ways you have found to make clothing care tasks more pleasant and consistent.

   Notes: _____

#3 Describe one of the principles of closet organization and what it means. Describe how its absence would limit the utility of your wardrobe.

   Notes: _____

#4 What does "preventive care" mean and why is it important?

   Notes: _____

Exercise 11–1 Closet Design

Draw a diagram of your closet. (It does not have to be perfect, just neat.)

Draw a diagram of how you could ideally improve the design and storage capacity.

Note any improvements you plan to make in the near future.

Exercise 11–2 Closet Reorganization

Name _____

Improve the organization and arrangement of the clothes in your closet and drawers.

• Record specific arrangement of clothes and their accessories.

• Record any improvements you were able to make at this time.

• Record your feelings about the project, during and after.

(Note: If possible, take a photograph of your finished arrangement.)

Exercise 11–3 Care Labels

Name_____

Look for labels in the neckline and waistline of clothes you are wearing.
• Identify the clothing item, fiber, and fabric names.
• Record care instructions and any additional information.
• Work with a classmate and identify as above.

You – Clothing Item	Fiber	Fabric	Care Instructions	Additional Information

Classmate – Clothing Item	Fiber	Fabric	Care Instructions	Additional Information

Exercise 11–4 Care Labels

Name_____

Look in your closet. Select five to ten favorite pieces of clothing, and five to ten less favorite pieces of clothing.
- Identify the clothing items, fiber, and fabric names.
- Record care instructions and any additional information.
- Consider how care required may have influenced your preferences.

	Clothing Item	Fiber	Fabric	Care Instructions	Additional Information
Favorite Clothes	1.				
	2.				
	3.				
	4.				
	5.				
	6.				
	7.				
	8.				
	9.				
	10.				
Less Favorite Clothes	1.				
	2.				
	3.				
	4.				
	5.				
	6.				
	7.				
	8.				
	9.				
	10.				

Conclusions:

Exercise 11–5 Local Store Experience

Name_____

Look in a local clothing store for a variety of labels and hangtags — from ten to fifteen different labels or tags.

• Identify the clothing item, fiber, and fabric names.
• Record care instructions and any additional information.

Clothing Item	Fiber	Fabric	Care Instructions	Additional Information
1.				
2.				
3.				
4.				
5.				
6.				
7.				
8.				
9.				
10.				

Exercise 11–5 Local Store
Experience (*continued*)

Name _____

Look in a local supermarket for a variety of laundry products — from five to eight different products.

• Identify the product name and function.
• Read through and record notes about consumer information provided on the package.
• Draw conclusions regarding the helpfulness of the information.
• Be prepared to discuss your experience and conclusions.

Product	Function	Consumer Information	Conclusions
1.			
2.			
3.			
4.			
5.			
6.			
7.			
8.			

Exercise 11–6 Interview

Name _____

- Interview three to five family members and/or friends regarding laundry or dry-cleaning accidents.
- Make notes of each accident/incident.
- Be prepared to relate the most interesting accident/incident you are told.

Interview #1

Interview #2

Interview #3

Interview #4

Interview #5

Chapter
12
Smart Shopping

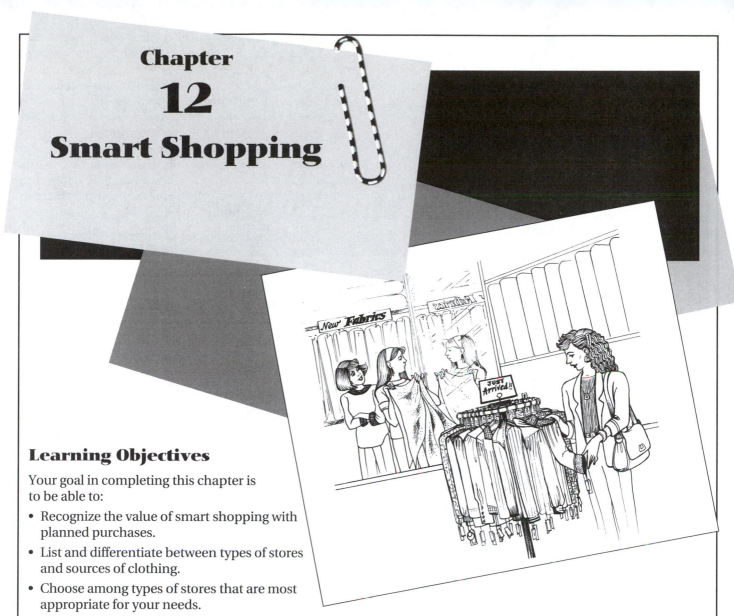

Learning Objectives

Your goal in completing this chapter is to be able to:

- Recognize the value of smart shopping with planned purchases.
- List and differentiate between types of stores and sources of clothing.
- Choose among types of stores that are most appropriate for your needs.
- Understand the value of making a shopping list.
- Describe how to use the telephone to assist in shopping.
- Identify when to shop and when not to shop.
- Describe what to wear and what to take shopping.
- Describe how to select merchandise and how to interact with sales associates.
- Explain how to check for proper fit in clothing.
- Define specific fitting standards.
- Recognize characteristics of quality in clothing.
- Define sales terms and types of sales.
- Appreciate the value of try-on time and dress rehearsals with new clothing.
- Be prepared to practice your rights and responsibilities in making returns.

Preview Main Points

1. Rely on smart shopping skills and strategies.
2. Knowing about the many types of stores and clothing sources available to you will help you in finding your clothing needs.
3. Practice shopping strategies that prepare you to make wise purchases.
4. Develop sales savvy with an understanding of sales terms, types of sales, and procedures.
5. Rely on private try-on times and dress rehearsals to become familiar and comfortable with new clothing.
6. Understand your rights and responsibilities as a consumer in the process of returns.

1.

Rely on smart shopping skills and strategies.

Open your closet doors for a long look. Don't be discouraged if the contents look skimpy. You've pared your wardrobe down to the bones — to what really works for you. What you need now is an accurate mental image of what's in your closet. This mental image will give you direction for planning, shopping, and purchasing wisely — for adding new pieces that will continue to work together for you to your advantage.

Think of it this way. When you buy a piece of furniture, you envision your whole house, then the room and how that piece of furniture will look and work in that room. It should be the same with your wardrobe. Just as a piece of furniture becomes part of the interior design, part of the artistic composition, a piece of clothing becomes part of your exterior design and a part of your personal artistic composition.

When you have a mental image of your wardrobe and shop with that wardrobe accurately in mind, when you see an item that catches your eye, you will know immediately if you need it, will really use it, and if it will fit into and contribute to your existing wardrobe. This puts you in charge.

With an increased awareness and understanding of yourself and your wardrobe needs, you can avoid the accumulation of wardrobe orphans, and you can feel secure in the knowledge that the clothing in your closet will present you attractively and appropriately wherever you go and whatever you do. Your wardrobe will help you achieve your goals and objectives.

As you implement your wardrobe plans, learn what stores and catalogs cater to your needs, preferences, and ability to buy.

2.

Knowing about the many types of stores and clothing sources available to you will help you in finding your clothing needs.

Go to the stores where you generally shop and visit others in the area where you live. Do some comparison shopping. Compare the clothing styles and values. Ideally, choose one item carried by many clothing stores. Visit several stores, locating the item in as many as possible, noting its price and quality. Compare the same item in the same brand wherever possible. Compare the same item in different brands. Determine which stores carry the most variety, in the best quality, at the best or widest price range. There are scores of different types of stores to visit. Some are recognizably different. Others are becoming increasingly difficult to differentiate between, as distinctions have become blurred in recent years. (See Table 12–1, pages 354 through 355, and Figure 12–1.)

Through this process of comparison shopping, you will discover which stores suit your personal style and provide the type of clothing you want at the price you are willing and able to pay. With each store you scout, consider the following points:

- The type and variety of merchandise carried in the store.
- The amount of money you have available to spend on clothing.
- The convenience of shopping at that store location.
- The type of sales associates the store employs.
- The types of services the store provides.
- The business practices of the store or retailer.

Be a comparison shopper, but don't overcompare at the expense of gas, time, and energy. Shop for the brands you have been pleased with in the past, but be open to new options. Finding the best bargain for your clothing dollar is a game of sorts, and you come out the winner.

Department Stores

Department stores sell a wide assortment of merchandise for the individual and the home. Merchandise is organized into separate departments according to type — ladies' sportswear, lingerie, furniture, boys' wear, toys, handbags, cosmetics, and so forth. Like a collection of many small stores under one roof, department stores offer one-stop shopping. Volume buying and plenty of floor space allow department stores to carry a range of styles, colors, sizes, qualities, and prices.

For decades, department stores have been the dominant retailers in major metropolitan areas, with smaller branch stores serving suburban areas. Examples include Bon Marche, ZCMI, A & S, Meier and Frank, and Filene's. Many, including J. C. Penney's, Macy's, Sears, Dillard's, and Bloomingdales, are located nationwide. Department stores often serve as anchor stores within a larger shopping mall.

Department stores operate on cash or credit, with most stores offering their own line of credit to customers. Department stores usually make free services and conveniences available to their shoppers, including telephone and mail order, delivery, alterations, and personal shopping services. The cost to the store to offer these services without charge, however, is reflected in the price of the merchandise, which is moderate to high.

You need not limit yourself to shopping in departments designated for women but should also consider the teens', men's, and boys' departments as well.

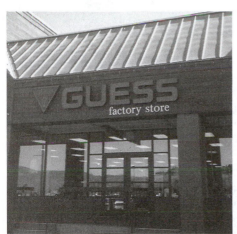

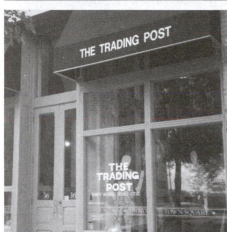

Figure 12–1a–j.

Table 12–1 Store Types

Store Types	Advantages	Disadvantages
Department stores	• Attractive, comfortable environment • Has the largest variety of departments and apparel • Wide range of prices and quality • Many services and conveniences • More likely to refund money on a returned garment purchase • Freedom to browse without pressure to buy • Excellent sales	• Slightly higher prices because of selection and services • Layout of stores and location of so many departments can be confusing • Branches of department stores may not offer as complete a line of merchandise as the central store • The cost of a more liberal return policy is often reflected in merchandise pricing • Large selection may put impulse buyers into debt
Specialty stores	• More personal attention to each shopper • Willing to special order • New fashions available sooner • More moderate-priced specialty shops in operation • Knowledgeable salespeople • Variety within the specialty	• May require more time and effort to assemble an outfit or cluster • Exchanges may be limited • Constant attention of clerks, difficult to browse • Quality varies • Range of prices is narrow and less flexible than that of department stores
Boutiques	• Unique merchandise • Knowledgeable salespersons • Individual customer service • High fashion • Often high quality	• All sizes not always available in each style • Often higher prices • Limited selection
Supermarkets and drugstores	• Clothing items that more often need to be replaced can be purchased while grocery shopping or filling a prescription • Locations are many and more convenient	• Generally cannot try on clothing • Often prepackaged clothing, more difficult to determine quality • Less variety • Super stores can be confusing
Discount stores	• Low prices all year • Can save 20–70 percent off regular retail price • Most operate on a cash or credit basis • Most have an exchange or refund policy • Usually have fitting rooms	• Styles majority of people are wearing • Clothing quality varies from low to moderate • Huge stores can be confusing • Self service • Large crowds • Unpredictable inventories due to a rapid product turnover • A full range of sizes may not be available
Off-price stores	• React quickly to market demands • Everyday discounts • Large selection • New merchandise is stocked daily • Organized into departments	• Store buys only items they can get a good deal on, unpredictable inventory • Many stores must cut or remove designers' labels • No personal attention or customer service • Often have no fitting rooms

Table 12–1 Store Types (*continued*)

Store Types	Advantages	Disadvantages
Factory outlet stores	• A designer's line may be available • Greater savings than many other discount stores • Same brands as available in department stores • Can find up-to-date clothes you need closer to the actual season • Generally good quality	• Sometimes located in remote or rural areas • May not take credit cards • Generally do not accept returns • Little to no improved customer service
Membership stores and wholesale clubs	• Low prices • Convenience when buying other items • Store will usually provide refunds	• Limited selection • Must pay a membership fee or add some percentage to the sale • Few or no services • Rapid turnover
Thrift stores	• Rare and out-of-date merchandise • Often in good condition • Good bargains if you know what to look for	• Limited selection • Less service • Takes time to find quality merchandise
Army/navy surplus stores	• Create a unique, military-style outfit • Less expensive than apparel made to look like military clothing • Garments are made to last • Stores usually take credit cards	• Unpredictable inventories • Military sizes are different
Damaged goods stores	• Many items may be fixed or worn as-is • Very inexpensive	• Imperfect clothing • No returns • Shopping for what you want is time consuming
Telephone/mail order	• Saves time and traveling expenses • Pay by credit card, check, or cash on delivery • Convenient — shop whenever and wherever you like • Large selection of catalogs and styles • Makes comparison shopping easy	• Must pay shipping costs • Cannot try clothes on • Difficult to judge quality • May cost extra to return an item • Merchandise may not be immediately available • Some mail order companies may not be legitimate
Home sale	• Personal attention • Informal	• Limited merchandise • Can feel obligated or pressured to purchase
Electronic shopping (television and computer)	• Convenient • Charge by telephone • Saves time and traveling expenses	• Home shopping shows generally use high-pressure sales tactics • Must pay shipping costs • Cannot try clothes on • Difficult to judge quality • Not everyone has a computer, a VCR, or cable television

These sections offer classic styles, quality construction, more dramatic textures and patterns in additional sizes, generally at lower cost than women's apparel, and often in better quality. Petite women often find shirts, jeans, and sweaters in sizes to fit from the boys' and teens' departments. Larger women will find men's blazers and shirts that fit more comfortably from the men's department. If you're looking for T-shirts, a jogging suit, a boxy-style blazer or jacket, women of all sizes can find good buys in the men's department. Accessories from these departments — such as gloves, scarves, and sunglasses — may suit the needs of women as well.

Specialty Stores

Specialty stores generally sell a specific type of merchandise, comparable to one department in a department store — such as ladies' apparel. Specialty stores cater to a relatively smaller clientele or narrower target market to fill a specific need. Some are larger, but many are small and owned by one or a few persons, some of whom may function as salespeople as well, fully informed about their merchandise and customers. Specialty stores are traditionally known for specialized service.

Examples of ladies' specialty stores include names like Classy Lady, RaNays, and Leonard's. Specialty stores that have evolved into national chains include The Limited, Limited Express, The Gap, Lane Bryant, Motherhood Maternity, and Naturalizer Shoes. Their private-label clothing has taken on brand recognition.

Specialty stores may even limit merchandise to a single brand or designer label. Pendleton, Liz Claiborne, and Ralph Lauren are examples of such stores. Mail-order operations — such as Talbots, Ann Taylor, Banana Republic, and Eddie Bauer — join the ranks of specialty shops with service-oriented stores in urban and mall locations.

Boutique is the name given to a relatively small and highly specialized shop — sometimes a small shop within a department store — that features innovative fashions in limited quantities at relatively higher prices. Each boutique tends to have a distinct atmosphere and a unique style of apparel and/or accessories to achieve a complete look. A boutique often has its own designer or uses a free-lance designer to provide fashions exclusive to the store.

Lingerie stores feature underwear and sleepwear for women of all ages and types. They can be, however, a good source of less expensive evening wear, lounge wear, sportswear, and swimwear in limited quantities. Elegant gowns and robes are often appropriate for parties and formal events. Loungewear in comfortable sweatshirt fabric, leotards, and body suits can be worn for exercise, play, and to the beach.

Dancewear stores sell leotards, dancing shoes, and hosiery. This is another good source for swimwear and also for summer shoes.

Sporting goods stores carry durable sportswear and outerwear, raincoats, and boots. They are particularly good places to find functional clothing for sports as well as play, such as jogging suits and bathing suits. Stores that specialize in outfitting the equestrian are relatively inexpensive suppliers of jeans, boots, and western outfits.

Craft shops and craft fairs are spilling over with hand-made clothing and accessories. Great care goes into the making of each item, such as hand-woven sweaters, hand-painted shirts, and hand-sewn leather moccasins. The artist is often on hand to take special and custom orders.

Import stores sell clothing, accessories, and baskets imported from the Orient, Middle East, Africa, and/or South America. Traditional styles, colors, and fabrics are generally all-season, relatively inexpensive, and difficult to find elsewhere. Handcrafted items are generally of good quality and made from materials not often found locally. Oriental shops carry imported items such as silk embroidered jackets, dresses, and specialty pieces like black patent Mary Jane flat-soled shoes. Pier One is a national chain of import stores featuring merchandise from the Orient.

Discount Stores

Discount stores are generally large establishments that sell merchandise at prices lower than in retail stores. These are departmentalized, self-service stores with about twenty percent of sales coming from apparel and shoes. Discount stores appeal to those shoppers who value savings over service. Lower prices can be found all year on all items in the store. National chain discounters include K Mart, Wal-Mart, and Target.

Off-price stores sell manufacturer overruns, slow sellers, and leftover goods at deep discounts from several different designers. These no-frills stores generally have low overhead and may pay for merchandise with cash on delivery, allowing them to sell for less than retail. The clothing may be from last season or the current season, or they may be slightly irregular. National chains include T.J. Maxx, Loehmann's, Marshalls, Burlington Coat Factory, Syms, Filene's Basement, Dress Barn, and Hit or Miss.

Factory outlet stores are exactly what they sound like — a single factory's or manufacturer's products are sold from an outlet store owned by the manufacturer or a broker. Cutting out the "middle man" keeps prices low — up to eighty percent less than retail year-round. The majority of merchandise is made up of the manufacturer's excess, irregulars, and flawed merchandise called "seconds." Factory outlet stores often operate from locations away from downtown and mall shopping areas.

Clearance stores are a merchant's version of a manufacturer's outlet store. Having decided to get their fair share of the sale's pie, clothes ready for clearance are shipped to a specific location and made available at significantly reduced prices.

Army/navy surplus stores carry military clothing and a variety of related goods acquired by bidding for the government's surplus stock. These clothes are built for durability and sell at some degree of discount.

Sample shops sell clothing formerly used by a sales representative for a particular manufacturer. Designer apparel is sold at or below wholesale cost, usually only a few times a year. The majority of sample clothing is size 6 or 8, and rarely is anything available over size 12.

Fabric discount stores carry surplus items, irregulars, and seconds that allow for the low prices.

Membership stores, also known as **wholesale or warehouse clubs** are a cross between a department store and a discount store, but require a membership fee granting the right to purchase anything in the store. Memberships are fairly easy to obtain. Membership stores sell only clothing that they may obtain in large volume and can sell for a low price. Fast-growing chains include Price Club, Sam's Club, Pace, and Costco.

Damaged goods stores sell items that have been damaged during manufacturing, shipping, fires, floods, and other disasters. Some of the clothes may be worn as-is while others need to be cleaned or repaired.

Supermarket Stores

Supermarkets are primarily food stores, but many have expanded to include general merchandise, including basic clothing items. Like department stores, they have become one-stop-shopping facilities. Similarly, **drug and variety stores** sell primarily drugs and cosmetics but also carry clothing as a convenience to shoppers. Both types of stores carry prepackaged items such as hosiery, underwear, and beach sandals. Both have evolved into national chains such as Albertsons, A & P, Kroger, Safeway, and Smith Food King.

Specialty superstores generally offer only one to three types of merchandise in huge quantities at discount prices lower than any other stores in the area. They dominate the market for their specific type of merchandise within the region. Companies such as The Limited and Talbots are among the first in this category.

Hypermarkets are enormous and feature virtually all types of merchandise including clothing — in theory 80 percent of the general consumer's needs in the form of time-tested, fast-moving products. Carrefour and Wal-Mart's Hypermart USA are examples of this growing trend in selling.

Used/Secondhand Stores

Used or secondhand stores traditionally sell donated clothing. Some may be well-worn while other articles may be fashionable and worn once or twice before being passed on. Because yesterday's fashions soon become today's trend clothes, secondhand stores are popular with price- *and* fashion-conscious shoppers.

Vintage clothing stores sell used and new apparel that is often faddish in style. The clothing sold may come from manufacturers' closeouts, the military, or previous wearers, and is arranged in bins in a store with a style all its own.

Antique clothing stores carry pricey, older clothing with historical value. Styles from the Victorian and Edwardian eras are among the classics to be found in these stores.

Thrift shops are operated by churches, hospitals, and charity organizations such as the Salvation Army, either full-time or annually. These sell donated, used items as well as some new articles that may have been donated by a department store or boutique. All profits from the sales go to a charitable purpose.

Auctions are held to sell the possessions of someone who has passed away, a family who is moving, or another private party. "Dead parcel" branches of the U.S. Postal Service also conduct auctions to sell bins of unclaimed clothing, furniture, and other lost or damaged mail. The buyer must purchase an entire numbered bin for the few desired items it contains. Postal auctions are held approximately eight times per year.

Estate sales place high priority on selling furniture. They can, however, be a good source for high-quality clothing at bargain prices. Estate sales are operated by a professional who appraises and sells the contents of a household. They are similar to garage sales, with the exception being that the merchandise is of better quality and everything in the house is being sold.

Rummage sales and garage sales feature some of the lowest prices available in clothing for the entire family. Shopping early will ensure a greater selection of classic styles and vintage clothing. The sellers are usually quite anxious to make a sale, so bargaining is possible.

Flea markets, or swap meets, offer people a place to sell merchandise on a part-time basis and without a high investment. Flea markets are usually held on weekends in a large parking lot, large open building, or race track. Traveling salespeople set up a booth or table and sell anything from tube socks to fake Rolexes to brand-name clothing. The open-market atmosphere is fun, but let the buyer beware; merchandise is not guaranteed or returnable.

Dry cleaners almost always have unclaimed clothing in storage and would like to discard it. By asking permission to rummage through the piles of forgotten clothes, you will be doing the cleaner a favor while finding many great treasures. Make offers comparable to secondhand prices.

Resale or consignment stores accept slightly worn or never-worn clothes from the consumer who bought them to resell as secondhand. The consignee and the store owner generally split the selling price of the item, fifty-fifty. At a consignment store, a shopper can often find a higher class atmosphere and high-quality merchandise one or two seasons old.

Renting clothes is an economical way to wear high-fashion gowns, furs, and jewelry for a special occasion. Rather than buying something expensive that will be worn only once or a few times, customers can make a statement by renting an outfit that will be remembered long after the event is over at a fraction of full cost.

Direct to the Home

Telephone/mail-order catalog companies use catalogs to sell their merchandise to consumers. No longer limited to serving rural populations with little interest in fashion, they target the various types of professional women in various stages of life. There are literally hundreds of specialty catalogs available, including J. Crew, Clifford & Wills, Spiegel, and Carol Reed. Merchandise is shipped to your home in a week or less. Many department stores and specialty stores have added separate catalog divisions in addition to their traditional retail operations. Examples include Sears, Nordstrom, Neiman Marcus, Bloomingdale's, Ann Taylor, and Page Boy Maternity.

Figure 12–2. Catalogs are becoming more popular as shopping options for the modern consumer. (*Courtesy of L. L. Bean, Inc.*)

In-home selling offers merchandise sold out of a residence location. Manufacturers pay individuals a percentage to sell a line of clothing, generally from their own homes. The manufacturers also supply advertising materials, samples, racks, and hangers. The homemaker is encouraged to invite friends, family, and acquaintances to shop out of her home. Long-time leader in this venture is Avon. Doncaster is an American company featuring cluster groups of coordinates at upper-moderate prices. Madeleine Direct evolved from a German-based catalog company distributing in America and features fashion-forward classic clothes with a distinctively European flair.

Electronic shopping has arrived at home via television, video, and computer. Shopping at home on TV shopping channels like the Home Shopping Club and QVC have become a major force in their own right. It is comfortable, quick, and easy. When you see something you like on screen, you call the 800 number and order with your credit card before the offer is taken off the air. More and more designers, as well as department stores and major media companies, are catching on to consumer enthusiasm and exploring the possibility of their own home shopping shows. Video catalogs are available that take you on a tour of a store in a faraway place and then allow you to mail-order merchandise. Video catalog channels are about to become the marketing story of the decade. A personal computer can link up to data bases that give information on products and ordering. The possibilities are endless as technology is ever-increasing.

Miscellaneous Sources of Clothing

Custom-made clothing may be purchased directly from professional tailors — in Hong Kong for example. The country's free port, low taxes, and one of the world's largest pools of tailoring talent make this an excellent place to buy custom-made suits, shirts, and coats at about half the price you would pay an American tailor. The best bet in getting the perfect fit in your favorite style would be to visit the tailors in Hong Kong. However, there are also traveling Hong Kong tailors who will show you fabric samples, take your measurements, and send your suit a few weeks later; and many tailors have mail-order operations.

Hand-me-downs are usually thought of in terms of a large family passing clothing along from one child to the next; however, passing clothing on among adults is also a smart way to expand a wardrobe. Friends and family who have changed sizes, careers, or life-styles may have clothes unworn but worth wearing.

For example, *"I love my family, but I hate their presents,"* confided my student. *"How can I tell them I don't like the clothes they give me?"*

You don't tell them. They might feel terrible, and you'll feel worse. You do, however, need to teach them what you like in clothes.

A clothing gift can present a package of problems for a variety of good reasons. Maybe the clothes don't fit. Maybe you dislike the color, fabric, or style. A friend recounted the reaction of her daughter upon receiving a fuzzy angora sweater from an aunt. Tears welled in the child's eyes, revealing her utter disappointment, as she quietly said, "Oh Mother, you know how I hate hairy things."

Maybe the gift is something you don't really need or want. A young man told how he anticipated getting a much-needed pair of work shoes, but his new bride proudly presented him with an elegant pair of black leather wingtips. "They're just like my good ones," he blurted out. "I don't need another pair."

Maybe the item of apparel doesn't go with anything you already own. Maybe you have nowhere to wear it. One husband candidly commented, "What am I supposed to do with this?"

All too often we select a gift according to our own preferences, needs, and wants, without giving serious consideration to those of the receiver.

This brings me to the problem of guilt. If the giver is a good friend or family member, you may feel obligated to wear the clothes, regardless of how you look or feel in them. On the other hand, you may refuse to wear them, thus offending the giver and feeling doubly guilty yourself.

To avoid these problems, learn to drop a few careful hints about your needs and preferences. Don't keep your desires to yourself. "Daydream" out loud instead.

Keep a wardrobe planning list and a file of clippings illustrating desired items. Show them to your family once in a while. I predict the people who've been wondering what to get you will want to help you achieve your goals by giving you something on your list.

Comment periodically on the clothing worn by others — "I really like . . ." or "that doesn't work for me because. . . ." Always include that one-liner why, and gradually family members will gain a better understanding of your needs and preferences. It's also important to let them know if your tastes have changed. How about, "I used to love rust, but lately I prefer plum and dark purple."

There's no guarantee these methods will get you exactly what you want for your birthday, but your chances are certainly better than before.

TIP

☞

FROM THE PROS

Gifts are an important source of clothing, and you need to like and make good use of gifts. However, gifts can present problems.

3.

Practice shopping strategies that prepare you to make wise purchases.

❦

The first guideline for smart shopping is to buy only what you need. Make a list of items you need to complete your cluster or add on to your expanded wardrobe. Be specific about the item, its style, color, fabric, what you expect it to go with, and the estimated cost. Keep your list in your closet area, perhaps tacked to the inside of your closet door — or in your purse or planner.

Prioritize your list according to each item's importance.

For example, *perhaps you need a blazer and slacks, but both are expensive. Decide which you need most and put it at the top of your list.*

Shopping can be distracting due to people, displays, and merchandise all around you. Your shopping list will:

- Keep you on target.
- Help you pass up tempting displays.
- Keep you from getting sidetracked into departments you don't need.
- Prevent you from impulse buys that whittle away your budget and keep you from being able to buy the item you really need.

Don't make your list too long. You want to shop for several items each trip to save time, but don't let yourself get so tired or rushed you buy something you really don't need — or something that's only close to what you need. If charcoal is what you need, don't settle for navy or black. Review your list before you go shopping and then stick to it.

Plan Ahead

Whether shopping at regular prices, discounts, or sale prices, plan ahead. Armed with your cluster plansheet and shopping list you are ready to preplan your shopping trip. It's easy to get tired when shopping, but having a cluster plan in mind makes all the difference in any shopping excursion. You don't spend the entire day running around from store to store accomplishing nothing. Knowing the stores available in your area, and the ones that suit you best, you can zero in on the ones you think are the most likely to have what you want. Further prioritize your list according to the stores and departments in stores, so you get to the most important, difficult-to-find, or fast-selling items first and save on retraced steps and zigzagging back and forth across town.

Do Your Homework

There is an incredible selection of clothing and accessories to choose from. It can be very confusing. To get a preview of what's in the stores, shop through a few fashion magazines and catalogs.

Remember that what you see in many fashion magazines is more extreme than real-life people are intended to wear, more so than what will be found in most stores. Leaf through the magazines several times, focusing on one detail of design, dress, or accessory at a time. Pull out pictures of clothing you are attracted to and put them into your style file for future reference.

Call it research or snoop shopping, but study store windows and floor displays. Browse inside the store. See how the clothes are being put together. Note the styles, colors, fabrics, and patterns. Study which accessories are being shown.

Use the Telephone

Call ahead and around to stores to see if they have what you want — in the brand, style, size, and color — or if they can get it for you. Ask for directions to the store, particularly if you live in a large city. Ask about store hours, parking, credit card, check, layaway, and return policies. Consider ordering from the store catalog rather than going into the store in person. Ask to speak to the manager or department buyer if you feel you aren't getting the right answers or service.

T I P
❦
F R O M   T H E   P R O S

If time is at a premium, rely on the telephone, telephone book, and store catalog or newspaper advertisements. This approach to shopping is particularly effective when ordering replacement or duplicate items such as stockings, lingerie, and cosmetics. Save a sales slip and refer to the information on it when placing your order. Larger stores often deliver free of charge. However, if time is really tight, a reasonable delivery charge is worth the service to you.

Shopping Alone or with a Friend

Take a very good friend or family member shopping with you only when you want a second opinion or need someone to stifle your impulse to buy. Even then, make sure that it is a person whose opinion you respect, someone who understands you, someone who will be objective and brutally honest with you, and someone who will not be a distraction. It may help if that person's personal style is similar to yours. Shop alone on longer shopping trips. Your time will be spent more efficiently. Include children only on short trips for gifts or personal items of their own to avoid overexposure to the vastly tempting array of merchandise.

Personal Shopping Service

Take advantage of personalized shopping services that may be available for extra help if time is short, if you are shopping out of town, or if the item you want is hard to find. The personal shopper can take your list over the phone and assemble everything in one dressing room. You simply join her to try on and make your decision. Make sure the personal shopper is qualified, and remember, she is a sales associate for one store, and that one store may not have all you need.

When to Go Shopping

Don't shop when you are tired, ill, stressed, or depressed. Nothing will look right to you, your judgment will be impaired, or you will settle for anything just so you can go home. Try not to shop just after eating when your figure is filled out more than usual. Don't shop at the last minute for something you need, or when you're rushed. You'll buy something out of frustration or desperation and end up with an expensive mistake. If you're leaving on vacation, don't worry about getting all the items you need before you go. Vacation time is a wonderful time to do a bit of shopping.

Shop when you're feeling in the mood and energetic. Do allow yourself enough time to avoid being hurried into making a decision. Allow at least two to three hours for serious shopping. More expensive items deserve more time to consider. If you hate to shop, schedule a once-a-season excursion. Shop in season if you need the best selection. Shop after the season if you need the best buy. If you're putting together a whole cluster, you'll need an entire day to complete it, including accessories. Anticipate your needs and buy ahead if you see exactly the right thing.

Stores are generally more crowded at lunchtime, late afternoon, during the early evening hours, on weekends, and on special sale days. Plan your shopping time when stores are the least crowded, usually weekday mornings before 11:30 early in the week, between 2:30 and 4:00 p.m., at dinnertime between 5:30 and 7 p.m., and late evening, after 8:30. You'll find that salespeople have more time to give you undivided attention then. You'll feel you have more time to make decisions. Shop when it rains, when everyone else stays home. It's a great time to have your favorite store all to yourself. If shopping is an ordeal for you, it may be worth it to you to take a morning or two off from work and do it properly.

What to Wear Shopping

Don't go out for any serious shopping if you look messy. Nothing you try on is going to look good to you. Take time to fix your hair and put on makeup, if you usually wear it. Dress in something you like and feel good wearing. (See Figure 12–3.)

Dress comfortably but attractively. Wear lingerie that supports your figure properly. Wear hosiery if you're shopping for dress clothes. Don't wear high heels. They weren't made for walking. When your feet hurt you can't concentrate on anything else. Wear comfortable, slip-on, lower-heel shoes for soon-to-be-tired feet — but make them shoes that will look good with the clothes you're going to try on.

Wear whatever you might be trying to match or coordinate with. When you have to try on clothing, wear

Figure 12–3. Dressing comfortably for shopping makes it more enjoyable and successful. *(Courtesy Eddie Bauer; photographer G. Remington)*

clothes that slip easily on and off. Don't wear lots of layers you have to repeatedly take off and put back on. Keep it simple. Avoid wearing anything with lots of zippers, buttons, hooks, or buckles. A loose-fitting, flared skirt is nice to wear if there are no private fitting rooms available. You can simply try on a skirt or pants under the skirt you're wearing.

What to Take Shopping

Don't weigh yourself down, but do carry a large shoulder bag or zippered tote bag to hold your cash, checkbook, credit cards, shopping list, small notebook, fabric swatches snipped from seam allowances of current clothing, or garments to color match. Take a calculator, measuring tape, even a map if you're unfamiliar with the area. Take a sheer scarf to cover your head and keep makeup off the merchandise. It'll save your hair as well. Take any special underwear needed to give you the right fit. If you plan to try on something to go with clothes you already own, take the older clothes along. It's better to have the real thing than to try to remember or imagine what it looks like. If you're shopping for tops to go under a jacket, take the jacket with you to evaluate the combination of styles, colors, and textures. Take essential accessories to test the looks of an outfit.

Store Layout

Become familiar with the store's layout. Don't hesitate to ask for directions if you are unsure about the location of particular items. Go directly to the department or area of the store that houses the item you need. Stay focused. After you've accomplished your shopping goal you can browse at your leisure, feeling satisfied that your shopping trip was time well spent.

Selecting the Merchandise

Locate the items you want to try on. Check color, quality, and care of these items, discarding any that don't meet your standards. (See Table 12–2.) Make sure garments fit your life-style, personal style, budget, and existing wardrobe. Discard those that don't fit. Walk through the store again, carrying the pieces you are interested in. Find coordinating pieces. Regardless of whether you're interested in the coordinates, you will get a better idea of how the piece will actually look when an outfit is complete.

Sales Assistance

Allow or invite a clerk or sales associate to help you only when you're ready, but don't be intimidated by her suggestions. Remember: Her goal is to sell anything; your goal is to buy right for you. If you're not ready, simply say, "I'm still looking, thank you," or "I'll let you know when I'm ready." This goes double in the fitting room. Don't be pressured into making a decision. You've got lots of things to look at and consider before you decide to buy or not to buy. Demand good service. Be specific about what you need. Don't assume that all salespeople are equally familiar with or knowledgeable about the merchandise. Ask for whoever knows the characteristics of the various brands, for specifics about a particular brand, for advice about fit or the care of the fabric, and so forth.

TIP
FROM THE PROS

Get acquainted with and befriend the sales associates. They can alert you to incoming merchandise and upcoming sales. You'll have first choice to both new and sale priced merchandise. Once acquainted with you and your needs or preferences, some will pull pieces they know meet your needs and schedule a time for you to come in and try them out. This type of personal attention is rare and worth cultivating.

The Fitting Room

- Locate the largest private fitting room, preferably one with three-way, full-length mirrors.

- Try clothing on as close to the way you'll wear it as possible, with the appropriate underwear, accessories, and so forth.

- See how clothes look on you as you walk, sit, bend, raise arms overhead, stretch, swing. Check the front, back, and side views of the garment. If you are trying on activewear, go through the appropriate motions. Look at yourself as you squint: What areas stand out? (See Table 12–3, page 364.)

- Feel the fit and comfort of the clothes. Close your eyes. Do the clothes feel good? Do they feel tight or twisted any place? If so, open your eyes and focus on those areas. Does the garment lie smooth or do wrinkles indicate poor fit? Does the garment hang straight?

- Check fit and quality by examining each part of the garment by sight and feel. Check the neck and collar, which are hardest to alter but most readily observed by others. Check the shoulders, upper back, chest, bust, sleeves. Check darts, seamlines, grain, closures, design details, waistline, and hemline.

- Walk into the corridor or main selling areas. Look at yourself eight to ten feet from the mirror. Distance gives you a realistic view of what others will see. Check the color in different lighting. Dressing rooms are notorious for poor lighting and mirrors. Make sure you look the way you want to be seen.

Fitting Cues

In the fitting room or when fitting home-sewn garments, check the garment for wrinkles. Wrinkles provide clues about fit. There are two types of wrinkles: tight and loose.
Tight wrinkles mean the garment is too small.

- Tight horizontal wrinkles mean the garment is too small around the body.

- Tight vertical wrinkles mean the garment is too short.

Loose wrinkles mean the garment is too big.

- Loose horizontal wrinkles mean the garment is too long at that point.

- Loose vertical wrinkles mean the garment is too big around the body.

Fitting Standards

People have different standards of fit. Some insist on custom fit, others require minor changes in ready-to-wear, still others are completely satisfied with clothing right off the rack. You must determine what standards you will accept. The standards given in Table 12–4, pages 365 through 366, are universal.

Table 12–2 Finding Quality in Ready-to-Wear *Buy the Best You Can Afford*

	Definition and General Info	Good Quality Indicators	Poor Quality Indicators
Fabric	All fibers, natural, manmade, and combinations of the two, can be made into fabrics of different quality — low to high.	Good quality fabric feels good, is free of flaws, and the weave holds together. The fabric is appropriate for the garment: firm enough to support the shape of garment for tailored styles or pliable enough to drape, gather, or flare for soft clothes.	Poor quality fabric may be flimsy, scratchy, or brittle. It may have fewer threads per square inch and be full of sizing or other fillers which wash out.
Grain Line	Grain line refers to the direction of the yarns in the woven cloth and the loops in knitted fabrics. Grain controls the way fabric hangs on the body. Clothing cut off-grain looks pulled to the sides, puckered, twisted, saggy, baggy, or unbalanced.	Good quality lengthwise grain lines run perpendicular to the floor at center front and center back of the garment. Quality crosswise grain lines are parallel to the floor across the chest, upper back, and hip. Bias grains run exactly diagonally. Quality linings and facings will also be cut on the grain. If a garment is cut on grain but does not fit properly, the grain line will slope or bow out of line. Altering should correct both fit and grain line.	Poor quality grain lines will not be parallel, perpendicular, or exactly diagonal to the floor, but somewhere in between. Garments cut off-grain will never hang right on the body in spite of pressing and adjusting. Washing usually makes off-grain worse.
Cut	Less expensive clothing is cut to use less fabric. Quality clothing is often cut using more fabric, with wider seam and hem allowances and more variety in design.	Good quality cuts match stripes and plaids and place prints artistically.	Poor quality cuts mismatch stripes and plaids and may place bold prints poorly, drawing attention to body areas you'd rather minimize.
Construction	Top quality construction produces good fit and smooth lines, allowing observers to concentrate on the wearer.	Quality construction produces smooth, secure, flat collars, cuffs, lapels, plackets, casing, waistbands, zippers, and button openings. Quality construction results in nonbulky, straight, and smooth gathers, pleats, tucks, vents, darts, and slits.	Poor quality construction creates puckers and twists that draw attention to themselves and the body parts where they lie. Poor quality construction produces seams and darts that pucker or twist, collars or lapels that bubble or ripple, design features that are bulky or won't lie flat.
Pressing	Pressing can flatten or shape fabrics.	A well-pressed garment holds its original shape and is free of wrinkles, folds, bubbles, puckers, or pleats not in the original design.	Poor quality pressing can ruin the fit of the finest clothes, shrinking, stretching, or creasing the wrong areas.

Table 12–3 General Fitting Information

	Fit	Sizing	Shopping
Undergarments	Undergarments should: • fit comfortably close — no binding or constricting • never ride up or down • be large enough: for example, too tight bras cause pain Straps and elastic openings should: • be adjustable • not cut into body causing bulges • never show	Different brands and styles will fit differently, so try several sizes. People may need different sizes after pregnancy, illness, exercise, weight gain, and so forth.	Periodically ask department or specialty store professionals to fit you. Learn from the pros. Once you know how to shop for undergarments, check at discount and chain stores as well as at sales. Catalogs and lingerie shops may have a wider range of sizes and styles. Always try on bras and slips to check fit.
Outergarments	Outerwear requires "wearing ease" to allow movement. When trying garments on, pinch excess fabric. Clothes that fit will have ease: 2–4" chest, 1–1½" waist, 2–4" hips. The armhole will not constrict or bind. Larger people tend to need more ease. Additional "design ease" may be built into garment, which is a matter of style and taste. Make sure minimum ease is present. Remember: Too tight and too loose clothing make people look bigger.	Try larger and smaller sizes because manufacturers' and designers' sizes differ. When your top and bottom are not the same size, buy separates in different sizes. Buy a larger size if you plan to wear the item over more than one layer or if it is cotton, linen, or silk, which may shrink 2–3 percent.	Find stores, brands, and designers that fit you, then shop for them. Continue looking after you find a few favorites. Ask people wearing what you like where they shop. Consider phone orders from catalogs or store ads. Catalogs may offer more sizes than stores. If in doubt, order two sizes and return the one that doesn't fit.
Shoes	Toe: Shoes should be ½" longer than longest toe. Check by pressing thumb on tip of shoe and wiggling toe. Sides: Sides of shoe should fit smoothly against sides of feet. Ball: Widest part of shoe should fit widest part of foot, the ball. Arch: The shoe's arch should match your arch without pressure. Heel: The heel should be comfortably snug and stay in place when walking. If shoes gap at sides while you are walking, they are too wide. Make sure the foot doesn't slide forward or the heel move up and down.	Shoe sizes vary among manufacturers, so don't depend on size to find the best fit. Ask the clerk to measure both feet since few feet are exactly the same. Buy to fit the larger foot and put an innersole pad in the other shoe if necessary.	Shop for shoes later in the day when feet are swollen; buy when feet are largest. Catalogs often have a wider range of sizes than regular stores. Shoes can get mixed up at the store, especially during sales. Make sure you leave with a matched pair.

Table 12–4 Specific Fitting Standards

Garment Area or Detail	Fitting Standards
Necklines	Should fit around the base of the neck unless designed otherwise, without cutting into the neck, wrinkling, or gapping. Wide or lowered necklines should lie flat and snug on the chest.
Collars and neckbands	Should fit comfortably around the neck. When buttoned, one finger should fit easily into the neckline. One-half inch of a shirt collar should show above a suit collar at center back.
Shoulder seams	Should lie flat on top of the shoulder, bisect the neck and shoulder, and end at the joint unless design lines dictate otherwise. Shoulder pads should appear natural, well placed, and not too small or too large.
Armholes	Should not bind, gap, or cut into the arm, but allow easy movement. Unless design lines dictate otherwise, the lowest point should be 1 to 2 inches below the armpit.
Armhole seams	Should cross the shoulder at the joint and follow the back arm crease unless design dictates otherwise. Jacket armhole seams may extend ½ to 1 inch and coat seams 1 to 1½ inches beyond the shoulder joint.
Sleeves	Should lie smooth around the arm with 1½-inch ease. One finger should fit easily under short sleeves, and elbows should have plenty of room to move in long sleeves. Elbow darts or fullness should be over elbow. Long sleeves should end at the wrist bone when the arm is bent at the elbow, and be no longer than the bend of the wrist when the arm is hanging straight. Short sleeves should add to the pleasing proportions of the bodice. Set-in sleeve caps should have no puckers or wrinkles, and the fullness should be even between front and back.
Upper back	Should fit smoothly with no bubbles, wrinkles, or bulges with enough ease to make movement comfortable.
Waists and waistbands	Should fit comfortably when standing, yet have 1- to 1½-inch ease for sitting. Two fingers should slip easily inside the waistband.

Basic Lines

Table 12–4 Specific Fitting Standards (*continued*)

Garment Area or Detail	Fitting Standards
Seams	
Center front and back seams	Should be perpendicular to the floor and be centered on the body. They should not curve or pull to the side.
Side seams	Should appear perpendicular to the waist and to the floor with no pulling or curving.
Lengthwise grain	Should follow front and back seams unless the skirt is cut on the bias. Should hang down the center of the sleeve above the elbow and down the crease of slacks.
Crosswise grain	Should parallel the floor at the hem, hip, upper arm, upper back, and chest.
Design Features	
Lapels	Should lie flat and be symmetrical. Should not gap open.
Darts	Should point toward and end 1 to 1½ inches from the fullest part of the curve being fitted. Should taper and end smoothly.
Pockets	Should lie flat without pulling or gapping open.
Closures	Should be straight and smooth without pulling, curving, or gapping. Front button closures should have one button at the fullest part of the bust.
Gathers	Should be even and tiny with no bunching or grouping. Gathers should fall evenly.
Pleats, slits, tucks, and vents	Should hang flat, closed, and straight against the body, opening only for movement. Should not pull open.
Linings	Should be cut on grain, not show, lie smooth, yet allow for ease of movement.
Clothing Articles	
Jackets	Should have room to fit easily over shirts and sweaters, to button without strain.
Coats	Should be roomy enough to fit over suits and jackets. Hems should fall about 1 inch longer than skirts.
Skirts	Should have 2-inch ease around the hips, should hang straight from the waist rather than cup around stomach, buttocks, or thighs. Skirt hems should be in proportion to the figure without crossing the widest part of the calf.
Pants and trousers	Should hang smoothly from the waist with ample room for the abdomen, thighs, and buttocks and with correct length for crotch. If wrinkles appear in pants when standing straight, check fit. Hems should brush the top of shoes in front, tapering to the top of heels in back unless designed otherwise.

Quick Fixes

When clothing doesn't fit quite right, try these tips.

- Add or replace shoulder pads. Replace the outdated gigantic shoulder pads of a few years ago with smaller pads.
- Adjust the length of sleeves by hemming, rolling, or pushing them up.
- Add scarves, jewelry, belts, or other garments to change the look.
- Layer with sweaters or jackets.
- Shorten the hem.
- Move a button or hook to allow more or less ease.

Altering to Get a Better Fit

Alteration is the process of changing certain parts of a garment to fit a particular person. Sometimes, minor alterations by a skilled person can make a garment look custom-made.

- Insist that the alterationist, not the salesperson, do the fitting.
- Once you know what should be altered, ask about prices, which vary widely. Ask for a total price rather than by piece or by hour.
- Determine when you can pick up your altered clothes. Some alterations can be completed while you are shopping, others require several days or weeks.
- Ask the alterationist to check and repair all buttons, buttonholes, snaps, hooks, and belt loops.
- Ask that loose threads be removed.
- If the buttons are unusual, ask the store to order additional ones.
- Try the garment on before leaving the store. Make sure it fits properly.

After Leaving the Fitting Room

- Return unwanted merchandise to the sales associate if she has not been in steady attendance and taken clothes away. She will rehang and restock your rejects.
- Take the merchandise you have chosen to buy to the check-out desk, pay the sales associate, and thank her. Ask about return policies just in case.
- Care for your new purchases by having them folded or hung carefully in protective bags. If you plan to continue shopping and won't need the new clothes for coordinating, store them carefully in the trunk of the car rather than carrying them around and adding more purchases. They will perform better if handled less. Or ask the sales associate to hold them until you are ready to leave.
- If you found a hard-to-fit item like slacks that fits you well, buy several pairs in different colors. The extra cost now will be off-set in time and money savings in the future.
- Save brand tags from clothes that fit you well. Write the store or catalog name on the tag to simplify the next search.

4.

Develop sales savvy with an understanding of sales terms, types of sales, and procedures.

There was a time when you could set your calendar according to the sales. There were the big semi-annual events in January and July, and smaller sales timed around the various holidays — Washington's birthday, May Day, Mother's Day, Veterans' Day, and so on. Now there are sales every day. There's always something on sale. The reason behind this is competition. Every store competes for the customer's attention. Sales attract customers, and customers buy the merchandise. Just as stores make sales work for them, you can make sales work for you.

Almost all merchandise has a time each year when new styles are introduced and selection is best. Likewise, nearly all merchandise goes on sale at some time during the year.

These times occur on a regular schedule. As new styles are about to arrive, the older styles must go to create room — and the sale begins. (See Table 12–5, page 369.)

How to Read the Ads

Advertising is part of everyday life. (See Figure 12–4.) A good ad can lead you quickly to what you're looking for, saving you hours or days of searching around for it. An ad, however, can also confuse and confound you. It can rush you off to buy something simply because the ad looked or sounded so appealing.

Sale ads can be the trickiest type to deal with because we all like a sale and because the ads often use words we don't fully understand. Learning what these terms mean protects you. This helps you determine whether the purchase is good or not — whether you're saving money or not.

Sale is the word that signals regular store merchandise has been marked down. Initial markup on merchandise pays for store overhead, personnel, services, maintenance, and so forth. Later markdowns to move remaining merchandise may range from 10 or 20 percent to 25, 30, 50, and 75 percent below regular retail price. As a shopper, you need to be aware that some stores mark up simply to mark down. The markdown does not represent a real price break. Find out how long the merchandise has been available. If it's only been available for a week or a month, it's probably not a true markdown.

Regularly priced implies that if an item is marked "regularly $30," and is "now $19," the $30 price must be what the item sold for before the markdown. It might, however, mean the sale price is only temporary, and the item will return to a higher price when the sale ends. "Regularly priced" may also mean the item was priced so high initially that the sale price represents true value and not a marked down discount.

Figure 12–4. Some ads don't mention essential price information for fashion-forward merchandise. *(Courtesy Neiman Marcus)*

Table 12–5 Season and Sales Calendar

Clothing Item	Jan.	Feb.	Mar.	Apr.	May	June	July	Aug.	Sept.	Oct.	Nov.	Dec.
Boots	¢	¢						$$	$$			
Coats	¢		¢				$$	$$	$$	¢		¢
Cosmetics	¢						¢					
Dresses	¢		$$	$$	¢	¢		$$	¢/$$		¢	
Evening clothes	¢									$$	$$	¢
Fabrics	¢		$$				¢	$$	$$			
Furs	¢	¢						¢	¢	$$	$$	
Gloves	¢	¢							$$			
Handbags	¢	¢	$$		¢		¢		$$	¢		
Hats		¢	$$	¢			¢	$$				
Hosiery		¢	¢			¢				¢		
Housecoats				¢								
Jewelry	¢	¢				¢					$$	
Lingerie	¢				¢		¢	$$		$$		
Luggage			¢							¢		
Rainwear				¢		¢			$$			
Robes	¢			¢						$$		
Scarves	¢		$$						$$			
Shoes	¢		$$		¢		¢	$$		¢		¢
Skiwear			¢					$$				
Sleepwear	¢		$$				¢	$$				
Suits	¢			$$			¢	¢	$$			
Sweaters	¢								$$			
Summerwear				$$			¢	¢	¢			
Swimwear			$$				¢	¢			$$	
Umbrellas	¢								$$			
Underwear	¢				¢	¢		$$				
Winterwear	¢	¢						$$	$$			

$$ New, best selection
¢ On sale, best prices

Selling at cost is a ploy unless the item is an intentional loss leader. No business can stay in business if it is continually "selling at cost." Investigate further.

List price, suggested retail price, and below list price are phrases manufacturers may use in recommending a reasonable selling price. You, however, cannot know if a tag price is evidence or the illusion of a good deal. Look beyond suggested list prices. Look only at the sale price and compare it to prices of similar merchandise at competing stores.

Comparable value refers to merchandise that is similar to but not identical to merchandise selling at a comparable or higher price. The retailer feels it has a $30 item comparable to a $50 item somewhere else. You may be getting a good buy, but it pays to compare for yourself.

Irregulars are items for sale with a slight flaw or defect in the color, weave or knit, or size. It may be a dirt mark that makes the item irregular. While you know the item isn't perfect, you may not be able to determine what the defect is. It is important to discover the flaw so you can assess its effect on the use or wear-life of the garment. In the case of minor flaws, barely visible, you can save significantly without concern. Hosiery, underwear, and sleepwear are regularly available as "irregulars."

Seconds are generally items for sale that are more visibly flawed than an irregular, such as a run, tear, mend, or color loss. Consider carefully before you buy.

As is refers to merchandise that has been damaged. It is for sale as it currently is, without improvement or repair.

Everything Must Go! This phrase means the retailer wants or needs very badly to sell out every item in the store. The question to ask is, "Why?"

Wholesale buying is not generally available to consumers. Advertising of this sort may actually refer to average merchandise at average price, not real wholesale rates.

Below wholesale means the seller claims to have bought the merchandise for below even wholesale price and can, therefore, pass the savings on. Investigate before buying. Check for irregulars and seconds.

Types of Sales

Knowing the meaning behind these sale names helps you understand the nature of the sale.

Preseason sales take place soon after new merchandise arrives and before the need for it really arrives — such as boots in August and swimsuits in February or March. Preseason sales are usually limited to a few items. Save department store catalogs from the previous year to determine if the preseason sales offer you any bargain prices.

Promotional sales occur early in the season — February for spring, July for fall — when selection is good. They're designed to get you to buy early. Items may be sold at a reduced price, only to go up later when the item becomes regularly available. Expect reductions of 15 to 20 percent. If merchandise is held over from the previous year, the markdown should be at 30 percent off.

One-day sales are considered promotional but for a limited period of time. Regular merchandise is reduced for the period of one day, 10 to 15 percent, possibly higher. After the sale day, prices go back up to the norm. Bargains are available, but you'll have to brave the crowds to do it.

Special purchase sales take place at any time and feature new merchandise bought at a lower price from the manufacturer and brought into the store at a reduced price. Items are often of lower quality, but may be pre- or post-season goods. Be cautious.

Stimulating sales are intended to stimulate selling during slow periods of time. They may go by differing names — August Coat Sale, January White Sale, Anniversary Sale, and so forth. In truth, the After-Christmas and After-Easter sales are held not so much to move the merchandise and make room for the new, as they are to lure the customers back into the stores in what would otherwise be a slack selling season.

Clearance sale refers to regular store merchandise offered at a lower price to clear it out. This should be goods that are going out of style, left over from the previous season, or discontinued. Markdowns are generally 25 to 50 percent. It is not a true clearance sale if new merchandise has been brought in for the sale. Investigate. Ask questions.

End-of-season clearance sales held in January/February and July/August traditionally offer the biggest markdowns with bargains galore because merchandise has to be cleared out to make room for the coming season's new merchandise. Most seasonal sales begin long before the current season is over. This is prime time to pick up wardrobe classics.

Warehouse sales occur when merchandise is marked down and sold out of a retailer's warehouse. Merchandise is not available in stores at the reduced price.

Manufacturer's closeout occurs when a company needs to get rid of a large amount of merchandise. Perhaps the product is discontinued, perhaps reorders did not come in, or production was late and retail stores refused delivery. The company offers the merchandise at a discount as low as 50 percent off the regular price — often the wholesale price.

Liquidation sale or going-out-of-business sale implies the store owner is going out of business and needs to dispose of or liquidate all merchandise. Be wary. This type of sale may last for months, even years, being a standard way of doing business for less scrupulous companies. Stores that continually feature liquidation sales often offer lower-quality merchandise at prices still too high.

On Sale

If economy is important to you, "on sale" is the best way to get quality clothing for less money. Don't, however, go to a sale if you don't need anything. A sale tag doesn't give you a green light to buy. Sales racks are often stocked with clothes in styles, colors, or fabrics that are unflattering at any price.

To shop the sales like the pros, begin by doing your homework — your research. Scout your favorite stores early in the season. Scan the catalogs. Become familiar with what is being sold and at what prices. Don't hesitate to shop department stores and specialty shops you consider too pricey. Sale priced, you can get high-quality clothing and an improved image at a lower cost. Try on the best possible choices. Make notes on the merchandise — styles, makes, colors, and sizes. Get the name of the department manager. Then wait for the end-of-season clearance sales to be advertised. Credit cardholders for department and specialty stores usually receive notice in advance through the mail. Many give cardholders an additional discount on already reduced items. Then call the department manager and ask if the items you are interested in are still available — at that store or from a branch store.

On the first day of the sale you'll find the best selection still available. On the last day, however, you'll get the best prices — sometimes slashed two or three times for super savings. Shop first for sportswear, then dresses and shoes. These items sell first. Wait for accessories like belts and scarves that sell slower. If you're tempted to buy a fad item, buy only if it's cheap!

Before you buy, ask about the store's return policy on sale items. Refund policies on sale items may be different from regularly priced merchandise. If all sales are "final" or "as is," you won't be able to return or exchange anything.

Don't let lower prices tempt you into buying for the sake of buying a bargain you don't need or can't use. Make sure that what you buy on sale meets your needs and standards.

Invest in basics and classics on sale. Look for wardrobe neutrals in all-season fabrics and fabric weights that suit your climate. Look for pieces that expand a cluster of clothes you know works well for you.

Ask for a rain check if the store runs out of the sale item you want. This reassures you the store didn't lure you in with the false promise of a bargain and then try to sell you something else — a common practice called "bait and switch."

A calendar of sales can help you plan your clothing purchases. (See Table 12–5.)

TIP
❧
FROM THE PROS

Watch for a shift in focus from sales to positive promotions that will create a sense of excitement in retail stores. Some of the new strategies will likely include multiple pricing, where you "buy one, get one free." By-invitation-only sales will be promoted to top charge customers. Closed-to-the-public trunk shows are increasing in popularity. Look for free-gift-with-purchase offers to perk up sales in less promoted departments, like career wear. Giveaways are bound to be creative.

5.

Rely on private try–on times and dress rehearsals to become familiar and comfortable with new clothing.

❧

After any shopping excursion, and before you put anything away, while you're still excited about what's new, take time to become familiar and comfortable with new clothes and accessories — make friends with them. The time is well spent and great fun if you'll mix and match the new pieces with clothes and accessories you already own. Find out how well your new clothes work together with those already in your wardrobe.

On that occasion, don't just try to imagine how an outfit will look. Comb your hair, touch up your makeup, then try it on in every combination you can think of. Confirm the many ways you thought you could wear them. Discover new ways. Who knows, you may put together something that, while unusual or unexpected, works perfectly. Experiment with combinations you won't have time to try out when it's time to get ready and go.

For example, *if a jumper is new, try it on over a favorite blouse or shirt. Button up the shirt and add a soft bow at the neck, now a necklace. Then open the shirt at the neck and try a second shirt over all, leaving it open down the front like a jacket. Roll up the sleeves for a super-casual look. Try the jumper with canvas shoes and later with boots. Take time to get the feel of each new look. Make it yours. Sit in it. Climb the stairs in it. View it from all angles. Clown around in front of the mirror in it. Make a list of each new look that works. Take your time and think it through. Months later you don't want to lament, "Oh, I wish I had worn it that way."*

If the additions to your wardrobe give you a definitely new image — a change in your former personal style, you might be smart to break them in slowly. Don't wear every new item at once. Wear only part of a new outfit to begin with. That way you won't overwhelm family or friends with all of what's new. On the other hand, some women are completely overwhelmed when family or friends make a big to-do over new clothes or a new image. They retreat back into the security of the old clothes or the old image and the new clothes never come out of the closet again. Better to give family and friends or colleagues a little time to get used to the new you.

For example, *if you get a new cluster and you're not comfortable with the new jacket, start out wearing the new skirt or the blouse. Next time add the new sweater or vest. By the time you finally come on with your new jacket, the skirt and blouse are old friends. People will have noticed, possibly even remarked about them, and they won't be shocked by the whole new you. Chances are, comments will be somewhat more reserved and you won't feel so overwhelmed.*

The point of this at-home fashion show is to become comfortable in new clothes and make them yours before trying them out in front of the family or in public. You're smart not to show off a garment that still needs to be altered. The same goes for a garment that demands something more to make it work. You'll only be disappointed if your audience can't share your vision of the finished look and is therefore less enthusiastic.

Dress Rehearsal

For a wonderful feeling of self-confidence when a special occasion calls for new clothes, it makes good sense to hold a "dress rehearsal" in the days before the event. You could wear the new clothes to a less important occasion first, but you run the risk of a rip or a stain. It's safer to audition the outfit at home, in front of a full-length mirror. Get yourself ready — accessories, makeup, and all. Do the usual bends, stretch, and turns. Get acquainted, make friends.

6.

Understand your rights and responsibilities as a consumer in the process of returns.

You say you bought a coat and the lining ripped loose the very first time you wore it? Or you purchased a dress that shrunk three sizes the very first time you washed it? You say you're upset?

Rights and Responsibilities

You have a right to be upset. As a consumer, you also have the right to recourse — the right as well as the responsibility to return unsatisfactory merchandise.

If you do not accept that responsibility but sit in angry silence instead, vowing never to shop at that store again, your opinion becomes a "lost statistic." Let your opinion count. When you return an item, you effectively communicate to merchants your feeling about the apparel or product. This is the only way to improve the quality and help insure the availability of better merchandise in the future.

To stay in business, merchants must please you, the consumer. At the same time, however, you should recognize that returned merchandise means extra expense to the store, since such merchandise must be reticketed and returned to the racks or be sent back to the manufacturer. This extra cost is passed on to you.

Consumers should request to return merchandise only when the action is truly warranted. If you have second thoughts about something you bought and wisdom says you need to return it, look for a defect of any kind —

in fabric, construction, or fit. It may give you a bargaining chip you can legitimately use to get your money back. Consumers who continually return merchandise simply because they "changed their minds" raise costs unnecessarily while they lower their credibility.

Merchandise tagged "damaged" or "as is" and sold at a reduced price leaves you out of luck should you change your mind about the item. Any attempt to return such goods is unwarranted. A notice of "all sales final" leaves you without recourse as well.

Returns are not legitimate if you care for a garment improperly and then attempt to return the damaged merchandise. It's dishonest to take an item on approval, wear or use it for a special occasion, and then return it. You may find that returns on evening wear are not allowed for exactly that reason.

Legitimate Reasons to Return

If you feel you have a valid reason to return an item, be prepared to point out the problem. In general, valid complaints concern the quality of workmanship. Poor quality fabric or thread, crooked, puckered, or broken seams, frayed seam edges and buttonholes, mismatched plaids or stripes, uneven or inadequate hems, faded or shrunken fabric, and loss of shape are all examples of valid complaints.

Some stores may even accept an item you've worn once if you are not satisfied with the fit, fabric, or style. This is a courtesy often left to the discretion of the store manager and one you should not abuse. If you are attempting to return a shirt that's fallen apart on the ninth day of an eight-day return policy, you may still be able to get satisfaction.

Some problems may not show up until after the first cleaning. Providing you followed the care instructions properly, you have a valid complaint. If you purchase an item in one store and soon after discover it in another store at a considerably lower cost, it's worth going back to the first store with proof of the lower price. Quite often, reputable stores will refund the difference rather than appear to have priced the item unreasonably — and to keep your business as well.

Similarly, you might purchase an item at full price and very soon after discover it on sale in the same store. Again, reputable stores will often refund you the difference. I once received an $80 refund on a suit. It never hurts to make the request.

Perhaps you have a valid complaint that involves service rather than merchandise. Perhaps you were annoyed by the lack of trained sales help, fitting rooms that were so small you tripped over yourself; nonexistent mirrors, price tags, or size tags; "women-pay-men-don't" alteration policies; or top-secret, restricted restrooms.

Whatever the issue, it's well worth your time to voice your complaint. In recent years there has been a significant increase in the number of consumer complaint departments, all in the interest of fostering good customer relations.

Return Policies

Save yourself time in a large store by calling first to ask whether your return goes back to the original department, to a refund desk, or to an adjustments department. Ask about general return policies. (See Figure 12–5.) If you haven't called ahead, look for return policies as soon as you get to the store. They may be posted near an entry door, at the credit desk, or near the cash register. If you don't readily spot them, don't hesitate to ask.

If you bought the item yourself, check the sales slip. Return policies may be printed there. A smart shopper always asks about a store's return policies before buying. If you don't like the store's return policy, don't buy there.

Stores are free to set their own return policies. Well-known national chain stores and department stores usually offer liberal return policies with generous grace periods of a month or more. Specialty stores and boutiques may be less liberal and allow only three to ten days to make a return. Certain items may not be returnable for hygienic reasons, including earrings for pierced ears, bathing suits, and hats.

Depending on the store, you may receive a cash refund, a refund in the manner in which payment was made, in-store credit on your charge account toward future pur- chases, or an exchange of goods. Stores try to accommodate customers who want to exchange what they got for what they want, but don't expect everything you want to be auto- matically available.

You may be required to present a receipt as proof of purchase. When buying for yourself or others, it's smart to save the sales slip, tickets, and tags for up to a year. The trouble that such a precaution takes turns into a help if later you want to make a return. A charge account can simplify the procedure, as it provides an automatic record of sales. Save an item's packaging until you're sure the item is satisfactory.

Many Happy Returns

- When making a return, it's best to avoid rush hours.
- To avoid potential problems, return merchandise in the closed bag or box.
- If you have sales receipts, take them along.
- Wear comfortable shoes and dress attractively. Neatly dressed customers get the best results.
- Go directly to the return desk or department where the item was purchased.

Figure 12–5. If you are uncertain about a garment, it's wise to ask about a store's return policy before purchasing. *(Courtesy Neiman Marcus)*

Get Extra Value with Private Labels

Shoppers often complain about the "sameness" of fashion merchandise as they go from store to store. "Everything looks the same," says one. "Major stores and even some boutiques carry the same brands, the same designers, the same styles, the same colors in the same fabrics. Everything's the same."

"I want something different, but not so different that I stick out like a sore thumb," says another.

Proliferation of designer labels and national brands, coupled with the stores' desire to profit from them, creates this "sameness."

If you look closer, however, something does differ from store to store. That something is private-label merchandise, and it's well worth noticing.

Private label refers to merchandise made exclusively for one store — clothing made to store specifications when special-ordered in large quantities. The clothes then carry the store's private label — usually the name of the store.

Examples include Macy's, Saks Fifth Avenue, ZCMI, Meier & Frank — all major department stores. Locally, you'll find items labled ZCMI Designer Sportswear, Nordstrom Point Of View and Nordstrom's Women's Tailored Clothing — each label indicating the department from which it is sold.

Private-label merchandise ensures that a store has something to offer that is different from the competition. It creates a distinct store image. Some retailers find that this type of exclusivity is attractive to customers.

And attractive it should be. Customers save money on private-label merchandise because the store buys in very large quantities, directly from the manufacturer. This cuts out the middleman and the savings are passed on to customers.

According to Debra Rapp, Fashion Coordinator at Nordstrom's in Salt Lake City, "Private label represents our commitment to value." Private-label prices are from 7 to 40 percent less when compared with similar national brand merchandise.

In most cases, customers get better quality merchandise for less money. In putting its own name on an item, a store is literally putting its reputation on the line. You know that management is going to offer quality merchandise.

"Our aim is to offer something of our own that spells quality," says Ellen Saltzman, vice-president and corporate fashion director of Saks Fifth Avenue, whose nationwide private-label program is one of the most extensive.

Another customer attraction is a store's commitment to fashion continuity. At Lord & Taylor, if an item sells well, they continue to offer it year after year, instead of discontinuing it as a conventional manufacturer would.

At Macy's, both classics and the latest fashions continue to be offered side by side, in virtually every department in every price range, all with the store's own label.

As Lord & Taylor spokeswoman Peggy Kaufman notes, "We will always carry a classic Shetland sweater, a basic cotton blouse, a cashmere sweater and a tweed skirt." And customers will be store-loyal for those clothes, because they may not be able to get them anywhere else. And therein lies the premise behind private labels.

- If possible, seek out the sales associate who originally helped you.
- If the sales associate doesn't have the authority to make an exchange or refund, see the department manager or buyer. From there, if necessary, go to the store manager.
- You may have to repeat your story several times before you reach the person who can help you.
- You may be tempted to stamp your feet, pound your fist, and shout your frustration. Better to be patient and keep your cool. A friendly smile, polite attitude, and calm but firm voice are likely to get you better results.
- Record the name of each person you talk to.
- Ask for a receipt or written confirmation if a store agrees to issue credit, mail a refund, or make a repair.

Power in the Printed Word

A well-written, courteous letter is another way to register possible complaints about merchandise or service. Call the switchboard for appropriate names and direct the letter to someone in upper management — that is, a person in a position able to do something about the problem. You can send copies of your letter to several individuals.

If the store fails to deal with your return or complaint satisfactorily, several agencies and organizations are available to help protect consumers' rights. Each works to test and improve standards of performance on products in many fields, including clothing and cosmetics. They welcome your input. If not able to help you with an individual problem, they may offer advice on what to do next or suggest another agency to contact.

These agencies and organizations include the local and national Better Business Bureau, the Federal Trade Commission, Food and Drug Administration, National Bureau of Standards, Consumer Affairs Council, American Society for Testing and Materials, National Retail Federation, and Consumer Product Safety Commission. The State Attorney General's Office may have a consumer protection division. Addresses can be obtained in your local library.

When all else fails, and you feel justified, you can seek satisfaction in a small claims court where you tell your story and accept the judge's decision. It has been my experience, however, that most stores are eager to keep your business and so go out of their way to help you.

Wardrobe Strategies
Review and End Note

In review, to build a workable wardrobe that meets your needs:

1. Rely on clothing as a resource, a tool that you can control and use to help you achieve your goals.

2. Rely on your clothing as an art form — personal pieces of wearable art.

3. Rely on separates in basic styles, clothes that are simple or plain in style lines and shape — adding an occasional costume and one-piece item as needed.

4. Rely on classic styles, clothes with design lines and shapes that fit and flatter most figures and are appropriate for many occasions — adding a current trend item as advisable.

5. Rely on wardrobe neutral colors, dulled or muted tones of every hue, as well as black, white, and gray — adding accent colors for interest.

6. Rely on all-season fabrics, light- to medium-weight woven and knit fabrics that you can wear at least three seasons or about nine months of the year — gradually adding seasonal clothing as needed.

7. Rely on solid colors and classic patterns, in small- to medium-scale prints, stripes, and plaids.

8. Rely on "tailored"-looking clothes for occasions when you need to appear more authoritative — softening the look for occasions when you need to appear more approachable and friendly.

9. Rely on a clothing cluster, a small group of coordinated clothes — possibly five to ten or twelve pieces, including accessories — then expand as needed and affordable.

10. Rely on a periodic wardrobe evaluation session.

11. Rely on proper clothing care to increase the value of this resource.

12. Rely on smart shopping skills and strategies.

The more you evaluate, experiment, and gain experience with your wardrobe, the more confident you'll get in your selection and coordination, the freer you'll feel, the more fun you'll have doing what comes naturally, and the less you'll worry about making clothing mistakes.

Fear of making a mistake keeps many women from moving ahead with wardrobe improvements or changes. Know that even the most talented and experienced people make fashion mistakes now and then. Don't berate yourself when you make a mistake. Believe in yourself instead. Remember that mistakes are best thought of as "steps up the ladder of learning" we all have to climb.

Fashion mistakes are usually the result of hasty or last-minute decisions. When you're in a hurry you don't take time to think things through. That's when you buy something you don't like, or can't use; something that doesn't fit, that's not worth the price. That's when you combine conflicting styles, colors that clash, or fabrics that fight for attention. By anticipating your needs and taking time to evaluate your outfits or finished appearance objectively, you can usually avoid making mistakes. With practice, you'll get so good it'll take only seconds.

Keep in mind that if you do make a mistake, it's a good sign that you're still learning. And when you resolve not to make that same mistake again, you come a little closer to your goal of creating the look that you like. Don't dwell on mistakes. Better yet, don't even think of them as mistakes but as lessons or experiences to learn from. Take a positive approach. With regular thought and practice, you may be surprised to see just how few mistakes you actually make.

T I P
FROM THE PROS

Above all, no matter how fashion savvy or sophisticated you may become, never take yourself or your appearance so seriously that you can't laugh at yourself. If all else fails, SMILE!

Review Main Points

Smart shopping skills and strategies, with mostly planned purchases, can result in a wardrobe that will present you attractively and appropriately and aid you in the achievement of your goals. An accurate mental image of what's in your closet will give you direction for planning, shopping, and purchasing wisely. Comparison shopping among the types of stores and clothing sources available to you will help you locate your clothing needs at the best dollar value. Specific shopping strategies prepare you to make wise purchases. Beginning with a shopping list, do your homework before you set out alone or with a friend or family member. Consider the best time to shop, what to wear and what to take along to facilitate your shopping success. Locate merchandise, rely on qualified sales assistance, and evaluate the fit of the clothing before you buy. An understanding of sales terms, types of sales and procedures will enhance your ability to get the best value for your clothing dollar. In a private try-on session at home, experiment with new clothing to become familiar and comfortable with it. Find out how well new clothes work together with those already in your wardrobe. Understand and exercise your rights and responsibilities as a consumer, returning a clothing item when you have legitimate reason.

Review Questions

1. _____ shopping, wherever possible, is an aid to getting the best value for your dollar.

2. A collection of many small stores under one roof, free services, and conveniences characterize _____ stores.

3. Departmentalized, self-service stores that sell merchandise at prices lower than retail describes most _____ stores.

4. _____ stores limit merchandise to a single type, brand, or designer label, catering to a relatiavely smaller clientele.

5. Second-hand clothing for resale is available at _____ stores, with approximately _____ the selling price of the item going to the previous owner.

6. _____ clothing stores sell donated clothes and are popular with both price and fashion conscious shoppers.

7. List four ways to do your homework prior to shopping to purchase.

   _____   _____

   _____   _____

8. Don't shop when you are _____, _____, or _____.

9. When going shopping for clothing, wear _____ shoes and clothes that are _____.

10. List four items to take with you when you go shopping for clothing.

    _____   _____

    _____   _____

11. List two types of quality factors to look for in clothing.

    _____   _____

12. In evaluating the fit and effect of a garment, you'll get a more realistic view of yourself by standing about _____ feet away from a mirror.

13. Tight horizintal wrinkles mean the garment is too _____ around the body, while loose vertical wrinkles mean the garment is too _____ at that point on the body.

14. Give three tips to improve the fit or appearance of clothing that doesn't fit well or flatter the figure.

_____.

_____.

_____.

15. Flawed or defective clothing for sale is labeled _____,

or _____.

16. Match the following sales to the words that describe them.

_____ pre-season sale   a) traditionally offer the best markdowns

_____ clearance sales   b) this sale may last for months

_____ liquidation sale   c) merchandise on sale before it's needed

_____ end-of-season sale   d) goods going out of style or discontinued

17. Which of the following words or group of words does not belong in the group? Circle the word.

Below Cost   Damaged   As Is   All Sales Final

18. Explain the purpose of a dress rehearsal with a new piece of clothing.

_____.

_____.

19. Give three tips for returning merchandise without a hassle.

_____.

_____.

_____.

20. Merchandise made exclusively for one store, made to specifications, and

carrying the store's name is known as _____ _____.

Discussion Questions

#1 What types of store or clothing sources are available in your area and what are the factors that attract you or gain your loyalty?

Notes: _____

_____

_____

#2 What could you do — or do you do — to improve the appropriateness of clothing gifts from your family?

Notes: _____

_____

_____

#3 What are some advantages and disadvantages in shopping the sales?

Notes: _____

_____

_____

_____

_____

#4 Thinking back, what is the best/worst clothing purchase you ever made, and what made it so?

Notes: _____

_____

_____

_____

_____

#5 What can you do to facilitate the return process — to make it a more pleasant experience?

Notes: _____

_____

_____

_____

_____

Exercise 12–1 Clothing Source Identification

Name_____

- Look at the clothing you are wearing.
- Identify each piece and where or how you acquired it.
- Identify the specific store or person as source.
- Identify the approximate original cost.
- Estimate fit and quality in terms of POOR, GOOD, and EXCELLENT.

Clothing Item	Source	Approx. Cost	Construction Quality	Fit Quality

Exercise 12–2 Wardrobe Source Identification

Name_____

- Look at the clothing in your closet and drawers.
- Select eight to ten pieces of clothing.
- Identify each piece and where or how you acquired it.
- Identify the specific store or person as source.
- Identify the approximate original cost.
- Estimate fit and quality in terms of POOR, GOOD, and EXCELLENT.

Clothing Item	Source	Approx. Cost	Construction Quality	Fit Quality

Exercise 12–3 Local Store Experience

Name _____

- Look in local stores, some where you regularly shop and at least one store new to you.
- Decide on a specific piece of clothing you would like or need to get — such as a shirt, skirt, pants, dress, coat, shoes — any one type of garment or accessory item.
- Find five that you are attracted to and think you'd like to buy.
- For each item, identify the following:

Clothing Item	Source	Cost	Fiber	Fabric	Color	Solid or Pattern	Care	Constr. Quality	Fit Quality	Advantages	Dis-advantages
1.											
2.											
3.											
4.											
5.											

- Having an accurate mental image of what's in your closet and drawers at home, which of the five items do you think will best meet your needs? Why?

_____

_____

- Having arrived home and now looking at clothes in your closet, do you believe the same item previously chosen will still best meet your needs? ☐ Yes ☐ No

Why? _____

Exercise 12–4 Comparative Shopping

Name _____

- Look in three different types of local stores — department, variety, specialty, discount, or secondhand stores.
- Decide on one type of clothing item to look for in all three stores.
- Evaluate the pieces of clothing and the stores in terms of POOR, GOOD, and EXCELLENT.

Store Type	Clothing Item	Quality	Fit	Fitting Room	Service Provided
1.					
2.					
3.					

Exercise 12–5 Cost-per–Wearing

Name_____

- Considering the item you selected in Exercise 12–4, estimate the number of times you might wear it over the period of one week, one month, one year, and three years.
- Figure out cost-per-wearing for the estimated three-year life of the garment.

_____ × 4 weeks = _____ × 12 months = _____
one week   one month   one year

× 3 years = _____ possible.
           total wearings

_____ ÷ _____ = _____
total wearings   cost of item   cost-per-wearing

- Given this estimated cost-per-wearing, do you believe this item would be a good purchase?

Exercise 12–6 Cost of Credit

Name _____

• Figure the cost of credit for the clothing item selected for Exercises 12–4 and 12–5, at the current rate for three months.

Example   Item: Leather jacket

Price: $250

Interest rate: 1.5% per month

Period of time for loan: 3 months

3 months × 1.5% interest rate per month = 4.5%

    a. _4.5%_   total interest

            4.5% × $250 (original cost) = $11.25

    b. _$ 11.25_   amount interest

             $11.25 + $250.00 (original cost) = $261.25

    c. _$261.25_ total cost of jacket

1.   Item:

     Price:

     Interest rate:

     Period of time for loan:

        a. _____ total interest

        b. $_____ amount interest

        c. $_____ total cost

2.   Item:

     Price:

     Interest rate:

     Period of time for loan:

        a. _____ total interest

        b. $_____ amount interest

        c. $_____ total cost

Exercise 12–7 Individual Needs

- Review Table 12–1.
- Put yourself in the place of purchasing clothing for one of the following individuals:

  - Infant
  - Toddler or preschooler
  - Elementary school youngster
  - Teenage student
  - Pregnant woman
  - Male high school teacher

  - Female, 72 years old, walks with a cane
  - Female bank vice-president
  - Female construction worker
  - Father at home with children
  - Single mother seeking employment
  - Female, 68 years old, with arthritis

- Look through your local telephone directory, selecting three stores you believe might offer merchandise appropriate for the individual you selected.
- Visit those three stores and evaluate actual merchandise available to meet the individual's needs.
- Report the individual's needs, store findings, and draw conclusions about clothing available.
- Be prepared to report your experience in class.

Glossary

Abstract patterns Arise from the artist's imagination and appear as splashes of color, as unrealistic free-form, or as flowing lines and shapes, with the possible suggestion of texture. They do not represent anything natural or man-made.

Accent colors Strong or intense color, brighter than most wardrobe neutral colors combined with them.

Accentuated neutral color schemes The harmony of any one chromatic hue in combination with one or more achromatic colors.

Achromatic colors Neutral colors without pigment, or without hue. They include black, white, and gray.

Add-ons Clothing pieces added on to an original cluster to expand the cluster.

Advancing Elements of design used in ways that appear to move toward or jump out at you are said to **advance**. They are generally dominant and noticed first.

Aesthetic clothing needs Needs described in terms of the artistic elements and principles of design.

After-image A physiological response to color. With prolonged viewing of an intense color, the eye becomes fatigued and automatically adapts itself by imposing an after-image in the complementary hue to rest the eye.

All-over arrangements Patterns that appear the same from any direction you look at them. They have a methodical, formal, regular rhythm, leading easily from one motif to another.

All-season fabrics Light- to medium-weight woven and knit fabrics that you can wear at least three seasons or about nine months of the year.

Analogous color schemes The harmony of two, three, or four hues that lie next to one another on the color wheel. All of the hues have one hue in common.

Analogous hues Colors that contain one hue in common. They lie next to one another on the color wheel.

Angular shapes Spaces enclosed with straight lines.

Asymmetrical balance Each side of a garment is different. The design space is broken into unequal parts.

Background area, or **negative space** Areas of solid color behind the motifs on a patterned fabric.

Background shapes Those formed by the outside edge of a motif in a pattern. Also, the body of a garment behind foreground shapes.

Balance The results of how lines, shapes, colors, textures, and patterns are used to break up an area or space and how they are distributed or grouped within a garment or an outfit. Balance is a principle of design.

Basics Clothing styles simple in design, with few details and no decoration. They do not attract attention to themselves.

Bell-shaped garments Clothing styles that combine straight lines in the top half of the garment with softly curved to full-rounded lines in the bottom half of the garment.

Body image Your perception of your physical self — the mental image and ideas you have about your body and its characteristics.

Border arrangements or **border prints** Appear right-side-up from only one selvage edge of the fabric. Dominant motifs in the pattern create a specific border along that edge.

Classic patterns Familiar patterns with continuous appeal. They are usually smaller in scale — small to medium, but not large. Classic patterns are more often rendered in wardrobe neutral colors.

Classic yang A category on the yin/yang continuum. The most feminine yang are characterized as practical, poised, orderly, and refined.

Classics Clothing styles that easily fit and flatter most figures and satisfy many clothing needs for many people.

Clo A unit of measurement used to communicate the insulating effect of clothing. The design and fit of a garment, as well as the number of layers, contribute to clo value, potential warmth, and body comfort.

Clothing/wardrobe management The process of evaluating and controlling the use and effect of [your] clothing on you and others.

Cluster A small group of coordinated clothes and accessories — from five to twelve basic pieces that can be combined in many ways to create many outfits.

Clustering A wardrobe strategy designed to guide you in selecting and coordinating clothing clusters to meet your wardrobe needs.

Cluster plansheets Charts that allow you to plan, evaluate, and review a cluster of coordinated clothes on paper before you begin to shop and at any time thereafter.

Color A physical sensation experienced when light rays of particular lengths stimulate the retina of the eyes. Color is an element of design.

Complementary color schemes The harmony of two hues that lie opposite one another on the color wheel. Complementary color schemes combine both warm and cool hues, and often lighter and darker values.

Complementary hues Colors most opposite or contrasting in character, one being warm and the other being cool. They lie directly opposite one another on the color wheel.

Composite type   One who borrows and blends both yin and yang characteristics. They cross over and borrow traits to meet different needs for different moods and occasions, roles, and goals.

Continuum   A continuous whole, quantity, or series, whose parts cannot be easily or separately discerned. Usually represents a progression from one extreme to another.

Cool hues   Colors that have shorter wavelengths, absorb more light, and appear to recede. They are generally positioned on the right side of the color wheel and include green, blue, and violet.

Costume clothes   Clothing styles that are detailed in design, decorated, or accessorized in ways that prevent their look from being changed easily.

Countering or **contrast**   Occurs when an element of design counteracts or contrasts with and, therefore, weakens, minimizes, or camouflages the effect of an existing characteristic.

Curved lines   These lines have some degree of roundness — from slight waves to full-rounded circles.

Curved shapes   These have some degree of roundness — from wavy free-forms to circles.

Decorative lines   Lines printed onto the fabric during manufacture, and formed when buttons, pocket flaps, trim, or special stitching is applied to the surface of the garment to change or enhance appearance.

Diagonal lines   Slant at an angle.

Diamond figure type   Wider in the midriff and waist area, narrower in the shoulders and hips/thighs, with a high hip curve and slim legs. The bust is often smaller and the buttocks flatter.

Diamond-shaped garments   Clothing styles designed with softly curved lines or fullness around the middle. They are narrower in the shoulder and at the hem, as compared to the waist. The waist is not generally defined.

Dominant   Whatever attracts the eye first and holds attention for a longer period of time.

Dramatic yang   A category on the yin/yang continuum. The most seldom seen yang are characterized as assertive, dignified, sophisticated, and possibly theatrical or exaggerated.

Dull, muted tones   Colors less intense or less saturated than pure hues. These tones contain a relatively lower concentration of clear pigment mixed with gray or its complementary color.

Elements of design   The medium of the art form. In dress, they include line, shape, color, texture, and pattern.

Emphasis   The use of line, shape, color, texture, and pattern to create a dominant focal point or center of interest in a garment or an outfit — a place on which the eye may rest attention. Emphasis is a principle of design.

Fabric finish   Any special treatment to a fabric that changes its characteristic texture or improves its performance — temporarily or permanently.

Fads   Impractical, novelty, or high-fashion items that tend to be short-lived and outdated within a few months. They often feature design lines and shapes that are relatively extreme in some way.

Fashion cycle   The predictable stages a clothing style goes through during its total time on the fashion scene, from its introduction and rise, to its peak and fall.

Fashion therapy   A facet of image management, with more attention directed to the improved effects of clothing on the wearer, rather than on the response of others.

Fiber   The basic structure in fabric — a single, slender, hair-like structure that can be made into thread, yarn, and finally fabric.

Figure types   Common combinations of figure variations — typical body shapes.

Figure variations   Variations from that so-called ideal figure used as a standard for comparison, for pattern making, and for clothing manufacture.

Foreground shapes   Those formed by design details on the surface of a garment, such as pockets, cuffs, plackets, and collars.

Four-way arrangements   Patterns that appear the same from four directions, given a quarter or 90° turn. Rhythm is regular. Matching can be done in either the lengthwise or crosswise direction.

Geometric patterns   Conform to the strict use of lines and recognized geometric shapes based on mathematical formulas and traditional woven fabrics.

Goals   Those things you want or hope to obtain or achieve in your life.

Harmony   The combined use of lines, shapes, colors, textures, and patterns in similar ways, appropriate for the purpose, idea, concept, or theme — with just enough variety to avoid boredom but not so much variety as to create conflict. Harmony is a principle of design.

Horizontal lines   Are placed across.

Hourglass figure type   Full-rounded upper body (shoulders and bust), a proportionally small waist, and full-rounded lower body (hips and buttocks).

Hourglass-shaped garments   A clothing style composed of softly rounded lines and a fitted waist, emphasizing the waist in comparison to the bust above and hips below.

Hue   The name of a color or specific color family, such as yellow, orange, red, violet (purple), blue, or green and its relative degree of warmness or coolness.

Ideal figure types   Figure appears similar in width in the shoulders and hips, with medium bust size and a small waist, a slightly curved abdomen, moderately curved buttocks, and slim thighs.

Image management The process of evaluating and controlling the effect of your appearance on you and others. Appearance includes dress, grooming, and body language.

Incomplete triad color schemes The use of only two colors in a triadic color scheme.

Ingenue yin A category on the yin/yang continuum. An ingenue is the most feminine yin and is characterized as forever young, delicate, gentle, innocent, and receptive.

Intensity, saturation, or **chroma** The relative degree of brightness or dullness of a hue. All hues on the color wheel are seen at natural or full intensity.

Inverted triangular figure type Figure is proportionally wider in the shoulders and narrower in the hips/thighs, with a high hip curve. They are generally larger in the bust, wider in the back, and flatter in the buttocks.

Inverted triangular-shaped garments (wedge) Clothing styles designed with predominantly straight lines, wider in the shoulders and narrower at the hem. Dominant line direction is diagonal.

Irradiation or **spreading** A physiological response to color that occurs when extremely contrasting colors are placed close to one another. Extremely light values with more light reflected appear to spread onto very dark values with few light rays reflected. A vibrating effect results.

Irregulars Clothing items with a slight flaw or defect that are sold at a lower-than-regular retail price.

Law of areas A time-tested guideline that states large areas of receding color or texture are more pleasing if balanced in combination with proportionally small advancing areas of another color or texture. Similarly, a small amount of trendy styling goes a long way and can pleasantly balance a large amount of classic styling.

Life-style Describes the way you live. It includes where you live, the geographical environment and natural resources; the general climate and the weather; how you live, including technological level and your finances; where you go; and who you're with and what you do. It can change over time.

Line A narrow, elongated mark which connects two or more points. Line encloses and divides space, creating shapes. Line is an element of design.

Lines in opposition Created when lines intersect, forming angles between opposing vertical, horizontal, and diagonal lines.

Lines in radiation Created when lines spread or radiate from a central point or area.

Lines in transition Created when one line changes direction smoothly into another direction, without sharp angles.

Man-made fibers Made from synthetic sources — primarily or completely from chemicals.

Monochromatic color schemes The harmony of one hue, often in several values.

Motifs Shapes or figures featured in a pattern.

Natural fibers Made from natural sources — plants, trees, or animals.

Near-complementary color schemes Colors from opposing sides of the color wheel — but not directly opposite one another. These color schemes include the following: analogous complementary, incomplete split complementary, single split complementary, double complementary, and double split complementary.

Neutral color schemes The harmony of one, two, or three achromatic neutrals.

Nonverbal communication Occurs through sight and touch. The visual image, personal appearance, or self-presentation communicates to everyone within view.

Novelty arrangements Pattern follows no specific or repeating pattern, but features irregularly spaced motifs.

One-way arrangements Pattern appears right-side-up from one direction only. Having a recognizable top and bottom, they are meant to be seen in their logical position on the body and not upside down.

Optical mixing A physiological response to color that occurs when small colored areas, such as a print, check, or stripe, are placed closely together. Each colored area tends to take on the color of the neighbor, and they visually blend within the eye.

Outlines Outside lines, created by the body's or the garment's outer edges. Also known as the silhouette.

Panel arrangements Pattern is designed in large but narrow sections arranged in only one direction. They reinforce the vertical direction and are intended to be used in one length without repeating.

Pastels Slightly dulled tints.

Pattern An arrangement of lines, shapes, and color on or in a fabric, including prints, stripes, checks, and plaids. Pattern is considered an element of design.

Patterns in fabric Formed in the fabric with threads or yarns, often dyed before weaving or knitting them.

Patterns on fabric Applied onto the surface of finished fabric using dyes. Techniques include printing, painting, spraying, appliqué, embroidery, and quilting.

Personal style Describes who you are, and in response to your life-style. It includes your personality traits and moods; your values, attitudes, and interests; your body build and personal coloring; and your clothing preferences. It evolves over time.

Physical clothing needs Clothing needed to preserve physical safety, health, and comfort, and to ensure survival.

Primary hues Red, yellow, and blue are primary hues. All other colors can be formed or created by mixing them.

Principles of design   The generally accepted guidelines or goals for any art form. They include balance, proportion and scale, rhythm, emphasis, harmony, and unity.

Private label   Merchandise made exclusively for one store, carries the store's name on the label. It is special-ordered in large quantities according to store specifications.

Proportion   The relationship of one part to another, and the parts to the whole. Proportion is a principle of design.

Psychological clothing needs   Clothing needed to foster and maintain a positive self-image, mental health, and psychological comfort.

Realistic, or **naturalistic, patterns**   Imitate or duplicate natural or man-made objects in a photographic manner — as they actually look.

Receding   Elements of design used in ways that appear to blend in or back away from you are said to **recede**. They tend to be subordinate, attracting less attention.

Rectangular figure type   Similar in width in the shoulders, waist, and hips/thighs. There is no defined waist curve or indentation.

Reinforcing or **repetition**   Occurs when an element of design repeats and therefore reinforces, strengthens, emphasizes, or exposes the effect of an existing characteristic.

Resource   Anything available which you can control and use to your advantage to help you achieve your goals.

Rhythm   The use of lines, shapes, colors, textures, or patterns to lead attention around the garment or the outfit. It is used to provide a transition between areas of the garment and unifies the entire design. Rhythm is a principle of design.

Romantic yin   A category on the yin/yang continuum. The most seldom seen yin, it is characterized as receptive, warm, charming, and responsive.

Rounded figure type   Above average-ideal weight range. This figure is larger and body lines are full-rounded curves.

Rounded- or **curved-shaped garments**   Clothing styles designed with curved lines and shapes, generally in the sleeves and/or skirt.

Sale   The price of regular store merchandise has been marked down.

Scale   The size relationship of one shape compared to another, of small, medium, and large. Scale is a principle of design.

Scarf or **bandanna arrangements**   Pattern forms a square to fill the size of a scarf. The pattern changes direction at the corners.

Secondary hues   Green, orange, and violet are secondary hues. They result from mixing two primary hues in equal amounts.

Seconds   Clothing items more visibly flawed than an irregular are sold at significantly reduced prices.

Self-actualization   The process of making something actual or real — bringing something into reality. The use of your abilities and resources in ways that maximize your potential to achieve your goals.

Self-competence   Specific abilities and skills or competencies you have mastered.

Self-confidence   Your belief, trust, and reliance on yourself.

Self-esteem   How you feel about yourself — your general feelings of self-worth based on self-image and influenced by the esteem others have for you.

Self-image   How you perceive the combination of all of your characteristics — your physical self including body image, your psychological self, social self, etc. How you see and judge yourself as a whole.

Separates   Clothes designed to cover only part of the body — top or bottom areas.

Shades   Low value colors, below or darker than natural — black has been added to the hue, absorbing more light.

Shape, or **form**   The area or space enclosed by a line, creating the outer edge or outline of an object. The outer edge or silhouette of a garment is a shape. Shape is an element of design.

Simultaneous contrast   A physiological response to color. Colors have an altering effect on one another — they appear to change in contrast to one another.

Social clothing needs   Clothing needed to develop and maintain a sense of acceptance, assignment, and belonging within society.

Spaced arrangements   Pattern appears as a single motif, or as a number of motifs, widely spaced or separated from any other motifs.

Sportive yang   A category on the yin/yang continuum. Sportive types are the most tailored or masculine yang, and characterized as assertive, casual, outgoing, and persistent.

Sporty yin   A category on the yin/yang continuum. Sporty types are the most masculine yin, and are characterized as friendly, casual, mischievous, and optimistic.

Straight lines   Crisp, flat, and rigid lines.

Structural lines   Lines woven or knitted into fabric during manufacture and lines created during construction of the garment, such as seamlines and foldlines.

Style file   A collection of pictured clothing styles arranged in a file according to garment types. A personal style file is created by cutting pictures of clothing from catalogs and magazines, to review and remind you of styles you like.

Stylized patterns   The designers' interpretation of natural or man-made objects. They reflect imagination rather than imitation.

Subordinate Whatever is less obvious or less important. Subordinate details hold attention for less time, as attention is always drawn back to whatever detail is dominant.

Symmetrical balance Both sides of a garment are the same. The design space is broken into equal parts.

Tailored A clothing style designed with predominantly straight lines, angular and tubular shapes, dulled and darker colors with stronger value contrast, firmer fabrics, and smaller patterns. Associated with yang characteristics.

Tertiary hues, or **intermediate hues** Yellow-green, blue-green, blue-violet, red-violet, red-orange, and yellow-orange are tertiary hues. They lie between a primary and a secondary hue, and result from a mixture of the primary and secondary hue on either side.

Tetrad color scheme The harmony of four colors spaced equidistant from one another around the color wheel.

Texture The surface characteristics of a fabric — the look, feel, sound, and hang or drape of the fabric. Texture is an element of design.

Thread or **yarn** A single fiber or several fibers spun or twisted into continuous strands for making into fabric.

Tints High value colors, above or lighter than natural value. White has been added to the hue, reflecting more light.

Trade names Brand names given to man-made fibers produced by a particular manufacturer, such as Dacron and Lycra. A trade name cannot be legally used for the same type of fiber produced by another manufacturer.

Trendy Designs that are extreme in some aspect of line, shape, color, texture, or pattern.

Triad color scheme The harmony of three colors spaced equidistant from one another around the color wheel.

Triangular figure type Narrower in the shoulders and wider in the hips/thighs, with a low hip curve. They are often smaller in the bust and waist, narrower in the back, and rounder in the buttocks.

Triangular-shaped garments Clothing styles composed of predominantly straight lines, they are narrower in the shoulders or waist and wider at the hem. Dominant line direction is diagonal.

Tubular figure type Slim to thin, angular figure, below the average weight range. They have few noticeable curves.

Tubular- or **rectangular-shaped garments** Straight lines in rectangular shapes and tubes around the body. Dominant line direction is vertical.

Two-way arrangements Pattern appears the same from only two directions, given a half or 180° turn. Motifs are stripes, are arranged in stripes, or are other geometric combinations.

Unity A sense of completeness. Nothing in the design or outfit is left out or unfinished. Unity is a principle of design.

Value The relative degree of lightness or darkness of a hue. Each pure hue has a natural or normal value, just as it appears on the color wheel.

Vertical lines Are placed up and down.

Visual, or **optical, illusion** A false perception or misinterpretation of the visual cues — something that deceives your eye when you look at it.

Wardrobe A larger group of clothes and accessories, generally brought together over an extended period of time, and serving all the needs of the owner. A completed wardrobe may include one expanded cluster or several small clusters.

Wardrobe evaluation The process of deciding what works in your wardrobe, what doesn't, and why — what you like, what you don't like, and why. The process involves weeding out what doesn't work, organizing what's left, and discovering how the clothes work together, coordinate, or combine. It may include a detailed inventory.

Wardrobe neutrals Generally dulled or muted tones and achromatic colors.

Wardrobing This continuous process involves evaluation, discarding of nonfunctional pieces, and the accumulation of new pieces. Planning occurs within all three phases.

Warm hues Colors that have longer wavelengths, reflect more light, and appear to advance. They are generally positioned on the left half of the color wheel, and include red, orange, and yellow.

Wear-life The expected wearing time of an article of clothing. Wear-life depends on how often and how hard the item is worn, the number of similar items you have on hand at any time, the care received in the closet and during cleaning, the classic or faddish styling of the garment, and the strength and quality of fabric and construction.

Wearable art A composition of lines, shapes, colors, textures, and patterns to be worn on the body.

Woolen yarns Made from short, rough fibers. They are softer, fuzzier, and weaker.

Worsted yarns Made from long, smooth fibers. They are firmer, smoother, and stronger.

Yang Oriental concept embodying advancing, assertive, authoritative, and dominant traits. In clothing, it relates closely to tailored styling.

Yin Oriental concept embodying receding, receptive, approachable, subordinate traits. In clothing, it relates closely to untailored styling.

Index

About the Author

Judith Rasband is the CEO of Conselle Corporation and Director of Image Management, an organization involved in the creation of educational materials on appearance-related topics. She combines thirty years of experience in fashion education and business.

Judith was born and raised in Washington State. She graduated in Home Economics Education from the University of Utah with honors as well as a love for and professional interest in clothing design, fashion styling, and family clothing management. A veteran educator, she has taught secondary-level, community college, and university courses in clothing selection and construction. She has practiced as a professional seamstress and consultant to private clients. While teaching at Brigham Young University, she earned a master's degree in Home Economics Education, specializing in the aesthetic, social, and psychological aspects of dress.

Judith wrote and self-syndicated a successful weekly newspaper column, *Images*, for ten years. She hosted weekly fashion segments on NBC's television affiliate in Salt Lake City while expanding her international speaking, teaching, and consulting business. Most recently, Judith has pioneered fashion video production, earning four-star reviews for her first efforts.

Previous publications as co-author included the text *Fitting and Pattern Alteration: A Multi-Method Approach* and trade book *Pregnant and Beautiful*. She is sole author of *Fabulous Fit* and *How to Clothe Your Family*. Among her upcoming writing plans are *Wardrobe Strategies for Men* and a complete text for professional image management consultants.